Lincoln and the Civil War

LINCOLN
and the
CIVIL WAR

A Profile and a History

Edited by

COURTLANDT CANBY

George Braziller, Inc.

NEW YORK · 1960

ACKNOWLEDGMENTS

The editor and publisher have made every effort to determine and credit the holders of copyright of the selections in this book. Any errors or omissions may be rectified in future volumes. For permission to use these selections, the editor and publisher make grateful acknowledgment to the following authors, publishers and agents, who reserve all rights for the matter reprinted:

From *Washington in Lincoln's Time* by Noah Brooks, and from *Lincoln in the Telegraph Office* by David Homer Bates, and from *Incidents and Anecdotes of the Civil War* by David Dixon Porter, and from *Memoirs of General William T. Sherman* by William T. Sherman; by permission of Appleton-Century-Crofts, Inc.

From *Diplomat in Carpet Slippers*, by Jay Monaghan, copyright © 1945, used by special permission of the publishers, The Bobbs-Merrill Company, Inc.

From *Lincoln Among His Friends* by Rufus Rockwell Wilson. Copyright 1942, by the Caxton Printers, Ltd., Caldwell, Idaho. Used by special permission of the copyright owners.

From *Conflict: The American Civil War* by George Fort Milton. Copyright 1941 by George Fort Milton. Published by Coward-McCann, Inc. N. Y. Used by permission.

From *Lincoln and the Civil War in the Diaries and Letters of John Hay*, edited by Tyler Dennett, copyright © 1939 by Dodd, Mead & Company, Inc.; and from *Lincoln the Liberal Statesman* by James G. Randall, copyright © 1947 by Dodd, Mead & Company, Inc.; and from *Lincoln the Pres-*

ident by James G. Randall, copyright © 1945 by Dodd, Mead & Company, Inc. Reprinted by permission of Dodd, Mead & Company, Inc.

From *A Stillness at Appomattox*, by Bruce Catton. Copyright 1953 by Bruce Catton. Reprinted by permission of Doubleday & Company, Inc.

From *Abraham Lincoln: The Prairie Years and The War Years*, One Volume Edition, copyright 1925, 1926, by The Pictorial Review Company; copyright, 1939, by Harcourt, Brace and Company, Inc.; copyright, 1953, 1954, by Carl Sandburg. Reprinted by permission of the publishers.

From *Abraham Lincoln: The War Years*, copyright, 1936, 1937, 1938, 1939, by Carl Sandburg; copyright, 1939, by Harcourt, Brace and Company, Inc. and reprinted with their permission.

From *The Day Lincoln Was Shot* by Jim Bishop, copyright © 1955 by Jim Bishop; and from *Reveille in Washington* by Margaret Leech, copyright 1941 by Margaret Leech Pulitzer; by permission of Harper & Brothers.

From *The Civil War and Reconstruction* (1937) by James G. Randall, by permission of D. C. Heath and Company.

From *The Lincoln Legend* by Roy P. Basler, © copyright 1935, by Roy P. Basler; by permission of Houghton Mifflin Company.

From *The American Political Tradition and the Men Who Made It* by Richard Hofstadter, copyright 1948 by Alfred A. Knopf, Inc.; and from *Lincoln on the Eve of '61* by Henry Villard, copyright 1940 by The Curtis Publishing Co., copyright 1941 by Oswald Garrison Villard and Harold C. Villard; and from *Lincoln and His Generals* by T. Harry Williams, copyright 1952 by Alfred A. Knopf, Inc.; and from *Abraham Lincoln* by Benjamin P. Thomas, copyright 1952 by Benjamin P. Thomas; by permission of Alfred A. Knopf, Inc.

From *Lincoln and His Generals* by T. Harry Williams, by permission of Hamish Hamilton Ltd., publishers of the British edition, for distribution in the British Commonwealth (apart from Canada).

From *Mary Lincoln: Biography of a Marriage* by Ruth Painter Randall, copyright 1953 by Ruth Painter Randall; and from *U. S. Grant and the American Military Tradition* by Bruce Catton, copyright 1954 by Bruce Catton; by permission of Little, Brown & Company; and from *Lincoln's War Cabinet* by Burton J. Hendrick, copyright 1946 by Burton J. Hendrick. Reprinted by permission of Little, Brown & Co.

From *Inside Lincoln's Cabinet: The Civil War Diaries of Salmon P. Chase*, edited by David Donald, copyright 1954, by David Donald, by permission of Longmans, Green & Company, Inc.

From *Lincoln and the South* by J. G. Randall, copyright 1946, by Louisiana State University Press, by permission of Louisiana State University Press.

From Nathaniel W. Stephenson, "Lincoln," in *The Cambridge History of American Literature*, W. P. Trent, John Erskine, Stuart P. Sherman and Carl Van Doren, editors, copyright, 1917-1943 by the Macmillan Company, used by permission of The Macmillan Company.

From *Statesmen and Soldiers of the Civil War* by Sir Frederick Maurice. Copyright 1926. Used by permission of F. M. P. Maurice.

From *Lincoln and the Press* by Robert S. Harper. Copyright 1951 by Robert S. Harper. Used by permission of McGraw-Hill Book Co., Inc.

From *Impressions of Lincoln and the Civil War* by Marquis Adolphe de Chambrun, copyright 1952 by Marquis Adolphe de Chambrun. Reprinted by permission of Random House, Inc.

From *The Emergence of Lincoln,* Volume II, by Allan Nevins, copyright, 1950 by Charles Scribner's Sons, by permission of Charles Scribner's Sons.

From *Rustics in Rebellion: A Yankee Reporter on the Road to Richmond, 1861-1865* by George Alfred Townsend, by permission of the University of North Carolina Press.

From *Lincoln and the Radicals* by T. Harry Williams, copyright, 1941 by the Regents of the University of Wisconsin, by permission of The University of Wisconsin Press.

From *Abraham Lincoln and the Fifth Column* by George Fort Milton, copyright, 1942 by Vanguard Press, Inc., reprinted by permission of the publishers, the Vanguard Press.

From *The Hidden Civil War: The Story of the Copperheads* by Wood Gray. Copyright 1942 by Wood Gray. Reprinted by permission of the Viking Press, Inc.

From *The Military Genius of Abraham Lincoln* by Colin R. Ballard, copyright 1952 by The World Publishing Company; and from *Abraham Lincoln: His Speeches and Writings,* edited by Roy. P. Basler, copyright 1946 by The World Publishing Co.; by permission of The World Publishing Company.

Contents

Editor's Note

Books and studies on Lincoln and the Civil War have been accumulating for almost a century. The sheer bulk of this literature as it exists today is enough to intimidate all but the most dedicated scholar. Yet as the centennial years approach, popular as well as scholarly interest in both subjects grows ever greater. How is the general reader or the student to find his way about in this literary jungle? How is he to pick and choose among the hundreds of titles, new and old?

I hope this book, with its novel approach to the presentation of history, may be of some help. I have made no attempt to add anything new or unusual to the already enormous literature on Lincoln and the Civil War. Instead, I have tried to present a tightly organized picture of Lincoln's presidency through selections from the more important titles already published in the field, the selections tied into each other by my own bridging passages. It has been my intention to render a double service: To offer a readable and satisfactorily detailed narrative for those who have neither the time nor the inclination to venture into the vast literature on the subject, and to stimulate as well as to suggest further reading for those who may care to undertake it.

If I have interjected more of my own writing than is usual in such a compilation, it is because I have determined to make the book something more than an anthology. The Civil War is a

*fascinating and significant episode in our history. In many re-
spects its problems are still our problems, as anybody who leafs
through this book will soon realize. In turning over hundreds of
studies in preparation for this volume I came to a rather unexpected conclusion. For the general reader (and I include myself
in that category), the very profusion and detail of the materials
available on the period tends to obscure, rather than to clarify,
the larger picture of the war and its meaning in our history. By
the same token I suggest that Lincoln has been generally viewed
as an isolated individual, heroic in proportions, but somehow
self-sufficient, aloof from the war. Lincoln and the war seem to
be only accidentally joined, whereas in actuality the two are one
and indivisible.*

*By marshalling my selections within a rigorously organized
framework, I have made every effort to bring out the larger
meaning or meanings of the war as a whole. And I have deliberately placed the emphasis of my book upon the last four years of
Lincoln's life—the war years—in order to underline the overriding importance of the war in Lincoln's career and of Lincoln to
the war. If I have succeeded in both respects, I will rest content.*

COURTLANDT CANBY
September, 1959

Introduction

The Making of a Leader

1809-1861

Who Is This Lincoln?

In 1860, with the country on the verge of civil war, Abraham Lincoln was elected to the presidency. He was little known outside of Illinois, and much misjudged where known; for under a mask of genial bonhomie, Lincoln was a complex and baffling man.

Who is this Lincoln? the country asked in 1860. And we in our turn must ask the same question. For only by learning more about Lincoln can we really begin to understand the Civil War. Lincoln made the war his war; he dramatized its meaning for millions of his countrymen and led them to victory through the most shattering crisis the United States has ever faced. And because of this he died, to paraphrase Stanton, a man for the ages. How the greatness buried deep within this unpretentious man welled forth to meet and then to surmount the crisis of the war, is the burden of this book. For Lincoln and the Civil War are inseparable; the one has little meaning without the other.

How did he appear to his contemporaries at the time of the Civil War? Shortly after Lincoln's death, Josiah G. Holland, his first biographer, questioned "multitudes of men who claimed to know Mr. Lincoln intimately" and found no two of them who agreed in their estimate of the dead President.[1] "The fact was," he wrote, "that he rarely showed more than one aspect of himself to one man. He opened himself to men in different directions."

[1] Reference notes are grouped together beginning on page 401.

13

*Holland then wryly set forth some of the contradictions he had
uncovered in his questioning—that Lincoln, for instance, was "a
very ambitious man, and that he was without a particle of ambition; that he was one of the saddest men that ever lived, and that
he was one of the jolliest men that ever lived . . . that he was the
most cunning man in America, and that he had not a particle of
cunning in him; that he had the strongest personal attachments,
and that he had no personal attachments at all . . . that he was a
man of indomitable will, and that he was a man almost without
a will; that he was a tyrant, and that he was the softest-hearted,
most brotherly man that ever lived . . . that his apparent candor
and fairness were only apparent, and that they were as real as his
head and his hands; that he was a boor, and that he was in all
respects a gentleman; that he was a leader of the people, and that
he was always led by the people; that he was cool and impassive,
and that he was susceptible of the strongest passions."*

*Though his face stares solemnly at us from a hundred books,
from calendars and advertisements and from the coins and bills
we handle every day, we do not know what Lincoln really looked
like. He disliked being photographed and "froze" stiffly before
the camera. No photographer ever caught the animation of that
mobile face nor its exaltation when fired with some universal
truth; nor could any portrait painter capture the personality behind those elusive features. "I have before me," wrote Horace
White, who knew Lincoln well, "a photograph of him taken at
Pittsfield, Illinois, during the campaign of 1858. It looks as I have
seen him a hundred times, his lantern jaws and large mouth and
solid nose firmly set, his sunken eyes looking at nothing yet not
unexpressive, his wrinkled and retreating forehead cut off by a
mass of tousled hair, with a shade of melancholy drawn like a
veil over his whole face. Nothing more unlike this can be imagined than the same Lincoln when taking part in a conversation,
or addressing an audience, or telling a story. The dull, listless*

features dropped like a mask. The melancholy shadows disappeared in a twinkling. The eye began to sparkle, the mouth to smile, the whole countenance was wreathed with animation, so that a stranger would have said: 'Why, this man, so angular and somber a moment ago, is really handsome.' "[2] *John Nicolay, one of Lincoln's secretaries, put it succinctly: "There are many pictures of Lincoln; there is no portrait of him."*[3]

Lincoln's contemporaries can bear witness to the baffling contradictions in his character, for Lincoln was continually confounding those who thought they knew him best. "Billy" Herndon, Lincoln's early friend and law partner, spent a lifetime after Lincoln's death trying to get the man down on paper. In his vivid way, Herndon wrote, "He was a sad-looking man; his melancholy dripped from him as he walked."[4] *And Francis Carpenter, the artist who spent some time in the White House in 1864, agreed that his "was the saddest face I ever knew. There were days when I could scarcely look into it without crying." Yet Charles A. Dana wrote, "His smile was something most lovely," and continued, "I have never seen a woman's smile that approached it in its engaging quality . . ." And Lincoln's laugh! "The 'neigh' of a wild horse on his native prairie," gushed Carpenter, "is not more undisguised and hearty."*

The curious fact is that Lincoln's gusto was as genuine as his melancholy. Twenty times in one evening, as the Marquis de Chambrun carefully noted, one mood might give way to the other.

Another contradiction that puzzled those who knew him best was his unusual combination of outward modesty with inner strength. "Humble Abraham Lincoln" he used to call himself in his early days in politics, striking an attitude which was at the same time both genuine and misleading. When Lincoln was President, Noah Brooks recalled, he always avoided referring to his own person except when acting in an official capacity, and used to speak of his position or office vaguely and modestly as "this place" or "here," as if he could not bear to associate himself with such an exalted office as the presidency. Before his death his "humbleness" had become a legend. Indeed, Lincoln's total lack of harsh aggressiveness was one of his most endearing qualities.

His characteristic humbleness was not in any sense a false modesty, a pose. Nor was it—as many presumed to their grief— the outward expression of a weak and unready character. One can guess that it sprang, rather, from a compassionate feeling for the wrongheadedness of the world and the frailty of men. His modesty was tinged, too, with a strong coloring of pessimism, born of long inner suffering; for, as Herndon said, Lincoln had a nature "as gentle as a woman's and as tender," and he had often been wounded. "Mr. Lincoln had not a hopeful temperament," wrote Brooks, "and, though he looked at the brighter side of things, was always prepared for disaster and defeat."

He had early singled out for himself the important questions and had no patience with the small, distracting conflicts of personality and detail which swallowed so much of the time and energy of other men. "He was certainly a very poor hater," wrote Leonard Swett, a fellow lawyer. "He never judged men by his like or dislike for them. . . . If a man had maligned him or been guilty of personal ill-treatment, and was the fittest man for the place, he would give him that place just as soon as he would give it to a friend."

On the other hand Lincoln had cunning. "Any man who took Lincoln for a simple-minded man would very soon wake up with his back in a ditch," wrote Leonard Swett, who had suffered many encounters with him at the bar. Elsewhere Swett wrote that Lincoln "handled and moved men remotely as we do pieces upon a chess-board. . . . He always told enough only of his plans and purposes to induce the belief that he had communicated all, yet he reserved enough to have communicated nothing . . . no man ever kept his real purposes closer, or penetrated the future further with his deep designs." And the journalist, Donn Piatt, observed, "There never lived a man who could say 'no' with easier facility, and abide by his saying with more firmness, than President Lincoln. His good-natured manner misled the common mind. It covered as firm a character as nature ever clad with human flesh, and I doubt whether Mr. Lincoln had at all a kind, forgiving nature. Such traits are not common to successful leaders. . . ."

Another of Lincoln's secretaries, John Hay, who worshiped the man, went even further. "It is absurd to call him a modest man," wrote Hay. "No great man was ever modest. It was his intellectual arrogance and unconscious assumption of superiority that men like Chase and Sumner could never forgive." Many were awed by the aura of strength about him, as they were terrified by his rare anger, which could be frightening. Dana noted the "impression of authority, of reserve force, Mr. Lincoln always gave to those about him," and Donn Piatt, echoing the words, wrote of the power of the man, arising from "a reserve force of intellectual ability." "Through one of those freaks of nature," Piatt concluded, "a giant had been born to the poor whites of Kentucky. . . ."

Yet the paradox remains, for this giant was truly humble. One might offer this in explanation: Although Lincoln knew his own superior strength, he had achieved the final insight: the tragic sense that the world is stronger than any one of us, that we are not the masters of life but that life is our master. There was no room for pride in Lincoln's strength; there was only humbleness.

In his early days, it is true, and even through the 1850's, he had been intensely ambitious. In a famous phrase, Herndon wrote, "He was always calculating, and always planning ahead. His ambition was a little engine that knew no rest. . . ." But the terrible burden of the war knocked the ambition out of him, replacing it with a deliberate, clearheaded, almost remote view of his soul-

destroying job, coupled with a passionate determination to see it through. His friends were often distressed by his cautious, pragmatic approach to every problem; his enemies were enraged by it and, misjudging, accused him of dangerous opportunism and of following rather than leading the people. Lincoln himself said, "I claim not to have controlled events but confess plainly that events have controlled me,"⁵ and would often confound his critics with the wry assertion, "My policy is to have no policy."⁶

It may have been fortunate that Lincoln preferred to grope his way forward without plan, for the Civil War was a great destroyer of plans. Instead, he stuck to general principles with bullheaded stubbornness, improvising the details as he went along, measuring his success by results alone. "If we had had a great man for the Presidency," he once said with typical irony, looking back on the election of 1860, "one who had an inflexible policy and stuck to it, this rebellion would have succeeded, and the Southern Confederacy would have been established."⁷

Lincoln's mind was cool, but there was passion deep down in the man; and it was the combination of these two—a rigorous mind riding herd on tumultuous passions—that perhaps explains the almost mystical intensity of his vision. His was a powerful mind; it worked slowly ("as if it needed oiling" said Herndon) but with rigorous logic; for Lincoln was eminently a rationalist. "In order to believe," wrote Herndon, "he must see and feel, and thrust his hand into the place. He must taste, smell, and handle before he had faith or even belief."

His mind in its late maturity was distinguished above all for its ability to penetrate beyond fact and flux to general principles and, ultimately, to the truth. "In debate," wrote Herndon, "he courteously granted all the forms and non-essential things to his opponent. Sometimes he yielded nine points out of ten. The nine he brushed aside as husks or rubbish; but the tenth, being a question of substance, he clung to with all his might."

It was the truth, as Lincoln saw it and was moved by it, that brought to the surface in rare outpourings of deep emotion the mystic, the prophet, the seer so deeply buried at other times beneath the logical fabric of his mind. As the ordeal of his country deepened, it was the preservation of the Union, the perpetuation of republican institutions in the United States and as a banner for the world, the defending of the hard-won rights of the people, which called forth his most profound response: ". . . that these dead shall not have died in vain—that this nation, under God, shall have a new birth of freedom—and that government of the people, by the people, for the people, shall not perish from the earth." *In such utterance, shaping into words the aspirations of the nation, lay the true greatness of the man. John Hay summed it up: "As . . . republicanism is the sole hope of a sick world, so Lincoln, with all his foibles, is the greatest character since Christ."*

Lincoln experts of our day, when discussing Lincoln's character, tend to reaffirm the mixed judgments of Lincoln's contemporaries rather than the ponderous biographers and popular story tellers of the late nineteenth century, for whom Lincoln was either a saint or a rather crude folk hero. Thus Richard Hofstadter, exhibiting the revisionist mood of the younger American historians, discovers in Lincoln's character a destructive conflict between his genuine humility and his assumption of the typically American role of the self-made man, which he played "with an intense and poignant consistency." The theme is a major one in Hofstadter's essay on Lincoln in The American Political Tradition, *from which this short selection has been taken.*[8]

Lincoln's simplicity was very real. He called his wife "mother," received distinguished guests in shirtsleeves, and once during his presidency hailed a soldier out of the ranks with the cry: "Bub! Bub!" But he was also a complex man, easily complex enough to know the value of his own simplicity. With his morbid compulsion for honesty he was too modest to pose coarsely and blatantly as a Henry Clay or James G. Blaine might pose. (When an 1860 campaign document announced that he was a reader of Plutarch, he sat down at once to validate the claim by reading the *Lives*.) But he did develop a political personality by intensifying qualities he actually possessed.

Even during his early days in politics, when his speeches were full of conventional platform bombast, Lincoln seldom failed to strike the humble manner that was peculiarly his. "I was born and have ever remained," he said in his first extended campaign speech, "in the most humble walks of life. I have no popular relations or friends to recommend me." Thereafter he always sounded the theme. "I presume you all know who I am—I am humble Abraham Lincoln. . . . If elected I shall be thankful; if not it will be all the same." Opponents at times grew impatient with his self-derogation ("my poor, lean, lank face") and a Democratic journal once called him a Uriah Heep. But self-conscious as the device was, and coupled even as it was with a secret confidence that Hay called "intellectual arrogance," there was still no imposture in it. It corresponded to Lincoln's own image of himself, which placed him with the poor, the aged, and the forgotten. In a letter to Herndon that was certainly not meant to impress any constituency, Lincoln, near his thirty-ninth birthday, referred to "my old, withered, dry eyes."

There was always this pathos in his plainness, his lack of external grace. "He is," said one of Mrs. Lincoln's friends, "the *ungodliest* man you ever saw." His colleagues, however, recognized in this a possible political asset and transmuted it into one of the most successful of all political symbols—the hard-fisted rail-splitter. At a Republican meeting in 1860 John Hanks and another old pioneer appeared carrying fence rails labeled: "Two rails from a lot made by Abraham Lincoln and John Hanks in the Sangamon Bottom in the year 1830." And Lincoln, with his usual candor, confessed that he had no idea whether these were the same rails, but he was sure he had actually split rails every bit as good. The time was to come when little Tad could say: "Everybody in this world knows Pa used to split rails."

Humility belongs with mercy among the cardinal Christian virtues. "Blessed are the meek, for they shall inherit the earth." But the demands of Christianity and the success myth are incompatible. The competitive society out of which the success myth and the self-made man have grown may accept the Christian virtues in principle but can hardly observe them in practice. The motivating force in the mythology of success is ambition, which is closely akin to the cardinal Christian sin of pride. In a world that works through ambition and self-help, while inculcating an ethic that looks upon their results with disdain, how can an earnest man, a public figure living in a time of crisis, gratify his aspirations and yet remain morally whole? If he is, like Lincoln, a man of private religious intensity, the stage is set for high tragedy.

Toward the Presidency

Lincoln was fifty-two when he assumed the presidency, and fifty-six when he died. All the earlier years were preparation.

Nevertheless, there were glimpses of the man he was to become in the long unfolding of his career; and in the many reverses he was to suffer there was a promise of his later wisdom. Born on a backwoods Kentucky farm on February 12, 1809, he sprang from a long line of restless pioneers who had been moving west from the Atlantic coast since the seventeenth century. The boy, growing up in primitive Indiana, was a familiar frontier type—"long, tall, and strong," lazy, a joker and a teller of stories, yet underneath, reticent, lonely and shy with women.

His adult life began in pioneer New Salem, Illinois. Although largely self-educated, he developed an early passion for writing, speaking and public life which brought him swiftly out of the log cabins of New Salem into the larger life of Springfield, the cosmopolitan little capital of the growing state. Here he lived for thirty years. Brash, confident and ambitious, his rise as a politician was rapid, too rapid perhaps for his own good. As a wheelhorse of the Whigs he quickly learned the tricks of the trade, first in the Illinois legislature where he served several terms, and then for one term in Congress. But his partisan attitude on the Mexican War lost him his following in Illinois and in 1849, bitterly disappointed, he retired to Springfield rather than suffer inevitable defeat. He was forty, and his political career was apparently at an end. In his own eyes he seemed to be a failure.

His personal life had been no happier. A fleeting romance with

Ann Rutledge in New Salem, the importance of which has been much exaggerated, ended with the girl's death. His stormy courtship in Springfield of Mary Todd, a vivacious and aristocratic belle from Lexington, Kentucky, led to their marriage in 1842, but life for this oddly disparate pair was not easy. Mary soon showed signs of that extreme instability which was to plague both of them for the rest of their lives.

For Lincoln, there was relief from family tensions in his long absences as an itinerant lawyer with the Eighth Judicial Circuit, which also brought him in touch with the life of his state. During these years Lincoln had developed into a highly successful lawyer, recognized as one of the leaders of the Illinois bar and much sought after by rich railroads, corporations and banks, as well as by municipalities and the state. His flourishing legal career was to prove no mean foundation for his coming venture into national politics.

The broad outlines of Lincoln's political and economic views in the years preceding his election to the presidency have been drawn by Richard Hofstadter.[9]

If historical epochs are judged by the opportunities they offer talented men to rise from the ranks to places of wealth, power, and prestige, the period during which Lincoln grew up was among the greatest in history, and among all places such opportunities were most available in the fresh territory north and west of the Ohio River—the Valley of Democracy.

Abraham Lincoln was nineteen years old when Andrew Jackson was elected President. Like most of the poor in his part of the country, Thomas Lincoln was a Jacksonian Democrat, and his son at first accepted his politics. But sometime during his eighteenth or nineteenth year Abraham went through a political conversion, became a National Republican, and cast his first vote, in 1832, for Henry Clay.

The National Republican (later Whig) Party was the party of

internal improvements, stable currency, and conservative banking; Lincoln lived in a country that needed all three. Doubtless
there were also personal factors in his decision. If the Democrats
spoke more emphatically about the equality of man, the Whigs,
even in the West, had the most imposing and affluent men. That
an ambitious youth should look to the more solid citizens of his
community for political guidance was natural and expedient . . .

Like his "influential and financial friends," Lincoln belonged
to the party of rank and privilege; it exacted a price from him. In
time he was to marry into the family circle of Ninian Edwards,
of whom it was once observed that he was "naturally and constitutionally an aristocrat and . . . hated democracy . . . as the devil
is said to hate holy water." Lincoln's connection with such a tribe
could only spur his loyalty to the democratic ways in which he
had been brought up; he never did "belong," and Mary Todd's
attitude toward him as a social creature was always disdainful. . . .

For public and private reasons alike he was touchy about attempts to link him with the aristocrats because of his Whig
affiliations, and once complained bitterly at being incongruously
"put down here as the candidate of pride, wealth, and aristocratic
family distinction."

And yet it was true that the young Lincoln fell short of being
an outspoken democrat. In the social climate of Illinois he ranked
as a moderate conservative. Running for re-election to the legislature in 1836, he submitted to a newspaper a statement of his
views which included the following: "I go for all sharing the
privileges of the government who assist in bearing its burdens.
Consequently I go for admitting all whites to the right of
suffrage who pay taxes or bear arms (by no means excluding
females)." Now, the Illinois Constitution of 1818 had already
granted the suffrage to all white male inhabitants of twenty-one or
over without further qualification, so that Lincoln's proposal
actually involved a step backward.

Lincoln's democracy was not broad enough to transcend color lines, but on this score it had more latitude than the democracy professed by many of his neighbors and contemporaries. One of the extraordinary things about his strangely involved personality is the contrast between his circumspectness in practical politics wherever the Negro was concerned, and his penetration of the logic of the proslavery argument, which he answered with exceptional insight. His keen onslaughts against slavery, in fact, carry the conviction of a man of far greater moral force than the pre-presidential Lincoln ever revealed in action. After 1854, when he renewed his study of the slavery question, Lincoln was particularly acute in showing that the logic of the defenders of slavery was profoundly undemocratic, not only in reference to the Southern scene, but for human relations everywhere. The essence of his position was that the principle of exclusion has no inner check; that arbitrarily barring one minority from the exercise of its rights can be both a precedent and a moral sanction for barring another, and that it creates a frame of mind from which no one can expect justice or security. . . .

In Lincoln's eyes the Declaration of Independence thus becomes once again what it had been to Jefferson—not merely a formal theory of rights, but an instrument of democracy. It was to Jefferson that Lincoln looked as the source of his political inspiration, Jefferson whom he described as "the most distinguished politician of our history." "The principles of Jefferson are the definitions and axioms of free society," he declared in 1859. . . . "Republicans," he added, in an utterly characteristic sentence which ought to be well remembered, "are for both the man and the dollar, but in case of conflict the man before the dollar." . . .

The Declaration of Independence was not only the primary article of Lincoln's creed; it provided his most formidable political ammunition. And yet in the end it was the Declaration that he could not make a consistent part of his living work. The

Declaration was a revolutionary document, and this too Lincoln accepted. One of his early public statements declares:

> Any people anywhere being inclined and having the power have the right to rise up and shake off the existing government, and form a new one that suits them better. This is a most valuable, a most sacred right—a right which we hope and believe is to liberate the world.

Having said so much, he did not stop:

> Any portion of such people that can may revolutionize and make their own of so much territory as they inhabit. More than this, *a majority of any portion of such people may revolutionize, putting down a minority, intermingled with or near about them,* who may oppose this movement. Such a minority was precisely the case of the Tories of our own revolution. It is a quality of revolutions not to go by old lines or old laws; but to break up both, and make new ones.

The principle is reiterated with firmness in the First Inaugural Address.

So Lincoln, the revolutionary theorist. There was another Lincoln who had a lawyer-like feeling for the niceties of established rules and a nationalist's reverence for constitutional sanction. This Lincoln always publicly condemned the abolitionists who fought slavery by extraconstitutional means—and condemned also the mobs who deprived them of their right of free speech and free press. . . . This Lincoln suppressed secession and refused to acknowledge that the right of revolution he had so boldly accepted belonged to the South. The same Lincoln, as we shall see, refused almost to the last minute even to suppress rebellion by revolutionary means. The contradiction is not peculiar to Lincoln; Anglo-Saxon history is full of it.

As an economic thinker, Lincoln had a passion for the great average. Thoroughly middle-class in his ideas, he spoke for those millions of Americans who had begun their lives as hired workers —as farm hands, clerks, teachers, mechanics, flatboat men, and rail-splitters—and had passed into the ranks of landed farmers, prosperous grocers, lawyers, merchants, physicians, and politicians. Theirs were the traditional ideals of the Protestant ethic: hard work, frugality, temperance, and a touch of ability applied long and hard enough would lift a man into the propertied or professional class and give him independence and respect if not wealth and prestige. Failure to rise in the economic scale was generally viewed as a fault in the individual, not in society. It was the outward sign of an inward lack of grace—of idleness, indulgence, waste, or incapacity.

This conception of the competitive world was by no means so inaccurate in Lincoln's day as it has long since become; neither was it so conservative as time has made it. It was the legitimate inheritance of Jacksonian democracy. It was the belief not only of those who had arrived but also of those who were pushing their way to the top. If it was intensely and at times inhumanly individualistic, it also defied aristocracy and class distinction. Lincoln's life was a dramatization of it in the sphere of politics as, say, Carnegie's was in business. . . .

For Lincoln the vital test of a democracy was economic—its ability to provide opportunities for social ascent to those born in its lower ranks. This belief in opportunity for the self-made man is the key to his entire career; it explains his public appeal; it is the core of his criticism of slavery.

There is a strong pro-labor strain in all of Lincoln's utterances from the beginning to the end of his career. Perhaps the most sweeping of his words, and certainly the least equivocal, were penned in 1847. "Inasmuch as most good things are produced by labor," he began:

> it follows that all such things of right belong to those whose labor has produced them. But it has so happened, in all ages of the world, that some have labored, and others have without labor enjoyed a large proportion of the fruits. This is wrong and should not continue. To secure to each laborer the whole product of his labor, or as nearly as possible, is a worthy object of any good government.

In Lincoln's day, especially in the more primitive communities of his formative years, the laborer had not yet been fully separated from his tools. The rights of labor still were closely associated in the fashion of Locke and Jefferson with the right of the laborer to retain his own product; when men talked about the sacredness of labor, they were often talking in veiled terms about the right to own. These ideas, which belonged to the age of craftsmanship rather than industrialism, Lincoln carried into the modern industrial scene. The result is a quaint equivocation, worth observing carefully because it pictures the state of mind of a man living half in one economy and half in another and wishing to do justice to every interest. In 1860, when Lincoln was stumping about the country before the Republican convention, he turned up at New Haven, where shoemakers were on strike. The Democrats had charged Republican agitators with responsibility for the strike, and Lincoln met them head-on:

> . . . I am glad to see that a system of labor prevails in New England under which laborers can strike when they want to, where they are not obliged to work under all circumstances, and are not tied down and obliged to labor whether

you pay them or not! I like the system which lets a man quit when he wants to, and wish it might prevail everywhere. One of the reasons why I am opposed to slavery is just here. What is the true condition of the laborer? I take it that it is best for all to leave each man free to acquire property as fast as he can. Some will get wealthy. I don't believe in a law to prevent a man from getting rich; it would do more harm than good. . . .

If there was a flaw in all this, it was one that Lincoln was never forced to meet. Had he lived to seventy, he would have seen the generation brought up on self-help come into its own, build oppressive business corporations, and begin to close off those treasured opportunities for the little man. Further, he would have seen his own party become the jackal of the vested interests, placing the dollar far, far ahead of the man. He himself presided over the social revolution that destroyed the simple equalitarian order of the 1840's, corrupted what remained of its values, and caricatured its ideals. Booth's bullet, indeed, saved him from something worse than embroilment with the radicals over Reconstruction. It confined his life to the happier age that Lincoln understood—which unwittingly he helped to destroy—the age that gave sanction to the honest compromises of his thought.

In retirement in Springfield after 1849 Lincoln had time to ponder. Many observers reported his long spells of abstraction during these five years, in which something incalculable happened to the man. When he returned to active politics in 1854, aroused "as he had never been before" by Douglas's Kansas-Nebraska Act, he seemed a different Lincoln. Political disappointment had purged him of partisanship for its own sake, and a long apprenticeship both in marriage and in politics had given him patience, skill and polish. The practice of law had taught him not only how to manage men, but also how to discipline his mind. Even the style of his thought and speech had changed; for the rant and rhetoric of his younger days had been replaced by the simple, terse, often impassioned utterance of his great period.

During his retirement the country, too, had changed. The re-opening of the slavery controversy in 1854 found the states more dangerously split than ever. Civil war in Kansas and the Dred Scott decision of 1857, which in effect opened the territories to slavery, greatly inflamed the sectional conflict. Lincoln's own Northwest, growing rapidly in wealth and power, was shifting its allegiance from the old South to the industrial states of the North-east as trade and travel began to flow along the new canals and railroads from west to east instead of down the southward-running rivers. This new alignment not only alarmed the South but gave the death blow to the national Whig party to which Lincoln still belonged. Already torn asunder over the slavery question, it was soon replaced by a new, ominously sectional party—the Republican—which Lincoln himself was to dedicate with the words: "A house divided against itself cannot stand."

In the slavery issue Lincoln had found a new means to further his political ambitions. But for the first time, ambition was now strongly tempered by principle. His position was relatively simple, and he held to it tenaciously. Its strength lay in his forthright recognition that slavery was not only an anachronism but also a moral evil which must at all costs be prevented from spreading beyond its present boundaries. He hammered at this theme. Compromise would no longer do; there must be no further surrender to the South; any extension of slavery must be considerd a threat to the future of the country. Contained, it would in time die out.

Lincoln realized, on the other hand, that slavery was a deeply rooted institution, enjoying the protection of the Constitution, and that it could not simply be destroyed overnight (as the abolitionists would have it) without grave danger to the country.

Personally favoring some form of gradual emancipation, Lincoln rejected war as a solution to the problem. Nor did he feel that war over slavery was inevitable, although many of his contemporaries so interpreted his "House Divided" speech of 1858.

Armed with these views, Lincoln in 1854 entered once more upon the national scene. Quickly he found himself in line for the Senate, pitted against Stephen Douglas. In 1856 he joined the newly organized Republican party and was almost nominated for the vice-presidency. Two years later he again ran for the Senate. But in effect the whole period from 1854 to 1858 was but a single campaign in which Lincoln sought to bring to the people of his state his message on the containment of slavery.

That he failed of election to the Senate both in 1855 and in 1858 proved unimportant. Even the famous Lincoln-Douglas debates of 1858 were of little significance from the standpoint of content. Limited to the fruitless question of slavery in the territories, they amounted, in the words of James G. Randall, to "an exhibition . . . a sparring for popular effect and party advantage"[10] between two wary politicians, both stepping gingerly around the deeper issues.

It was the vividly partisan newspaper reporting of the Lincoln-Douglas debates of 1858 which created a new familiarity with Lincoln's unusual personality, first among the people of his state and then throughout the entire country. And it was this reporting which made him a presidential possibility in 1860.

After his defeat in 1858, Lincoln returned to the law. But he was now nationally known and presidential talk grew around him. He continued to be active in the Republican party and throughout 1859 made occasional speeches in the West. In October of that year John Brown's fanatical raid on Harpers Ferry raised the slavery controversy to a new level of emotion.

In such an atmosphere, Lincoln's measured address at Cooper Union in New York City in February, 1860, was remarkable for its careful definition of the Republican position and its thoughtful examination of the history of the slavery issue as far back as the Constitutional Convention in 1789. The speech immensely increased Lincoln's reputation, this time in the east as well as in the west, and shortly thereafter his self-appointed managers brought about his nomination as Illinois' favorite son. It was at the Decatur Republican state convention that he was first dubbed the "rail-splitter" when his country cousin, old John Hanks, triumphantly appeared with two fence rails supposedly split by the young Lincoln. Shortly afterward came the Republican convention at Chicago. Benjamin Thomas, in his one-volume biography of Lincoln, describes Lincoln's nomination for the presidency.[11]

Proud to be host to the Republican convention, Chicago had prepared against its coming by erecting a rambling frame structure, known as the Wigwam, designed to hold ten thousand people. But even this would be too small, for besides the usual galaxy of delegates, professional politicians, newspaper reporters, and hangers-on, thousands of other persons planned to attend the convention. New York sent more than two thousand men to cheer for Seward. Pennsylvania was represented by fifteen hundred. Hundreds more came from New England. And from all over Illinois the Lincoln men poured in, taking advantage of the cheap railroad fares that Norman Judd had wangled. . . .

Lincoln's managers set up headquarters in the Tremont House. Their chief strategist was David Davis, of Bloomington. An enormous man, weighing more than three hundred pounds, rich, sagacious, indomitable, he was judge of the Eighth Circuit, which he had traveled with Lincoln for many years, sharing his room, roaring at his stories, sometimes chiding him for impoverishing the bar with his low fees, coming to appreciate his qualities of mind and character. On hand to assist Davis was a coterie of Lincoln's friends, many of them his associates on the circuit—Norman Judd, Stephen T. Logan, Leonard Swett, Joseph Medill, Jesse Fell, Republican gubernatorial nominee Richard Yates, Orville Browning, and a score of others.

No novices in the game of politics, they knew they faced a formidable but by no means hopeless task, for Lincoln's strength lay in his rivals' weaknesses. The acknowledged leader of the party was Seward, experienced, calculating, and somewhat cynical, a former Governor of New York, a United States Senator since 1848, and a forthright opponent of slavery extension. Backed solidly by the New York delegation, led by the smart manipulator Thurlow Weed, Seward was immensely popular. But he also had enemies, notably Horace Greeley, who, banned from the New York delegation, had contrived to be chosen a delegate from Oregon. Actually more of a compromiser than Lincoln, Seward by reason of his "higher law" and "irrepressible conflict" utterances was reputed to be a radical. . . .

Salmon P. Chase, of Ohio, twice Governor and once a United States Senator, not only was more radical than Seward and far less popular, but could not even command the full support of his own state. Conservative Edward Bates, of Missouri, had antagonized the German voters by consorting with the Know-Nothings. Simon Cameron, of Pennsylvania, had an unsavory reputation and, like Chase, was opposed in his own state delegation. Colorless John McLean, of the United States Supreme Court, was seventy-five years old.

Lincoln, on the other hand, did not enjoy sufficient prominence to have been marked either as a conservative or as a radical. He had no public record he must defend. His lowly birth and self-made attributes found favor with the masses. Six weeks before the convention Lincoln correctly appraised his situation when he wrote to a friend in Ohio: "My name is new in the field; and I suppose I am not the *first* choice of a very great many. Our policy, then, is to give no offence to others—leave them in a mood to come to us, if they shall be impelled to give up their first love." . . .

On the eve of the convention it appeared that Indiana might be persuaded to give Lincoln her twenty-six votes on the first ballot, and that a goodly number of Pennsylvania votes might be obtained on the second ballot if Lincoln's chances appeared good. Davis was dickering with all the finesse he could command, when a telegram came from Lincoln: "I authorize no bargains and will be bound by none." Lincoln's friends were confounded. From an experienced politician such an admonition was unthinkable. Did Lincoln mean to shackle them, they wondered, or was he writing for the record? "Lincoln ain't here," the perspiring Davis grunted, "and don't know what we have to meet." Davis proceeded to clinch the Indiana delegation with a promise of the Secretaryship of the Interior to Caleb B. Smith and the Commissionership of Indian Affairs to William P. Dole.

Into the vast pine-board Wigwam on the morning of Wednesday, May 16, trooped ten thousand people, while twice as many swarmed hopefully outside. . . . Pillars were wreathed with flags and bunting. Busts of notables stood in the corners. Portraits of statesmen and allegorical paintings of Justice, Liberty, and the like adorned the barren walls.

The first two days were devoted to routine business and the adoption of the platform. During recesses delegations met in caucus. The suspense became harrowing. The Seward men wished to ballot for President on Thursday afternoon, but the opposition effected a postponement. . . . Some time after midnight the Pennsylvania delegation, despite promises from Weed of tempting sums of money for campaign purposes if they would swing their strength to Seward, agreed to go for Cameron on the first ballot, McLean on the second, and Lincoln on the third. . . .

The Pennsylvanians were not won without a recompense. Davis promised Cameron a cabinet post. . . .

Conscious of the decisive part that crowd psychology might play in the morrow's session, one member of the Illinois delegation wished that the host of Seward shouters could be kept out of the Wigwam. Why not? asked somebody with a flash of inspiration. Ward Hill Lamon and Jesse Fell ordered a large supply of extra tickets printed and got them judiciously distributed to Lincoln men, all of whom were instructed to present them early. A Chicagoan reputedly able to shout across Lake Michigan was enlisted to take a strategic position in the hall and bellow lustily whenever Judd took out his handkerchief. Another man from Ottawa, equally endowed with vocal strength, was instructed to exercise his talent from another section of the Wigwam. Having done everything within their power, the weary Illinoisans snatched what sleep they could.

The convention reassembled at ten o'clock Friday morning. The hall was packed as usual. Outside, however, some extremely angry ticket-holders could not get in. For, while the Sewardites paraded, Lincoln's supporters had used their bogus tickets to advantage.

Nominations began at once, and as the name of Seward was presented, a tremendous shout went up—not all his friends remained outside by any means. But the racket merely served to inspire the Illinoisans. When Judd nominated Lincoln, their wild yell, according to one witness, "made soft vesper breathings of all that had preceded. No language can describe it. A thousand steam whistles, ten acres of hotel gongs, a tribe of Comanches, headed by a choice vanguard from pandemonium, might have mingled in the scene unnoticed." . . .

Bates, McLean, Cameron, and others were nominated, and the balloting commenced. After the long roll call the chairman announced the result: Seward 173½, Lincoln 102, Cameron 50½, Chase 49, Bates 48, with the remainder scattering. It looked henceforward like a two-way fight. Seward gained only 11 votes on the second ballot, while Lincoln picked up 79 as Pennsylvania, unmindful of McLean, swung a thumping 48 additional votes to Lincoln and he gained others elsewhere. Chase and Bates trailed with 42½ and 35 respectively.

The tension became almost unbearable as a clerk called the roll again. Hundreds of pencils kept tally. Lincoln steadily picked up. His vote reached 231½; 233 would nominate him. Joseph Medill, who had seated himself quietly among the Ohio delegation, leaned over to whisper to David Cartter, chairman of the Ohioans; "If you can throw the Ohio delegation to Lincoln, Chase can have anything he wants." Cartter, a stammerer, bounded up, exclaiming excitedly: "I-I a-a-rise Mr. Chairman, to a-a-nounce the c-ch-change of f-four votes, from Mr. Chase to Mr. Lincoln."

There was a moment's silence. Then the wildest yell of all was loosed. Men danced and jumped. Hats, handkerchiefs, banners, canes were tossed aloft. The noise lulled, only to swell again. A cannon on the roof let go with a salute. Boat whistles answered from the river. The city's bells joined in the din. Across the nation thousands of telegraph instruments commenced to chatter.

The sectional storm was now sweeping all before it. The Democratic party, once dominant in the national councils, began to break up on the dangerous reefs of secession. Gathered at Charleston three weeks before the Republican convention at Chicago, it had been unable to nominate a candidate, and lost the Southern extremists in a walkout which was the first move toward rebellion. In June various splinter groups of the party met again at Baltimore, and this time the Democratic party fell apart: the regular Democrats nominated Douglas of Illinois, the seceders John C. Breckinridge of Kentucky, while a moderate group of disgruntled old Whigs calling itself the Constitutional Union party named John Bell of Tennessee. With the opposition thus fragmented, a Republican triumph was assured. Nevertheless, the Republicans staged a noisy and exuberant campaign.

Following the election there were four anxious, wearing months in Springfield before Lincoln could take the oath of office. For the most part Lincoln maintained a policy of silence; but he was besieged by office-seekers, politicians, and the just plain curious.

Henry Villard, a young German correspondent for the New York Herald *and later a railroad magnate, reported on Lincoln during the fall of 1860.[12] At first he doubted Lincoln's capacity for leadership in the expected crisis, but within a month he had changed his opinion.*

Small as the number of attendants has been for some days—not over 160 per day—the receptions of the President are nevertheless highly interesting and worthy of detailed notice. They are held daily from ten A.M. to 12 Noon and from three P.M. to half-past five P.M. in the Governor's room at the State House, which has been for some time given up to the wants of Mr. Lincoln.

The appointed hour having arrived, the crowd moved up stairs into the second storey, in the southeast corner of which the reception room is located. Passing through a rather dark sort of doorway, the clear voice and often ringing laughter of the President usually guide them to the right door. The boldest of the party having knocked, a ready "Come in" invites them to enter. On opening the door, the tall, lean form of "Old Abe" directly confronts the leader of the party. Seizing the latter's hand with a hearty shake, Lincoln leads him in, and bids the rest to follow suit with an encouraging "Get in, all of you." The whole party being in, he will ask for their names, and then immediately start a running conversation. Although he is naturally more listened to than talked to, he does not allow a pause to become protracted.

He is never at a loss as to the subjects that please the different classes of visitors and there is a certain quaintness and originality about all he has to say, so that one cannot help feeling interested. His "talk" is not brilliant. His phrases are not ceremoniously set, but pervaded with a humorousness and, at times, with a grotesque joviality, that will always please. I think it would be hard to find one who tells better jokes, enjoys them better and laughs oftener than Abraham Lincoln.

. . . No restrictions, whatever, being exercised as to visitors, the crowd, that daily waits on the President, is always of a motley description. Everybody who lives in this vicinity or passes through this place, goes to take a look at "Old Abe." Muddy boots and hickory shirts are just as frequent as broadcloth, fine linen, etc. The ladies, however, are usually dressed up in their very best, although they cannot hope to make an impression on old married Lincoln. Offensively democratic exhibitions of free manners occur every once in a while. Churlish fellows will obtrude themselves with their hats on, lighted cigars and their pantaloons tucked into their boots. Dropping into chairs they sit puffing away and trying to gorgonize the President with their silent stares, until their boorish curiosity is fully satisfied. Formal presentations are dispensed with in most cases. Nearly everyone finds his own way in and introduces himself. Sometimes half a dozen rustics rush in, break their way through other visitors up to the object of their search and after calling their names and touching the Presidential fingers, back out again. . . .

Mr. Lincoln's personal appearance is the subject of daily remark among those who have known him formerly. Always cadaverous, his aspect is now almost ghostly. His position is wearing him terribly. Letters threatening his life are daily received from the South, occasionally, also, a note of warning from some Southerner who does not like his principles, but would regret violence. But these trouble him little compared with the apprehended difficulty of conciliating the South without destroying the integrity of his own party. The present aspect of the country, I think, augurs one of the most difficult terms which any President has yet been called to weather; and I doubt Mr. Lincoln's capacity for the task of bringing light and peace out of the chaos that will surround him. A man of good heart and good intention, he is not firm. The times demand a Jackson.

By February of 1861, seven southern states had already seceded from the Union. And Lincoln had to recognize that he was a minority President, a President who would have to take office with the knowledge that all of the South and a great part of the North had voted against him. Yet most authorities now agree that the unorganized majority—North and South—opposed disunion, and upon this helpless majority Lincoln would have to pin his hopes.

In the second volume of his The Emergence of Lincoln, *Allan Nevins has summed up the election.*[13]

Men might, as always, dispute the meaning of the election. On the surface it seemed to offer no clean-cut national verdict for anything; certainly not for Lincoln and the Republican tenets. Yet its central import was actually plain: The nation had taken a mighty decision—the decision that slavery must be circumscribed and contained. Lincoln's 1,866,000 followers wished to contain the institution within existing limits by a flat Congressional refusal to recognize it outside; the 1,375,000 adherents of Douglas wished to contain it by local-option type of popular sovereignty. But contained it would be, under either formula. No longer would a compact, determined Southern minority dictate national policy on the subject. The popular majority of the land had asserted itself, and a people's man, far stronger than the South supposed, stood ready to execute their will. Behind this decision that slavery had passed its flood tide and must henceforth stand still or recede, lay an implicit decision on the two rival assumptions that had divided South and North —one, the assumption that slavery was right and wholesome; the other, that it was wrong and deleterious. Slavery might persist indefinitely within the fifteen slave States, but as to its restriction, and as to the faith that it was in the path of ultimate extinction, the nation had come at last to an unavoidable determination.

From that decision there was but one appeal. Dreadfully clear now, to ears attuned to the future, sounded the drums and bugles.

Lincoln and the Civil War

1861-1865

1.

The Union Breaks Apart

Tension slackened during Lincoln's last weeks in Springfield. Of the fifteen slave states, eight still remained loyal to the Union in February of 1861, and all but one of these accepted Virginia's call for a peace convention to meet in Washington that month. In the meantime special Congressional committees had been searching for an acceptable compromise. From the Senate's Committee of Thirteen came the Crittenden proposal which would have restored the Missouri Compromise line to the Pacific, excluding slavery to the north of it but guaranteeing it to the south. But Lincoln continued to oppose any further extension of slavery into the territories. "Stand firm," he advised. "The tug has to come, & better now than any time hereafter."[1]

On February eighth, three days before the new President left for Washington, seven seceding states meeting at Montgomery, Alabama, adopted a constitution and the next day elected Jefferson Davis president. In the deep South, at least, secession was in full tide. In the first volume of Abraham Lincoln: The War Years, Carl Sandburg has provided an impressionistic sketch of the "divided house" that Lincoln was now called upon to rule.[2]

Only tall stacks of documents recording the steel of fact and the fog of dream could tell the intricate tale of the shaping of a national fate, of men saying Yes when they meant No and No when they meant Perhaps; of newspapers North and South lying to their readers and pandering to the cheaper passions of party, clique, and class interest; of the men and women of the ruling classes North and South being dominated more often than not by love of money, wealth, power, distinction, luxury, servants, jewels, and display beyond necessity or importance; of the Southern planters and merchants being $200,000,000 in debt to the North and chiefly to the money controllers of New York City; of the paradoxes involved in the Northern hope of the black man's freedom in the South; of the jealousy of Virginia and Kentucky slave-breeders, whose market was interfered with by the African slave-traders; of the race question that was one thing in the blizzard region of New England, where a Negro was pointed out on the streets as a rare curiosity, and something else again in the deep drowsy tropical South, where in so many areas the Negro outnumbered the white man; of the greed of Savannah and Mobile slave-traders, who mocked at the law prohibiting them from buying Negroes in Africa and selling those Negroes in Cuba for delivery in the Gulf Coast canebreaks and everglades; of how the prohibitory law as to fugitive slaves was mocked at and made a byword by abolitionists stealing slave property and running it North to freedom; of abolitionists hanged, shot, stabbed, mutilated, disfigured facially by vitriol, their home doorways painted with human offal; of the Northern manufacturer being able to throw out men or machines no longer profitable while the Southern planter could not so easily scrap his production apparatus of living black men and women; of the *New York Times* elaborately analyzing the Northern wage and money system as having "masses of disposable capital" while the assets of the South were fixed and frozen through the slavery system; of stock and bond markets becoming huge gambling enterprises in which fleeced customers learned later that the dice had been loaded; of a new mass production intricately organized in firearms and watch factories; of automatic machinery slightly guided by human hands producing shoes, fabrics, scissors, pins, and imitation jewelry sold by a chain of Dollar Stores; of a wilderness of oil derricks sprung up in western Pennsylvania, and the new gas engine of the French inventor Lenoir; of sky-climbing balloons soaring 23,000 feet and the prediction that soon there would be passenger balloons to Europe; of microscopically exact gauges to measure one ten-thousandths of an inch for you, sir; of such curious statistics as the Far Western State of Iowa having double the white population of South Carolina; of the persistent national vision of a railroad to the Pacific joining East and West coasts; of covered wagons heading west with the sign "Pike's Peak or Bust" and others returning with the sign "Busted by Gosh," of still other wagons emblazoned "Ho for California," "Oregon or Death," or "The Eleventh Commandment: Mind Your Own Business"; of five hundred westbound wagons a day passing through Fort Kearney, Nebraska; of horse stages taking passengers west across plains, desert, mountains, against thirst, heat, alkali water, sandstorms, Indians, bandits, breakdowns, in a regular twenty-three-day run from St. Louis to San Francisco; of the pony express running the United States mail from St. Joseph, Missouri, to San Francisco in eleven days, using five hundred horses and eighty riders, each taking the sacks an average of 133⅓ miles, carrying knife and revolver, riding three ponies to one stretch, sliding off one and hopping another, a living chain of human service going on day or night, in moonlight, under stars or in darkness, through rain, snow, sleet, over level prairies, hugging steep mountain trails and across desert paths laid through cactus and sage better known to the lizard and the coyote; of farming machinery that doubled or tripled the range of crop land one man could handle; of woman's household work lightened by labor-saving sewing machines, churns, egg-beaters, and like devices; of the casual and unquestioned statement that "two centuries ago not one person in a thousand wore stockings, one century ago not one person in five hundred wore them, and now not one person in a thousand is without them"; of Abraham Lincoln thumbing through his personal copy of *Blackwood's Magazine* and reading that in thirty years the population of the United States would double and in 1940 reach 303,000,000; of immense stretches of land where sod might yet be broken for unnumbered millions to come; . . . of the 260,000 free Negroes of the South owning property valued at $25,000,000, one of them being the wealthiest landowner in Jefferson County, Virginia; of at least one in every hundred free Negroes owning one or two slaves, a few owning fifty or more; of the Southern poor white lacking slaves, land, and the decent creature comforts of the Negro house servant, lacking the guarantees of food, clothing, shelter, and employment assured the Negro field hand; of the Southern poor white often clutching as his dearest personal possession the fact that he was not born black; of Northern factory hands and garment-trade workers paid a bare subsistence wage, lacking security against accident, sickness, old age, unemployment while alive and funeral costs when finally dead; of the vague hope across the South that the Northwestern States might join their Confederacy or form a confederacy of their own hostile to New England and allied to the South; of the one-crop Cotton States' heavy dependence on the Border Slave States and the North for food supplies, animal fodder, implements, and clothing; of the Cotton States' delusion that New England and Europe were economic dependents of King Cotton. . . .

Thus might run a jagged sketch of the Divided House over which Lincoln was to be Chief Magistrate. And now before he was yet sworn in came advice from the *New York Herald*, circulating 77,000 copies daily, earning profits of $300,000 a year, mentioned by President James Buchanan as "the most powerful organ in the country for the formation of public opinion." Its owner and editor, James Gordon Bennett, publicly, so the whole country might know, told Lincoln that instead of going to Washington for inauguration he should step out of the national picture and go home. "A grand opportunity now exists for Lincoln to avert impending ruin, and invest his name with an immortality far more enduring than would attach to it by his elevation to the Presidency," read the newspaper editorial. "His withdrawal at this time from the scene of conflict, and the surrender of his claims to some national man who would be acceptable to both sections, would render him the peer of Washington in patriotism." And having instructed the President-elect, the *Herald* added a warning: "If he persists in his present position, in the teeth of such results as his election must produce, he will totter into a dishonoured grave, driven there perhaps by the hands of an assassin, leaving behind a memory more execrable than that of Arnold —more despised than that of the traitor Catiline." . . .

It took Lincoln twelve days to reach Washington from Springfield, along a circuitous route that allowed for the maximum of speeches, receptions and banquets. He was not at his best. Faced with the crisis, his speeches were evasive and much too cheery. In Columbus, Ohio, amazement and ridicule greeted his statement that: "It is a good thing that there is no more than anxiety, for there is nothing going wrong . . . there is nothing that really hurts anybody."[3]

A few days later Jefferson Davis, down in Alabama, took the oath of office while cannon boomed and in the town's leading theater an actress danced upon the Stars and Stripes. After meeting Lincoln in New York City a keen observer wrote, ". . . he owned to me that he was more troubled by the outlook than he thought it discreet to show."[4]

Warned by his advisers of a plot to assassinate him while pass-

*ing through disaffected Baltimore, Lincoln, much against his in-
clination, allowed them to slip him through the city in disguise in
the dead of night. He arrived unheralded in Washington early on
the morning of February twenty-third.*

*Conditions in Baltimore reflected the fact that the Union was
not separating neatly into two halves. The populations of large
border areas were miserably torn in their loyalties. Maryland,
Kentucky, Missouri, Delaware, the western portion of Virginia,
even the southern parts of Ohio, Indiana and Illinois looked in
greater or lesser measure to the South, and many of these regions
were now uncertain which way to turn. To complicate matters,
much of this huge area, with a population larger than that of the
newly created Confederacy, was slave territory. To lose it, or
any substantial part of it, would be to risk defeat before the battle had fairly begun. Upon reaching Washington one of Lincoln's
first acts, therefore, was to meet with the delegates of the Peace
Convention, which had been sitting in that city for several weeks
under the chairmanship of old ex-President Tyler.*

*And then Lincoln had to face the mounting flood of office-
seekers, politicians, bigwigs, all clamoring for his attention. In*
Reveille in Washington *Margaret Leech describes the hectic first
days in Washington.*[5]

At six o'clock next morning, when the train from
Philadelphia pulled into the Washington depot, the conductor
might have been surprised at the sudden recovery of a sick gentleman, who on the preceding night had been quietly hustled into
a berth at the end of the last car. The gentleman, in a soft,
slouched hat, a muffler and a short, bobtailed overcoat, descended
spryly to the platform. His tall and lanky figure would have
made him an oddity in any gathering, and he had a plain, dark-
skinned, melancholy face, with a stiff new crop of chin whiskers.
He was closely attended by two companions, one of whom was

big and heavily built, with bulges under his coat in every place
where a man might carry arms; while the other was a short,
bearded fellow, with a wary, peasant face. As they passed along
the platform in the stream of sleepy-eyed travelers, they attracted
attention from only one person in the depot, a man who had
planted himself behind a pillar, and was peering out with a sharp,
worried expression. As the lanky stranger passed, this man seized
hold of his hand. "Abe," he cried in a loud voice, "you can't play
that on me!" "Don't strike him," the stranger hastily told his
escorts. "It is Washburne." The President-elect had arrived in the
capital of the United States. . . .

The original plan, that Mr. Lincoln should occupy a rented
house during the pre-inauguration period, had been changed on
the advice of Thurlow Weed, the political manager of New York
State. In a hotel, the incoming President would be accessible to
the people, and Mr. Weed himself had written to Willard's to
make the reservation. The best rooms in the house were, however, occupied when Mr. Lincoln made his unexpectedly early
appearance, and a New York capitalist had to be hastily dislodged
from the suite connected with Parlor Number 6, a large corner
apartment on the second floor, overlooking the Avenue and the
grounds of the Executive Mansion.

Mr. Seward was waiting at Willard's to receive the President-
elect and congratulate him on his safe arrival. He was somewhat
chagrined, Washburne thought, that he had not been up in time
to go to the depot. At eight o'clock, however, the senator and
the congressman sat down in high elation to breakfast, loading
their plates with the first run of Potomac shad. Mr. Lincoln had
retired to his rooms to rest. . . .

Mr. Lincoln breakfasted alone at nine in his parlor, and did
not appear until eleven, when he left the hotel under the escort
of Mr. Seward. Those solitary morning hours were the quietest
he was ever to know in Washington. He would live thereafter at

the mercy of the people, advancing eternally toward him in a jerking procession of faces.

The first duty of the President-elect was to pay his respects at the Executive Mansion. A special meeting of the Cabinet was in session, when the doorkeeper handed Mr. Buchanan a startling card. "Uncle Abe is downstairs!" the President cried, and hurriedly descended to the Red Room. He soon returned with the two Republicans. Mr. Lincoln was presented to the Cabinet, and paused for a few minutes' conversation before leaving to call on General Scott. . . .

Rumors that he was in town caused unprecedented sales of the *Evening Star,* which was out in the early afternoon with a description of his arrival at Willard's. Many people still remained skeptical. . . . Later, "squads of the incredulous" surged through the rain to meet the special train, and the Fourteenth Street entrance to Willard's was surrounded. The crowds were rewarded by the sight of the weary Presidential party, oppressed by the gloom of the Maryland threats and Lincoln's sudden departure. Mrs. Lincoln had become hysterical over the separation from her husband. Colonel Edwin Sumner was a very angry old soldier, thwarted in the performance of his duty; and Colonel Ellsworth had expected their train to be mobbed in Baltimore. To counteract the depression, Bob Lincoln had led the party in a rendition of "The Star-Spangled Banner," as the cars crossed the Maryland line.

Leaning on the arm of Mr. Seward, Mrs. Lincoln entered the hotel, and was received in the thronged hallway by the Messrs. Willard in person. Upstairs, the President-elect sprawled in an armchair with a beaming face, while his two spoiled boys, Willie and Tad, climbed over him. He had had a busy afternoon, for the tide of visitors had already set toward Parlor Number 6. General Scott, whom he had missed in the morning, had returned his call in full uniform, sweeping his instep with the yellow plumes of his hat as he bowed. Headed by Stephen A. Douglas, the Illinois senators and congressmen had paid their respects. Old Francis P. Blair had come in with his hatchet-faced son, Montgomery, who was hoping to be appointed Postmaster General. The Blair family, father and two sons, were a power in the Republican party. They were a fighting clan from the border slave States, Democrats who had swung into opposition to slavery. The elder Blair, formerly a famous newspaper editor and a member of Jackson's Kitchen Cabinet, was an acute politician who still wielded great influence behind the scenes. Frank, junior, former congressman, recently reelected, was a Free-Soil leader in Missouri; while Montgomery, like his father, now lived and intrigued in Maryland. Mr. Lincoln reposed great confidence in the senior Blair, and submitted to him, as well as to his chief adviser, Mr. Seward, a copy of his inaugural address.

Soon after his family's arrival, Lincoln was informed that the delegates to the Peace Conference desired to wait on him. He appointed the hour of nine to receive them, and drove off to a seven o'clock dinner at Seward's, where the Vice-President-elect, Senator Hannibal Hamlin of Maine, was also present. The long parlor hall at Willard's was lined with people when he returned; and, shaking hands on both sides, he was so interested, said the *New York Herald*, that he forgot to remove his shiny new silk hat.

Ex-President Tyler and the Honorable Salmon P. Chase of Ohio led the Peace delegates up the stairs to Parlor Number 6. Chase was as pompous as General Scott, and very nearly as antipathetic to slavery as Senator Sumner. Re-elected to the Senate after serving as governor of his State, he was the most prominent of the former Democrats in the Republican party. His rumored appointment to the Cabinet would satisfy the radicals, who were disgruntled with the conciliatory Seward. He was tall, imposing, and handsome, with the noble brow of a statesman. As he stood beside Mr. Lincoln, presenting the delegates, it was Chase who

looked the part of President of the United States, and Chase
would have been the first to think so. . . .

The next day was Sunday, and Mr. Lincoln attended St. John's
Church with Mr. Seward. Under the same guidance he visited the
Senate and the House on Monday, and also the Supreme Court;
but almost his entire time during the pre-inauguration week was
spent in the big, crowded parlor of the hotel suite. Willard's held
an unprecedented collection of men notable in public affairs, civil,
military, and naval. Republican leaders were there to confer, and
delegations to press their advice on the administration's policies
and Cabinet appointments. The Peace Conference was winding
up its session with resolutions that satisfied no one, and border
slave State men came to beseech guarantees that there would be
no Federal coercion. Past the new President, from early morning
until late at night, streamed minor politicians, place seekers, editors, reporters and handshakers. He was still unknown to the
passer-by in the street, but hundreds became familiar with his
features in Parlor Number 6. . . .

*As inauguration day approached many, including old General
Winfield Scott, hero of the Mexican War and now Commander-
in-Chief of the Army, feared violence. Scott deployed his troops
along the route of the inaugural procession, placed sharpshooters
in windows, and moved two batteries of artillery near the Capitol.
Wilder Dwight, an enthusiastic young major from Massachusetts,
described the scene in a letter.*[6]

WASHINGTON, March 4, 1861

Dear Father,—

This morning broke badly, but at noon the sky cleared. I remained quietly at Willard's, and was present when Mr. Buchanan
came to receive the President-elect, and saw the interview, which
was a formal one; then I saw Lincoln and Buchanan take their

carriage, and, by back streets, reached the Capitol grounds, and got a good place.

Soon Lincoln and Judge Taney, followed by Buchanan and the other judges, etc. appeared. The band played Hail Columbia. The crowd was immense. The Capitol steps were covered with uniforms, etc. Baker, of Oregon, for the Committee of Arrangements, announced that Mr. Lincoln would speak; and when Abraham rose and came forward and rang out the words, "Fellow-citizens of the *United* States," he loomed and grew and was ugly no longer. I was not very near, but heard him perfectly. The address you will read, and like, I hope. Its effect was very good. An immense concourse—thousands—stood uncovered and silent, except occasional applause; the voice clear and ringing; the manner very good, often impressive, and even solemn; the words I think to the point, direct and clear. The scene itself was of its own kind. And I must say its effect upon me was far greater than I had supposed.

When the address closed and the cheering subsided, Taney rose, and, almost as tall as Lincoln, he administered the oath, Lincoln repeating it; and as the words, "preserve, protect and defend the Constitution" came ringing out, he bent and kissed the book; and for one, I breathed freer and gladder than for months. The man looked a man, and acted a man and a President. So much for the inauguration.

Benjamin Thomas analyzes Lincoln's First Inaugural Address.[7]

Unrolling his manuscript and adjusting his spectacles, Lincoln faced the anxious crowd. His first words offered reassurance to the South. "I have no purpose, directly or indirectly, to interfere with the institution of slavery in the states where it exists," he declared. "I believe I have no lawful right to do so, and I have no inclination to do so." Just before adjournment Congress had passed a thirteenth amendment to the Constitution, forever guaranteeing slavery in the states from Federal interference, and Lincoln, having made a last-minute insertion in his manuscript, promised his support to this amendment. Since he thought such a guarantee was already implied in the Constitution, he said, "I have no objection to its being made express, and irrevocable." He would respect the constitutional provision for the capture and return of fugitive slaves.

Having sought to quiet Southern fears, Lincoln faced squarely the question of Federal authority. "No State, upon its own mere notion, can lawfully get out of the Union," he asserted. But what of those states which already considered themselves withdrawn? "I shall take care," said he, "as the Constitution itself expressly enjoins me, that the laws of the Union be faithfully executed in all the States. Doing this I deem to be only a simple duty on my part; and I shall perform it, so far as practicable, unless my rightful masters, the American people, shall withhold the requisite means, or, in some authoritative manner, direct the contrary." But there need be no resort to force or bloodshed in enforcing the laws. "The power confided to me will be used to hold, occupy, and possess the property, and places belonging to the government, and to collect the duties and imposts; but beyond what may be necessary for these objects, there will be no invasion— no using of force against, or among the people anywhere."

In the original draft of the address Lincoln had expressed a purpose to *reclaim* the public places and property already seized, but on the advice of his friend Orville H. Browning he changed this to "hold, occupy, and possess" government property. In line with suggestions of Seward and experienced old Francis Preston Blair, Lincoln toned down pledges regarding the maintenance of Federal authority and stressed promises of conciliation, so that the speech in its final form was as indulgent as he could make it without renouncing his constitutional duties. Where hostility to the government was so "great and so universal" as to prevent resident citizens from administering the Federal offices, no attempt would be made to force "obnoxious strangers" upon the people, Lincoln promised. "While the strict legal right may exist in the government to enforce the exercise of these offices, the attempt to do so would be so irritating . . . that I deem it better to forego, for the time, the use of such offices." The mails would be delivered unless repelled. The customs would be collected offshore (actually no effort was made to collect them). Defiance would not be met by force. While Federal authority would be upheld in principle, every possible concession would be made, in the hope that time and an atmosphere of friendliness would compose all differences.

Physically speaking, the states could not separate, Lincoln pointed out. They must remain face to face, and commercial and political relations must continue. Would such relations be more satisfactory after separation than before? Could aliens make treaties more easily than friends could make laws? Could treaties be better enforced among aliens than laws among friends? Why should there not be a patient confidence in the ultimate justice of the people? "If the Almighty Ruler of nations, with his eternal truth and justice, be on your side of the North, or on yours of the South, that truth, and that justice, will surely prevail, by the judgment of this great tribunal, the American people." Nothing could be lost by taking time.

"In *your* hands, my dissatisfied fellow countrymen, and not in *mine*, is the momentous issue of civil war. The government will not assail *you*. You can have no conflict, without being yourselves the aggressors. *You* can have no oath registered in Heaven to destroy the government, while *I* shall have the most solemn one to 'preserve, protect and defend' it."

Lincoln had meant to close with this paragraph, but Seward suggested some final "words of affection—of calm and cheerful confidence," and offered an additional paragraph of his own phrasing. The idea met Lincoln's hearty sanction, and he transformed the Secretary's graceless sentences into a moving and exalted plea: "I am loath to close. We are not enemies, but friends. We must not be enemies. Though passion may have strained, it must not break our bonds of affection. The mystic chords of memory, stretching from every battle-field and patriot grave, to every living heart and hearth stone, all over this broad land, will yet swell the chorus of the Union, when again touched, as surely they will be, by the better angels of our nature."

The day after his inauguration, Lincoln was told that the most important Southern stronghold still in Union hands, Fort Sumter in Charleston harbor, must be provisioned within six weeks or its troops withdrawn. The North already looked upon the Fort as a symbol of the Union itself. To the South the presence of a "foreign" force in the heart of the new Confederacy had become intolerable. And any attempt to supply and thus maintain the Fort might well lead to war. In the passage below Richard Hofstadter suggests that Lincoln's handling of the situation was deliberately designed to place the onus of starting a war—if there had to be a war—upon the South.[8]

Before Lincoln took office the issues upon which he was elected had become obsolete. Seven states of the deep South had seceded. The great question was no longer slavery or freedom in the territories, but the nation itself. The Union, if it was to be maintained, as Lincoln, an ardent nationalist, thought it must, could be defended only by the sort of aggressive war that few Northerners wanted to wage. Psychologically on the defensive, the North had to be strategically on the offensive. One of Lincoln's most striking achievements was his tactical and ideological resolution of this difficulty.

By all rational calculation the Confederacy had much to lose and nothing to gain by war. Its strategic aim was merely to preserve itself as an independent state, an end that could be lost in war and achieved in peace. The North, on the other hand, once compromise and reconciliation had failed, had to wage a successful coercive war in order to restore the Union. Northern public opinion, which was in fierce agreement on the desirability of maintaining the Union, was reluctant to consider what saving the Union might cost. There was no more unanimity in the North on waging the war to keep the Union than there had been in the South on seceding to destroy it. *Always there loomed the danger that an apparently unprovoked attack upon the Confederacy would alienate so many people in the Union and the world at large that it would hopelessly cripple the very cause for which the war would be fought.* Such an attack would certainly lose the support of the border states, still not withdrawn from the Union, which Lincoln was desperately eager to hold. He had deferred to this sentiment in his Inaugural Address. . . .

The situation had all the elements of a dilemma for both sides. But since Lincoln had to act first to save the fort [Sumter] from starving, his was the initial problem. He had promised to maintain the Union, and protect, preserve, and defend the Constitution. It was now too late to restore the Union by compromise, because the Republican leaders, with his advice and consent, had rejected compromise in December. To order Anderson to withdraw Fort Sumter's garrison at the demand of the Confederates was a tremendous concession, which Lincoln actually considered but rejected; it would be an implicit acknowledgment of the legality of secession, and the Union would, by his own recognition, be at an end; the moral stock of the Confederacy would go soaring. And yet a military assault to bring relief to the fort would be a dangerous expedient. If it failed, it would ruin the already diminished prestige of his administration; success or failure, it would be looked upon by peace advocates and the border states as wanton aggression. However, there was one way out: the Confederates themselves might bring matters to a head by attacking Sumter before Anderson should be forced by shortages to evacuate.

It was precisely such an attack that Lincoln's strategy brought about. On March 29, 1861 the Secretaries of War and the Navy were ordered to co-operate in preparing a relief expedition to move by sea on April 6. Governor Pickens of South Carolina was notified that an attempt would be made to supply Fort Sumter *"with provisions only,"* and not with arms, and was advised by Lincoln that "if such an attempt be not resisted, no effort to throw in men, arms, or ammunition will be made without further notice, or [sic] in case of an attack upon the fort."

To Northern opinion such a relief expedition would seem innocent enough—bringing food to hungry men. But to the Confederacy it posted a double threat: force would be used *if* the attempt to provision the fort were resisted; and should it not be resisted, an indefinite occupation by Union forces could be expected, which would weaken the Confederate cause at home and sap its prestige abroad, where diplomatic recognition was so precious. Lincoln had now taken the burden of the dilemma from his own shoulders and forced it upon the Southerners. Now they must either attack the fort and accept the onus of striking the first blow, or face an indefinite and enervating occupation of Sumter by Anderson's soldiers. Could any supposedly sovereign government permit a foreign power to hold a fort dominating the trade of one of its few great harbors? As Professor James G. Randall has observed, the logic of secession demanded that the Confederates take the fort or that the Union abandon it.

Major Anderson refused a demand for prompt evacuation. Knowing that the Union relief fleet was approaching, the Confederates on the morning of April 12 began firing upon Sumter, and thus convicted themselves by an act of aggression. They had not only broken the Union, they had attacked it; and the reception of the deed in the North was everything that Lincoln could wish.

On July 3 the newly appointed Senator from Illinois, Orville Browning (chosen to replace Douglas, who had just died), called upon Lincoln and held a conversation with him. Fortunately Browning kept a diary, and his entry for that evening reads:

> He [Lincoln] told me that the very first thing placed in his hands after his inauguration was a letter from Majr. Anderson announcing the impossibility of defending or relieving Sumter. That he called the cabinet together and consulted Genl Scott—that Scott concurred with Anderson, and the cabinet, with the exception of P M Genl Blair were for evacuating the Fort, and all the troubles and anxieties of his life had not equalled those which intervened between this time and the fall of Sumter. He himself conceived the idea, and proposed sending supplies, without an attempt to reinforce [,] giving notice of the fact to Gov Pickens of S.C. *The plan succeeded. They attacked Sumter—it fell, and thus, did more service than it otherwise could.*

If we may trust Browning, who was one of Lincoln's friends, it was the Confederate attack and not the military success of the expedition that mattered most. In a letter to Gustavus Vasa Fox, the extraordinary naval officer who had led the relief attempt, Lincoln concluded, "You and I both anticipated that the cause of the country would be advanced by making the attempt to provision Fort Sumter, even if it should fail; and it is no small consolation now to feel that our anticipation is justified by the result."

This realistic bit of statecraft provides no reason for disparaging Lincoln, certainly not by those who hold that it was his legal and moral duty to defend the integrity of the Union by the most effective means at his command. The Confederate attack made it possible to picture the war as a defensive one; for some time it unified Northern sentiment. Who can say with certainty that the war could have been won on any other terms?

Lincoln's "realistic bit of statecraft" enabled him, in his message to Congress on July fourth, to picture the war not only as a struggle to maintain the Union but also as a crusade to defend the democratic way of life—"man's vast future" as he so often called it—from a mortal attack. "This is essentially a people's contest," he said. *"On the side of the Union it is a struggle for maintaining in the world that form and substance of government whose leading object is to elevate the condition of men. . . . Our popular government has often been called an experiment. Two points in it our people have already settled—the successful* establishing *and the successful* administering *of it. One still remains—its successful* maintenance *against a formidable internal attempt to overthrow it. . . . Such will be a great lesson of peace; teaching men that what they cannot take by an election, neither can they take by a war; teaching all the folly of being the beginners of a war."*[9]

The attack upon Fort Sumter released the tension built up through many years of bickering. With the conflict now so clearly joined, there was a tremendous, almost joyous, upwelling of war fever, North and South. Virginia promptly left the Union, to be followed shortly by North Carolina, Arkansas and Tennessee. For the moment both sections were united as they would not be again through four long years of war.

Washington found itself exposed on the borders of a hostile nation. Cut off from the Union by rebellious Maryland, it expected any moment to be invaded from the South. The Sixth Massachusetts, coming to its rescue, was attacked by a furious mob in Baltimore as it passed through, resulting in the first blood-

*shed of the war. Then for a week no more troops arrived. It
was an anxious time in Washington. Across the Potomac Confederate campfires twinkled at night, while by day disloyal government workers and army and navy officers streamed out of the
city to join the enemy. Willard's hotel was deserted and the
avenues desolate except for sentries patrolling before the bar-
ricaded public buildings. In his office Lincoln paced up and down,
muttering, "Why don't they come? Why don't they come?" And
at last they came, the crack Seventh New York leading the way
for 10,000 troops.*

*On May 10, 1861, a young lady named Jane Stuart Woolsey
wrote a letter from New York City to a friend in Paris which
gives an unforgettable picture of the naïve enthusiasm and the
hysteria of those unreal, first days of the war.*[10]

I am sure you will like to hear what we are all
about in these times of terrible excitement, though it seems almost impertinent to write just now. Everything is either too big
or too little to put in a letter. . . . So it will be best perhaps not
to try to give you any of my own "views" except, indeed, such
views of war as one may get out of a parlor window. Not, in passing, that I haven't any! We all have views now, men, women and
little boys,
> "Children with drums
> Strapped round them by the fond paternal ass,
> Peripatetics with a blade of grass
> Betwixt their thumbs,"—

from the modestly patriotic citizen who wears a postage stamp
on his hat to the woman who walks in Broadway in that fearful
object of contemplation, a "Union bonnet," composed of alternate layers of red, white and blue, with streaming ribbons "of the
first." We all have our views of the war question and our plans
of the coming campaign. An acquaintance the other day took her

little child on some charitable errand through a dingy alley into a dirty, noisy, squalid tenement house. "Mamma," said he, "isn't this South Carolina?"

Inside the parlor windows the atmosphere has been very fluffy, since Sumter, with lint-making and the tearing of endless lengths of flannel and cotton bandages and cutting out of innumerable garments. How long it is since Sumter! I suppose it is because so much intense emotion has been crowded into the last two or three weeks, that the "time before Sumter" seems to belong to some dim antiquity. It seems as if we never were alive till now; never had a country till now. How could we ever have laughed at Fourth-of-Julys? Outside the parlor windows the city is gay and brilliant with excited crowds, the incessant movement and music of marching regiments and all the thousands of flags, big and little, which suddenly came fluttering out of every window and door and leaped from every church tower, house-top, staff and ship-mast. It seemed as if everyone had in mind to try and make some amends to it for those late grievous and bitter insults. You have heard how the enthusiasm has been deepening and widening from that time.

A friend asked an Ohio man the other day how the West was taking it. "The West?" he said, "the West is all one great Eagle-scream!" A New England man told us that at Concord the bells were rung and the President's call read aloud on the village common. On the day but one after that reading, the Concord Regiment was marching into Faneuil Hall. Somebody in Washington asked a Massachusetts soldier: "How many more men of your state are coming?" "All of us," was the answer. One of the wounded Lowell men crawled into a machine shop in Baltimore. An "anti-Gorilla" citizen, seeing how young he was, asked, "What brought you here fighting, so far away from your home, my poor boy?" "It was the stars and stripes," the dying voice said. Hundreds of such stories are told. Everybody knows one. You read many of them in the papers. In our own little circle of friends one mother has sent away an idolized son; another, two; another, four. One boy, just getting over diphtheria, jumps out of bed and buckles his knapsack on. One throws up his passage to Europe and takes up his "enfield." One sweet young wife is packing a regulation valise for her husband today, and doesn't let him see her cry. Another young wife is looking fearfully for news from Harper's Ferry, where her husband is ordered. He told me a month ago, *before* Sumter, that no Northman could be found to fight against the South. One or two of our soldier friends are surgeons or officers, but most of them are in the ranks, and think no work too hard or too mean, so it is for The Flag. Captain Schuyler Hamilton was an aid of General Scott's in Mexico, and saw service there, but he shouldered his musket and marched as a private with the Seventh. They wanted an officer when he got down there, and took him out of the ranks, but it was all the same to him; and so on, indefinitely. . . .

There was a dark time just after the Baltimore murders, when communication with Washington was cut off and the people in power seemed to be doing nothing to re-establish it. It cleared up, however, in a few days, and now we don't feel that the "social fabric"—I believe that is what it is called—is "falling to pieces" at all, but that it is getting gloriously mended. So, "Republicanism will wash"—*is* washed already in the water and the fire of this fresh baptism, "clothed in white samite, mystic, wonderful," and has a new name, which is *Patriotism*.

The accession of four more border states to the South, led by Virginia, enormously increased the size and power of the Confederacy. And with Virginia went Robert E. Lee, after refusing an offer to command the Union armies. The remaining border states now held the balance of power. It was not too difficult to hold Maryland and Delaware in the Union because of their geographical positions; but it took all of Lincoln's statesmanship, working largely in secret and behind the scenes, to save Kentucky and Missouri. In his lively The Military Genius of Abraham Lincoln, *written shortly after World War I, General Colin R. Ballard, an Englishman, opens with the delicate problem of the border states, then sets the stage for the first battle of the war, Bull Run.*[11]

Thus, Lincoln was compelled to base his strategy on the ruling principle that Washington and the border States must be held at all costs; this entailed leaving detachments to watch a front over 1,000 miles in length, and there was no concealment of the fact that the reasons for this were purely political.

This is a very important point, because it marks the first rift between his strategy and the orthodox faith—only a little rift as yet, but to grow into a chasm later on. The true faith is that attack is always the best means of defence, and that all forces should be concentrated to form a mass for offensive action; this mass should be directed against the main body of the enemy. Passive resistance can never be anything but a crime. A temporary attitude of defence, with a view to counter-attack, may be condoned only on the Jesuitical principle of doing evil that good may come; but it must be regarded with suspicion, and the counter-stroke must be prepared beforehand.

Now if this "grand principle of warfare" be applied to the present case it means that all the Federal forces should have been collected; they would form a steamroller which could crush Virginia and take Richmond; the rebellion would then collapse; meanwhile the border States would have to take care of themselves. "If you cut down a tree the branches will fall."

None of the critics has gone so far as to put this into words as a serious suggestion. They recognize that in a benighted country, where war is unknown, politics must have their say; much may be forgiven to the heathen in his blindness. But if in this instance Lincoln was more to be pitied than blamed it was the first symptom of political interference, and he must be watched in future.

Lincoln himself was quite shrewd enough to see that a passive defensive would guard his own States but would never crush the rebellion. He must therefore think out offensive measures of some kind.

Here he picked out as his chief asset Command of the Sea, and it was one which could be brought to bear on a weak point of the enemy. The capital of the South was locked up in plantations and slaves. There was little internal trade. Commerce, and with it finance, depended on keeping open communications with Europe. Five million bales of cotton had been shipped to England in 1860. At the same time the South was not rich in factories, and would want to draw munitions as well as other necessaries from abroad. A tight blockade would therefore cripple finance and cut off supplies: it would thus be a real offensive measure. The task was not an easy one; Lincoln deserves credit for seeing that it could be carried out and that no expense should be grudged that would make it effective. He proclaimed the blockade on April 19th, five days after the fall of Fort Sumter. It was true strategical foresight. The total coast-line to be watched was over 3,000 miles long and contained a couple of hundred harbours.

The Blockade. In 1860 the U.S. Navy had only forty-two vessels in commission, half of them sailing ships; but in those days, before ironclads, any merchantman could be transformed into a second-class man-of-war by putting a few light guns on board. By December 1861 there were 264 ships, and before the end of the war there were nearly 700.

Crews were recruited from the merchant service, who understood navigation and seamanship. The officers were accustomed to command and the men to discipline. Gunnery was not yet a fine art and could very soon be picked up. In the matter of personnel the navy was much better off than the army. Professor Paxson says: "Every village politician believed himself competent to be a colonel, if not a brigadier-general, while the public, unaccustomed to dwell on special fitness, assumed that military capacity was inherent in all. But few fancied themselves able to command a ship, and the navy was left, generally, to the control of experts." At their head was the Secretary, G. S. Welles, a good organizer.

The South had no navy to start with, and though a few vessels were improvised the actual fighting was confined to some duels which have attracted attention as romantic incidents. The real business was done by the blockade.

But, though sure, the blockade must take a long time to exert real pressure. The South, rich in food supplies, could maintain itself for a time, and it was only by degrees that the pinch was felt. And the scope of a navy is confined to the seas and the coast; the army of the South was as safe from the navy of the North as an elephant is from a whale. So, though the blockade was the main offensive, something must also be done on land if the rebellion was to be suppressed soon.

Land Operations. This brings us down to the scene of the campaigns.

A glance at the map shows that the range of the Alleghenies cuts the country into two, so, as might be expected, there were two distinct theatres of war.

A. The Western Theatre, its main features being the great rivers Ohio and Mississippi.

B. The Eastern Theatre, chiefly in Virginia. This was the more important from the fact that it contained both the capitals—Washington and Richmond. The main armies would naturally be found either defending their own capital or threatening that of the enemy.

The division between the two theatres was so complete that

operations in the one had little direct bearing on the other. This simplifies the narrative; attention can be concentrated on the East right up till July 1863, after which the story of the West can follow.

Numbers. At the outbreak of war the standing army of the United States numbered about 16,000 officers and men. Nearly all the men remained loyal to the Union, but most of them were scattered in the small forts which guarded the Indian frontier, and only 3,000 were available for service in the East. There were about 1,200 officers who had been trained at West Point; about one-third of these were Southerners, and, with few exceptions, they resigned their commissions and joined the army of the South.

Immediately after the fall of Fort Sumter the President issued proclamations calling for the following recruits:

Volunteers for three months' service	75,000
Volunteers for three years' service	42,000
Recruits for the Regular Army	22,000
Recruits for the Navy	18,000
Total . .	157,000

At first sight it looks like an error of judgment to have fixed so short a period as three months for any of the volunteers—an indication that Lincoln had very little idea of the task in front of him—in fact, a great lack of the foresight which is the first requisite in a strategist. It must, however, be noted that the appeal was made by Lincoln on his own responsibility, without consulting Congress, and as the President has no right to declare war or raise troops without the assent of Congress, he was stretching his powers quite as far if not farther than the limits intended by the Constitution. At the same time an extra session of Congress was summoned for July 4th, and as soon as it met the President sent a message asking for confirmation of his action and further power to raise the total to 400,000.

It seems that Lincoln did not want to fluster the nation, and especially the doubtful States; the call to arms must be posted in every village, and an appeal on too large a scale would give a handle to discontent, arouse alarm, and deter waverers. On the whole it appears that Lincoln himself saw a long way ahead, but did not consider the nation was yet fit to be taken into full confidence.

The system of recruiting was through the Governors of the various States. The President called on each State to supply a certain quota of the total required; the Governor then made his own arrangements for enrolling and collecting recruits. At first there was little difficulty, but later on, when the demands increased, there was a good deal of jealousy and the system did not work smoothly.

The call for recruits was oversubscribed, and 90,000 were accepted. Many, however, were absorbed in garrisons, and it was only by degrees that a surplus of 50,000 could be collected near Washington for offensive measures.

This force was divided into two. At Washington General McDowell had 35,000, organized in five divisions (Tyler, Hunter, Heintzleman, Runyon, Miles).

At Harper's Ferry, fifty miles to the north-west, was a detachment of 15,000 under General Patterson.

Reports showed that the enemy had also two forces, about 20,000 under Beauregard covering the important railway junction at Manassas; about 10,000 under J. E. Johnston facing Patterson. . . .

To sum up. As far as could be seen the factors were evenly balanced except that the Federals had a superiority in numbers, about 50,000 against 30,000; this was sufficient to decide Lincoln on an advance. It is as certain as anything can be that if he had held on without attacking he would have been condemned for throwing away a golden opportunity. . . .

Dispositions. At the beginning of July the information was fairly correct. . . . Beauregard could be outnumbered unless he were reinforced by Johnston. To prevent such reinforcement Patterson was ordered to move southwards and occupy the attention of Johnston, in the Shenandoah Valley, but without committing himself to a general engagement. This sounds simple, but is really one of the most difficult tasks in war. With a small mobile body the enemy can be harassed and threatened—later on Stonewall Jackson showed himself a master of such tactics. But Patterson's force was not sufficiently trained, nor well enough staffed, for such delicate work. He pushed southwards on July 2nd, and some skirmishing took place in the next few days. His reports showed that he was in close touch with Johnston, and therefore it was taken for granted that a sharp advance by McDowell would catch Beauregard unsupported. On July 11th and 13th McClellan defeated a Southern force in Western Virginia. The moment seemed therefore to have arrived for McDowell to advance. He left Washington on July 16th.

Public clamor for an advance on Richmond (which had succeeded Montgomery, Alabama, as the Confederate capital) was so insistent that Lincoln had ordered McDowell forward in a move which was confidently expected to end the war. For a week before the battle Mr. Horace Greeley's New York Tribune *had whipped up public excitement in the North with its repeated exhortation, "Forward to Richmond!" As the armies joined in combat, success for the North at first seemed assured; but then Johnston, having outwitted Patterson in the Shenandoah Valley, reinforced the Confederates at the crucial moment and Bull Run turned into a rout. The North was shocked into hysteria. The emotional and unstable Mr. Greeley promptly wrote Lincoln a private letter: "This is my seventh sleepless night—yours, too, doubtless—yet I think I shall not die, because I have no right to die. . . . Send me word what to do. I will live till I can hear it, at all events. If it is best for the country and for mankind that we make peace with the rebels at once, and on their own terms, do not shrink even from that. . . .*[12]

Lincoln afterward referred to this letter, which had been signed, "Yours, in the depth of bitterness," as "pusillanimous"; yet it was typical of the wild despair in the North at the time. Actually, neither side had been at all prepared for a major engagement, and the battle had been as hard on the rebels as it had been on the Yanks. It contributed dangerously, moreover, to Southern over-confidence, while at the same time it steeled the North for the far harder trials ahead. The war was not really to begin in earnest until 1862.

2.

Commander-in-Chief

---

*So far-flung were the operations of the Civil War, so shattering
its effects, so pervasive its implications that only in recent years
have we been able to gain a measure of perspective on it. The military aspects of the war in particular have been misunderstood.
The tactics of a Lee or a Jackson were so brilliant—probing and
feinting with their smaller, mobile forces; aiming wherever possible at the enemy's morale rather than at his numbers—that it is
hard for the armchair strategist to believe that the North stood
any chance of victory at all. Yet actually the North, despite its
blundering, always-too-late leadership, despite defeat after defeat,
was consistently on the offensive throughout the war around the
whole perimeter of the South.*

*This is the pivotal military fact of the war. The South sought
only to ensure its continued existence as an independent nation.
Its military planning was, therefore, primarily defensive. All it
could do was to keep the enemy off while hoping for a miracle in
the form of foreign intervention or the internal collapse of the
North. The North, on the other hand, was faced with a far more
difficult military task: the crushing of a rebellion. To win, it had
to invade the Confederacy, destroy its armies, and force the un-*

*conditional surrender of its government. An offensive operation
of this magnitude required strategic planning on a scale seldom
envisaged in Lincoln's day.*

*No wonder the North fumbled and hesitated. But in time a
winning strategy emerged; and behind this strategy lay the perti-
nacity and vision of one man. Lincoln is now recognized as the
first strategist of modern, total war. It took two Englishmen
studying our Civil War with the objectivity of the foreigner to
show us that the winning strategy was Lincoln's. General Ballard
(who wrote, "My case is that Lincoln kept a true course by
strength of character and the light of sheer genius") and Sir
Frederick Maurice, writing after World War I, were followed
by two American historians, Kenneth P. Williams and T. Harry
Williams, who completed the new picture of Lincoln as the
master strategist with Grant as his able second-in-command. In
his* Lincoln and His Generals, *T. Harry Williams gives the heart
of the argument.*[1]

The Civil War was the first of the modern total
wars, and the American democracy was almost totally unready to
fight it. The United States had in 1861 almost no army, few good
weapons, no officers trained in the higher art of war, and an inadequate and archaic system of command. Armies could be raised
and weapons manufactured quickly, but it took time and battles
to train generals. And it took time and blunders and bitter experiences to develop a modern command system. Not until 1864 did
the generals and the system emerge.

In 1861 the general in chief of the army . . . was Winfield Scott.
He was a veteran of two wars and the finest soldier in America.
But he had been born in 1786, and he was physically incapable
of commanding an army in the field. He could not ride, he could
not walk more than a few steps without pain, and he had dropsy
and vertigo. The old General dreamed wistfully of taking the

field. "If I could only mount a horse, I—" he would say sadly and pause, "but I am past that." . . .

There was not an officer in the first year of the war who was capable of efficiently administering and fighting a large army. Even Scott, had he been younger and stronger, would have had difficulty commanding any one of the big armies called into being by the government. All his experience had been with small forces, and he might not have been able to have adjusted his thinking to the organization of mass armies. The young officers who would be called to lead the new hosts lacked even his experience. Not only had they never handled troops in numbers, but they knew nothing about the history and theory of war or of strategy. They did not know the higher art of war, because there was no school in the country that taught it. . . .

One of the most ironic examples of American military unreadiness was the spectacle of Northern—and Southern—generals fighting in their own country and not knowing where they were going or how to get there. Before the war the government had collected no topographical information about neighboring countries or even the United States, except for the West. No accurate military maps existed. General Henry W. Halleck was running a campaign in the western theatre in 1862 with maps he got from a book store. With frenetic haste, the general set topographical officers and civilian experts to work making maps, but the resulting charts were generally incorrect. Benjamin H. Latrobe, the civil engineer, drew a map for a general going into western Virginia, but the best he could promise was that it would not *mislead* the expedition. General George B. McClellan had elaborate maps prepared for his Virginia campaign of 1862 and found to his dismay when he arrived on the scene that they were unreliable; "the roads are wrong . . . ," he wailed. . . .

At the head of the American military organization was the president, the commander in chief of all the armed forces of the nation. The man who was president when the war began had been a civilian all his life, had had no military experience except as a militia soldier in a pygmy Indian war, and in 1861 probably did not know even how to frame a military order. The president of the rival nation, the Confederate States, was a graduate of West Point, he had been in the regular army and had seen battle service in the Mexican War. Abraham Lincoln was a great war president; Jefferson Davis was a mediocre one. Nowhere in the history of war is there a better illustration of Clausewitz's dictum that an acquaintance with military affairs is not the principal qualification for a director of war but that "a remarkable, superior mind and strength of character" are better qualifications.

With no knowledge of the theory of war, no experience in war, and no technical training, Lincoln, by the power of his mind, became a fine strategist. He was a better natural strategist than were most of the trained soldiers. He saw the big picture of the war from the start. The policy of the government was to restore the Union by force; the strategy perforce had to be offensive. Lincoln knew that numbers, material resources, and sea power were on his side, so he called for 400,000 troops and proclaimed a naval blockade of the Confederacy. These were bold and imaginative moves for a man dealing with military questions for the first time. He grasped immediately the advantage that numbers gave the North and urged his generals to keep up a constant pressure on the whole strategic line of the Confederacy until a weak spot was found—and a break-through could be made. And he soon realized, if he did not know it at the beginning, that the proper objective of his armies was the destruction of the Confederate armies and not the occupation of Southern territory. His strategic thinking was sound and for a rank amateur astonishingly good.

During the first three years of the war, Lincoln performed many of the functions that in a modern command system would be done by the chief of the general staff or by the joint chiefs of staff. He formulated policy, drew up strategic plans, and even devised and directed tactical movements. Judged by modern standards, he did some things that a civilian director of war should not do. Modern critics say that he "interfered" too much with military operations. He and his contemporaries did not think that he interfered improperly. In the American command system it was traditional for the civilian authority to direct strategy and tactics. . . .

Much of Lincoln's so-called interfering with the conduct of the war occurred in the first years of the conflict, when he believed, with some reason, that he was more capable of managing operations than were most of the generals. When the war started, he was inclined to defer to the judgments of trained soldiers. He soon came to doubt and even scorn the capabilities of the military mind. He asked of the generals decision, action, fighting, victory. They replied with indecision, inaction, delay, excuses. He became oppressed by the spectacle, so familiar in war, of generals who were superb in preparing for battle but who shrank from seeking its awful decision. "Tell him," he wrote in preparing instructions for one general, "to put it through—not to be writing or telegraphing back here, but put it through." He wanted victories, but he got more letters than victories, letters from generals who wrote back that they could not put it through unless Lincoln provided them with more men and more guns . . . and still more. . . .

Lincoln never discarded his judgment to others in choosing generals. But he was willing to discard his judgment of what was good strategy and take the opinion of any general whom he considered to be able. He was willing to yield the power to direct strategic operations to any general who could demonstrate that he was competent to frame and execute strategy. Lincoln sensed that there was something wrong in the command system. Somewhere, he thought, there ought to be a division of function be-

tween him and the military. But where should the line be drawn?
And who was the general to whom he could confide the power
to control? Lincoln was to go through some bitter and agonizing
experiences before he got the answers to these questions. In the
process, he and the army and the nation were to learn a lot about
command. By 1864 the United States would have a modern command system. Lincoln did not know it in 1861, but he was going
to make a large and permanent contribution to the organization of
the American military system.

*The Civil War really began after Bull Run. Both North and
South realized at last that a long, bitter war lay ahead; and now
Lincoln's protracted search for a fighting general began. For a time
McClellan seemed to be the man, but for a variety of reasons,
which are still very much a matter of controversy, he failed. Perhaps the chief reason (one that the men of '61 could not have been
expected to understand) was that McClellan, essentially an eigh-
teenth-century gentleman, thought in terms of a restricted, lei-
surely war of maneuver, fought by professional soldiers. But the
Civil War was to be a cruel war in which civilians were to play
a large part. The subtle weakness of McClellan's approach was
most vividly demonstrated in the Peninsula campaign, for which
Sir Frederick Maurice supplies the background. The selection is
taken from his* Statesmen and Soldiers of the Civil War.[2]

   Lincoln's answer to the defeat of Bull Run was a
call for 500,000 volunteers for three years, and an exercise of certain of his Presidential powers which caused many Senators and
Congressman to make wry faces. He also brought General Mc-
Clellan from Western Virginia, where he had gained a substantial success, to command the troops around Washington. McClellan was then thirty-nine years old. He had been an officer of the
Engineers in the United States Army and had served with credit

on General Scott's staff during the Mexican War. On leaving the army, he had been first chief engineer and then vice-president of the Central Illinois Railway. . . .

McClellan was undoubtedly a good soldier. Lee after the war declared that of the Union generals the ablest was "McClellan by long odds"; but Lee knew McClellan only as an opponent. Grant also after the war declared: "If McClellan had gone into war as Sherman, Thomas, or Meade, had fought his way along and up, I have no reason to suppose he would not have won as high distinction as any of us." Grant had opportunity of knowing of McClellan's performances both as a commander of troops in the field and as a commander-in-chief in relations with a Government, and his judgment is probably the more correct of the two.

When McClellan was brought to Washington he was a young man of attractive manner and appearance; he had real gifts of organization and leadership, and was quickly not only respected but loved by his men. He became the idol of the press, which dubbed him the "Young Napoleon"—a nickname not without reference to his habit of issuing somewhat flamboyant proclamations to his troops. Everyone from the President downwards was anxious to serve and help him. As he wrote to his wife, "I find myself in a most strange position here, President, Cabinet, General Scott, all deferring to me. By some strange operation of magic I seem to have become a power in the land." In October General Scott resigned, and Lincoln made McClellan Commander-in-Chief. All this seems to have turned the General's head. He was lacking in the elements of courtesy to the President, of whom the best he could say was, "He is honest and means well," while admitting that Lincoln had gone out of his way to be civil to him. After the first enthusiasm for him had cooled there was a good deal of political intriguing against him, and McClellan, finding the difficulties which he had himself in great measure created becoming too much for him, classed, in his anger, all the administration in Washington as "unscrupulous and false."

McClellan's organization of the army proceeded apace, and the public expectation of it and him were high. But time passed, the army did not move, and expectation changed first to impatience and then to outspoken criticism. On October 21 an ill-managed affair at Ball's Bluff, on the Potomac above Washington, ended in a disastrous repulse of the Federal troops. One of the results of this repulse was the establishment of a Congressional committee of inquiry, which developed into a committee on the conduct of the war. The proceedings of this committee were often injudicious, and they were periodically a thorn in Lincoln's side. Two of its principal members were hostile to McClellan, and disposed to think that Lincoln was wanting in energy in the conduct of the war. Partly from this source and partly from other quarters, the pressure on the President for some definite military action increased.

With Congress clamoring for action and with a general who would not move and who kept his plans, if he had any, to himself, Lincoln was placed in a difficult position. "This poor President!" wrote W. H. Russell, the British war correspondent, in October. "He is to be pitied; surrounded by such scenes, and trying with all his might to understand strategy, naval warfare, big guns, the movements of troops, military maps, reconnaissances, occupations, interior and exterior lines, and all the technical details of the art of slaying."[3]

McClellan was indeed difficult. As early as November, 1861, angered by one of the President's attempts to influence strategy, he brutally snubbed Lincoln and Seward and began openly to insult the president whom he called "nothing more than a well-meaning baboon."

Then in December McClellan fell ill. The army had not budged. "All quiet on the Potomac," once an expression of confidence, became a popular jeer. Lincoln, in despair, took over the command himself for a time; but then it appeared that McClellan after all did have a plan—the Peninsula campaign. He wanted to move toward Richmond from a base on the Virginia rivers. Lincoln, preferring a frontal attack on the Confederate army at Manassas, reluctantly gave McClellan his way on condition that he leave sufficient troops behind to cover Washington. In early March, as McClellan began to move, word came to Washington that the Confederate ironclad Merrimac *was ravaging Union shipping near Norfolk. This crisis passed when the Union* Monitor *neutralized the threat in the first battle in history between armored warships.*

Historians still wrangle over the Peninsula campaign. Was its failure to be blamed on Lincoln and Stanton as bungling amateurs, or on the incompetence of McClellan? Most historians today stand with Lincoln who performed with imagination in a difficult and unprecedented situation.

The controversy centers around Lincoln's disposition of McDowell's corps of the Army of the Potomac, numbering 35,000 men. In clear violation of Lincoln's order, McClellan had sailed for Virginia leaving behind a skeleton force far too weak to protect Washington. When Lincoln discovered this, he promptly ordered McDowell's force at Fredericksburg withheld from McClellan in order to cover the capital. McClellan, embittered by what he considered an injustice, laid siege to Yorktown on the Peninsula, but demanded more men and more guns before he would attack. The Confederates settled the issue for him by evacuating the city. Lincoln, Stanton and Chase, who had come down to the Peninsula to find out why the campaign was lagging, personally directed the capture of Norfolk which resulted in the final destruction of the Merrimac. *And when the army had at last moved up to within five miles of Richmond, McClellan, still calling for reinforcements, busied himself building bridges across the Chickahominy. A division of McDowell's corps was finally sent to him while the rest of the corps was ordered to advance upon Richmond from the north in a pincers movement coordinated with McClellan's army to the South.*

At this crucial point Stonewall Jackson appeared in the Shenandoah Valley and in a series of brilliant moves threatened Washington itself. Should Lincoln allow McDowell to move upon Richmond as planned, or should he withhold McDowell from the Peninsula in an attempt to trap Jackson in the Valley? He chose the latter course, and McDowell might well have succeeded in smashing Jackson had it not been for the slowness of Banks and Frémont.

In the meantime McClellan had been checked at Fair Oaks before Richmond by a sudden blow from General Joseph E. Johnston. Although reinforced with troops after the Valley campaign had ended, he continued to hesitate, complaining of the rains. (Lincoln once said, "McClellan thinks that Heaven always sends rain on the just and never on the unjust.")[4] *McClellan was attacked instead by General Robert E. Lee and Jackson with a drive which developed into a seven days' battle. Lee continued to attack while McClellan executed a masterful withdrawal to the banks of the James, fighting by day and moving by night. In effect, the Peninsula campaign was over.*

Under great pressure to dismiss McClellan, Lincoln visited him at Harrison's Landing on the James. There, curiously enough, the President received from McClellan a personal letter full of unsolicited political advice. Somewhat later McClellan was ordered to withdraw to Washington, which was once again threatened by Jackson.

General Ballard, reviewing the Peninsula campaign and quot-

ing extensively from McClellan's reminiscences (McClellan's Own
Story), *gives his own decided views on the relations between Lincoln and the general.*[5]

It is not unusual to find a general complaining about
the Government. Plenty of similar cases can be quoted from history. The general always wants just a little more—more men,
more munitions, more supplies, while the Government, responsible to the country for finance, has to keep a watchful and sometimes suspicious eye on expenditure. Wellington was often at
loggerheads with the Cabinet, but, bitterly as he complained, he
never accused a fellow countryman of a deliberate intention to
ruin his campaign.

April 1st. On the steamer to Fort Monroe. "I did not feel
safe till I could fairly see Alexandria behind us. If I remained
there I would be annoyed very much and perhaps be sent
for from Washington."

Then comes the arrival in the Peninsula and his scheme is fairly
started.

April 3rd. "I hope to get possession of Yorktown day after
to-morrow. I see my way very clearly, and, with my trains
once ready, will move rapidly."

April 5th. "I feel sure of to-morrow. I have, I think, provided against every contingency, and shall have the men well
in hand if we fight to-morrow."

April 6th. "Things quiet to-day; very little firing."

"I received an order detaching McDowell's Corps from my
command. It is the most infamous thing that history has recorded."

April 8th. "I have raised an awful row about McDowell's

Corps. The President very coolly telegraphed me yesterday that he thought I had better break the enemy's lines at once. I was much tempted to reply that he had better come and do it himself."

April 11th. "I am sure that I will win in the end in spite of all their rascality. History will present a sad record of these traitors who are willing to sacrifice the country and its army for personal spite and personal aims."

May 14th. A dispatch to the President. "I cannot bring into actual battle against the enemy more than 80,000 men at the utmost, and with them I must attack in position, probably entrenched, a much larger force, perhaps double my numbers."

Note the date of this, May 14th. This was how McClellan envisaged his prospects; ten days later the President had to decide whether to send McDowell to chase Jackson or to send him to reinforce McClellan for an attack on double his numbers in a strong entrenched position.

May 17th. "I am now at this present moment involved in a great many different orders for parties to move out at daybreak on reconnaissances." (Nothing happened on May 18th.)

"During the day and night of May 30th a very violent storm occurred. . . . The enemy seeing the unfavourable position in which we were placed threw an overwhelming force upon the position occupied by Casey's Division."

This refers to the battle of Fair Oaks. It is interesting to note that the rains which had constantly made the roads impassable for McClellan were seized by the enemy as a good opportunity for attacking. . . .

June 7th. "I shall be in perfect readiness to move forward and take Richmond the moment McCall reaches here and the ground will admit the passage of artillery."

June 13th. "On the 12th and 13th Gen. McCall's Division arrived."

June 14th. "All quiet in every direction. Weather now very favourable."

June 25th. "I incline to think that Jackson will attack my right and rear. The rebel force is stated at 200,000. But if the result of the action, which will probably occur to-morrow or within a short time, is a disaster, the responsibility cannot be thrown on my shoulders; it must rest where it belongs."

For once McClellan was right in foretelling an action to-morrow. It was the beginning of the Seven Days.

"On the 26th, the day upon which I had decided as the time for our final advance, the enemy attacked our right in strong force, and turned my attention to the protection of our communications and depots of supply."

There are over six hundred pages, very much to the same effect, with some account of the enthusiasm of the army whenever "little Mac" appeared upon the scene.

The extracts are from dispatches and private letters written at the time, but the book was compiled by McClellan about twenty years later, and he apparently saw nothing that needed explanation or correction. We see a careful and energetic organizer; perhaps no man could be found better able to train an army and lead it to the bank of the Rubicon. But there he came to a dead stop.

He has been accused of hesitation, over-caution, timidity, but none of these words really fits. Hesitation is certainly wrong; McClellan never hesitated about anything in his life; it is quite a mistake to picture him trembling on the brink and trying to screw up courage for the plunge. Not a bit of it. The river was impassable—of course, it was—and nobody but a fool would attempt it till to-morrow. Timidity is not the right term; he was physically brave; his assurance is shown by the calm way in which he pursued his own path regardless of suggestions, appeals, or even definite orders; his letters to the Government contain terms which are far from timid, and might be called impertinent. There certainly was caution, plenty of it, but even this word is not satisfying, because from his point of view the caution was quite justifiable. Perhaps we can get nearest to it by saying that his organizing faculties were overdeveloped, and he was governed by an overwhelming desire to complete his preparations. His victory must be certain and complete. . . .

Numbers. "So soon as I feel that my army is strong enough." This brings us to the matter of numbers. In [the] table . . . will be found his estimates, of his own forces as well as of the Confederates. In the other column are given the actual figures, extracted from the Official Records, which were very carefully compiled and may be taken as correct. But to get the *effective* strength of the Federals we ought to subtract about one-fifth of the gross numbers, for their states included servants, grooms, and various non-effectives.

Forces in the Peninsula.

Date	McClellan's Estimate	Actual Numbers
April 7th	South "100,000 possibly more"	13,000 reinforced to 53,000
"	North "40,000 for attack"	108,000

May 14th	South "Probably double my numbers"	53,000
"	North 80,000	128,000
June 25th	South 200,000	86,000
"	North about 90,000	128,000

Looking at the actual figures we see that an addition of 35,000 (McDowell's Corps) would give the Federals a very fine superiority of numbers over the Confederates. Lord Wolseley is quite right in saying that McDowell's 35,000 would have put McClellan in a position to gain a decisive victory. But the whole question is whether McClellan would have used them. To answer this reference must be made to McClellan's own estimate; an addition of 35,000 on any date does not bring him up to the enemy's strength. "So soon as *I* feel that my army is strong enough I will attack." This answers the question quite clearly— McClellan would not have attacked. If any one doubts this let him study McClellan's book; I have read it several times (not for pleasure) and each time confirms my conviction that McClellan would not have attacked.

The Strategist. Starting from the premise that McClellan would not attack, it is only a short step to the next argument. *Lincoln knew that McClellan would not attack.*

Lord Charnwood says that Lincoln had not the gift of rapid perception, but "when he had known a man long or been with him or against him in important transactions, he sometimes developed great insight and sureness of touch." For eight months he had been studying McClellan, and by going over the ground once again I believe we can get an idea of the thoughts in the mind of the Strategist.

We see the President after Bull Run, resolute, unflinching, but sadly at a loss in the search for a commander of his forces. To him enters the young general, brimming over with ideas and energy. Order is evolved out of chaos, troops are disciplined, forts spring up, and Washington is made secure. Easy to imagine how Lincoln's heart warmed as he saw the progress that was made.

Then just a little cloud—the Confederate batteries on the Potomac. It appeared that these were trifles, which must await the good pleasure of the general who was busy with big things.

When the general fell ill in December the President was refused admission to his bedside, though the general admits he was doing business with his own staff. There was no certainty when he would recover; he might not recover at all. The President thought he had a right to seek counsel from other officers. McDowell was one of these, and he has left a record of the consultations; Lincoln was terribly despondent, his words were: "If something was not done soon the bottom would be out of the whole affair." . . .

On January 12th McClellan "mustered strength enough to be driven to the White House, where my unexpected appearance caused very much the effect of a shell in a powder magazine." His account of the Cabinet Meeting which followed is worth all the money that any one pays for his book. Chase said the Cabinet wanted to know McClellan's plans—"the uncalled-for violence of his manner surprised me, but I determined to avail myself of it by keeping perfectly cool." The President calmed down the uncalled-for violence, and McClellan scored off everybody.

On January 22nd was issued the "President's General War Order No. 1": "That the 22nd day of February 1862, be the day for a general movement of the land and naval forces of the United States against the insurgent forces." This order has been condemned as "a curious specimen of puerile impatience." In ordinary circumstances it would be so, but the circumstances were not ordinary; the Head of the State had exhausted every means of persuasion and argument (I think he had lost his temper, and I hope so); nothing was left but to force a decision by order, and the drastic terms in which it was couched were intended to shake McClellan out of his serenity. It succeeded in extracting a proposal for action—a movement by sea.

Lincoln hesitated. He could understand the argument that an attack on Richmond would draw the Confederates away from Washington, but instinct already whispered that McClellan would not attack. On the other hand, the senior officers told him that the Peninsular Scheme offered the only hope of early success. Conscious of his own ignorance of the science of war, he accepted their decision.

Then came McClellan's statement of the troops to be left behind. Lincoln must have kicked himself (he deserved it) for neglecting to go into details before McClellan sailed. But there was no more hesitation; he was responsible to the country for the safety of Washington, and that must be his first consideration. There was, however, a possibility that McClellan would act when he found himself face to face with the enemy, so Lincoln set himself patiently to make the best of things. On April 9th he wrote a long letter:

"MY DEAR SIR,—Your despatches complaining that you are not properly sustained, while they do not offend me, do pain me very much. . . . After you left I ascertained that less than 20,000 unorganized men, without a single field battery, were all you designed to be left for the defence of Washington and Manassas. . . . My implicit order that Washington should, by the judgment of all the commanders of army corps, be left entirely secure, had been neglected. It was precisely this that drove me to detain McDowell. . . . And allow me to ask you. Do you really think I should permit the line from Richmond via Manassas Junction to this city to be entirely open except what resistance could be presented by less than 20,000 unorganized troops? . . . I suppose the whole force which has gone forward for you is with you by this time. And if so I think it is the precise time for you to strike a blow. By delay the enemy will relatively gain on you—that is he will gain faster by fortifications and reinforcements than you will by reinforcements alone. And once more let me tell you that it is indispensable to you that you strike a blow. I am powerless to help this. You will do me the justice to remember I always insisted that going down the bay in search of a field, instead of fighting at or near Manassas, was only shifting and not surmounting a difficulty; that we should find the same enemy, and the same or equal entrenchments at either place. The country will not fail to note, is now noting, that the present hesitation to move upon an entrenched enemy is but the story of Manassas repeated. I beg to assure you that I have never written you or spoken to you in greater kindness of feeling than now, nor with a fuller purpose to sustain you, so far as in my judgment I consistently can. But you must act."

The unexperienced lawyer summed up in three lines the situation which the professional soldier was constitutionally incapable of realizing. "By delay the enemy will relatively gain on you— that is he will gain faster by fortifications and reinforcements than you will by reinforcements alone."

The reply of the professional soldier to this was that though the official states showed he had over 100,000 men, "I had— after deducting guards and working parties—much less than 40,- 000 for attack."

By the middle of May McDowell had been reinforced up to 40,000 and was moving from Fredericksburg. Then came the news that Jackson was driving Banks to the Potomac, and the great question arose, should McDowell be sent to Richmond or to the Valley?

"In war men are nothing; it is the Man who is everything."
This was one of those exaggerations in which Napoleon delighted,
to emphasize the value of genius as compared with mere numbers.
Nearly every military writer has quoted it when talking of the
brilliance of Lee and Jackson. But in the case of Lincoln some
of them have fallen into the pit that they have digged for others.
They do a little sum in arithmetic to prove that McClellan would
have taken Richmond; therefore Lincoln was wrong—an interfering politician.

Lincoln could do simple arithmetic. Had he not, as a child,
done sums on a spade with a lump of chalk? After adding up the
numbers he looked beyond them at the Man. If he had seen a
Grant, a Sheridan, a Sherman, there would have been no hesitation and McDowell would have marched southwards at once.
But all he saw was McClellan, sitting in eternal rain, and facing a
strong position held by 200,000 of the enemy. Was Lincoln
wrong?

"In war men are nothing; it is the Man who is everything." Let
me underline those words before asserting that Lincoln was not
only justified, but more than that—he provides a perfect example
of a true appreciation of Napoleon's maxim.

*"The fact is the people have not yet made up their minds that
we are at war with the South," said Lincoln after Antietam.
"General McClellan thinks he is going to whip the Rebels by
strategy; and the army has got the same notion. They have no
idea that the War is to be carried on and put through by hard,
tough fighting, that it will hurt somebody; and no headway is
going to be made while this delusion lasts."[6] Committed to the
offensive, Lincoln needed a ruthless general who would seek out
and destroy the enemy's forces. Since John Pope had a reputation for aggressiveness, Lincoln had brought him from the west
to command a new army, the Army of Virginia, formed by re-
grouping the troops in and around Washington and in the Val-*

ley. Eventually most of McClellan's troops were thrown into this new force. Lincoln also needed a strategic director for this far-flung war, a job he had been shouldering himself since March. From the west, again, he had summoned General Henry W. Halleck, and had made him general-in-chief in July. But Halleck soon lost his nerve and rapidly degenerated into little better than a "first-rate clerk,"[7] *as Lincoln put it later. The war was right back on Lincoln's hands again.*

Perhaps the low point came at the time of the second battle of Bull Run in August, 1862, when the dashing Pope allowed himself to be outmaneuvered and crushed by Lee and Jackson while McClellan, in a fit of pique at having been pulled out of the Peninsula, deliberately dawdled nearby in Alexandria. Where McClellan's command ended and Pope's began nobody knew, and Halleck had no control over either general. As Pope's defeated forces streamed back into panicky Washington Lincoln absorbed them again into the Army of the Potomac and placed the discredited McClellan in command of the defenses of the capital. At least, Lincoln recognized, McClellan was "an organizer and a good hand at defending a position."[8] *The Cabinet was flabbergasted.*

Unfortunately, this new appointment gave McClellan another chance at Lee, when the Southern commander moved up into Maryland. Although Antietam has been accounted a Union victory, McClellan's generalship was poor and he allowed Lee to escape. Again he dawdled, inventing one excuse after another for his inaction. In October, when he complained that his horses needed rest, Lincoln wired, "Will you pardon me for asking what the horses of your army have done since the battle of Antietam that fatigue anything?"[9] *Finally in November, his patience exhausted, Lincoln dismissed McClellan.*

"The Little Napoleon" had many faults, but as Sir Frederick Maurice suggests, perhaps the most crucial one was his "inca-

pacity to establish relations of trust and confidence with Lincoln[10] *who was, after all, his commander-in-chief. Lincoln's choice now fell on Ambrose Burnside, a modest and attractive man who seemed on his record to be eminently suited for the job, although he had twice before refused it. Burnside planned to make a dash for Richmond, but there were the usual fatal delays which allowed the enemy to concentrate across his path at Fredericksburg. What followed has been described by T. Harry Williams.*[11]

Burnside determined to cross at Fredericksburg early in December and fight a decisive battle with the Confederate army. His decision was bad. Even if he got his army over the river, he would have to attack the Confederates on grounds of their choosing and where they had nearly every advantage. The terrain around Fredericksburg was a natural defensive position, and the Confederates had increased its strength with field fortifications. So strong was the Confederate line that Lee did not seriously oppose Burnside's crossing. The Confederate commander wanted the Union army to get across and dash itself to pieces in attacks on his works. Burnside was walking into a military trap. He crossed his army, and on December 13 fought the bloody battle of Fredericksburg. His one slim chance of victory was to break the Confederate line at some point with an assault in depth. But he did not commit his troops in massive numbers at any point. Rather he sent them in in what almost might be called piecemeal attacks. Every Union attack was repulsed with heavy losses. At the end of the day, over 12,000 Union troops were killed, wounded, or missing.

Before the battle, Burnside was in a state of nervous depression. He seemed to doubt himself and his plan. He knew that others doubted him. Many of his officers, notably Hooker, openly criticized his generalship. After the battle, he broke down almost completely. One general found him in his tent convulsed by agony. "Oh! oh those men! oh, those men!" he cried. He pointed over the river: "Those men over there! I am thinking of them all the time." He talked wildly about leading his old corps in a suicidal charge, but his officers talked him out of the idea. He convinced himself that his principal officers were opposed to him and had disobeyed his orders. He could whip the enemy if he had reliable generals, he declared, but lacking them he would have to give up and retire to the north side of the Rappahannock. He cried when he gave the order to recross the river. . . .

Burnside was willing to shoulder all public responsibility for the defeat. A few days after the battle, he heard that the government was being criticized for making him fight at Fredericksburg against his will. He telegraphed Lincoln for permission to come to Washington and Lincoln granted it. Burnside arrived in the capital at ten o'clock on a Saturday night. He went to a hotel, and sent his secretary to the White House to inquire if Lincoln would see him then or the next morning. The secretary found Lincoln in bed but unable to sleep because of dyspepsia. The President said he would pull on his "breeches" and see Burnside at once. Burnside then went to the White House. He told Lincoln that he would publish a letter taking all the blame for Fredericksburg. Lincoln was relieved and pleased. He said that Burnside was the first general he had found who was willing to relieve him of a particle of responsibility. . . .

Burnside, too, had failed and had to go; but the Army of the Potomac had fought magnificently at Fredericksburg. It had at last become a seasoned fighting machine. Neither McClellan, beloved by its soldiers, nor Burnside could use this great force as it should be used. In the meantime, perhaps because the army had been poorly led, restiveness grew among its officers. Some, fanatically loyal to McClellan, had been openly insubordinate to Pope and *Burnside. Some had talked boldly, too, of the need for a national dictator, and none more boldly than "Fighting Joe" Hooker who, as T. Harry Williams has written, was "a military intriguer of a high order."*[12] *It was a profound surprise, therefore, when Lincoln chose Hooker to succeed Burnside. If Hooker was the man he needed, he would take him, braggadocio and all; but not without the warning contained in this masterly letter.*[13]

EXECUTIVE MANSION
WASHINGTON, January 26, 1863

Major-General Hooker:—
General.

I have placed you at the head of the Army of the Potomac. Of course I have done this upon what appear to me to be sufficient reasons. And yet I think it best for you to know that there are some things in regard to which, I am not quite satisfied with you. I believe you to be a brave and skilful soldier, which, of course, I like. I also believe you do not mix politics with your profession, in which you are right. You have confidence in yourself, which is a valuable, if not an indispensable quality. You are ambitious, which, within reasonable bounds, does good rather than harm. But I think that during Gen. Burnside's command of the Army, you have taken counsel of your ambition, and thwarted him as much as you could, in which you did a great wrong to the country, and to a most meritorious and honorable brother officer. I have heard, in such a way as to believe it, of your recently saying that both the Army and the Government needed a Dictator. Of course it was not *for* this, but in spite of it, that I have given you the command. Only those generals who gain success, can set up dictators. What I now ask of you is military success, and I will risk the dictatorship. The government will support you to the utmost of its ability, which is neither more nor less than it has done and will do for all commanders. I much fear that the spirit which you have aided to infuse into the Army, of criticizing their Commander, and withholding confidence from him, will now turn upon you. I shall assist you as far as I can, to put it down. Neither you, nor Napoleon, if he were alive again, could get any good out of an army, while such a spirit prevails in it.

And now, beware of rashness. Beware of rashness, but with energy, and sleepless vigilance, go forward, and give us victories.

Yours very truly

A. LINCOLN

Lincoln visited the army fairly often. These trips provided much-needed relaxation from the cares of Washington. In April, 1863, he descended upon Hooker's army near Fredericksburg, probably to find out what Hooker's plans were. The journalist Noah Brooks, Lincoln's friend, described the jaunt. The selection is from Washington in Lincoln's Time.[14]

At Hooker's headquarters we were provided with three large hospital tents, floored, and furnished with camp bedsteads and such rude appliances for nightly occupation as were in reach. During our stay with the army there were several grand reviews, that of the entire cavalry corps of the Army of the Potomac, on April 6, being the most impressive of the whole series. The cavalry was now for the first time massed as one corps instead of being scattered around among the various army corps, as it had been heretofore; it was commanded by General Stoneman. The entire cavalry force was rated at 17,000 men, and Hooker proudly said that it was the biggest army of men and horses ever seen in the world, bigger even than the famous body of cavalry commanded by Marshal Murat.

The cavalcade on the way from headquarters to the reviewing-field was a brilliant one. The President, wearing a high hat and riding like a veteran, with General Hooker by his side, headed the flying column; next came several major-generals, a host of brigadiers, staff-officers, and colonels, and lesser functionaries innumerable. The flank of this long train was decorated by the showy uniforms and accoutrements of the "Philadelphia Lancers," who acted as guard of honor to the President during that visit to the Army of the Potomac. The uneven ground was soft with melting snow, and the mud flew in every direction under the hurrying feet of the cavalcade. On the skirts of this cloud of cavalry rode the President's little son "Tad," in charge of a mounted orderly, his gray cloak flying in the gusty wind like the plume of Henry of Navarre. The President and the reviewing party rode past the long lines of cavalry standing at rest, and then the march past began. It was a grand sight to look upon, this immense body of cavalry, with banners waving, music crashing, and horses prancing, as the vast column came winding like a huge serpent over the hills past the reviewing party, and then stretching far away out of sight.

The President went through the hospital tents of the corps that lay nearest to headquarters, and insisted upon stopping and speaking to nearly every man, shaking hands with many of them, and leaving a kind word as he moved from cot to cot. More than once, as I followed the President through the long lines of weary sufferers, I noticed tears of gladness stealing down their pale faces; for they were made happy by looking into Lincoln's sympathetic countenance, touching his hand, and hearing his gentle voice; and when we rode away from the camp to Hooker's headquarters, tremendous cheers rent the air from the soldiers, who stood in groups, eager to see the good President. . . .

On the 9th the First Corps, commanded by General Reynolds, was reviewed by the President on a beautiful plain at the north of Potomac Creek, about eight miles from Hooker's headquarters. We rode thither in an ambulance over a rough corduroy road; and, as we passed over some of the more difficult portions of the jolting way, the ambulance driver, who sat well in front, occasionally let fly a volley of suppressed oaths at his wild team of six mules. Finally Mr. Lincoln, leaning forward, touched the man on the shoulder, and said:

"Excuse me, my friend, are you an Episcopalian?"

The man, greatly startled, looked around and replied:

"No, Mr. President; I am a Methodist."

"Well," said Lincoln, "I thought you must be an Episcopalian, because you swear just like Governor Seward, who is a church-warden." The driver swore no more.

As we plunged and dashed through the woods, Lincoln called attention to the stumps left by the men who had cut down the trees, and with great discrimination pointed out where an experienced axman made what he called "a good butt," or where a tyro had left conclusive evidence of being a poor chopper. Lincoln was delighted with the superb and inspiriting spectacle of the review that day. A noticeable feature of the doings was the martial music of the corps; and on the following day the President, who loved military music, was warm in his praise of the performances of the bands of the Eleventh Corps, under General Howard, and the Twelfth, under General Slocum. In these two corps the greater portion of the music was furnished by drums, trumpets, and fifes, and with most stirring and thrilling effect. In the division commanded by General Schurz was a magnificent array of drums and trumpets, and his men impressed us as the best drilled and most soldierly of all who passed before us during our stay.

I recall with sadness the easy confidence and nonchalance which Hooker showed in all his conversations with the President and his little party while we were at his headquarters. The general seemed to regard the whole business of command as if it were a larger sort of picnic. He was then, by all odds, the handsomest soldier I ever laid my eyes upon. I think I see him now: tall, shapely, well dressed, though not natty in appearance; his fair red and white complexion glowing with health, his bright blue eyes sparkling with intelligence and animation, and his auburn hair tossed back upon his well-shaped head. His nose was aquiline, and the expression of his somewhat small mouth was one of much sweetness, though rather irresolute, it seemed to me. He was a gay cavalier, alert and confident, overflowing with animal spirits, and as cheery as a boy. One of his most frequent expressions when talking with the President was, "When I get to Richmond," or "After we have taken Richmond," etc. The President, noting this, said to me confidentially, and with a sigh: "That is the most depressing thing about Hooker. It seems to me that he is overconfident."

One night when Hooker and I were alone in his hut, which was partly canvas and partly logs, with a spacious fireplace and chimney, he stood in his favorite attitude with his back to the fire, and looking quizzically at me, said, "The President tells me that you know all about the letter he wrote to me when he put me in command of this army." I replied that Mr. Lincoln had read it to me: whereupon Hooker drew the letter from his pocket, and said, "Wouldn't you like to hear it again?" I told him that I should, although I had been so much impressed by its first reading that I believed I could repeat the greater part of it from memory. That letter has now become historic; then it had not been made public. As Hooker read on, he came to this sentence:

You are ambitious, which, within reasonable bounds, does good rather than harm; but I think during Burnside's command of the army you took counsel of your ambition, and thwarted him as much as you could, in which you did a great wrong to the country and to a most meritorious and honorable brother officer.*

Here Hooker stopped, and vehemently said: "The President is mistaken. I never thwarted Burnside in any way, shape, or man-

* Brooks seems to have quoted from an inaccurate version of Lincoln's Letter to Hooker. *Editor.*

ner. Burnside was preeminently a man of deportment: he fought
the battle of Fredericksburg on his deportment; he was defeated
on his deportment; and he took his deportment with him out of
the Army of the Potomac, thank God!" Resuming the reading of
Lincoln's letter, Hooker's tone immediately softened, and he finished it almost with tears in his eyes; and as he folded it, and put
it back in the breast of his coat, he said, "That is just such a letter
as a father might write to his son. It is a beautiful letter, and, although I think he was harder on me than I deserved, I will say
that I love the man who wrote it." Then he added, "After I have
got to Richmond, I shall give that letter to you to have published."

*Although Hooker managed to lure the Confederates out of
their impregnable position at Fredericksburg, he, too, was to
prove unequal to his task. In nine days of swinging maneuver the
Rebels, despite their inferiority in numbers, boldly kept him on
the defensive, then inflicted on him a decisive defeat at Chancellorsville. When Lincoln heard the news his face turned ashen (almost the same color, Brooks noted, as the gray wallpaper behind
him).*[15] *But the Rebels had lost Stonewall Jackson at Chancellorsville, an army in himself.*

*Nevertheless, Lee kept the initiative, and in a dramatic move
aimed at the demoralization of his enemy, pushed north around
Washington into the heart of the Union. The climax of the war
had come, but Hooker, who had lost his nerve after Chancellorsville, tried to avoid the inevitable clash. First he proposed an
attack upon Lee's rear guard at Fredericksburg. Warned by Lincoln of the risk of "being entangled upon the river, like an ox
jumped half over a fence, and liable to be torn by dogs, front
and rear,"*[16] *Hooker shifted his ground and offered to march upon
Richmond. At this Lincoln lost patience "I think Lee's army and
not Richmond is your sure objective point."*[17]

By the end of June Lee's army was thrusting into Pennsylvania.

The North was in a panic; Lee's stratagem was working. But Lincoln, cool-headed as ever, saw his chance to smash the Southern army while it was far from its base, and perhaps end the war at a blow. At this point Hooker quarreled petulantly with Halleck over reinforcements and offered to resign. Much to Hooker's surprise, the President accepted the resignation with alacrity and at the most crucial point of the war placed George Meade, a solid and dependable soldier, in command. Under Meade, the Army of the Potomac groped northward, made contact with the Rebels more or less by accident at Gettysburg, and closed in battle. Three days of confused fighting followed.

This was the climactic contest of the war. Although strategically unimportant, Gettysburg was the first decisive victory for the North. It was the "high tide of the Confederacy," and has given rise to more poetry, fiction and armchair controversy than any other single battle of our history. It was a close struggle, from the opening skirmishes to Pickett's desperate charge on the third day when the "flower of old Virginia" fell in defeat.

A few days after Gettysburg the news flashed east that Grant had taken the great Mississippi fortress of Vicksburg. The crucial western theater had been weakened when Lee moved north instead of west. The mistake showed the limitations of his strategic thinking, for it was at Vicksburg rather than at Gettysburg that the Confederate cause was lost.

Wild rejoicing in the North greeted the double victory. In a letter written from Wilmington, Delaware, on July 7th, 1863, William Lusk conveyed the electric excitement of this great release.[18]

HEADQUARTERS DELAWARE DEPARTMENT
WILMINGTON, DEL., July 7th, 1863

Dear, dear Cousin Lou:

I said I would write you so soon as the full purport of the

good news was ascertained. And now that it has all broken upon us, although my heels are where my head ought to be, I will try and fulfil my engagement as coherently as possible. We have had the dark hour. The dawn has broken, and the collapsed confederacy has no place where it can hide its head. Bells are ringing wildly all over the city. Citizens grin at one another with fairly idiotic delight. One is on the top of his house frantically swinging a dinner bell, contributing thus his share of patriotic clamor to the general ding-dong. Bully for him! How I envy the heroes of Meade's Army. It would be worth while to die, in order that one's friends might say, "He died at Gettysburg." But to live to hear all the good news, and now to learn that Vicksburg has surrendered, is a little too much happiness for poor mortal men. I can laugh, I can cry with joy. All hysterical nonsense is pardonable now. Manassas, twice repeated, Fredericksburg and Chickahominy! Bless them as the cruel training that has made us learn our duties to our country. Slavery has fallen, and I believe Heaven as well as earth rejoices. Providence has tenderly removed that grand old hero, Jackson, before the blow came, that the one good, earnest, misguided man might be spared the sight of the downfall of a cause fanaticism led him to believe was right. . . . These enthusiastic citizens of Wilmington, not content with bell-ringing, have taken to firing cannon, and the boys, to help matters, are discharging pistols into empty barrels. The people in a little semi-slaveholding State, when not downright traitors, are noisily, obstreperously loyal, to a degree that New England can hardly conceive of. My letter must be short and jubilant, I cannot do anything long to-day.

Just dance through the house for me, and kiss every one you meet. So I feel now. Good-bye.

Affec'y.,

WILL.

The North celebrated, but only Lincoln seems to have grasped the true significance of Gettysburg. The war might have been won on those fields; but once again Lee had been allowed to escape. Once again a commander had failed. General Ballard points up the moral:[19]

It might be imagined that the President, of all men, would be overjoyed with the news of victory. It was an undeniable and glorious victory, on a big scale, wiping out at one blow the disappointments of the Peninsula, Bull Run, Fredericksburg, and Chancellorsville. The danger that had so closely menaced the cities of the North was now averted: the reputation of Lee and his army for invincibility was shattered: the fighting power of the Union army was proved and its moral ascendancy established. The political gains were enormous: it justified the action of the Government and strengthened its position. It silenced the croaking of the ravens who had been demanding peace at any price. It was a snub to the prophets at home and abroad who had been declaring the cause of the Union to be hopeless.

Such thoughts might well have filled the President's mind to the exclusion of all others—at least in the first intoxication of victory. Yet, so far from this being the case, Lincoln's mind was filled with nothing but disappointment. He penned to the victor words far harsher than he had ever addressed to McClellan, Pope, Burnside, or Hooker—and in them we see how truly he judged past events, how clearly he foresaw events to come. From the past he judged the stubborn pride of the South, the brilliance of Lee, the valour of the Confederate soldiers, and he saw that though the Union had won a battle it had not yet won the war. He saw how Lee would again fall back behind the rivers and forests and mud of Virginia, he saw the struggle and sacrifice of blood that would be entailed in crushing that wonderful army. His forecast filled him with horror and dismay.

And here, in the early days of July, Lee's army was within easy reach. Meade had 60,000 veterans flushed with victory and 20,000 fresh men had joined him. Lee could scarcely have more than 40,-000, suffering from a heavy defeat; his road was blocked by an unfordable river; he must stand to fight. As Lincoln himself had said; "Lee's army and not Richmond is your sure objective point." The capture of that army might well finish the war.

This thought seems to have flashed into Lincoln's mind from the first and was not prompted by any one else. He spent some time on July 6th at the telegraph office listening to Meade's reports, and on his return home at 7 p.m. he sat down and wrote to Halleck. "I left the telegraph office a good deal dissatisfied. You know I did not like Meade's phrase: 'Drive the invaders from our soil!'" A clear indication of the main idea of his strategy— *not to drive away the enemy but to prevent him getting away.*

Next day he wrote—"We have certain information that Vicksburg surrendered to General Grant on the 4th of July. Now, if General Meade can complete his work, so gloriously prosecuted thus far, by the literal or substantial destruction of Lee's army the rebellion will be over."

Throughout the following days he was torn with anxiety. About noon on the 14th news came in that Lee had escaped. Rhodes says: "Lincoln could hardly restrain his irritation within bounds. On the spur of the moment he gave vent to his feelings in a letter to Meade which on second thoughts he did not sign or send."

The letter was as follows:

"I am sorry to be the author of the slightest pain to you. You fought and beat the enemy at Gettysburg, and of course, to say the least, his loss was as great as yours. He retreated, and you did not, it seems to me, pressingly pursue him. You had at least 20,000 veteran troops with you and as many more raw ones within supporting distance, all in addition to those who fought with you at Gettysburg; while it was not possible that he had received a single recruit, and yet you stood and let the river run down, bridges be built, and the enemy move away at his leisure without attacking him. Again, my dear General, I do not believe you appreciate the magnitude of the disaster involved in Lee's escape. He was within your easy grasp, and to have closed upon him would, in connexion with our other successes, have ended the war. As it is the war will be prolonged indefinitely. If you could not safely attack Lee last Monday, how can you possibly do so south of the river, when you can take with you very few more than two-thirds of the force you then had in hand? It would seem unreasonable to expect, and I do not expect, that you can now effect much. Your golden opportunity is gone, and I am distressed immeasurably because of it."

But Lee had escaped. The letter would have rendered Meade's position intolerable—in fact would have amounted to dismissing him, which would look like ingratitude to the soldiers who had fought so hard at Gettysburg. It is all very well to shoot a general after a failure, *pour encourager les autres,* but to do so after a victory would not have a steadying effect on the nerves of his successor. So Lincoln let the sun go down on his wrath and faced the gloomy future with grim courage.

3.

Grant and Victory

With the capture of Vicksburg the entire Mississippi was in Union hands. One of Lincoln's fundamental strategic aims, the encirclement and isolation of the Confederacy, had been virtually accomplished. For the blockade of the Atlantic ports was beginning to be effective, and now Grant had cut the Confederacy's overland lifeline to the outside world—the route for foodstuffs from Texas, Arkansas and Louisiana as well as for sorely needed manufactured goods from Europe via Mexico. Triumphantly, Lincoln wrote in August: "The signs look better. The Father of Waters again goes unvexed to the sea."[1]

But the Vicksburg campaign had been a hard one. It had taken almost a year and all of Grant's incomparable tenacity to wrest from Rebel hands the last 250 miles of the river, dominated by the almost impregnable fortress. Naval assaults in May and June of 1862 had failed. In the fall Grant had tried an approach by land. Benjamin Thomas carries on the Vicksburg story.[2]

Vicksburg, the key to this stretch of river, was a natural citadel. Situated on a commanding bluff, two hundred feet above the water, it was protected in the rear by rough terrain. The few roads followed the heavily timbered ridges, and a rank growth of vines and canebrakes made the ravines impenetrable. Stagnant pools of water breathed miasma. The Confederates had lined the riverbank with heavy guns. Redoubts surrounded the city.

In November 1862, when Grant marched south from Memphis to attack, the enemy had cut his rail communications and destroyed his supply depot at Holly Springs. Twice Sherman was repulsed with heavy loss at Chickasaw Bluffs, and Grant, deciding that Vicksburg must be taken from the south, but fearing to run his transports past the heavy batteries, cut loose from his base and crossed to the west bank of the Mississippi. Here he tried to bypass the city by digging a canal across a great bend in the stream; but mud, mosquitoes, and swamp fever plagued his tough Midwestern troops as Confederate batteries on the waterfront harassed them.

Rumors came to Washington that Grant was drinking again. Murat Halstead, of the *Cincinnati Commercial*, wrote to Chase: "You do once in a while, don't you, say a word to the President, or Stanton, or Halleck, about the conduct of the War?

"Well, now, for God's sake say that Genl Grant, entrusted with our greatest army, is a jackass in the original package. He is a poor drunken imbecile. He is a poor stick sober, and he is most of the time more than half drunk, and much of the time idiotically drunk. . . ."

The prim Chase sent Halstead's letter to Lincoln with the comment that the *Cincinnati Commercial* was an influential paper, and that such reports about Grant were becoming too common to overlook.

Lincoln sent Congressman Washburne, Governor Yates of Illinois, and Adjutant General Lorenzo Thomas to investigate Grant's conduct. Washburne was Grant's fellow townsman from Galena; he and Yates had been Grant's most active sponsors; the investigators reported the general and his command in excellent order. Charles A. Dana, whom Stanton sent to Mississippi as an observer, likewise found nothing to complain about. When a delegation came to Lincoln to demand Grant's dismissal, the President used a jest to stall them off. "If I knew what kind of liquor Grant drinks," he said, "I would send a barrel or so to some other generals." But the attacks on Grant became so persistent and so bitter that Lincoln confided to Nicolay: "I think Grant has hardly a friend left, except myself."

Thwarted for three months by terrain, Grant decided to risk the scowling batteries above the river. Moving his army down a series of bayous and streams west of the Mississippi to a point some fifty miles below Vicksburg, he ordered Rear Admiral Porter to run his ironclads, steamers, and barges past the city. In pitch-darkness on the night of April 16, Porter's flotilla cut loose from its anchorage and drifted silently downstream, fires banked and lights extinguished. The flash of a heavy cannon split the night. Guns roared along the bluff as the Confederates discovered Porter's ships. The gunboats thundered back. The Union vessels hugged the shadows of the shore as the Confederates set fire to houses on the riverbank to light the stream. Smokestacks trailed sparks and flame as the flotilla, full steam ahead, churned on down the river with slight damage. By the end of April 1863 Grant had his army south of Vicksburg and was ready to attack.

General John C. Pemberton commanded some 35,000 Confederate troops in Vicksburg and along the railroad south of it. General Joseph E. Johnston, in command of all the Confederate forces in the West, had almost as many more around Jackson, the capital of Mississippi. Grant had superiority in numbers, but, bereft of communication with the North, he must live off the hostile country. Behind him flowed the broad river, commanded above and below him by the enemy. A serious defeat might mean the annihilation or surrender of his army.

On May 11 Grant cut loose from his base and telegraphed Halleck: "You may not hear from me for several days." Except for an occasional report from General Stephen A. Hurlbut at Memphis, Lincoln's chief knowledge of Grant's movements for the next two weeks came from items in Southern newspapers that were acquired by capture or exchange, and from Confederate semaphore messages intercepted by Army of the Potomac signalmen, who had broken the Confederate code.

At last, on May 25, a report forwarded by Hurlbut from General John A. Rawlins, Grant's chief of staff, brought Lincoln official information that Grant had fought and won five battles in three weeks, capturing the town of Jackson, forcing General Johnston to draw off, and driving Pemberton behind the Vicksburg redoubts. Admiral Porter telegraphed by way of Cairo: "There has never been a case during the whole war where the Rebels have been as successfully beaten at all points. . . . It is a mere question of a few hours & then with the exception of Pt. Hudson which will follow Vicksburg the Mississippi will be open its entire length."

Victory did not come that easily, however, for Pemberton had been ordered to hold Vicksburg at all costs. Two frontal attacks failed, and Grant settled down to a siege. Night and day his batteries pounded the city, while Porter's gunboats shelled it from the river. Citizens and soldiers burrowed into the hillsides as Grant pushed ever closer with saps and mines. Gaunt hunger stalked the city streets. Grant had Vicksburg in his clutch unless Johnston could bring troops to raise the siege. . . .

Vicksburg fell. When Lincoln heard the news from Gideon Welles, Secretary of the Navy, he threw his arms around the bearded Welles and exclaimed, "What can we do for the Secretary of the Navy for this glorious intelligence? He is always giving us good news. I cannot in words tell you of my joy over this result. It is great, Mr. Welles! It is great!"[3]

Lincoln's strategy for the western theater envisaged a two-

pronged attack: the opening up of the river from the north and from the south, and an advance through the mountains into Tennessee to pry open the gateway to the heart of the Confederacy at Chattanooga. The latter would also effect the rescue of the Unionists around Knoxville. Grant's capture of Vicksburg accomplished half the task and established him as a general worth watching. Five months later his victory at the battle of Chattanooga completed the plan and made him a national hero. Lincoln was now ready to move Grant to the east as commander of all the Union armies.

Grant's emergence as a leader had taken time. In the distant west, even more than in the east, Lincoln struggled year after year with generals who got the "slows," who bickered among themselves instead of fighting the enemy, who made unreasonable demands for reinforcements and supplies and then lost their nerve in battle. If Halleck or McClellan could not straighten them out, Lincoln would step in. "During the entire war," wrote one of his telegraph operators, "the files of the War Department telegraph office were punctuated with short, pithy despatches from Lincoln."[4]

After the dismissal of Frémont in November, 1861, western operations came under Halleck at St. Louis and Buell in Kentucky. During December, with McClellan sick, Lincoln tried to get both to move forward in concert, but little happened. In January of the new year he wrote, "It is exceedingly discouraging. As everywhere else, nothing can be done." He admonished both generals: "Delay is ruining us."[5] *Then, unexpectedly, there was a victory. Carl Sandburg tells the story.*[6]

On February 6 of '62 Commodore Foote and his gunboats escorted a line of steamboats up the Tennessee River carrying eighteen regiments under Brigadier General Ulysses S. Grant. They crowded the decks watching the scenery, 18,000 troops, corn-huskers, teamsters, rail-splitters, shopmen, factory hands, college students, from Iowa, and Nebraska, from Illinois, Indiana, Ohio, Missouri, many of them not yet old enough to vote. . . .

The gunboats stopped at Fort Henry, filled it with exploding shells, and troops marched in and took its Confederate flag. The garrison had left for Fort Donelson, twelve miles away on the Cumberland River. Grant marched his army this twelve miles across country to Fort Donelson in fair weather, so warm and balmy that thousands of soldiers threw away their blankets, overcoats, or both.

Foote took his gunboats up to the Ohio River, up the Cumberland, and exchanging shots with the Fort Donelson guns was disabled so that he had to steam upriver. This left Grant with 27,000 troops, counting new arrivals, to contest with 18,000 troops inside a fort. . . .

Before the fighting began a cold wind came, snow fell, the roads froze, and in ten-above-zero weather men fired and loaded their muskets, and in the night huddled and shivered, seeking fences, brushes, trees, logs, to keep off the wind. Neither side dared light a bivouac fire. Men and boys were found next morning frozen stiff.

Grant went aboard Foote's flagship to arrange for the gunboats, though disabled, to keep up the best fire they could from a distance so as to worry the cannoneers in the fort. Riding back from this conference, Grant found his right wing battered and wavering. Some word dropped led him to order Confederate prisoners searched. They were carrying three days' rations in their haversacks. Grant sent word along the line that the enemy in desperation was trying to cut its way out and retreat. "Gentlemen, the position on the right must be retaken." . . .

Nearly all the correspondents mentioned the personal quality of the individual soldiers on both sides. They had come for fighting and they fought. "Cold and hungry, with garments stiff with frost, the soldiers were still hopeful and firm," wrote one. "I did not find a single discouraged man, or one who, if he were so, would admit it. The universal sentiment was, as bluff Colonel Oglesby expressed it, 'We came here to take that fort, and we will take it. . . .'" The Richmond Dispatch correspondent wrote, "The enemy are represented to have fought nobly, far better than the Northern soldiers have ever fought before; but most, if not all of them, were from the West, sturdy farmers and backwoodsmen, and, like ourselves, accustomed to the use of arms."

On Sunday, February 16, 1862, telegrams began trickling into the War Department at Washington. General Simon B. Buckner, commanding Fort Donelson, had sent a messenger to Grant asking for "terms of capitulation" and Grant replied: "No terms except an unconditional and immediate surrender can be accepted. I propose to move immediately upon your works." And the Confederate commander was surrendering the fort and 13,828 prisoners. The battle losses were: Union, 500 killed, 2,108 wounded, 224 missing; Confederate, 231 killed, 1,534 wounded.

The victory clinched Kentucky to the Union, gave a foothold in Tennessee, sent Union armies two hundred miles forward into enemy territory. More than anything else it lighted up the gloom of the North. Over the country were outpourings of people to celebrate with bonfires, fireworks, bells ringing, whistles blowing, meetings, speeches, subscriptions for the wounded. "Men embraced each other on the street."

Halleck, now in command of the western armies, took all the credit for the victory and later on tried to get Grant removed for failing to keep in touch with him. But the North had a new

*hero in "Unconditional Surrender Grant," and Lincoln, on his
own initiative, promoted him to major general.*

*Then Grant made a mistake. In April, 1862, moving farther
south along the Tennessee River, he was surprised by a Confederate force at Shiloh and barely held his own in a battle which
was the bloodiest of the war to that time. Unjustly, Grant was
blamed for the slaughter. A.K. McClure tells how, as spokesman
for a number of leading Republicans, he visited his friend the
President to urge Grant's removal.*[7]

Not only in Washington, but throughout the loyal
states, public sentiment seemed to crystallize into an earnest demand for Grant's dismissal from the army. His victories at Forts
Henry and Donelson, which had thrilled the country a short
time before, seemed to have been forgotten, and on every side
could be heard the emphatic denunciation of Grant because
of his alleged reckless exposure of the army, while Buell was
universally credited with having saved it. . . .

I did not know Grant at that time; had neither partiality nor
prejudice to influence my judgment, nor had I any favorite
general who might be benefited by Grant's overthrow, but I
shared the almost universal conviction of the President's friends
that he could not sustain himself if he attempted to sustain
Grant by continuing him in command. . . . So much was I impressed with the importance of prompt action on the part of
the President after spending a day and evening in Washington
that I called on Lincoln at eleven o'clock at night and sat with him
alone until after one o'clock in the morning. He was, as usual,
worn out with the day's exacting duties, but he did not permit
me to depart until the Grant matter had been gone over and many
other things relating to the war that he wished to discuss. I
pressed upon him with all the earnestness I could command the
immediate removal of Grant as an imperious necessity to sustain

himself. As was his custom, he said but little, only enough to
make me continue the discussion until it was exhausted. He
sat before the open fire in the old Cabinet room, most of the time
with his feet up on the high marble mantle, and exhibited unusual distress at the complicated condition of military affairs.
Nearly every day brought some new and perplexing military
complication. He had gone through a long winter of terrible
strain with McClellan and the Army of the Potomac; and from
the day that Grant started on his Southern expedition until the
battle of Shiloh he had had little else than jarring and confusion
among his generals in the West. He knew that I had no ends
to serve in urging Grant's removal, beyond the single desire to
make him be just to himself, and he listened patiently.

I appealed to Lincoln for his own sake to remove Grant at
once, and, in giving my reasons for it, I simply voiced the
admittedly overwhelming protest from the loyal people of the
land against Grant's continuance in command. I could form no
judgment during the conversation as to what effect my argu-
ments had upon him beyond the fact that he was greatly distressed
at this new complication. When I had said everything that could
be said from my standpoint, we lapsed into silence. Lincoln remained silent for what seemed a very long time. He then
gathered himself up in his chair and said in a tone of earnestness
that I shall never forget: *"I can't spare this man; he fights."*

*Pope began to move down the Mississippi while Shiloh was
being fought. By June of 1862 the Union armies had reached
Memphis. The lower reaches of the river had been secured in
April when Farragut and Porter ran by the forts and captured
New Orleans. Only the middle stretch of the river dominated by
Vicksburg remained to be conquered.*

*Though the river war was going well the war in the mountains
was discouraging. While Buell slowly approached Chattanooga*

in September, a Confederate army under Bragg suddenly in-
vaded Kentucky. Buell withdrew to the Ohio River to protect
his bases, and after the threat was removed, he seemed in no
hurry to resume his Tennessee campaign. In October, Halleck,
now general-in-chief in Washington, wrote Buell impatiently,
speaking for Lincoln, "He does not understand why we cannot
march as the enemy marches, live as he lives, and fight as he
fights, unless we admit the inferiority of our troops and our
generals."[8]

On October twenty-third, shortly before Lincoln got rid of
McClellan, Buell was removed and William S. Rosecrans, sup-
posed to be a "fighting" general, was placed in his command.
But "Old Rosy" turned out to be excitable, touchy, and slow
again. He redeemed himself with a partial victory at Murfrees-
boro (Stone's River) at the turn of the year; but then there was
more trouble. Sandburg takes up the narrative.[9]

Having fought a drawn battle at Murfreesboro in
the first week of January, 1863, General Rosecrans kept the
Army of the Cumberland at that same place in Tennessee for
six months, fortifying, drilling, setting no troops into motion to
stop Confederate armies from hitting Grant at Vicksburg, letting
three brigades of Confederate cavalry get away to raid and
terrorize southern Indiana and Ohio.

Stanton and Halleck kept sending letters and telegrams to
Rosecrans, trying to get the Army of the Cumberland into
action. Rosecrans kept asking for supplies, revolving rifles,
cavalry. Late in June of '63 Rosecrans marched his forces through
rough and broken country, and by September 9 had, without
a battle, maneuvered the Confederate army under Bragg out of
Chattanooga and put his own troops into that strategic center.
While on this operation Rosecrans wrote to Lincoln early in

August reciting conditions: bad roads, bad weather, cavalry weakness, long hauls for bridge material.

"I think," Lincoln replied, "you must have inferred more than General Halleck has intended, as to any dissatisfaction of mine with you. I am sure you, as a reasonable man, would not have been wounded could you have heard all my words and seen all my thoughts in regard to you. I have not abated in my kind feeling for and confidence in you. I have seen most of your despatches to General Halleck—probably all of them."

The President then told of the anxiety he had been through while Rosecrans stayed inactive as Grant was threatened at Vicksburg by Johnston's army, which might any day have been joined by Bragg's army. Soon after, "despatches from Grant abated my anxiety for him, and in proportion abated my anxiety about any movement of yours."

Then still later Lincoln had seen a Rosecrans dispatch arguing that the right time to attack Bragg would be after the fall of Vicksburg. "It impressed me very strangely, and I think I so stated to the Secretary of War and General Halleck. It seemed no other than the proposition that you could better fight Bragg when Johnston should be at liberty to return and assist him than you could before he could so return to his assistance." And now that Johnston's army was relieved from watching Grant at Vicksburg "it has seemed to me that your chance for a stroke has been considerably diminished, and I have not been pressing you directly or indirectly."

The President then gently asked Rosecrans about supplies and horses, as though preparations were costing as much as real action, and closed the letter: "And now be assured once more that I think of you in all kindness and confidence, and that I am not watching you with an evil eye." . . .

High praise of Rosecrans as a strategist rang in many quarters after the long marches and maneuverings by which he had arrived

at Chattanooga while Bragg lay to the south. At first Rosecrans
felt good, elated, over his position. Then reports came indicating
that Bragg had received reinforcements and more were coming,
that Bragg had his army well concentrated while Rosecrans'
forces were scattered over a fifty-mile line. Rosecrans did not
know that Bragg, as one of Davis's most trusted commanders,
was getting all the large and small armies that the Richmond
War Department could order to his help, that General Lee had
been to Richmond and arranged with Davis for Longstreet
with 20,000 troops from the Army of Northern Virginia to be
sent by railroad down across the Carolinas and up into far
northern Georgia to the help of Bragg. This gave Bragg 70,000
troops as against Rosecrans' 57,000.

The two armies grappled at Chickamauga Creek near Crawfish
Spring on September 19 of '63. . . .

"Sunday morning, the 20th of September, the President
showed me [John Hay] Rosecrans' despatches of the day before,
detailing the first day's fighting, and promising a complete
victory the next day. The President was a little uneasy over
the promise, and very uneasy that Burnside was not within supporting distance."

Late that Sunday afternoon came a telegram from Dana at
Chattanooga: "My report to-day is of deplorable importance.
Chickamauga is as fatal a name in our history as Bull Run."

*The defeated army streamed back to Chattanooga, pursued by
the Rebels. In Washington there was consternation. Lincoln en-
couraged Rosecrans to hold Chattanooga at all costs while urging Burnside, who had been operating with a small Union army
in East Tennessee and had earlier entered Knoxville in triumph,
to come to Rosecrans' support. Stanton, trying to decipher a
message from Rosecrans giving his reasons for the defeat, snorted,*

"I know the reasons well enough. Rosecrans ran away from his fighting men and did not stop for thirteen miles."[10]

There was some truth in the charge; but a few days after the battle Rosecrans wired from Chattanooga, *"We can hold this point."*[11] In the meantime Burnside had gone off on a tangent of his own. Lincoln wrote out a telegram: *"Yours of the 23d is just received, and it makes me doubt whether I am awake or dreaming. I have been struggling for ten days . . . to get you to go to assist General Rosecrans in an extremity, and you have repeatedly declared you would do it, and yet you steadily move the contrary way."*[12] Again he never sent the message.

Too many generals had failed. In mid-October of 1863 Lincoln placed Grant at the head of all departments and armies in the west, a significant appointment which was the first, long-overdue step in the creation of a more efficient system of command in all theaters. Grant immediately removed Rosecrans and put George Thomas, "The Rock of Chickamauga," in his place. Grant then hurried to Chattanooga by train and horseback and began to take energetic steps to lift the siege. In the "battle above the clouds" Hooker (who had been rushed to the west with reinforcements) overran Lookout Mountain dominating the city. Next Sherman thrust unsuccessfully at Bragg's right in an attempt to push him off another strongly held height, Missionary Ridge. To relieve the pressure on Sherman, Grant ordered a diversion against the rifle pits guarding the base of the ridge at its central point. Then the miracle happened as the troops, without orders, stormed up the precipitous side of the ridge against Bragg's army, which broke and fled. The taking of Missionary Ridge has been called the Pickett's charge of the Union armies.

To the north, Longstreet was still threatening Nashville. In December, 1863, Sherman drove him into Virginia, and Unionist East Tennessee, to Lincoln's joy, was free at last. Lincoln's grand strategic objectives had been achieved, and it was all Grant's do-

ing. The Mississippi had been opened; and beyond Chattanooga lay Georgia and the heart of the Confederacy. At last Lincoln had found a general who could and would fight. In February, 1864, Lincoln appointed Grant general-in-chief of all the Union armies.

Shortly after he first met the new general-in-chief Lincoln said, "He's the quietest little fellow you ever saw. . . . The only evidence you have that he's in any place is that he makes things git! Wherever he is, things move!"[13] Margaret Leech has described the White House reception on March 8, 1864, at which Lincoln and Grant met for the first time.[14]

Near the door of the Blue Room the advance of the column of callers was suddenly checked. The President, after cordially wringing the hand of one visitor, detained him in conversation. He was a short, scrubby officer, stooped and sun-burned, with rough, light-brown whiskers, and he appeared scarcely worthy of signal attention. There was something seedy about him; the look of a man who is out of a job, and takes too much to drink. The stars on his shoulder straps were tarnished. But a buzz ran through the Blue Room. Everyone began to stare at the man who stood awkwardly looking up at the President, while arriving guests jostled in confusion outside the doorway. General Grant and Mr. Lincoln were meeting for the first time.

Seward hurried to the rescue. He presented the general to Mrs. Lincoln, and led him through a lane of eager faces into the crowded East Room. Grant's entrance turned the polite assemblage into a mob. Wild cheers shook the crystal chandeliers, as ladies and gentlemen rushed on him from all sides. Laces were torn, and crinolines mashed. Fearful of injury or maddened by excitement, people scrambled on chairs and tables. At last, General Grant was forced to mount a crimson sofa. He stood there bashfully shaking the thrusting hands that wanted to touch success and glory—Donelson, Vicksburg, Chattanooga—personified in a slovenly little soldier, with a blushing, scared face. . . .

On the day after Grant's arrival, he was formally presented with the commission of lieutenant-general. The grade had been revived by recent act of Congress, with the tacit understanding that it would be bestowed on Grant. It was high military honor from a republic which had been chary of permitting its heroes to place a third star on their shoulder straps. To witness the presentation, Grant brought along his son Fred, a boy of fourteen, who had been through the siege of Vicksburg. He was also accompanied by two aides and by General Halleck, who had all but forced him out of the service in 1862. The President and the gentlemen of the Cabinet assembled, and, in reply to Mr. Lincoln's short speech, Grant painfully stammered out a few lines he had penciled on a half sheet of note paper. In his embarrassment, he seemed scarcely able to read his own writing; but the composition, with its reference to his heavy responsibilities, the noble armies of the Union and the favor of Providence, was entirely original with himself. He had omitted the compliments to the Army of the Potomac, which the President had asked him to pay.

The next day Grant paid a visit to General Meade's headquarters at Brandy Station. Mr. Welles, observing him at the Cabinet meeting on his return, found him deficient in military bearing and dignity, but more business-like than he had formerly appeared. Grant had been fortified by a great decision. He had completely changed his plans, abandoning his cherished intention of leading the Western armies on a campaign to Atlanta. The President had told him that the country wanted him to take Richmond. Grant said that he could do it, if he had the troops. In his stubborn heart, he felt the strength to resist the political pressure of Washington, and he had resolved that his place was with the Army of the Potomac. On the third evening after his arrival in the capital, he left for Nashville, to sever his relations with the troops which he had led to victory. As he traveled westward on the cars, the orders were issued which placed him in command of all the armies of the Union. . . .

T. Harry Williams assesses Grant as the greatest general of the Civil War.[15]

Grant's war service before 1864 had been an ideal training experience for the job of general in chief. He was a better war director because he had come up the hard and long way. He had started as a small unit commander and then had gone on to bigger commands as he had proved on the field that he could handle larger responsibilities. He learned self-confidence from his successes and patience and determination from his failures. His experience with small commands was fortunate for Grant. It taught him the importance of looking after such things as ammunition supplies and means of transportation—the prosaic vital things that can make or break an army. Most valuable of all, he first encountered the problems of army administration on a small scale and mastered one set before he met another and more complex one. He learned administration from the regimental level up, which was a better way than if he had suddenly been placed in charge of a huge army as McClellan had been. . . .

Grant was, judged by modern standards, the greatest general of the Civil War. He was head and shoulders above any general on either side as an over-all strategist, as a master of what in later wars would be called global strategy. His Operation Crusher plan, the product of a mind which had received little formal instruction in the higher art of war, would have done credit to the most finished student of a series of modern staff and command schools. He was a brilliant theatre stategist, as evidenced by the Vicksburg campaign, which was a classic field and siege operation. He was a better than average tactician, although like even the best generals of both sides he did not appreciate the destruction that the increasing firepower of modern armies could visit on troops advancing across open spaces.

Lee is usually ranked as the greatest Civil War general, but this evaluation has been made without placing Lee and Grant in the perspective of military developments since the war. Lee was interested hardly at all in "global" strategy, and what few suggestions he did make to his government about operations in other theatres than his own indicate that he had little aptitude for grand planning. As a theatre stategist, Lee often demonstrated more brilliance and apparent originality than Grant, but his most audacious plans were as much the product of the Confederacy's inferior military position as his own fine mind. In war, the weaker side has to improvise brilliantly. It must strike quickly, daringly, and include a dangerous element of risk in its plans. Had Lee been a Northern general with Northern resources behind him, he would have improvised less and seemed less bold. Had Grant been a Southern general, he would have fought as Lee did.

Fundamentally Grant was superior to Lee because in a modern total war he had a modern mind, and Lee did not. Lee looked to the past in war as the Confederacy did in spirit. The staffs of the two men illustrate their outlook. It would not be accurate to say that Lee's general staff were glorified clerks, but the statement would not be too wide of the mark. Certainly his staff was not, in the modern sense, a planning staff, which was why Lee was often a tired general. He performed labors that no general can do in a big modern army—work that should have fallen to his staff, but that Lee did because it was traditional

for the commanding general to do it in older armies. Most of
Lee's staff officers were lieutenant colonels. Some of the men on
Grant's general staff, as well as the staffs of other Northern generals, were major and brigadier generals, officers who were capable of leading corps. Grant's staff was an organization of experts
in the various phases of strategic planning. The modernity of
Grant's mind was most apparent in his grasp of the concept that
war was becoming total and that the destruction of the enemy's
economic resources was as effective and legitimate a form of
warfare as the destruction of his armies. What was realism to
Grant was barbarism to Lee. Lee thought of war in the old
way as a conflict between armies and refused to view it for
what it had become—a struggle between societies. To him,
economic war was needless cruelty to civilians. Lee was the last
of the great old-fashioned generals, Grant the first of the great
moderns.

*Not only did Lincoln now have a general whom he could trust,
both as a fighter and as a strategist, but for the first time the outlines of a modern command system had begun to emerge. Grant,
as general-in-chief, chose to remain with Meade and his army in
the field. Meade thus in effect became Grant's chief-of-staff in
the field while Halleck, who had never really been anything else,
was now officially named chief-of-staff at Washington. And behind these men was Lincoln, Commander-in-Chief by virtue of
his presidential office.*

*Grant's plan called for a simultaneous advance by four separate
armies. While the Army of the Potomac moved against Lee and
Richmond, Sherman, now in command in the west, was to advance upon Atlanta from Chattanooga. At the same time Butler
with a smaller force, in order to distract Lee, was to threaten
Richmond from the southern Peninsula while Sigel was to march
southward in the Valley. Actually, owing to the incapacity of*

*Butler and Sigel, little was done on the Peninsula or in the Valley.
The hard fighting lay between Grant and Lee, while Sherman,
fencing with Johnston, pushed him relentlessly back toward Atlanta.*

*The Wilderness, Spotsylvania, Cold Harbor—the long, gruel-
ing Virginia campaign dragged on. Grant hammered at Lee, always entrenched, always brilliantly defensive, and could neither
hold him in battle nor destroy him. The two armies sidled south-
eastward toward Richmond. The casualties were enormous, the
combat unrelenting. Feinting around Richmond to keep Lee from
holding there, Grant drove at Petersburg to its south, railway hub
of the Confederacy, but could not get in before Lee had reinforced its weak defenses. This was in mid-June of 1864. Then
came the siege of Petersburg. The longest of the war, it lasted for
nine months, right up to the end. The enemy was endlessly stubborn, and the North was nearing exhaustion. This was the "dark
summer" of '64, the low point; and only Sherman's capture of
Atlanta on September second, and Savannah on December tenth
kept the North in the war.*

*A brief vignette from Bruce Catton's best-seller, A Stillness at
Appomattox, pictures Lincoln's anguish in the White House while
the bloody fighting continued.*[16]

Washington was many miles away, and little was
known there about how the fighting was going, except that the
army was constantly calling for more men and more food and
ammunition. But the real storm center was the White House.
Here was Lincoln, sleepless and gaunt and haggard, his tough
prairie strength tried now as never before. He had once characterized another man, who could see no wrong in human slavery,
by musing that he supposed the man did not feel the lash if it
were laid on another man's back instead of on his own. That kind

of insensitivity he himself did not have, and the fact that he
lacked it was his greatest asset and his heaviest cross.

He could feel what hit somebody else, and however remote the
quiet rooms in the White House might be from the fearful jungles
below the Rapidan, all of the lines led back here, because here
was held the terrible power to still the tempest or make it go
on to the very end. Lincoln could pardon condemned soldiers
who fell asleep at their posts, or who broke and ran for it in the
heat of action—he called these latter his "leg cases," saying that a
brave man might be cursed by cowardly legs which he could not
keep from bearing him back out of danger—and he was the man
who with a word could have stopped all the killing, and he had
to will that the killing go on.

Now . . . the great wagon trains were lumbering down to
Fredericksburg, every day and every night, and the white ash and
charred twigs of the Wilderness were dropping on disfigured
bodies which no one would ever name, while long columns of
weary men went blindly into new fights that would be worse than
what they had just come away from; and Lincoln sat late at
night with a volume of Shakepeare's tragedies, and to a friend he
read the lines of Macbeth's despair:

> Tomorrow, and tomorrow, and tomorrow
> Creeps in this petty pace from day to day
> To the last syllable of recorded time,
> And all our yesterdays have lighted fools
> The way to dusty death. . . .

*Early's raid up into Maryland was Lee's last desperate effort
to shake Grant from his neck by creating a diversion. When General Early, on July eleventh, stabbed briefly at the outer defenses
of Washington, Lincoln came momentarily under fire as he stood
on a parapet to view the action.*

The Virginia campaign and Early's raid on Washington have been used by Sir Frederick Maurice to illustrate the satisfactory command ararngements between Lincoln and his new general-in-chief.[17]

Grant's appointment had been hailed with enthusiasm in the North, and the hopes which it aroused ran high. The appearance of a new commander in war is generally the signal for an outburst of popular acclamation. But a public always greedy for results quickly becomes impatient if it does not get them, and impatience is apt to change to disappointment and anger. When Grant's eagerly expected advance began and was followed by the long lists of casualties from the battlefields of the Wilderness, Spotsylvania, and Cold Harbor, grief produced anxieties which turned to grumblings against the new Commander-in-Chief. These grumblings had their political reactions which, with the approach of the presidential election, were of importance. . . .

A few days after the ill-planned and costly assault at Cold Harbor [Lincoln] told Grant: "I have just read your dispatch. I begin to see it. You will succeed. God bless you all." Here was a reinforcement to Grant worth many thousands of men. Lincoln, having made up his mind to keep Grant, supported him when he most needed support; he saw that Grant was wearing out Lee's army and holding to it so tight that it could not manœuvre, and told him that he both understood and approved. Two months later, August 16, 1864, when Grant's assaults upon Lee's lines at Petersburg had failed, when despondency in the North had again become general, and the demands for a peace of accommodation were increasing, Lincoln again wrote: "I have seen your dispatch expressing your unwillingness to break your hold where you are. Neither am I willing. Hold on with a bulldog grip, and chew and choke as much as possible."

This message, which gave Grant as clear an endorsement of his policy as any soldier could desire, is the more remarkable in that it followed on a mistake of Grant's which might well have shaken the President's confidence in him, and was sent at a time when Lincoln's political difficulties were probably greater than they were at any other period of the war.

When Grant moved the Army of the Potomac across the James to the siege of Petersburg, he was no longer well placed to supervise and direct the other forces of the Union. He had left a force in the Shenandoah Valley to block that favorite line of Confederate invasion, but this force, unskillfully handled, had been manœuvred in the middle of June out of the Valley by a Confederate contingent under Early, who promptly marched for the Potomac, crossed it, and moved on Washington, arriving before the capital on July 11. Now Early's force was far more formidable than Jackson's which had created such alarm two years before, and the garrison of Washington in July 1864 was far more weak than that which McClellan had left when he sailed for the Yorktown peninsula. Yet the contrast of the effect in Washington of Early's and Jackson's raids is remarkable. Grant had, of course, been informed of Early's progress and had dispatched troops to cover Washington, but the information had come to him somewhat tardily, and the troops had not arrived when Early was in Maryland and within a day's march of the scantily garrisoned forts covering the capital. In spite of this there were none of the hectic and ill-considered orders which Lincoln and Stanton had showered upon their perplexed generals in 1862. Instead, we find Lincoln telegraphing to Grant on July 10: "General Halleck says we have absolutely no force here fit to go to the field. He thinks that, with the 100-days men and the invalids we have here, we cannot defend Washington and scarcely Baltimore. . . . Now what I think is that you should provide to retain your hold where you are certainly, and bring the rest with you personally, and make a vigorous effort to destroy the enemy's forces in this vicinity. I think there is really a big chance to do this if the movement is prompt. This is what I think upon your suggestion, and is not an order."

The calls upon Lincoln for help against the bold raider came from all parts of Maryland and of Pennsylvania in '64 as they had in '62, but they were very differently answered. Here is his reply to one urgent appeal for troops: "I have not a single soldier but who is being disposed by the military for the best protection of all. By latest accounts the enemy is moving on Washington. Let us be vigilant, but keep cool. I hope neither Washington nor Baltimore will fall." Neither Washington nor Baltimore fell, though it is possible that Early might have been able on July 11 to get some troops into the capital for a few hours. Actually he retreated on learning that the transports with Grant's troops had arrived off Washington. Grant well knew that the reinforcements he had sent would be ample to drive Early back, and he knew, too, that the purpose of the raid was to cause him to weaken his pressure on Petersburg. Therefore he replied to the President's suggestion that he should come himself to Washington with more troops: "I think, on reflection, it would have a bad effect for me to leave here." Lincoln accepted that decision without question, and that acceptance—and indeed the whole incident—displays his implicit confidence in Grant, a confidence due not to blind trust but to the effect upon Lincoln's mind of close and continuous observation of the soldier's methods and actions. Most of Lincoln's correspondence with Grant begins with the words, "I have seen," or, "I have read your dispatch," and as proof that very little escaped the President's eye it may be mentioned that once when during the siege of Petersburg the usual supply of Richmond newspapers did not reach Washington, Lincoln promptly telegraphed to know the reason for the intermission. Grant was well aware that there was in Washington one ready to support him when he needed help, to give him a hand if he tripped, to remove him if he failed. Lincoln left Grant to his task, but he did not leave him without control and assistance.

Early's raid, which might under a looser system of conducting war have saved Richmond, as it was saved in '62, had no military results for the Confederacy save the material and supplies which he captured, and this was due to the relations Lincoln had established with his Commander-in-Chief. In fact the one serious military consequence of the raid was Grant's determination to close finally the famous covered way from Virginia into Maryland, which had so vexed his predecessors and eventually himself. For that purpose, and at Lincoln's instigation, he personally supervised the preparation of Sheridan's expedition, which not only prevented the Confederates from again using the Valley as a means of relieving the dangers to Richmond, but deprived Lee's army in the lines of Petersburg of its most convenient granary.

I have said that Grant personally directed the preparation for the last campaign in the Shenandoah Valley at Lincoln's instigation. He had told Halleck from his headquarters before Petersburg what he wanted done, and on reading this communication Lincoln at once telegraphed to him: "I have seen your dispatch in which you say, 'I want Sheridan put in command of all the troops in the field with instructions to put himself south of the enemy and follow him to the death. Wherever the enemy goes let our troops go also.' This I think but . . . I repeat to you that it will not be done nor attempted unless you watch it every day and hour and force it." Promptly came the answer, "I start in two hours for Washington," and Sheridan was started on his enterprise.

The sequel showed how truly Lincoln had sized up the situation and the men around him. One visit from Grant did not suffice, for the cautious Halleck and the nervous Stanton were holding Sheridan's ardor in chains. Grant gives us an account of this second visit: "On the 15th of September I started to visit General

Sheridan in the Shenandoah Valley. My purpose was to have him attack Early and drive him out of the Valley and destroy that source of supplies for Lee's army. I knew that it was impossible for me to get orders through Washington to Sheridan to make a move, because they would be stopped there, and such orders as Halleck's caution (and that of the Secretary of War) would suggest would be given instead. . . . When Sheridan arrived I asked him if he had a map showing the positions of his army and that of the enemy. He at once drew one out of his pocket, showing all roads and streams and the camps of the two armies. He said that if he had permission he could move so and so (pointing out how) and he could 'whip them.' . . . I asked him if he could be ready to get off by the following Tuesday. This was on Friday. 'Oh yes,' he said, he 'could be off before daylight on Monday.' I told him then to make the attack at that time and according to his plan." Again we see the fallacy of supposing that Lincoln left Grant entirely to himself. Sheridan's Valley campaign was due primarily to his initiative and judgment. He no longer intervened as he had done in May '62; he had learned how to intervene wisely and opportunely.

In his U. S. Grant and the American Military Tradition *Bruce Catton discusses Grant's winning strategy from a broader point of view.*[18]

That hard advance from the Rapidan to the James, made at such frightful cost, and those dreary weeks in the Petersburg trenches that had seemed to be sheer useless waste and tragedy—these had been essential in the grand strategy of the last year of the war. They had compelled the Richmond government to keep facing north while Sherman and Thomas took the Confederacy to pieces behind its back. Thousands of soldiers in the Army of the Potomac died before Sherman ever reached Atlanta or made his fabulous, all-destroying march to the sea, but they had made his conquests possible. In the end, as Sherman moved grimly on to the consummation of his design, Davis could do no better than go to Georgia and make speeches to oppose him.

Few of Grant's subordinates served him as well as did Sherman and Thomas. Banks ran into trouble with his Red River expedition and hurried back to New Orleans in disgrace, having done no more than keep thousands of good Union soldiers from pulling their weight that final summer. Ben Butler failed utterly, trying to come up the south bank of the James River while Grant and Meade marched down from the Rapidan, and the blow that might have taken Richmond and ended the war ahead of time became a dismal fiasco. Generals Franz Sigel and David Hunter failed, in succession, to close the Confederacy's great granary and strategic highway in the Shenandoah Valley, and their failure added months to the fighting required of the Army of the Potomac.

Unfortunately, for a while those failures were all that people could see. They came just when the terrible casualty lists from Virginia were at their worst, and the combination strained Northern endurance to the uttermost. In midsummer Lincoln himself believed that he would not be re-elected, and like nearly everyone else he assumed that a lost election would mean a lost war. But just when things looked worst, Sherman captured Atlanta, and bluff old Admiral Farragut damned the torpedoes and broke his way into Mobile Bay, and Phil Sheridan burned out the beautiful and dangerous garden spot of the Shenandoah, destroying the Confederate army that had defended the place—and, in the end, it was Southern endurance that broke. . . .

The house was coming down, and after four stormy years of life the Southern Confederacy, with all the dreams that possessed it, was entering the darkness of blown-out stars and echoing night, leaving the unbroken fabric of the American Union dyed with an ineradicable streak of passion and remembered glory.

4.

Lincoln's Cabinet

On August 7, 1863, John Hay, one of Lincoln's secretaries, noted in his diary: "The Tycoon [Lincoln] is in fine whack. . . . He is managing this war, the draft, foreign relations, and planning a reconstruction of the Union, all at once. I never knew with what tyrannous authority he rules the Cabinet, till now. The most important things he decides & there is no cavil."[1] And Salmon P. Chase, Secretary of the Treasury, wrote: "We . . . are called members of the Cabinet, but are in reality only separate heads of departments, meeting now and then for talk on whatever happens to come uppermost. . . ."[2] Navy Secretary Gideon Welles reported that Cabinet meetings were "infrequent, irregular, and without system."[3]

Traditionally, the Cabinet had been a council of state, but Lincoln was an overburdened and unsystematic administrator who preferred casual, often individual talks with his advisers rather than formal meetings. Though under pressure of war he failed to use the full potentialities of his Cabinet, at least he had chosen strong men for his official advisers. For better or for worse, they managed to play important parts in the crisis.

Burton J. Hendrick's Lincoln's War Cabinet is perhaps the outstanding book on the subject. Hendrick discusses Lincoln's selection of his Cabinet.[4]

It was a matter of frequent remark with Abraham Lincoln that the cabinet which, in completed form, he submitted to the Senate on March 5, 1861, was essentially the same as the one he had selected on November 7, 1860, the day following his election. In the construction of his official family Lincoln displayed the qualities that were to distinguish his administration. Independence of opinion, absolute reliance on his own judgment, a willingness to listen to advice, a readiness to compromise, so long as the main object was achieved, and a logically thought out scheme of action—all these well-known Lincoln characteristics were ultimately brought to bear in making this, his first great decision. The original choice of counselors was made on Lincoln's own initiative, with no broader outlook on the national field than could be obtained from the window of his little shabby law office in Springfield. In after years Lincoln liked to relate the story to his favorite intimates. One of them, Gideon Welles, has left an account in Lincoln's own words, incidentally, giving the first close-up picture we have of Lincoln after his election to the Presidency. He spent the evening of that fateful November 6, 1860, in the telegraph office at Springfield, the superintendent having placed the room at his exclusive disposal. "I was there without leaving, after the returns began to come in until we had enough to satisfy us as to how the election had gone. I went home, but not to get much sleep, for I felt then, as I never had before, the responsibility that was upon me. I began to feel at once that I needed support—others to share with me the burden. This was on Wednesday morning, and, before the sun went down, I had made up my cabinet. It was almost the same that I finally appointed."

True as was this statement of the case, the selection of the cabinet was not the simple process that Lincoln's words imply. Probably no President underwent such anguish in organizing an administration as the one elected on the eve of the Civil War. Though the new department heads had been chosen before the

sun went down November 7, the cabinet, in definite form, was
not complete even on the day of inauguration. When Lincoln, on
February 11, 1861, began his journey to Washington, only two
cabinet members had been offered appointments and had accepted
them. While the somewhat drab inaugural procession was advancing on March 4 from the White House to the ceremonies in front
of the domeless Capitol, the most important post, that of Secretary
of State, was still hanging in suspense. When the completed list
reached the Senate the following day, five nervous expectant
statesmen obtained the first official news of their selection.

*Although characterized by extreme diversity of views (which
was to make trouble later) the Cabinet members had all voted
Republican in 1860. The differences within the Cabinet represented cleavages within the Republican party itself, and Lincoln's
struggle to hold this diverse group of men together was only a
small part of his larger problem of maintaining, under the leadership of the Republican party, enough unity in the North to fight
an effective war. J. G. Randall explains some of the difficulties
facing Lincoln in choosing such a cabinet.[5]*

It has been noted . . . how Lincoln was not uninfluenced by agreements in the party convention of 1860 which have
been construed as promises of cabinet appointments to Simon
Cameron of Pennsylvania and Caleb B. Smith of Indiana. In addition to these obligations, he had so profited by the friendliness of
certain men that they may naturally have thought they had claims
upon his favorable consideration. Among such were Gideon
Welles of Connecticut, Montgomery Blair of Maryland, and Cas-
sius Clay of Kentucky. Thus the bestowal of rewards for party
service for which the successful candidate had reason to be personally grateful was a potent, though unwelcome, element in
Lincoln's choice.

But these "conditions . . . fairly implied" were only the beginning of Lincoln's worries. The very nature of his party, precarious, unrepresentative of the whole nation, never before victorious in a presidential election, presented complications. Already it was a party of factions, and these factions cut deep into practical Republican affairs in every important state.

Nor were the factions merely intrastate. The severe antipathies between the Seward element and the Chase element, and between Seward and Welles, related precisely to those problems of broad national policy that were to become the peculiar harassment of the incoming administration. To all this was added the task of recognizing Southerners in a "black Republican" cabinet while keeping due regard for other sections, especially New England, whose claims were natural enough but whose chances of genuinely agreeing on a selection were slight. It was not merely a question of "a New England member" but *what* New England member, and so on throughout the country. Cabinet positions meant power. To politicians they meant plums. By many they were regarded as doors to patronage. The question of a man's special fitness for a particular job in governmental administration was exceedingly difficult to work into the cabinet-making pattern: it was a subordinate factor in Lincoln's actual selection.

To the surprise of many, Lincoln included in his slate most of his disappointed rivals for the presidency. When told, "They will eat you up," Lincoln replied, "They will be just as likely to eat each other up."[6] Prophetic words!

Benjamin Thomas gives thumbnail sketches of the members of the Cabinet as it was finally constituted.[7]

Early in December, Lincoln offered Seward the portfolio of the State Department. Seward hesitated. "The wily old scarecrow," as Henry Adams described him, with his slouching, slender figure, his mussy clothes, his beaked nose and shaggy eyebrows that gave him the profile of a canny macaw, still regarded himself as the real leader of the party. Lincoln was utterly untried, Seward thought, and scarcely to be trusted with grave issues in such a perilous time. Could Seward work most effectively within or outside the cabinet? The astute New Yorker dispatched his political henchman, Thurlow Weed, to Springfield to learn more about Lincoln's opinions. On the day that South Carolina seceded, Weed and Lincoln were closeted, discussing patronage and policy, and Weed attempting to determine to what degree the inexperienced Illinoisan would accept Seward's advice.

Next on Lincoln's list came Salmon P. Chase. Tall, erect, with a finely shaped head and level blue eyes that lent a certain majesty to his appearance, Chase's sterling honesty qualified him for the Treasury. Touchy, ambitious, unbending, he was a leader of the antislavery radicals.

Long-bearded, prudent Edward Bates, of Missouri, was chosen for Attorney General. Shy, reserved, and of old-fashioned courtliness, he was a pensive, unimaginative man, slender of body, thin through the shoulders, but with a rugged face, dominated by heavy brows and prominent nose over a copious beard. An antislavery lawyer of the strict-construction school, he would speak for the border-state loyalists.

To give the critical border states a generous measure of representation, Lincoln selected shrewd, pinch-faced Montgomery Blair, of Maryland, for Postmaster General. A son of old Francis P. Blair of Andrew Jackson's celebrated "kitchen cabinet," a graduate of West Point, who, turning to law and politics, had defended Dred Scott before the Supreme Court, Montgomery Blair was prominent among the Union element in Maryland, just as his brother "Frank" Blair, Jr., once a slaveholder, was now a leader of the free-soil forces in Missouri. The Blairs—clannish, contentious, and politically adept—wielded immense influence.

Lincoln settled on Gideon Welles, of Connecticut for Secretary of the Navy. Actually, Welles was the choice of Vice-President-elect Hannibal Hamlin, whom Lincoln consulted in Chicago regarding New England's representation in the cabinet. Testy, opinionated, and humorless, Welles affected a heavy beard and a thick, pomaded, light-brown wig that gave him the appearance of Father Neptune. A former Democratic editor, an "old granny" according to his enemies, utterly inexperienced in naval matters but with the good sense to accept the expert and energetic guidance of his brilliant young assistant Gustavus Vasa Fox, Welles would prove to be a capable and conscientious administrator.

In choosing a Secretary of the Interior, Lincoln respected David Davis's pledge to Caleb B. Smith, a plodding party liegeman with influence in his own state of Indiana, but indistinguished otherwise.

Most vexatious to the harassed President-elect was the question of what to do with Simon Cameron, a rich, dominating, behind-the-scenes wire-puller to whom politics had been a profitable business. Tall and slim, with delicate features and a sort of foxy wariness, Cameron controlled a powerful faction in Pennsylvania, but was opposed by men equally strong. Soon after the election Lincoln, honoring Davis's promise, assured Cameron of a cabinet post—the Pennsylvania boss preferred the Treasury. Then, when immediate pressure was brought to bear against Cameron, and Lincoln was reminded of some of his questionable deals, the President-elect withdrew the offer. But Cameron had allowed it to reach the press; his pride and prestige would suffer if Lincoln failed to follow through. Cameron's friends and enemies hounded Lincoln week by week. At last, when the rival Pennsylvania faction became fearful that their state might be passed over altogether, and withdrew their opposition, Lincoln, perhaps against his better judgment, made Cameron Secretary of War.

Almost from the time of Lincoln's election he had known generally the men he would select, but fearing that he would be "teased to insanity to make changes," he did not tender some of the positions until he reached Washington. Meanwhile some desperate maneuvering took place, for the Seward and Cameron factions disliked Chase because of his radicalism. Welles looked upon the suave Seward as a conniver, and many party stalwarts abhorred the powerful and ofttimes mischief-making Blairs.

On the eve of Lincoln's inauguration his carefully chosen slate threatened to crash when Seward withdrew his acceptance of the Department of State, refusing to serve with Chase. "I cannot afford to let Seward take the first trick," commented the harried Lincoln as he forced the capricious New Yorker to reconsider.

Lincoln excluded all Illinoisans from his cabinet because he himself came from that state, but Norman Judd and many others who had helped to promote his candidacy were rewarded with lesser jobs. Some old-line Whigs grumbled that the three representatives of their party—Seward, Bates, and Smith—were outnumbered by the former Democrats—Chase, Welles, Blair and Cameron; but Lincoln reminded them that his own Whig antecedents restored the balance.

The furor occasioned by Lincoln's election convinced some of the most bitterly partisan Republicans that one cabinet post should be offered to an out-and-out Southerner as a gesture of good will. Lincoln did not see how any true Southerner could serve without dishonoring his convictions, but he was willing to try. As early as November he made overtures to James Guthrie, of Kentucky, a Democrat and former Secretary of the Treasury under Pierce, who pleaded age and infirmities. Lincoln's next choice was John A. Gilmer, of North Carolina, who consulted with Southern colleagues in Congress, turned down the President-elect's offer, and eventually became a Confederate Congressman. Others whom Lincoln considered proved unacceptable on one score or another, so that he finally settled for Bates and Blair. Outside the border states, however, their appointment did no good; staunch Southerners considered them renegades.

Hendrick takes the analysis of Lincoln's Cabinet a step further.[8]

"At night. President Lincoln's first cabinet meeting," Edward Bates noted in his Diary for March 6, "Intended, I suppose, to be formal and introductory only. In fact, uninteresting." Inevitably this group of ill-assorted statesmen must have felt some awkwardness at their first assembling. They were far from being a mutual-admiration society. Three of them, Chase, Blair, and Welles, were confronting a "Premier" who, for the preceding four months, had used all his resources of intrigue, and even of intimidation, to keep them out of the intimate White House circle. And of his maneuverings all three were well aware. But even Chase, Blair, and Welles, although they had a common bond of accord in hostility to the Secretary of State, were not entirely companionable themselves. Welles and Blair, it is true, could rub elbows on congenial terms; Welles's friendship with the Blair family, beginning in the Jacksonian era, and cemented afterward by cordial association at Silver Spring, had laid the basis of a co-operation that survived the Lincoln administration. They were almost the only friendly couple in the cabinet. Both men, however, had little regard for Chase. All three had another aversion in common—the lanky Pennsylvanian who had finally succeeded, with the help of Seward and David Davis, in slithering into the Secretaryship of War. To Edward Bates, who found that first evening's proceedings so "uninteresting," not one of his associates embodied his ideal of a statesman. Welles was probably the only one for whom he felt any personal attraction. Cameron himself did not find a single friend at Lincoln's board unless his marriage of convenience with Seward—soon to be dissolved—put the Secretary of State in that class. Caleb B. Smith was isolated, both by his own unimportance and by the methods he had used to obtain his seat. Seward, from the first, refused to take any of his fellow members seriously. Not one of them, in his view, was to play any figure in the general conduct of affairs. His failure to dominate Lincoln in cabinetmaking had taught him nothing. Perhaps Thurlow Weed had learned, in Lincoln's phrase, that Seward had not been nominated at Chicago, but that statesman's behavior, in the very first business that faced the administration, showed that Seward had not taken the lesson deeply to heart. . . .

In his letters to Lincoln, Seward had shown little modesty. Even toward the leader most concerned, he did not hesitate to assume a superior attitude. "I, my dear sir," he wrote Lincoln on February 24, "have devoted myself singly to the study of the case here with advantage of access and free communication with all parties of all sections. I have a common responsibility and interest with you and I shall adhere to you faithfully in every case." Only a few days before, in suggesting changes in the inaugural address, Seward had expressed similar ideas to his nominal chief. "Only the soothing words which I have spoken have saved us and carried us along thus far. Every loyal man and indeed, every disloyal man in the South, will tell you this." To others, Seward's letters were written in the same strain. Those to Mrs. Seward portray himself as the one man pursuing a steady, definite purpose amid the accumulating ruins. "All parties, north and south, cast themselves upon me." "My future responsibilities have already begun." "I have assumed a sort of dictatorship for defense, and am laboring night and day." "It seems to me that, if I am absent only three days, this administration"—the letter was written in January 1861, so the reference is to the Buchanan regime—"the Congress and the District would fall into consternation and despair. I am the only hopeful, calm, conciliating person here."

"Mad men North and mad men South are working together to produce a dissolution of the Union by civil war. The present [Buchanan] administration and the incoming [Lincoln] are united in devolving on me the responsibility of diverting these disasters."

If Lincoln felt chagrin at Seward's statement that he had an equal responsibility with him in "saving" the Union, and that his course during the interim from election to inauguration had succeeded in turning over to the new President a government still secure, there is no record to indicate the fact. But that he seriously differed with Seward in his proposals for counteracting secession there is abundant evidence.

Seward was playing a dangerous game. Once strongly antislavery, his growing conviction that compromise and conciliation alone would solve the crisis had led him far from the official Republican position laid down by Lincoln, moderate as that was. And since Seward still considered himself to be the leader of the Republican party, conflict between Lincoln and the Secretary of State seemed almost inevitable.

At the very first meeting of the Cabinet the explosive problem of Fort Sumter had been thrown at the perplexed and untried advisers. Margaret Leech pictures the Cabinet in this crisis:[9]

Day after day, the dismayed gentlemen of the Cabinet assembled in the President's office with its worn carpet and plain, heavy furniture. They sat around a long oak table, covered with a green baize cloth, and listened to the advice of the experts: Army officers, who discouraged the relief at Fort Sumter; Navy men who believed that it could be successfully carried out. Even granted that an expedition was feasible, it was not an easy matter to resolve to undertake it. The Sumter question had become a powder magazine, and only one of the President's advisers, Mr.

Montgomery Blair, was eager to drop a match in it. High above the fireplace, an old engraving of Andrew Jackson stared down on Lincoln and his Cabinet.

On March fifteenth Lincoln asked for written opinions. Five ministers were for evacuation, two against it. On that same day, without consulting Lincoln, Seward told Justice Campbell, a Southern member of the Supreme Court, that Sumter would be evacuated. He knew that Campbell would pass this on to the three Confederate commissioners then in Washington, whom Lincoln had refused to see. Seward repeated his assurances to Campbell on at least two other occasions, thus giving the South reason to cry perfidy when the attempt to provision Sumter was finally made. The historian James Ford Rhodes wrote, "The assurances to Campbell were simply those of an officious Secretary of State whose vanity had grown by what it fed on until now he deluded himself with the idea that he and not another was the executive of the nation."[10]

In the meantime Lincoln had sent various private emissaries to Charleston to test the sentiment there. On the basis of their reports, he made up his mind to try to hold Sumter. After a state dinner on March twenty-eighth he asked the Cabinet ministers to remain. He had just received from General Scott a recommendation to evacuate the fort, based upon purely political grounds. Hendrick describes the scene:[11]

It was to discuss this recommendation that Lincoln had summoned the banqueters from the state dining room. However bland Seward might appear on this critical evening, there were probably few of his colleagues who doubted that Scott's views on Sumter and Pickens had been inspired by the Secretary of State. Montgomery Blair, in the midnight cabinet meeting, could not restrain his indignation. He burst out in a violent tirade against Scott, accusing him of deserting his proper field. "Mr. President," said Blair on this occasion, "you can now see that General Scott, in advising the surrender of Fort Sumter, is playing the part of a politician, not of a general. No one pretends that there is any military necessity for the surrender of Fort Pickens, which he now says it is equally necessary to surrender. He is governed by political considerations in both recommendations." In making these remarks on the general's motives, Blair kept his eyes fixed on Seward. He might as well have named "Seward" instead of Scott in his denunciation. All his colleagues—including Seward himself—knew who was the object of his wrath. Blair never concealed, then or afterward, his conviction that, in presenting this humiliating document to Lincoln, Scott was carrying out Seward's instructions.

The President requested his cabinet to assemble on the following day, March 29. At that council he held his second session on Sumter. This disclosed a striking change of opinion from the one that had been expressed just two weeks before. Every member, except Seward and Caleb Smith, now advised immediate relief. Probably the President's own attitude largely explains this change. It was apparent to all that the President's determination was fixed. Irrespective of anything his cabinet might say, Fort Sumter was to be relieved. The sole constitutional responsibility rested on the President, and he was ready to assume it. . . .

On that same March 29, Lincoln sent orders to Secretary of War Cameron to prepare a relief expedition to Sumter ready to sail if necessary as early as April 6.

Seward had promised Justice Campbell a final and definitive decision on the relief of Fort Sumter by the first of April. In view of his earlier assurances, the Secretary of State now found himself in an embarrassing position. He alone, he felt, could preserve the peace; but Lincoln stood in his way. Seward saw only one solution: to transfer the executive power from the misguided Lincoln into his own, more capable hands. On the morning of April first the President found the following extraordinary letter on his desk.[12]

SOME THOUGHTS FOR THE PRESIDENT'S CONSIDERATION, APRIL I, 1861.

First. We are at the end of a month's administration, and yet without a policy, domestic or foreign.

Second. This, however, is not culpable, and it has even been unavoidable. The presence of the Senate, with the need to meet applications for patronage, have prevented attention to other and more grave matters.

Third. But further delay to adopt and prosecute our policies for both domestic and foreign affairs would not only bring scandal upon the administration, but danger upon the country.

Fourth. To do this we must dismiss the applicants for office. But how? I suggest that we make the local appointments forthwith, leaving foreign or general ones for ulterior and occasional action.

Fifth. The policy at home. I am aware that my views are singular and perhaps not sufficiently explained. My system is built upon this *idea*, namely, that we must

CHANGE THE QUESTION FROM ONE UPON SLAVERY, OR ABOUT SLAVERY, FOR A QUESTION UPON UNION OR DISUNION.

In other words from what would be regarded as a party question, to one of *Patriotism or Union.*

The occupation or evacuation of Fort Sumter, although not in fact a slavery or a party question, is so *regarded.* Witness the temper manifested by the Republicans in the free states, and even by the Union men in the South.

I would therefore terminate it as a safe measure for changing the issue. I deem it fortunate that the last administration created the necessity.

For the rest I would simultaneously defend and reinforce all the forts in the Gulf, and have the navy recalled from foreign nations to be prepared for a blockade. Put the island of Key West under martial law.

This will raise distinctly the question of *Union* or *Disunion*. I would maintain every fort and possession in the South.

For Foreign Nations

I would demand explanations from Spain and France, categorically, at once.

I would seek explanations from Great Britain and Russia, and send agents into Canada, Mexico and Central America, to rouse a vigorous continental spirit of independence on this continent against European intervention.

And, if satisfactory explanations are not received from Spain and France,

Would convene Congress and declare war against them.

But whatever policy we adopt there must be an energetic prosecution of it.

For this purpose it must be somebody's business to pursue it and direct it incessantly.

Either the President must do it himself, and be all the while active in it, or

Devolve it on some member of the cabinet. Once adopted, debates on it must end, and all agree and abide.

It is not my especial province.

But I neither seek to evade nor assume responsibility.

Lincoln needed Seward. He could easily have dismissed him for his presumption in attempting to take over power that could not

*belong to him. It is to Lincoln's credit that he pocketed the letter
and told no one about it. It was not to come to light until more
than twenty-five years after the war. He did draft the following
reply, but scholars now believe he never sent it.*[13]

EXECUTIVE MANSION, April 1, 1861

Hon. W. H. Seward.
My dear Sir:

Since parting with you I have been considering your paper
dated this day, and entitled "Some Thoughts for the President's
Consideration." The first proposition in it is, "*First*, We are at the
end of a month's administration, and yet without a policy either
domestic or foreign."

At the beginning of that month, in the inaugural, I said: "The
power confided to me will be used to hold, occupy, and possess
the property and places belonging to the government, and to collect the duties and imposts." This had your distinct approval at
the time; and, taken in connection with the order I immediately
gave General Scott, directing him to employ every means in his
power to strengthen and hold the forts, comprises the exact
domestic policy you now urge, with the single exception that it
does not propose to abandon Fort Sumter.

Again, I do not perceive how the reinforcement of Fort Sumter would be done on a slavery or a party issue, while that of Fort
Pickens would be done on a more national and patriotic one.

The news received yesterday in regard to St. Domingo certainly brings a new item within the range of our foreign policy;
but up to that time we have been preparing circulars and instructions to ministers and the like, all in perfect harmony, without even a suggestion that we had no foreign policy.

Upon your closing propositions—that "whatever policy we
adopt, there must be an energetic prosecution of it.

"For this purpose it must be somebody's business to pursue and
direct it incessantly.

"Either the President must do it himself, and be all the while active in it, or

"Devolve it on some member of his cabinet. Once adopted, debates on it must end, and all agree and abide"—I remark that if this must be done, I must do it. When a general line of policy is adopted, I apprehend there is no danger of its being changed without good reason, or continuing to be a subject of unnecessary debate; still, upon points arising in its progress I wish, and suppose I am entitled to have, the advice of all the cabinet.

Your obedient servant,
A. Lincoln

After Lincoln's display of firmness, in whatever form it took, Seward made an about-face, gave up his ambitions, and thereafter served his chief with loyalty and devotion. "Executive force and vigor," he wrote two months after the incident, "are rare qualities. The President is the best of us. . . ."[14] *Indeed, such good friends did they become that the jealousy of the rest of the Cabinet was increasingly aroused. "Premier" Seward, Welles complained, discouraged regular meetings of the Cabinet and yet managed to see Lincoln alone almost every day.*[15]

One member of the Cabinet soon lived up to the unsavory reputation with which he had entered the administration. An investigation of Simon Cameron's War Department brought to light not only maladministration but also widespread corruption, especially in contracts for horses. Although Cameron had not profited personally, the fact that he favored Pennsylvanians for jobs had become notorious. In order to ingratiate himself with the powerful antislavery radicals, he presumed to advocate in his annual report to Congress the freeing of the slaves and their use as soldiers, without consulting Lincoln in advance. The President thereupon quietly banished him to Russia as Minister to the Czar.

As Cameron's successor in the War Department, Lincoln chose Edwin Stanton, former Attorney General in Buchanan's cabinet

and lately legal adviser to Cameron. The appointment was surprising, for Lincoln had never forgotten a crushing snub Stanton had administered to him in Cincinnati before the war when both were lawyers. As late as 1861, moreover, Stanton had publicly referred to Lincoln as a "low, cunning clown."[16] As usual, Lincoln had suppressed his personal feelings. He realized that Stanton had the makings of the driving, ruthless administrator he desperately needed in this key post.

Stanton had been intimate with McClellan, but turned on the general the very day after his confirmation as Secretary of War. When Stanton joined the Cabinet, the radical Republicans in the Senate, led by Ben Wade and Zach Chandler from the midwest and Charles Sumner, the austere abolitionist from Massachusetts, felt they had the instrument they needed to destroy McClellan. The radicals and McClellan had one thing in common: they both despised the administration. McClellan, who was almost pathologically suspicious of those "wretched politicians" in Washington, wrote: "There are some of the greatest geese in the cabinet I have ever seen."[17] And the radicals, convinced that the administration's "softness" toward Democrats like McClellan was endangering the war effort, were boldly determined to transfer the entire control of the war to Congress. Congress alone, they felt, was capable of pushing through to victory under their relentless leadership. Lincoln must be shorn of power.

Of the members of the Cabinet, the radicals approved only Stanton and Chase, for the majority of the Cabinet supported Lincoln's program for the restoration of the Union rather than for the elimination of slavery. As the Secretary of the Treasury had lost influence in the government, he had turned more and more toward the radicals and their extreme antislavery position.

After the collapse of the Peninsula campaign and the second disaster at Bull Run, the intrigue against McClellan came to a head. Even Lincoln was inclined to believe that McClellan had

wanted Pope to fail at Bull Run, and had deliberately withheld re-
inforcements which might have turned defeat into victory. Hen-
drick carries on the story.[18]

        Stanton and Chase, and their congressional cohorts, attributed the full blame to McClellan. His fortnight's delay in beginning the northward movement of his army, his failure, once this army had landed on the Potomac, to rush them to Pope's hard-pressed contingents—here, they cried (and the criticisms to which the proceedings gave rise have not yet died down), was the explanation for the Federal rout. Here was more of that pro-slavery "treason" which had paralyzed the Union armies for the preceding ten months. McClellan, of course, had his defenders then, as he has today. He had changed his base from southern to northern Virginia, he declared, with all possible dispatch. In fact, his skill in withdrawing from the James, in face of a hostile army, his admirers have always hailed as one of those maneuvers at which he was so great a master. To get his men to the scene of active operations in the time allotted, they declare, was beyond human power. Had McClellan been guilty of the crime of which he was accused—that of deliberately withholding his troops and thus insuring Federal defeat—only a firing squad could have meted out the appropriate penalty. That mild-mannered Christian gentleman, Salmon P. Chase, advocated this as the one desirable solution of the McClellan problem. "Chase," notes Gideon Welles, said that "he deliberately believed McClellan ought to be shot, and should, were he President, be brought to summary punishment."

This conviction made Chase a willing partner in the plan which Stanton set in motion for McClellan's destruction. That the program also endangered the existence of the cabinet did not deter either man. All through August, Stanton and Chase had been bringing pressure to bear on Lincoln to this end. They did not

seek merely to reduce McClellan's command. Only utter disgrace
—his retirement to civil life—would be deemed adequate punishment for his crime. Stanton had gone as far as his authority warranted, to accomplish this result. Probably no military man of
high rank ever received a more cutting reply than when McClellan in late August telegraphed Stanton, asking what his status was.
At that time his army had been taken from him and transferred
to Pope. Just what then, he asked of the Secretary, did he command? "General McClellan," came the answer, "commands that
portion of the Army of the Potomac that has not been sent forward to General Pope's command." As only one hundred men,
many of whom were ill, remained with McClellan at the time,
this official announcement may be regarded as one of those
studied insults for which Stanton had so brilliant a gift. Writing
to Thaddeus Stevens, expressing his satisfaction with Stanton's
reply, Chase remarked, "This is late, but well, though not well
enough." A more fitting disposition of McClellan, Stanton and
Chase had been cogitating for some time. It came to a head on
Saturday, August 30. News had just arrived from Pope, telling
of a great Federal victory; he had defeated and was pursuing
Stonewall Jackson to his destruction. Pope's message was utterly
untruthful, though possibly he believed it himself; in fact, the
wily Confederate leader was luring Pope into an ambush, where
in due course he entrapped and destroyed him.

Chase had heard only Pope's version, when on the afternoon
of that day he came into the office of Gideon Welles and handed
him a paper, which he asked the Navy head to sign. The document was written in Stanton's familiar backhand scrawl and to it
the names of Stanton and Chase, with their official titles, had been
appended. Both Mr. Bates, Attorney General, and Mr. Smith,
Secretary of the Interior, Chase informed Welles, had signified their willingness to add theirs. The paper was addressed to
the President of the United States. "The undersigned," it read,

"feel compelled by a profound sense of duty to the government and the people of the United States, and to yourself as your constitutional advisers, respectfully to recommend the immediate removal of George B. McClellan from any command in the armies of the United States. We are constrained to urge this by the conviction that after a sad and humiliating trial of twelve months and by the frightful and useless sacrifice of the lives of many thousand brave men and the waste of many millions of national means, he has proved to be incompetent for any important military command, and also because by recent disobedience of superior orders and inactivity, he has twice imperilled the fate of the army commanded by General Pope and while he continues in command will daily hazard the fate of our armies, exhibiting no sign of a disposition or capacity to restore by courage and diligence the national honor that has been so deeply tarnished in the eyes of the world by his military failures. We are unwilling to be accessory to the destruction of our armies, the protraction of the war, the waste of our national resources, and the overthrow of the government, which we believe must be the inevitable consequence of George B. McClellan being continued in command, and seek, therefore, by his prompt removal to afford an opportunity to capable officers under God's providence to preserve our national existence."

Probably American history offers no parallel to this document. In the first place, it was most undignified in substance and manner. It was not an official paper, though signed by two cabinet members and addressed to the President, but a stump speech. In the most approved Stantonian style, it assumed as true all the charges then in open and whispered circulation in Washington—that McClellan was responsible for Pope's defeat, that he had deliberately withheld forces that would have ensured his victory, that he was plotting the overthrow of the government. The unasked-for advice was also an insult to Lincoln. It informed the President, in so many words, that, if he did not at once dismiss McClellan from "any command" in the Federal army, the signers—and Stanton and Chase believed they could count on at least five of the seven cabinet members—would resign their portfolios and disrupt the administration. The declaration that they would be "unwilling to be accessory" to the national calamities that would follow McClellan's retention in any command could have no other meaning. Indeed, Chase, in discussing the subject with Gideon Welles in this and subsequent interviews, avowed such to be the purpose. Chase, writes Welles, said that the letter "was designed to tell the President that the administration must be broken up or McClellan dismissed. The method was an unusual one, but the case itself was unusual." "Why not take the matter up in face to face conversation with Mr. Lincoln," Welles asked, "instead of putting the matter so uncompromisingly in writing?" Nothing could be gained, Chase replied, by discussing matters of such consequence personally with the President. "Argument was useless. It was like throwing water on a duck's back. A more decisive expression must be made and that in writing." Both Stanton and Chase had in fact already used verbal persuasion without result; this letter, which was virtually an ultimatum, had therefore been prepared. . . .

Had the ultimatum succeeded, Lincoln's whole plan of a coalition cabinet would have gone adrift. The scramble that would have taken place for the control of the administration would have endangered the whole Union cause. This revolution would have triumphed—that is, the Lincoln cabinet of August 1862 would have fallen in ruins—except for one man. The old-fashioned but shrewd gentleman then filling the post of Secretary of the Navy saw the meaning of the step at a glance and stiffened his puritanical back against it. Stanton and Chase clearly understood that Welles's accession was indispensable. Though Stanton had enrolled four members of the cabinet in his palace revolution—a majority—the demonstration was not quite so impressive as it appeared on the surface. His only really strong ally was Chase. The other two, Caleb B. Smith and Bates, exercised little influence in the administration. Smith was practically a cipher; neither by character nor by ability did he enjoy the respect of his associates or the public; his career was approaching its end, and, in fact, he retired from the cabinet four months after signing the Stanton-Chase manifesto. Edward Bates was a more important convert, though he, a man without a political party, and filling a minor cabinet place, did not add great strength to the uprising. One wonders why Bates, who was a wise, honest man, with a strong sense of official propriety, permitted himself to be drawn into the intrigue. He despised both Chase and Stanton and always bracketed them as unfaithful to the President and as selfish pursuers of their own ambitions. It is also true that Bates was not overemphatic in his admiration of Lincoln. "The President," he notes on December 31, 1861—and this remained his view to the end—"is an excellent man, and in the main wise, but he lacks *will* and *purpose*, and, I greatly fear, has not *the power to command.*" He thought designing men took advantage of Lincoln's "amiable weakness," that "he lacked nerve to apply the remedy," that "if he had more *vim*" he would have dismissed Stanton from the cabinet. In the matter of McClellan, Bates in particular regarded Lincoln as inept and vacillating. Yet Chase was wrong in telling Welles that Bates would sign the paper. He was too judicially minded to endorse Stanton's wild charges, though, as presently became evident, he was willing to sign an appeal couched in more appropriate language.

Stanton and Chase had no hope of bringing Blair into the intrigue, and Seward, who with Blair had supported McClellan, had conveniently gone off on a long trip. Although Bates was finally persuaded to sign a milder version of the ultimatum, Welles,

*whose support was vital, steadfastly refused to have anything to
do with the remonstrance; and so the whole matter was dropped
before it had come to Lincoln's attention.*

*The staunch Secretary of the Navy, who knew perfectly well
that the intrigue was aimed (as he wrote) at ultimate "control"
of the administration, had averted a serious crisis.[19] Lincoln himself of course was out of patience with McClellan, but as usual he
saw further than Stanton and Chase. When McClellan's organizing genius was once more needed to re-form the beaten troops
around Washington after the rout at Bull Run, Lincoln did not
hesitate to return the general to command. The Cabinet was
stunned. Hendrick continues.[20]*

Of all the assembled statesmen, Stanton showed the
greatest emotion. As Welles records, the Secretary of War was
"trembling with excitement." He was big with news, which he
announced "in a suppressed voice." McClellan, he informed his
colleagues, had been restored to command of the Army of the
Potomac! Consternation and amazement followed the declaration. At the height of the discussion, the tall, gaunt figure of the
President entered, calm and controlled, yet evidently laboring under a great strain. All the perturbed cabinet faces turned in his
direction. Was it true that McClellan had been replaced in his
old position? Yes, Lincoln quietly answered, it was true. His delay in reaching the cabinet meeting had been caused by his absence in consultation with that military chieftain. He and General
Halleck had called at McClellan's house, routed him out before
breakfast, and ordered him to take command of the Federal armies
stationed about Washington. In response to the anxious expressions on every face—which, in the case of Stanton and Chase,
amounted to surly glares—Lincoln said that he had done what
seemed best under all the circumstances.

"No order to that effect," said Stanton, "has been issued from
the War Department."

Lincoln turned on his insolent subordinate with that cold finality he could use at times most effectively. "The order is mine," he replied, "and I will be responsible for it to the country." He acknowledged all McClellan's shortcomings. The general had "the slows" and was not to be depended on for aggressive fighting. But he was a good engineer, a splendid organizer of armed forces; he knew, better than any man, conditions that then surrounded Washington, and no man in the nation was so competent for the immediately pressing task—that of reconstituting the demoralized hordes then pouring into the Washington forts, and whipping them expeditiously into a fighting force.

The most serious cabinet crisis of the war came in December, 1862. The McClellan intrigue had been an abortive attempt at a "palace revolution" within the Cabinet, but this was to be a determined assault upon the administration from without, a bold move among the Republicans in Congress, spearheaded by the radicals, to wrest executive and military control of the war from the President.

After the Republican losses in the fall elections and the bloodletting at Fredericksburg which followed, their mood grew uglier. The final dismissal of McClellan in November was not enough to satisfy the radicals. The next step would be to replace Lincoln's coalition Cabinet with a group of faithful radicals, which would of course include Chase and Stanton. The point of immediate attack was to be Seward. He had supported McClellan, and had opposed the Emancipation Proclamation, by now administration doctrine. The first volume of Seward's diplomatic correspondence, moreover, published inopportunely at this time, had shocked even Lincoln with its revelation of Seward's "softness" toward the South in the crisis of 1861.

The Republican senators met in caucus on December sixteenth and seventeenth. The mood was revolutionary; hard, ugly words were thrown at Seward, and at Lincoln himself. But milder coun-

*sels prevailing, the senators finally agreed merely to call upon
Lincoln for a "partial reconstruction" of the Cabinet. Thirty-one
out of thirty-two Republican senators signed the remonstrance.
Seward, hearing of it, sent in his resignation. Lincoln declared
himself "more distressed than by any event in my life." He told
a friend, "They wish to get rid of me, and I am sometimes half
disposed to gratify them."[21] J. G. Randall describes the denouement.[22]*

Lincoln was presented with no mere tempest in a
teapot. He was face to face with a challenge to his position and
leadership, but this was not all. He was at a crisis which involved
the success of the government and the fate of the nation. Even
if, in response to selfless prompting, he should step out, what of
the country and of the cause he was serving? The President's unhappy state of mind was not merely personal. Already the question of his own leadership had been canvassed in his mind. He had
pondered dispassionately whether he ought to yield to another,
supposing that were constitutionally possible, and had decided
that such action was not indicated as the solution of the nation's
difficulties. Yet he must stay in office as a real and not a merely
nominal leader. If senators could push him around, his effective-
ness would be seriously weakened, with the possibility of further
disaster to the Union cause. He could not forget that in the minds
of conservative men it was the radicals who had been responsible
for the unhappy outcome of Fredericksburg. The men who were
using the caucus of Republican senators as their instrument were,
as Browning said, the President's "bitterest enemies"; they were
"doing all in their power to break him down." They were the
"ultra, radical, unreasoning men who raised the insane cry of on
to Richmond in July 1861, and have kept up a war on our generals ever since—who forced thro the confiscation bills, and ex-
torted from the President the proclamations and lost him the con-

fidence of the country. . . ." Fearing that popular indignation
would fall upon their heads, thought Browning, they were "intent upon giving it another direction." . . .

Lincoln's technique, or diplomacy if that is the word, rose to
the occasion. It was arranged that a committee of the senators
should call on the President on the evening of Thursday, December 18, and state their demands. Patiently the nation's Executive
listened while senators presented the case against Seward—his
lukewarmness and responsibility for failure. "To use the P[r]est's
quaint language, while they believed in the Prest's honesty, they
seemed to think that when he had in him any good purposes, Mr.
S.[eward] contrived *to suck them out of him unperceived.*"

Lincoln arranged that the senatorial committee (nine men selected to represent the Republican caucus) should meet him again
on the evening of Friday, December 19. That morning, beginning
at 10:30, he had a long and earnest session of his cabinet. Enjoin-
ing secrecy, he reported the resignation of Seward and his son
and the conference with the senators. The President stated how
"shocked and grieved" he was to hear the senators' objections to
Seward, knowing as he did how there had never been any dis-
agreements in the cabinet "though there had been differences,"
and how their confidence and zeal had "sustained and consoled"
him.

Having given the cue for the cabinet's attitude—co-operation
with the President and among themselves—Lincoln made an
adroit move which disarmed the critics and doubters. He contrived it so that when the senatorial committee of nine came again
they found themselves confronted by the whole cabinet except
Seward. One effect of this was that Chase, who had talked with
some of the senators in the anti-Seward sense, found himself in
a situation in which he could not do otherwise than confirm the
President's statement of essential harmony in the cabinet. The
mere confronting of the legislators with the cabinet, in a meeting

of which Lincoln was moderator, gave the President a notable advantage. It was one thing for senators to use strong language in a caucus; it was quite another to do it face to face with President and cabinet. When questioned directly by the President, only four of the solons stuck to their guns in insisting upon Seward's removal.

As with the senators, so with the secretaries. For any cabinet member to associate himself with a senatorial drive against a colleague would put him clearly in the wrong. "This Cabinet," said Stanton, "is like yonder window. Suppose you allow it to be understood that passers-by might knock out one pane of glass— just one at a time—how long do you think any panes would be left in it?" At length the meeting of President, cabinet, and senators broke up "in a milder spirit" than when it met. The senators had shot their bolt, yet no explosion had occurred.

Thus ended Friday. Next day Washington buzzed with rumors that the whole cabinet had resigned and the President was in receipt of a number of new slates. Holding another cabinet meeting, Lincoln found himself in possession of another resignation. What happened is best told in the language of Gideon Welles: "Chase said he had been painfully affected by the meeting last evening, . . . and . . . informed the President he had prepared his resignation. . . . 'Where is it?' said the President quickly, his eye lighting up in a moment. 'I brought it with me,' said Chase, . . . 'Let me have it,' said the President, reaching his long arm and fingers toward C., who held on, . . . reluctant to part with the letter, . . . Something further he wished to say. but the President . . . did not perceive it, but took and hastily opened the letter. 'This,' said he, . . . 'cuts the Gordian knot.' . . . 'I see my way clear.'" In his prairie phrase, Lincoln could ride; "I have got a pumpkin in each end of my bag," he said.

Having maneuvered the situation to precisely the point which he desired, and having arranged it so that both secretaries stayed in town, Lincoln now addressed to Seward and Chase identical notes mentioning their resignations and adding that the public interest would not admit of their acceptance. He therefore requested each to resume his duties. Seward promptly complied; Chase, not forgetting the President's gratified look at the cabinet meeting, asked leave to "sleep on it." On the same day that his resignation was presented (Saturday, December 20) he wrote out a letter asking that the resignation be accepted and advancing the view that both he and Seward could serve better as private citizens. He gave the matter further thought over a painful Sunday; then on Monday, December 22, he sent the President two letters. Enclosing the Saturday letter, he stated that he had changed his mind and would resume his post.

The crisis passed. The important members of the Cabinet remained in office, although Caleb B. Smith, Secretary of the Interior, was replaced by an equally unimpressive politician, John Palmer Usher. If not defeated, the Republican senators had been deflated. Clearly Lincoln had emerged as the dominant figure in his cabinet. But the coalition, shakier than ever, was about to fall apart. Hendrick summarizes the breakup.[23]

The year 1864 proved to be a critical one in the history of the Lincoln cabinet. Before its end the reorganization which had been threatened so many times had become an accomplished fact. The change, however, represented no triumph for the Sumners, the Wades, the Chandlers, and the Greeleys who had struggled and intrigued so fiercely for a whole presidential term to gain control of affairs. The reconstruction was the work not of attacks from without, but of dissensions within. By December 1864, only two of the seven whom Lincoln had appointed on March 5, 1861, remained around his council table. William H. Seward and Gideon Welles still occupied their familiar, if somewhat uneasy, seats. But Salmon Portland Chase and Montgomery Blair had succumbed to the political complications of Lincoln's second presidential campaign, and Edward Bates, in his seventy-second year, had retired to a comfortable old age in St. Louis. The mere fact that Chase's was the most spectacular resignation indicates the extent to which the radical attempts to reorganize the cabinet to their advantage had miscarried.

That the cabinet disintegrated in 1864 was not surprising; the really astonishing thing was that it had held together so long. No such uncongenial or contentious group had ever assembled beneath the White House roof. Lincoln's conception of a coalition was politically sound, but on the personal side it inevitably led to trouble. For the most part Lincoln's councilors were forceful men, with their own programs, their own ambitions, their own vanities, jealousies, obstinacies, and defects of temper. Each had his set of ideas and his personal following, and on few matters had any two agreed. The criticism constantly made that the cabinet was not a "unit," that each of its members went his own way and lived by himself in a watertight compartment, was largely justified. An inner bloc—Blair, Welles, and Bates—did remain on approving personal terms, but that was the only element of harmony. Perhaps a qualification to this statement should be made in the case of Blair and Bates, who had little personal regard for each other, and who at times sharply disagreed in matters of politics and the conduct of the war. Still, these two positive characters generally held the same views on important questions— such, for example, as Reconstruction and the future of the Negro —belonged to the same wing of the party, and so may be linked with Welles as forming an anti-Chase, anti-Seward, and anti-Stanton entente. From the Diaries of Chase and Welles, and from the memoranda of Blair, could be culled an entertaining anthology of elegant extracts in which their fellow statesmen are described, over and over again, as deceitful, scheming, avaricious of power, and disloyal to the President. Both Welles and Bates esteemed Chase an ignoramus in matters of finance—a judgment that posterity does not accept; while Blair did not hesitate to denounce the Secretary of the Treasury as a "traitor" to Abraham Lincoln. The feelings all three entertained for Stanton were unutterable. The elder Blair's conviction that Stanton would "betray any man, no matter what his obligations to him, if he stood in the way of his selfish and ambitious schemes" was likewise that of his son. In the last year of their official association, Blair and Stanton were not on speaking terms. They would enter the cabinet room, take their seats without the usual greetings, and sit throughout the session oblivious of each other's presence. Relations between Blair and Seward were scarcely more cordial. The stories of wild altercations in cabinet that now and then reached the newspapers were usually exaggerated, but material in plenty existed for the reportorial talent to build upon. Maunsell B. Field once complained to Seward that he was keeping no diary, thereby depriving posterity of a most illuminating record. It would contain little, Seward replied, except a squalid account of quarrels within the cabinet, and would disgrace the nation if ever exposed to public view. Real patriotism demanded silence.

It was the quarrel between Chase and the Blairs that finally broke up the coalition Cabinet. The Blairs were a pugnacious lot: Postmaster General Montgomery Blair of the Cabinet, his brother "Frank" Blair, Jr., boasting a brilliant record both as congressman and as a general, and their father, old Francis P. Blair, the elder statesman. "When the Blairs go in for a fight," said Montgomery, "they go in for a funeral."[24] They had several bones of contention with Chase. He had been pushing his presidential ambitions with morbid intensity, and his men had invaded the Blair states, Maryland and Missouri. The campaign, moreover, had begun to turn on the issue of reconstruction.

While the Blairs stood with Lincoln, Chase of course sided with the radicals who were outraged by the moderate tone of Lincoln's postwar plans. Posing busily as the reluctant candidate, Chase had actually turned the Treasury into a political machine with Jay Cooke's fiscal department turning out vast quantities of pro-Chase publicity. There was a campaign biography, a speaking tour, and a rash of laudatory articles and editorials and finally, in January 1864, an official announcement of the candidacy.

Yet it was said that only two people really believed in the campaign: Chase himself and his fascinating daughter Kate. As a social leader of Washington society, Kate did everything in her feminine power to promote it. Lincoln, to whom Chase had begun to condescend as the gulf between them widened, smiled at it all. "I am entirely indifferent as to his success or failure in these schemes," he said, "so long as he does his duty at the head of the Treasury Department."[25] But in February Chase's backers got out a flagrantly anti-Lincoln circular which the President could not ignore. Chase himself disavowed the "Pomeroy Circular" and offered to resign, but it destroyed what little public support he had been able to build up, and gave the Blairs their opportunity.

Frank Blair, returning from the army, took up his seat in Congress and opened a violent attack upon Chase, charging his department with corruption in its handling of trade with the conquered areas of the South. On February twenty-seventh, in an inflammatory speech, he demanded an investigation of the charges. Hendrick takes up the narrative.[26]

By this time the Blair-Chase contention had reached a stage of fever heat almost without parallel in the eighty years' history of Congress. The attack of February 27 proved to be a mild affair compared with the philippic that the younger Blair delivered two months afterward. Those who gathered in the upper house on April 23 understood, by a glance in the gallery, that the anticipated storm was not exclusively the affair of the younger Blair, but of the whole Blair family. There conspicuously sat the venerable head of the clan, freshly arrived from Silver Spring, and by his side his sprightly daughter Betty Lee, a handsome, smiling, valiant sister, all eager to cheer on one brother, while he engagingly vituperated the cabinet colleague of another. The remaining gallery seats were occupied, for news had leaked out of the forthcoming performance; the Senate almost en masse abandoned its own quarters and crowded in to the House, as it usually did on the promise of rough-and-tumble excitement in the lower chamber. Certain new developments had added fuel to Blair's sufficiently fiery temperament. The repeated refusals of the Garfield Committee to investigate Chase's "trade permits," even when directed to do so by the House, seemed partisanship of the most unscrupulous kind. The Jay Cooke newspapers— heavily endowed with Treasury advertising—had started a campaign of unrestrained mud-slinging against the Missouri soldier-statesman. The Chase cohorts in Missouri had sought to turn the tables on Frank by accusing him of grafting in government contracts and conducting an illicit trade in supplying whiskey and other drinkables to the army. The House did appoint, on Blair's demand, a committee to investigate these charges. The report dismissed them as calumnies and brought forth a fact that made Frank a popular hero once more, for it showed that the document on which his enemies had relied to support their statement was a forgery.

In his speech Frank placed this forgery directly at the door of Secretary Chase, for the crime, he said, if not instigated by the Secretary himself, was clearly the work of his agents. The scene was one of the most turbulent that the House had ever staged. Most of the members were on their feet the larger part of the time, Chase's friends yelling demands for order, Blair's adherents coming to his support with shouts of "good," "go ahead," "keep it up"; Speaker Colfax, completely losing control of the body, kept viciously pounding his gavel, declaring the speaker "out of order," ordering him to stop—in vain, for the House overruled his parliamentary decisions, perhaps because the show was too enjoyable a one to be shut off on technicalities. Who was responsible, asked Frank, for these "forgeries" against him published in certain newspapers? "These dogs have been set on me by their master, and since I have whipped them back into their kennels I mean to hold their master for this outrage and not the curs who have been set upon me." Many of the charges had been put in circulation by a newspaper "pensioned by the Secretary of the Treasury. . . . I am simply endeavoring to show the motives which caused me to oppose Mr. Chase and which opposition caused him to retort upon me by an assault upon my character and reputation by the forgeries committed and disseminated by his understrappers."

"The gentleman is out of order!" shouted Speaker Colfax, bringing down his gavel with a mighty bang. "You're all right!" responded the Blair supporters. "Go ahead," and Frank did, ignoring the presiding officer's interruption.

Frank Blair came to a blistering finale, then stalked out of the House to return to his army post, leaving the radicals furious and the ordinarily statesmanlike Chase in "a fearful rage," his face ashen, his voice hoarse, his body shaking with anger. Some in Congress blamed Lincoln for countenancing the speech, but the President was able to satisfy his accusers that he was guiltless.

The virulence of the attack reacted against the Blairs and in September forced Lincoln to accept Montgomery's resignation in the interests of party harmony. Chase had gone earlier. In June, much to the Secretary's surprise and mortification, Lincoln had accepted one of his innumerable resignations with a curt note which amounted to a dismissal. Nobody except Stanton regretted his departure; and though Blair took his own dismissal with good grace, Chase publicly nursed his grievances against Lincoln. Even after Lincoln had swallowed his dislike for the man and appointed him Chief Justice of the Supreme Court in December, Chase and his daughter began to lay plans for 1868. "Oh, how little great men can be!" as one editor summed up Chase's strange career.[27]

The reconstituted Cabinet played a less important role in national affairs, though Lincoln used it frequently as a testing ground for his ideas. One such meeting is described in reportorial detail by Jim Bishop in his recent book, The Day Lincoln Was Shot.[28] *It was April 14, 1865, the last day of Lincoln's life. In this morning meeting, Frederick Seward was to take the place of his father for the Secretary of State had been severely injured in a carriage accident. The nation on that day, with Appomattox behind it, was eagerly awaiting news of Johnston's surrender of his southern army to General Sherman. But in effect the war was over. It was Good Friday, and many were attending church.*

The President did not attend on this day. He sat at the small table between the big sunny windows chatting with the members of the Cabinet and greeting guests as they arrived for this important meeting. This one, he knew, would set the tone for the future of the South—and, by that token, the future of the North—and what was decided here today could hardly be thwarted by Congress before December, a cushion of eight months.

And so he was extra jovial in his greeting, standing to shake hands with a newcomer like General Grant, at which point the Cabinet members broke into applause. The two men sat near the window and chatted, while the other men broke into conversational groups. Frederick Seward came in, told the President that his father was improving slowly, then stepped away to permit Colonel Horace Porter to greet Mr. Lincoln.

The Secretary of the Navy, Mr. Welles, came in and sat in his

Cabinet chair at the big table. He was puffing from the exertion of walking up the steps and down the long corridor. The Secretary of the Interior, John P. Usher, sat across from Welles and talked of spending a good part of the summer in Indiana. The newest member of the Cabinet, Hugh McCulloch, Secretary of the Treasury and the butt of Lincoln's gentle jokes about money, stood by himself at the start of his third Cabinet meeting, as though waiting to be asked to talk to someone. The curly-bearded snob from Ohio, Postmaster General William Dennison, did not ask him nor anyone else.

James Speed, the Attorney General, with a head like a ball anchor with moss dripping from the bottom, nodded to Mr. Lincoln and the President asked everyone to be seated at the Cabinet table. All hands were present except Secretary of State Seward who was represented by his son; Vice President Andrew Johnson, who *might* have been invited but wasn't; and Secretary of War Stanton, who often arrived late.

The President sat almost sideways at the head of the table so that he could cross his legs, and opened the meeting by asking if there was any news of General Sherman. There was none, said General Grant softly, when he had left the War Department. No news from Sherman meant no news of surrender from General Joseph Johnston. The President said that he had a feeling that there would be news before the day was out.

He started to tell a story, in a soft, deprecating way, about a recurring dream he had had, and he had engaged the attention of his appointees when Mr. Stanton arrived, dropping his hat and coat in the anteroom, and apologized for being late. He said that he had hoped to bring great news of General Sherman, but he had none.

The story was not picked up again, and Lincoln channeled the talk toward reconstruction. Stanton, busy removing sheafs of papers from his portfolio, said that, unless there was disagreement, he would like to announce the cessation of the draft to the country. He felt that it would lift the morale in all quarters, and help the country to realize that we all had to get back to work. Everyone was in agreement on this matter, and Stanton added that General Grant had spent a busy two days saving the country enormous sums of money by cutting the size of the army and by canceling army contracts.

The President said that it was pretty well agreed that the war was done, and that he needed suggestions regarding the best procedure to follow in the South. He was going to be saying those words, in different form, several times in the next three hours because he had no intention of adjourning this meeting for lunch or for any other reason until the skeleton outline of reconstruction had been erected.

Frederick Seward said that he had discussed this matter with his father before he left home this morning and, while it was extremely painful for his father to talk at all, the old gentleman had asked that the Cabinet consider ordering the Treasury Department to take charge of all Southern customs houses at once and to begin to collect revenues; he also felt that the War Department should garrison or destroy all Southern forts now; that the Navy Department, as a matter of precaution and a show of determination, should order armed vessels to drop anchor in all Southern ports and, at the same time, take possession of all navy yards, ships and ordnance; that the Department of the Interior should, without delay, send out Indian agents, pension agents, land agents and surveyors and set them to work reassessing Southern land; that the Post Office Department should reopen all post offices and re-establish all mail routes; that the Attorney General should busy himself with the appointing of proper judges and the reopening of the courts; in sum, that the Government of the United States should resume business in the South and that, at the same time, it should take care that that constituted authority and private citizens were not molested or impeded in their tasks.

The President smiled. The man from the sick bed had said an enormous amount in one breath, and the dissection of each of these suggestions would require considerable agreement among the men around the table. Seward was aware of this, just as he was aware that the Secretary of War would be at this meeting with his own suggestions for picking up the broken states and reassembling them.

The meeting droned on. Mr. Lincoln listened, made suggestions, brought departments together in their thinking, and, when energies appeared to flag, he brought up another point in the Seward doctrine.

"We must reanimate the states," he said. He admitted to the gentlemen that he was relieved that the Congress was not in session and, by indirection, signified that he had no intention of calling it into special session.

Ideas caromed smartly around the green table, some clicking with all hands, some finding no proponents except the original sponsor. Communications would have to be re-established between the South and the North at once. Once the arteries were functioning, the next step would be to see that nourishment flowed through them and Mr. Stanton suggested that the Treasury Department be empowered to issue permits to all who wished to trade, and that he, at the War Department, order the Southern ports to receive all trading vessels.

Old Gideon Welles stroked his beard and thought that he saw Stanton reaching for postwar Navy power.

"It would be better," he said, "if the President issued a proclamation stating the course to be pursued by each of the several departments."

This was an oblique warning to Stanton to leave naval matters to the Department of the Navy. Some of the men concentrated on wartime measures which could now be dropped. Stanton lifted his sheaf of papers and, raising his head slightly so that he could see through the lower part of his glasses, asked the Cabinet to listen to a plan which he had drafted "after a great deal of reflection" regarding reconstruction in the South.

He read the first part, pausing rarely to interpret, about the assertion of Federal authority in Virginia. Some of the members made penciled notes on pads set before them. When the reading of this section was finished, Mr. Welles reminded everyone present that the state of Virginia, which was used as a model in Mr. Stanton's document, already had a skeleton government and a governor.

The President, watching his flexing foot, said that the point was well taken. Stanton looked at the President to see whether the first section would be debated before he was allowed to proceed. Lincoln apparently was waiting to hear the rest of it. He had asked the Secretary of War to draw this thing up, and it was felt that the result would be a dilution of Lincoln's soft approach and Stanton's harsh one.

"I will see," said Stanton, "that each of you gets a copy of this."

The second section was then read and this part dealt with the re-establishment of the several state governments. Some of the members felt that there was more Stanton vengeance than Lincoln mercy in its proposals and Welles, as unofficial spokesman for the Stanton opposition, denounced it as "in conflict with the principles of self-government which I deem essential."

Mr. Stanton replied that he realized that the matter needed more work and more study, but that he had been asked to draw this up in time for the meeting and had done his best. Young Frederick Seward asked if it wouldn't be possible for all hands to be given a copy of the paper, so that it could be studied thoroughly and, at a subsequent Cabinet meeting, the President could have the best thinking of all members.

Mr. Lincoln nodded solemnly and said that he expected each man to "deliberate on this matter carefully."

Welles said that, as he saw the problem—taking Virginia as a hypothetical case—it was important, on the one hand, that the state government be representative of what the people of the Old Dominion wanted in a government, and yet equally important that the people be persuaded not to elect the very men who had instigated the rebellion in the first place.

Postmaster General Dennison said that Welles had stated the thing that he was worried about, and Mr. Stanton agreed. The sense of the members was that the best way to act would be to disenfranchise by name the leaders of the rebellion, political and military, and to leave the people of each state to choose from the men who were left.

Mr. Lincoln said little at this stage of the long meeting. He looked sadly and longingly at each man, and then looked back at his foot.

"We still acknowledge Pierpont as the legitimate governor of Virginia," Mr. Stanton said.

"There will be little difficulty with Pierpont," said Dennison.

"None whatever," Mr. Stanton said.

Pierpont had assented to the breaking off of West Virginia as a separate state and the de facto recognition of Pierpont as Governor of Virginia was involved.

Stanton blandly proposed that the states of North Carolina and Virginia be united under one state government, but the majority of the Cabinet members opposed the thought, claiming that the war had been fought to reunite the states, not to remake them.

Each messenger who tiptoed into the room was greeted with lighted expressions, but these dimmed quickly when it turned out that the news was not of General Johnston. There was no way that the men in that room could know that men in another room to the South were, at this moment, coming to a surrender decision. The messengers kept coming into Lincoln's big office, and each saw the same expectancy.

At one stage, in a lull, the President remembered his unfinished story about the recurring dream and he told the Cabinet that everything would turn out all right because of it.

"What kind of a dream was it?" said Mr. Welles.

"It relates to your element, the water," the President said. "I seemed to be in some indescribable vessel and I was moving with great rapidity toward an indefinite shore." Lincoln seemed to fear that the men might ridicule his dream, so he added: "I had this dream preceding Sumter, and Bull Run, Antietam, Gettysburg, Stone River, Vicksburg and Wilmington."

"Stone River was certainly no victory," said General Grant. "Nor can I think of any great results following it."

Lincoln agreed, but maintained that the dream usually presaged good news and great victories. "I had this strange dream again last night," he said, "and we shall, judging from the past, have great news very soon. I think it must be from Sherman. My thoughts are in that direction. . . ."

The talk turned to the leaders of the Confederacy and what to do with them. Mr. Stanton felt that, as Americans, they were traitors to their country and he could not see how anyone could put another interpretation on the matter.

Posmaster General Dennison, a roguish glint in his eyes, said, "I suppose, Mr. President, that you would not be sorry to have them escape out of the country?"

"Well," said Lincoln, leaning backward and trying to look serious, "I should not be sorry to have them out of the country, but I should be for following them up pretty close, to make sure of their going."

This led to an informal discussion of the many shades of

opinion from the Senate and House on the subject of what to do with the leaders of the rebellion.

"I think it is providential," the President said, "that this great rebellion is crushed just as Congress has adjourned, and there are none of the disturbing elements of that body to hinder and embarrass us. If we are wise and discreet we shall reanimate the states and get their governments in successful operation, with order prevailing and the Union re-established before Congress comes together in December. . . ."

That came from his head. This, from his heart:

"I hope that there will be no persecution, no bloody work after the war is over. No one need expect me to take any part in hanging or killing these men, even the worst of them. Frighten them out of the country, open the gates"—throwing up both arms and fluttering his fingers—"let down the bars, scare them off, enough lives have been sacrificed."

5.

The Political War

"In his conduct of the war," wrote Leonard Swett in 1866, Lincoln "acted upon the theory that but one thing was necessary, and that was a united North."[1] *Faced with the divisive passions of four long, bitter years of war, Lincoln had to call upon every ounce of his tact, strength and wisdom to hold the North together. James G. Randall writes about Lincoln's political war in his* Lincoln the Liberal Statesman.[2]

All the world is familiar with Lincoln the emancipator, the author of the Gettysburg address, the timeless spokesman of democracy. Few of us are acquainted with Lincoln the baboon, the imbecile, the wet rag, the Kentucky mule. Yet these are typical examples of the names heaped upon him in those cruel days when high office brought him less of glory than of insult and abuse within the ranks of the nation he was struggling to save from dissolution. Some of these utterances, voluminously given in contemporary correspondence long since forgotten, are presented here not for their own sake, but as evidence of the extent to which a leader may be reviled in his own time and yet go down in memory as a national hero. One does not take the full measure of the man's character unless he remembers that while

Lincoln was battling a formidable enemy in arms and studying to avert international disaster, foes within his own political household were like choking fingers at his throat.

In the thinking of the nation Lincoln is remembered by what his friends have said of him, for the most part after his death. This is fortunate. If, like Wilson, he were remembered by what enemies have said, the picture would be amazingly different. For in the eyes of contemporaries Lincoln was a President who offended moderates without satisfying extremists, who issued a tardy and incomplete emancipation proclamation after showing a willingness to conserve slavery, who suppressed civil rights, headed a government marred by corruption, bungled the war, and then lost the peace, his postwar policy being blocked by congressional leaders in his lifetime before being wrecked in the reconstruction period. These denunciations are preserved only in fading manuscripts and yellowing newspapers, while Lincoln's fame is a living thing, as if Fate had been struck with remorse and had made a belated effort to even the scales.

There were three main political groupings in the North: The "peace" Democrats and disloyal Copperheads on one side, the radical Republicans on the other (sometimes carrying the "war" Democrats with them), and in between both the moderate Democrats and Republicans. Of the two extremes, the most dangerous to Lincoln were the radical Republicans within his own political family. In the end they triumphed over him. "To be wounded in the house of one's friends," he told Noah Brooks, "is perhaps the most grievous affliction that can befall a man."[3]

The passage below, taken from T. Harry Williams' Lincoln and the Radicals, analyzes the wartime divisions within the Republican party.[4]

No polyglot army of an ancient emperor ever exhibited more variety than did the Republican Party in 1860.

Within its diverse ranks were radicals and abolitionists who wanted to destroy every vestige of slavery, moderates who would have been content to restrict its expansion into the territories, Whigs, Free-Soilers, and antislavery Democrats, Eastern manufacturers who hoped for a protective tariff and Western farmers who favored free trade, hardened machine politicians and visionary reformers. Two threads of unity bound this heterogeneous coalition into the semblance of a national organization. Each constituent part was opposed, although with varying intensity, to the institution of Negro slavery. And the party broadly represented the social ideology of the "free," capitalistic society of the North, whose ruling middle class felt it must strike down the political power of the slavocracy in order to complete its economic control of the nation.

There was a right and a left wing in the party even before 1860. The moderates were typified by Lincoln, the courtly Orville H. Browning of Illinois, James R. Doolittle of Wisconsin, and Vermont's venerable Jacob Collamer. They advocated the gradual extinction of slavery, compensated emancipation, and colonization of the Negroes in another land. They detested slavery, and believed the institution could not survive the strain of a long civil war. But they also feared and distrusted the revolutionary ardor of the radicals and the spirit of fanaticism that was inherent in the abolitionists. They opposed the wartime abolition of slavery except as a final measure of military necessity to prevent the disruption of the Union. Hence the conservatives fought from the beginning the hasty plans of the radicals to bring about immediate emancipation. Temperamentally they objected to the reforming zeal of the radicals. Furthermore, unlike the abolitionists, they had some appreciation of the practical difficulties that would follow the sudden liberation of several million slaves. The conservatives were reasonable, able men, but their very virtues rendered them incapable of coping with the determined radicals in a revolutionary period. In contrast to the radicals, the moderates were negative and vacillating, lacking a cohesive program of consistent action.

The radicals were the real driving power in the party. They were the men whom young John Hay, Lincoln's secretary, who had encountered their fierce prototypes of the French Revolution in his superficial reading, dubbed the Jacobins. Aggressive, vindictive, and narrowly sectional, the radicals hated slavery with a bitter personal feeling. But more than slavery they hated its political representatives, the proud cavaliers who had dominated Congress in the fifties and who had scourged the sputtering radical minority with polished gibes. Unlike many of the moderates, the Jacobins welcomed the outbreak of civil war as the longed-for opportunity to destroy slavery and to drive the "slave traders" from the national temple. In 1861 they had opposed attempts at compromise which might have averted secession. Conciliation of the sections would have deprived the Republican Party of its excuse for being; would, thought Michigan's Zachariah Chandler, "rupture" the organization. Chandler worked vigorously against compromise, and calmly welcomed the holocaust: "Without a little blood-letting, this Union will not . . . be worth a rush!" The radicals stood for instant emancipation, the confiscation of "rebel" property, the use of colored soldiers, civil and, when it should become expedient, political equality for the Negro. They loved the Negro less for himself than as an instrument with which they might fasten Republican political and economic control upon the South. Closely associated with the Jacobins, but more sincerely radical, were the abolitionists. Fanatical and impractical, their motto was that of all revolutionaries. "Let there be justice even though the heavens crumble." The abolitionists, within yet beyond the party, often forced the radical politicos to adopt a more extreme position than the exigencies of the moment warranted.

The Jacobins were led by master politicians. In the House of Representatives, caustic, terrifying, clubfooted old Thaddeus

Stevens ran the Republican machine, hurling his devastating taunts equally at Democrats, Republican laggards, the president, and "the vile ingredient called conservatism, which is worse than secessionism." In the Senate the radical leaders were Ohio's "Bluff Ben" Wade, endowed with a brutal wit, who had first won fame by offering to meet the Southern hotspurs upon the field of honor with squirrel rifles at thirty paces as the weapons; grim, furious Zack Chandler, "Xanthippe in pants," who bossed Michigan politics with an iron hand and a liberal supply of liquor; and Charles Sumner of Massachusetts, handsome, scholarly, and humorless, despised by many radicals for his cant, but valued as an impressive show-window display. . . .

Almost from the day when armed conflict began, the radical and conservative factions clashed over the purposes of the war. Lincoln and the moderates attempted to make the restoration of the Union the sole objective; and they would have restored it, if possible, without at the same time destroying slavery. Senator Browning, who often acted as Lincoln's spokesman, asserted in July, 1861: "For one, I should rejoice to see all the States in rebellion return to their allegiance; and if they return, if they lay down the arms of their rebellion and come back to their duties and their obligations, they will be as fully protected, now and at all times hereafter, as they have ever been before, in all their rights, including the ownership, use, and management of slaves."

In the president's mind, the preservation of the American experiment in government overshadowed all other questions. He regarded emancipation as incidental to this larger issue, to be resorted to as a last desperate measure, and then to be initiated by himself as an exercise of the war powers of the executive rather than by Congress. His intense conviction that secession must be crushed at all costs even impelled him to throw overboard considerations of party regularity. By inviting Northern Democrats and Border State slaveholders to accept prominent positions in the administration, he endeavored to enlarge the Republican organization into an all-inclusive Union party, a "popular front" whose one resolution was to end the war quickly and re-establish the nation.

Against this mild program the Jacobins inveighed, ranted, and sneered. Many of them felt that Lincoln was only a well-meaning incompetent who lacked the "inclination to put down this rebellion with the strong hand required." The radicals were determined that the war must not end without the death of slavery. "We cannot afford to go over this ground more than once," wrote aristocratic Charles Francis Adams of Massachusetts. "The slave question must be settled this time once for all." Impetuous George W. Julian, leader of the Indiana radicals, exclaimed that the war would be "an empty mockery of our sufferings and sacrifices" if slavery were spared. "Bluff Ben" Wade declared that "if the conflict continues thirty years and bankrupts the whole nation, I hope to God there will be no peace until we can say there is not a slave in this land." The fervid outbursts of radicals like Julian and Wade against the president's policy were dictated by coolheaded consideration of political expediency. If after a short war the Southern states returned to the Union with the institution of slavery still intact and the political control of the slaveholders unshaken, Republican influence in the government would be nullified and the economic revolution vexatiously delayed. A victory achieved upon Lincoln's plan, protested frank Martin Conway of Kansas, "must inevitably result in restoring the domination of the slaveholding class," and hence could "bring no lasting peace." "What!" cried a Western radical, "bring back the rebel States, into full fellowship as members of the union, with their full delegations in both Houses of Congress. They, with the pro-slavery conservatives of the Border States and the Democrats of the Northern states, will control Congress. Republicans and Republican principles will be in the minority and under law, and this latter state would be worse than the former—worse than war itself . . ."

The wily Lincoln surrendered to the conquering Jacobins in every controversy before they could publicly inflict upon him a damaging reverse. Like the fair Lucretia threatened with ravishment, he averted his fate by instant compliance. In 1865 L. Maria Child observed, perhaps ironically, "I think we have reason to thank God for Abraham Lincoln. With all his deficiencies," he had been a man "who was willing to grow."

When the war came, the North closed ranks behind Lincoln. Even the radicals bowed to the majority and approved Lincoln's policy of a war for the restoration of the Union. But as the conflict dragged on and war fever abated, both radical Republicans and Peace Democrats began to come out in open opposition to the administration and to each other. A growing conviction among the radicals that nothing less than a "total" war against slavery and the whole social system of the South would ensure victory for the North led them to the extreme position that anybody with opposing ideas was either woefully misled or downright traitorous. Enthusiastic at first about McClellan, they turned against him when his endless procrastination began to look to them like a concealed "softness" toward the South. Finally they helped to hound him out of his command. Lincoln's tolerance of Democrats in the army and in the government wore their patience still further, for the idea, held by Democrats and moderate Republicans alike, that the Union might be restored by force of arms without abolition of slavery in the South seemed to the radicals more and more like a reductio ad absurdum.

Several incidents early in the war fed their growing mania. In August, 1861, General Frémont, an abolitionist, issued on his own authority a proclamation freeing the slaves of rebels in the western territory under his command. Lincoln enraged the radi-

cals by countermanding this flagrant invasion of the executive power; and when the President dismissed Frémont in November for sheer military incompetence, the radicals were beside themselves. Finally, on October twenty-first the Union suffered a minor defeat at Ball's Bluff with unexpectedly high casualties, including the loss of the popular Colonel Edward D. Baker. The radicals unjustly blamed the fiasco on the alleged treason of the commanding officer, Democratic Charles P. Stone.

In his diary for October 26, 1861, John Hay noted: "This evening the Jacobin club, represented by Trumbull, Chandler and Wade, came up to worry the administration into a battle."[5] In December, with McClellan sick and the war at a standstill, the angry radicals returned to Congress determined to force their views upon the administration. They soon found the instrument they needed in the joint Committee on the Conduct of the War, set up as a result of a debate over a resolution to investigate Bull Run and Ball's Bluff. The Committee was dominated by the powerful and ruthless Ben Wade, with Zach Chandler as second in command. The Democratic members were largely ignored, except for War Democrat Andrew Johnson of Tennessee, who in any case left Congress early in 1862 to become military governor of his state. After Stanton was appointed Secretary of War in January of 1862 the Committee worked hand-in-glove with him. T. Harry Williams examines the Committee and its work.[6]

Until the Committee was created the Jacobins were in the dark regarding the plans of the president and his military advisers; they knew almost nothing of the real condition of the military forces or of the secrets of army administration. The radicals could never have initiated and carried on their struggle against Lincoln without the vital information which the Committee furnished in its jaundiced reports. It became the spearhead of the radical drive against the administration. It investigated the principal military campaigns, worked to undermine Democratic and conservative officers, interfered boldly with the plans of commanders, and bullied Lincoln into accepting the radical program. It was the most potent weapon wielded by the Jacobin cabal in the successful campaign to make radicalism instead of moderation the political faith of the nation. Yet its creation caused not a ripple of attention. Many conservatives voted for the measure without realizing the significance of the agency they were helping to establish. . . .

At its first meeting the Committee decided to conduct all its hearings in secret, and the members swore not to reveal any information given by witnesses. This restriction was designed primarily to prevent military plans and intelligence from reaching the enemy through public channels. The bosses of the Committee, however, played fast and loose with their own rule whenever a political advantage was to be gained. They divulged their confidential information to the radical machine. At times they even inspired propaganda campaigns in the radical press with secret reports from the Committee's archives. In another ruling adopted at an early meeting the Committee determined that for the purpose of taking testimony a quorum was not necessary. This enabled one or two Republican members to examine witnesses at any time. Officers appearing in answer to a summons would find to their surprise only Wade and Chandler present. . . .

The secret hearings invested the Committee with powers unlike those of other similar investigative bodies, and gave color to the charge that its sessions savored of Star Chamber methods. When the Committee set out to accomplish the downfall of a conservative general, its first step was to call a parade of witnesses who were known enemies of the suspected officer and who supplied a mass of hostile if inaccurate evidence. Finally the Committee summoned the general himself. He appeared alone before the Committee's bar, without benefit of legal counsel. He was not given an opportunity to examine the previous testimony; he might guess but could not know that grave charges had been made against his character and loyalty. He knew nothing of the specific nature of these charges, unless the Committee chose to give him a vague explanation. Thus Wade once told General Stone, suspected by the radicals of treason, that the Committee had evidence which impugned his loyalty. But the chairman refused to acquaint Stone with the exact nature of the indictments against him. As a result the agonized and innocent officer was forced to present an inadequate, general defense. . . .

The Committee, despite the secret sessions and the sinister epithets of its enemies, was not in any legal sense a court. It possessed no judicial powers and could pass no sentence. Rather it was a grand jury which reported to the president officers it believed guilty of incompetence and treason. The Committee, explained Wade, rendered no final judgments on military men: "We only state what, in our opinion tends to impeach them . . . and then leave it to better judges to determine." This was not quite an accurate statement, as the Committee always attempted to bully the judge, Lincoln, into making the right decision.

Since from McClellan down most of its officers were Democrats, the army was suspected by the Committee of preparing at the first favorable opportunity to force a negotiated peace upon a vacillating administration, a peace which would leave slavery intact in the South. While the Committee probed relentlessly for a treason which never existed, the officers haled before it were uncommonly stiff-necked about what they considered unwarranted interference in the affairs of the military. Their training had not prepared them for the hazards of civilian control.

The Committee's investigation of the conduct of the war was not only damaging to the army but proved to be a blind for its own misconduct. After a grossly biased trial, General Stone spent over six months in jail although innocent of the accusations hurled against him after Ball's Bluff. The charges against Fitz John Porter after Second Bull Run were equally unfounded, but the court-martial verdict was not reversed for years. Halleck, Buell and McDowell, all Democrats, were plagued by the Committee. Meade was brought under scrutiny, and Grant would have been next had not Sherman's capture of Atlanta rescued him.

On the other hand the radicals succeeded in rehabilitating their hero, Frémont, and would never say a word against those Republican generals, Pope and Hooker. In the end they approved Burnside, who turned radical to curry favor with them. And in publicizing their views the radicals, and Stanton too, proved to be the most expert propagandists of the war. They subjected McClellan to a lengthy interrogation in 1863, and then released a report on the conduct of the war which, as a piece of special pleading, was almost as hard on their titular chief, Lincoln, as it was on the Democratic opposition.

Opposition came easily to the Democrats, for the war had not been of their making. They had believed in the traditional art of compromise which had averted so many crises in the past. Most remained loyal, but the growing dominance of the radical Republicans deepened their disillusion. And as always it was slavery that was the great divider. While the Republicans were distressed by Lincoln's reluctance to turn the war into a crusade against slavery, the Democrats on the other hand feared that if the radicals succeeded in destroying slavery, a flood of undisciplined Negroes would invade the North with dreadful consequences for business and labor. The Democrats were disturbed, moreover, by the growing tendency of the administration toward centralization and its gradual abrogation of civil liberties. With some justice they feared that the Republicans, in the name of war unity, might attempt to break up their party. Many Democrats, discouraged by the growing triumph of radical Republican policies, began gradually to move from disillusion to unrest, and a minority flirted with treason.

Disaffection, both Republican and Democratic, was reflected in the problem of raising an army, always a delicate gauge of the popular mood. The passage is from Nathaniel Stephenson's Lincoln and the Union.**⁷

In 1861, when the tide of enthusiasm was in flood, and volunteers in hosts were responding to acts of Congress for the raising and maintenance of a volunteer army, Cameron reported in December that the Government had on foot 660,971 men and could have had a million except that Congress had limited the number of volunteers to be received. When this report was prepared, Lincoln was, so to speak, in the trough of two seas. The devotion which had been offered to him in April, 1861, when the North seemed to rise as one man, had undergone a reaction. Eight months without a single striking military success, together with the startling defeat at Bull Run, had had their inevitable effect. Democracies are mercurial; variability seems to be part of the price of freedom. With childlike faith in their cause, the Northern people, in midsummer, were crying, "On to Richmond!" In the autumn, stung by defeat, they were ready to cry, "Down with Lincoln."

In a subsequent report, the War Department confessed that at the beginning of hostilities "nearly all our arms and ammunition" came from foreign countries. One great reason why no military successes relieve the gloom of 1861 was that, from a soldier's point of view, there were no armies. Soldiers, it is true, there were in myriads; but arms, ammunition, and above all, organization were lacking. The supplies in the government arsenals had been provided for an army of but a few thousand. Strive as they would, all the factories in the country could not come anywhere near making arms for half a million men; nor did the facilities of those

* From *Abraham Lincoln and the Union,* by Nathaniel W. Stephenson, Volume 29, THE CHRONICLES OF AMERICA, pp. 142 ff. Copyright and permission Yale University Press, New Haven, Connecticut.

days make it possible for munition plants to spring up overnight. Had it not been that the Confederacy was equally hard pushed, even harder pushed, to find arms and ammunition, the war would have ended inside Seward's ninety days, through sheer lack of powder.

Even with the respite given by the unpreparedness of the South, and while Lincoln hurriedly collected arms and ammunition from abroad, the startled nation, thus suddenly forced into a realization of what war meant, lost its head. From its previous reckless trust in sheer enthusiasm, it reacted to a distrust of almost everything. Why were the soldiers not armed? Why did not millions of rounds of cartridges fall like manna out of the sky? Why did not the crowds of volunteers become armies at a word of command?

The violence of the outcry against Lincoln's removal of Frémont in November, 1861, was by no means confined to the radicals and showed how jittery the people had become. Later disclosures of corruption in Cameron's War Department (which led to his replacement by Stanton) fed their fears. The war was getting on everybody's nerves and Lincoln, freely called a "dictator" and an "imbecile," became the scapegoat. Stephenson continues his examination of recruiting and shifts in the popular mood.[8]

Stanton made at least one great blunder. Though he had been three months in office, and McClellan was still inactive, there were already several successes to the credit of the Union arms. The *Monitor* and *Virginia (Merrimac)* had fought their famous duel, and Grant had taken Fort Donelson. The latter success broke through the long gloom of the North and caused, as

Holmes wrote, "a delirium of excitement." Stanton rashly concluded that he now had the game in his hands, and that a sufficient number of men had volunteered. This civilian Secretary of War, who had still much to learn of military matters, issued an order putting a stop to recruiting. Shortly afterwards great disaster befell the Union arms. McClellan, before Richmond, was checked in May. Early in June, his peninsula campaign ended disastrously in the terrible "Seven Days' Battles."

Anticipating McClellan's failure, Lincoln had already determined to call for more troops. On July 1st, he called upon the Governors of the States to provide him with 300,000 men to serve three years. But the volunteering enthusiasm—explain it as you will—had suffered a check. The psychological moment had passed. So slow was the response to the call of July 1st, that another appeal was made early in August, this time for 300,000 men to serve only nine months. But this also failed to rouse the country. A reinforcement of only 87,000 men was raised in response to this emergency call. The able lawyer in the War Department had still much to learn about men and nations.

After this check, terrible incidents of war came thick and fast —the defeat at Second Manassas, in late August; the horrible drawn battle of Antietam-Sharpsburg, in September; Fredericksburg, that carnival of slaughter, in December; the dearly bought victory of Murfreesboro, which opened 1863. There were other disastrous events at least as serious. Foreign affairs were at their darkest. Within the political coalition supporting Lincoln, contention was the order of the day. There was general distrust of the President. Most alarming of all, that ebb of the wave of enthusiasm which began in midsummer, 1861, reached in the autumn of 1862 perhaps its lowest point. The measure of the reaction against Lincoln was given in the Congressional election, in which, though the Government still retained a working majority, the Democrats gained thirty-three seats.

If there could be such a thing as a true psychological history of the war, one of its most interesting pages would determine just how far Stanton was responsible, through his strange blunder over recruiting, for the check to enthusiasm among the Northern people. With this speculation there is connected a still unsolved problem in statistics. To what extent did the anti-Lincoln vote, in 1862, stand for sympathy with the South, and how far was it the hopeless surrender of Unionists who felt that their cause was lost? Though certainty on this point is apparently impossible, there can be no doubt that at the opening of 1863, the Government felt it must apply pressure to the flagging spirits of its supporters. In order to reinforce the armies and to push the war through, there was plainly but one course to be followed—conscription.

The government leaders in Congress brought in a Conscription Act early in the year. The hot debates upon this issued dragged through a month's time, and now make instructive reading for the present generation that has watched the Great War. The Act of 1863 was not the work of soldiers, but was literally "made in Congress." Stanton grimly made the best of it, though he unwaveringly condemned some of its most conspicuous provisions. His business was to retrieve his blunder of the previous year, and he was successful. Imperfect as it was, the Conscription Act, with later supplementary legislation, enabled him to replace the wastage of the Union armies and steadily to augment them. At the close of the war, the Union had on foot a million men with an enrolled reserve of two millions and a half, subject to call.

The Act provided for a complete military census, for which purpose the country was divided into enrollment districts. Every able-bodied male citizen, or intending citizen, between the ages of twenty and forty-five, unless exempted for certain specified reasons, was to be enrolled as a member of the national forces; these forces were to be called to the colors—"drafted," the term was—as the Government found need of them; each successive draft was to be apportioned among the districts in the ratio of the military population, and the number required was to be drawn by lot; if the district raised its quota voluntarily, no draft would be made; any drafted man could offer a substitute or could purchase his discharge for three hundred dollars. The latter provision especially was condemned by Stanton. It was seized upon by demagogues as a device for giving rich men an advantage over poor men.

George Fort Milton, in his Abraham Lincoln and the Fifth Column, *discusses some of the weak points of the conscription system.*[9]

Both exemption by the drafted man's "commutation" —paying $300 cash—and that through furnishing a substitute were sanctioned by an act of the Congress, and thus were covered with the cloak of virtue by the authorities. President Lincoln made a merit of necessity, and claimed pride in the fact that the money revenues of the Provost Marshal General's office, through the $300 fees, were so great that the administrative expenses of enrollment and draft required no appropriation by the Congress. . . .

There were 86,724 men called in the draft who purchased exemption by commutation. The number of substitutes furnished, according to the *Official Records of the Union and Confederate Armies,* was 118,010, the two together making 204,734. This number of men used their purses to escape personal military service under the cloak of the absolution, perhaps tacit approval, of the law. The number was large enough, one authority says, "to include all men of wealth and their sons who were drafted, and most of the moderately well-to-do tradesmen and farmers as well. Since the method was so respectable, practically all who were able to do so availed themselves of it." This reference was to men of means who were drafted, not to the well-to-do in general. The Union forces had tens of thousands of such men and boys who had rushed to enlist, and fought splendidly through the war.

It is fitting to point out that procuring exemption from the draft became an organized business. On September 1, 1863, Thompkins and Co., No. 645 Broadway, New York City, advertised in the papers that "the New York Draft Assurance Association will this week, for $10, guarantee any undrafted party exemption from the draft. For $25 we will furnish any drafted party with an acceptable substitute. At these rates, we simply take the risks of an ordinary life insurance company." These schemes sound strange today, yet late in 1864 the War Department officially validated and gave its approval to the insurance plan.

There were other devices which never received the official nod. A new class of grafters, tricksters, and dealers in sharp practice sprang up, called "exemption agents." These had runners to bring patrons to their offices, while scores set up shop in the lobbies of the New York City Hall, and offered affidavits at 50 cents apiece. Physical disabilities were at a premium; young men who were prematurely gray claimed to be over the age limit. Many eligibles made their ways to Memphis, New Orleans, and other places under the control of occupying troops, but beyond the zone of operation of the enforcement machinery of the Enrollment Act.

The number of deserters cannot be ascertained with precision, but it has been carefully estimated by army authorities. The figure, checked against the *Official Records*, comes to 421,625. This number is more than double the total of those who purchased commutation or furnished substitutes. It represents men who had no legal bar to punishment, but were called criminals for the action they took to evade military service.

The figures of desertion are divided between the men who had been enlisted and had done some troop service, put at 260,399, and the draftees who failed to report, numbering 161,286. Provost Marshal General Fry estimated that about a quarter of the listed army desertions were "unintentional"; and that perhaps 30 per cent of failures of drafted men to report were similarly not culpable, or were repaired by their reporting later. Applying these corrections, the figures would be 195,255 deserters from the army, and 112,901 drafted men who did not report, or a total for the two categories of 308,156 actual deserters.

This is a formidable figure. It affords statistical proof of the general dislike of the draft. The Copperhead fifth column aided and abetted but it did not cause the "long, persistent, sullen, often virulent and sometimes violent resistance"—to quote Shannon—"which was encountered in practically every State of the Union whenever any draft was made at any period of the war."

Not only did the defects of the system make it unpopular, but many considered the Conscription Act unconstitutional, an unwarranted invasion by the central government of the prerogatives of the states. There was open resistance in New York City, and the Pennsylvania coal fields were in flaming anarchy for over a year. Stephenson tells the story of the famous New York City draft riots.[10]

The occasion was the beginning of the first draft under the new law, in July, 1863, and the scene of the rebellion was the City of New York. The opponents of conscription had already made inflammatory attacks on the Government. Conspicuous among them was Horatio Seymour, who had been elected Governor of New York in that wave of reaction in the

* From *Abraham Lincoln and the Union*, by Nathaniel W. Stephenson, Volume 29, THE CHRONICLES OF AMERICA, pp. 168 ff. Copyright and permission Yale University Press, New Haven, Connecticut.

autumn of 1862. Several New York papers joined the crusade. In Congress, the Government had already been threatened with civil war if the act was enforced. Nevertheless, the public drawing by lot began on the days announced. In New York the first drawing took place on Saturday, July 12th, and the lists were published in the Sunday papers. As might be expected, many of the men drawn were of foreign birth, and all day Sunday, the foreign quarter of New York was a cauldron boiling.

On Monday, the resumption of the drawing was the signal for revolt. A mob invaded one of the conscription offices, drove off the men in charge, and set fire to the building. In a short while, the streets were filled with dense crowds of foreign-born workmen shouting. "Down with the rich men," and singing, "We'll hang Horace Greeley on a sour apple tree." Houses of prominent citizens were attacked and set on fire, and several drafting offices were burned. Many negroes who were seized were either clubbed to death or hanged to lamp posts. Even an orphan asylum for colored children was burned. The office of the *Tribune* was raided, gutted, and set on fire. Finally a dispatch to Stanton, early in the night, reported that the mob had taken possession of the city.

The events of the next day were no less shocking. The city was almost stripped of soldiers, as all available reserves had already been hurried south when Lee was advancing toward Gettysburg. But such militia as could be mustered, with a small force of federal troops, fought the mob in the streets. Barricades were carried by storm; blood was freely shed. It was not, however, until the fourth day that the rebellion was finally quelled, chiefly by New York regiments hurried north by Stanton—among them the famous Seventh—which swept the streets with cannon.

The aftermath of the New York riots was a correspondence between Lincoln and Seymour. The latter had demanded a suspension of the draft until the courts could decide on the constitu-

tionality of the Conscription Act. Lincoln refused. With ten
thousand troops now assembled in New York, the draft was
resumed, and there was no further trouble.

*Suspension of the privilege of habeas corpus by presidential
proclamation in 1862 was finally legalized by Congress in 1863.
But long before this the Democratic opposition had hardened
against the administration. Arbitrary arrests as a result of the
suspension of habeas corpus, war weariness, the change of war
policy implied in the preliminary emancipation proclamation,
had done their work. In the fall elections of 1862 the Republican
party came close to defeat. The tragic slaughter at Fredericksburg
in December deepened the crisis. By the turn of the year 1862-
1863 the great Army of the Potomac was dangerously restive,
and the midwest, heart of the Democratic opposition, was in turmoil. Guerrilla bands openly ranged the most disaffected areas
while defiant Peace Democrats in the assemblies of Illinois and
Indiana and in peace conventions elsewhere called for an immediate armistice.*

*Republican Governor Yates of Illinois used a trick to dissolve
his rebellious assembly and was answered by a mammoth peace
meeting in Springfield itself. In Indiana Governor Morton, a
strong supporter of the war who had built up an efficient military
establishment of his own, had to resort to dictatorial methods to
control his state. By January, 1863, he was facing a rebellious
Democratic legislature which refused to pass appropriation bills
or any other legislation in an obvious attempt to force him to re-
linquish control of his military machine. In Indiana, at least, the
political war had come close to a shooting war. George Fort
Milton carries on Morton's story.*[11]

The Democratic leaders had calculated shrewdly.
There would seem little question that once the Copperhead legislature was called back into special session, it would force through

its measure to take over the control of Morton's military establishment. But there was no special session. The Governor did not announce that he had no intention of summoning one. But the weeks passed, and then the months, and the anti-Morton solons were still at home.

What the Governor had done was to abandon the normal pattern of constitutional government in the State of Indiana. The reason he gave for this was that it was the only way to save the Union cause. Once let the Butternuts and the Copperheads emasculate his authority and Indiana would become worse than neutral. Therefore Oliver P. Morton ruled the State as a despot, subject to control by neither legislature, nor court, nor public opinion. From the spring of 1863 until January, 1865, when a new and Radical legislature assembled, Morton was the dictator of Indiana, and did whatever he willed.

This was an extraordinary development for an Anglo-Saxon political society. From time immemorial it had been almost a sacred maxim of this race of free people under representative government that the power of the purse must control. The safeguard of the people's liberty had ever been regarded as their right to grant, or refuse to grant, money sought by the executive—whether king, or President, or governor. Now, for the first time since the days of James II, an Anglo-Saxon community was conducted without obtaining the approval of the legislature for taxes raised and money spent.

There seemed no limit to which this Radical dictator would not go to effect his ends. The State had to have money, and Morton used every conceivable device to drag it in. The State arsenal he had set up had never been legislatively authorized or adopted, so in a technical sense it remained his private personal property. He sold large quantities of its production of weapons and ammunition to the Federal Government, and it returned a profit of about $75,000 a year. The State treasurer, a Democrat, demanded that these funds be put in the official treasury. Morton refused, and instead put them in a private safe in his private office.

He harassed the county governments wherever the Republicans had the control, to get them to appropriate from county funds for the purposes of the State. A good deal of money came in this way, and went into his own strongbox.

But it was far from enough, so the money-seeking dictator journeyed to the capital on the Potomac again and again, club in one hand and empty purse in the other. His appeals to Chase, and to Fessenden when the latter succeeded as Secretary of the Treasury, ran into the stone wall of a bureaucratic conception of public funds. They refused his pleas, saying that it was patently illegal to pay out Federal funds to a State. He appealed to the White House, but Abraham Lincoln who had not hesitated to employ the draft felt that he could not stretch his powers as President— either the great residual group or the almost illimitable powers as Commander in Chief under which he had freed the slaves—to send Treasury funds into the Governor's private care.

But not so Edwin M. Stanton, who made short shrift of matters of constitutionality, and issued orders to send $250,000 to Indianapolis. Morton gave him a jubilant and hypocritical warning: "If the cause fails, we shall both be covered with prosecutions." Stanton answered: "If the cause fails, I do not wish to live."

The disaffected Democrats were roughly divided into an eastern branch led by Governor Horatio Seymour of New York and the western Peace Democrats, dominated by the notorious Clement L. Vallandigham, whose magnetic personality and undoubted talents covered a dangerous fanaticism. The eastern Democrats played the part of a loyal opposition throughout the war, but in the west the party became increasingly tainted with outright disloyalty. As a congressman Vallandigham bitterly attacked what he and his group described as the unconstitutional acts of the administration. In January of 1863, in the closing weeks of the session, he arose to taunt the supporters of the war: "Defeat, debt, taxation, sepulchres, these are your trophies. In vain the people gave you treasure, and the soldier yielded up his life. . . . The war for the Union is, in your hands, a most bloody and costly failure. . . . And you have not conquered the South. You never will. . . . What then? Stop fighting. Make an armistice— no formal treaty. Withdraw your army from the seceded States. . . ."[12]

Leaving Congress, Vallandigham visited Governor Seymour in New York, then opened a peace campaign which led to his arrest and trial in May. The Vallandigham case became a cause célèbre. Although there were hundreds of arbitrary arrests under the Lincoln administration, it dramatized more than any other the conflict between the rights of the individual under the Constitution and the necessity for stern measures in a country torn by civil war. Robert S. Harper, in his Lincoln and the Press, *describes the arrest of Vallandigham.[13]*

Clement L. Vallandigham, his term in Congress having expired, took his fight to the people. Puffed by editorial praise of the peace papers and flattered by the flood of publicity that followed his every movement, he ranted and raved against Lincoln, apparently daring the government to arrest him.

General Burnside, transferred to command of the Department of the Ohio after his defeat at Fredericksburg, kept his eye on Vallandigham. On April 13, 1863, he issued General Order No. 38, which said in part:

. . . hereafter all persons found within our lines who commit acts for the benefit of the enemies of our country will be

tried as spies or traitors, and if convicted will suffer death.
. . . The habit of declaring sympathies for the enemy will
no longer be tolerated in this department. Persons committing such offenses will be at once arrested, with a view to
being tried as above stated or sent beyond our lines into
the lines of their friends.

Burnside's order was the subject of widespread comment in
the Democratic press. That it was aimed at Vallandigham, there
could be no doubt, and he prepared for a showdown. The peace
wing of the Democratic party was especially strong at Mount
Vernon, in Knox County, Ohio, and he announced he would
speak there on May 1.

Every effort was made to publicize the meeting. A stand was
set up in a field, decorated with pictures of butternuts, one of
the insignia worn by Peace Democrats. Newspaper reports say
thousands heard Vallandigham. Hundreds wore Copperhead
badges, made from pennies. A large banner carried by a township
delegation bore the words: "The Copperheads Are Coming." . . .

General Burnside sent members of his staff in civilian dress to
hear Vallandigham. They carried their reports back to the General, and Vallandigham returned to his home at Dayton. Word
got around that Burnside's men had been at Mount Vernon, and
arrest of Vallandigham was expected momentarily.

General Burnside sent a full company of the 115th Ohio Regiment to Dayton by special train, leaving Cincinnati shortly before midnight on May 4. Upon arrival at Dayton at three o'clock
in the morning, the soldiers marched to the Vallandigham home,
and an officer pounded on the door.

Vallandigham poked his head from a second-floor bedroom
window. The officer said they had come to arrest him and demanded admittance. Vallandigham replied he would not open the
door and began to call in a loud voice, "Asa! Asa! Asa!" His cry

was answered by a pistol shot fired from a rear window, a pre-arranged signal to his friends. The soldiers broke into the house and found Vallandigham in his nightshirt. The officer told him to get into his clothing. Fire bells were ringing all over the city, and a crowd began to gather in front of the house.

Vallandigham was marched off to a waiting train, taken directly to Cincinnati, placed in a military prison, and there all visitors were denied access to him.

The arrest left Dayton in an uproar. By noon, wagons and carriages filled with Vallandigham followers were arriving in town. At dusk, a mob of five or six hundred men, hooting and yelling, attacked the office of the *Dayton Daily Journal*, a Republican newspaper that despised Vallandigham. Bullets broke the windows of the building, and blazing torches were tossed inside.

Fire started in the *Journal* building and spread rapidly. It destroyed a hat store, a shoe store, the office of a church publication, a livery stable, a meat market, and a leather store. The firemen were helpless. Their engines had been put out of commission and the hose slashed to ribbons.

City officials telegraphed to Cincinnati for troops, and Burnside had a company in Dayton by ten o'clock. With engines repaired under protection of soldiers, firemen finally halted the conflagration. . . .

Vallandigham spent his first day in prison writing an address to the Democrats of Ohio and managed to get it into the hands of his party press. Dated "military prison, Cincinnati, May 5th, 1863," it said in part:

> I am here in a military bastile for no other offense than my political opinions, and the defense of them, and of the rights of the people, and of your constitutional liberties. Speeches made in the hearing of thousands of you in de-

nunciation of the usurpations of power, infractions of the Constitution and laws, and of military despotism, were the sole cause of my arrest and imprisonment. I am a Democrat —for the Constitution, for the law, for the Union, for liberty—this is my only "crime." For no disobedience to the Constitution; for no violation of law; for no word, sign, or gesture of sympathy with the men of the South, who are for disunion and southern independence, but in obedience to their demand as well as the demand of northern abolition disunionists and traitors, I am here in bonds today; but "Time, at last, sets all things even!"

On May sixth a military commission tried Vallandigham for disloyalty under Burnside's General Order Number 38, and sentenced him to prison for the duration, refusing a writ of habeas corpus. Although somewhat embarrassed by the general's arbitrary action, Lincoln stood by Burnside's decision. In a characteristic move, he softened the effect of the blow by commuting the sentence to banishment beyond the Union lines. Vallandigham was thrust unceremoniously into the hands of unwilling and embarrassed Confederate officers and eventually made his way to Canada. Stephenson discusses the implications of the case.[*][14]

It seems quite plain that the condemnation of Lincoln on this issue of usurpation was not confined to the friends of the Confederacy, nor has it been confined to his enemies in later days. One of Lincoln's most ardent admirers, the historian Rhodes, condemns his course unqualifiedly. "There can be no question," he writes, "that from the legal point of view the President should have rescinded the sentence and released Vallandigham." Lincoln, he adds, "stands responsible for the casting into prison of citizens of the United States on orders as arbitrary as the *lettres-de-cachet* of Louis XIV." Since Mr. Rhodes, uncompromising Unionist, can write as he does upon this issue, it is plain that the opposition party cannot be dismissed as through and through disunionist.

The trial of Vallandigham made him a martyr and brought him the Democratic nomination for Governor of Ohio. His followers sought to make the issue of the campaign the acceptance or rejection of military despotism. In defense of his course Lincoln wrote two public letters in which he gave evidence of the skill which he had acquired as a lawyer before a jury by the way in which he played upon the emotions of his readers.

Long experience [he wrote] has shown that armies cannot be maintained unless desertion shall be punished by the severe penalty of death. The case requires, and the law and the Constitution sanction, this punishment. Must I shoot a simple-minded soldier boy who deserts, while I must not touch a hair of a wily agitator who induces him to desert? This is none the less injurious when effected by getting a father, or brother, or friend into a public meeting, and there working upon his feelings till he is persuaded to write the soldier boy that he is fighting in a bad cause for a wicked administration and a contemptible government, too weak to arrest and punish him if he shall desert. I think that in such a case to silence the agitator and save the boy is not only constitutional, but, withal, a great mercy.

His real argument may be summed up in these words of his:

You ask, in substance, whether I really claim that I may override all the guaranteed rights of individuals, on the plea of conserving the public safety—when I may choose to say the public safety requires it. This question, divested of the phraseology calculated to represent me as struggling for an arbitrary prerogative, is either simply a question who shall decide, or an affirmation that nobody shall decide, what the public safety does require in cases of rebellion or invasion.

The Constitution contemplates the question as likely to occur for decision, but it does not expressly declare who is to decide it. By necessary implication, when rebellion or invasion comes, the decision is to be made, from time to time; and I think the man, whom for the time, the people have under the Constitution, made the commander-in-chief of their army and navy, is the man who holds the power and bears the responsibility of making it. If he uses the power justly, the same people will probably justify him; if he abuses it, he is in their hands to be dealt with by all the modes they have reserved to themselves in the Constitution.

Lincoln virtually appealed to the Northern people to secure efficiency by setting him momentarily above all civil authority. He asked them in substance, to interpret their Constitution by a show of hands. No thoughtful person can doubt the risks of such a method; yet in Ohio, in 1863, the great majority—perhaps everyone who believed in the war—accepted Lincoln's position. Between their traditional system of legal juries and the new system of military tribunals the Ohio voters made their choice without hesitation. They rejected Vallandigham and sustained the Lincoln candidate by a majority of over a hundred thousand. That same year in New York the anti-Lincoln candidate for Secretary of State was defeated by twenty-nine thousand votes.

How civil rights can best be maintained in time of war without unnecessary hardship is still a problem today. The bitterness of a civil war provoked extreme measures in both the North and

South, yet on the whole the Lincoln administration handled its problems with restraint and wisdom. This is James G. Randall's conclusion in the passage below from his The Civil War and Reconstruction.[15]

Lincoln's practice fell short of dictatorship as the word is understood in the fourth decade of the twentieth century. He did not think of suppressing his legislature and ruling without it. He did not pack his Congress, nor eject the opposition. There was nothing in his administration comparable to a Napoleonic *coup d'état* or a Cromwellian purging of Parliament. No party emblem was adopted as the flag of the country. No rule for the universal saluting of Lincoln was imposed. There was no Lincoln party constituting a super-state and visiting vengeance upon political opponents. Criminal violence was not employed *sub rosa* after the fashion of modern dictatorships. No undue advantage was taken of the emergency to force arbitrary rule upon the country or to promote personal ends. Lincoln half expected to be defeated in 1864. The people were free to defeat him if they chose at the polls. The Constitution was indeed stretched, but it was not subverted.

Freedom of speech and of the press were not extinguished under Lincoln. Though Vallandigham was banished in 1863 for making a speech, he spoke frequently and with equal violence in 1864 without molestation. Being without restraint, his utterings were less effective. In this matter one must avoid the historical fault of generalizing from selected instances. There were, it is true, a number of newspaper suppressions or suspensions by officers acting under Lincoln. The Chicago *Times*, an anti-Lincoln sheet, was suspended by military order of General Burnside (June, 1863) because of "disloyal and incendiary sentiments," but Burnside's act was not promoted by the Lincoln administration. The order was promptly revoked by the President, the paper being permitted to resume. In May, 1864, the New York *World* and the *Journal of Commerce* were suspended for publishing a bogus proclamation of the President calling for 400,000 men and naming a day of public humiliation and prayer. The perpetration of this hoax was not so much a deliberate falsifying by the management of the papers (though their anti-administration bias was evident) as it was a trick by one Howard to rig the stock market. On the third day after the suspension the papers were allowed to resume. Various other newspapers, including the Louisville (Kentucky) *Courier*, the New Orleans *Crescent*, the *South* of Baltimore, the Baltimore *Gazette*, and the Philadelphia *Evening Journal*, were suppressed or suspended. The larger fact, however, is that the government as a general rule refrained from control of news, both on the positive and negative side. It did not pursue the policy of forcing the publication of "inspired" articles; nor did it maintain a censorship. Scores of newspapers throughout the country, including some that were very prominent, continually published abusive articles during the Lincoln administration without encountering the suppressing hand of government. Lincoln's view as to the appropriate course to be taken toward newspapers was expressed as follows in a letter to General Schofield: "You will only arrest individuals and suppress assemblies or newspapers when they may be working palpable injury to the military in your charge, and in no other case will you interfere with the expression of opinion in any form or allow it to be interfered with violently by others. In this you have a discretion to exercise with great caution, calmness, and forbearance."

Ignoring the papers, allowing them to "strut their uneasy hour and be forgotten" as President Wilson expressed it, proved as a rule effective in regions where pro-Lincoln sentiment was active; while in localities where the opposite sentiment prevailed, suppression would have failed of its purpose by promoting sympathy for the victims. The Civil War was fought, as a recent writer has pointed out, "with the enemy at our gates and powerful secret societies in our midst without an Espionage Act."

Criticism of the Lincoln administration resolves itself into a question of standards and ideals, viewed in the light of Anglo-Saxon traditions and with reference to conditions which subjected the government to difficulties of the most serious nature. As the Civil War was unique in its proportions and intensity, so was the Lincoln administration unique in its methods. That it swerved from the course of democratic government and departed from the forms of civil liberty is obvious; that it stretched and at times seemed to ignore the Constitution is evident. The arbitrary arrests cannot be passed over lightly: to do so would allow too small a value to civil guarantees. On the other hand a search of the full record will show that anything like a drastic military régime was far from Lincoln's thoughts. The harshness of war regulations was often tempered by leniency. The President was generous in releasing political prisoners, whom he refused to treat as war criminals, and in the suppression of anti-governmental activity the government under Lincoln was milder than that of Wilson, though facing greater provocation. As for dictatorships after recent European models, the pattern simply does not fit the Lincoln government. The word "dictator" in its post-World-War connotation would be utterly inappropriate if applied to the Civil War President.

Though most Democrats were loyal, a minority of extremists dabbled in subversion and might well have done serious damage to the Northern war effort if they had been better organized. Their efforts were carried out through various secret societies, centered inevitably in the middle west where the peace sentiment was always strongest. Although the glamorous exploits of individual Confederate spies like Mrs. Rose O'Neal Greenhow

*and Belle Boyd have received a great deal of attention, the secret
societies were, potentially at least, far more dangerous because
of the wider scope and impact of their activities. Organized with
the traditional secret oaths, rituals, passwords and ascending
degrees, outwardly (and as far as the general membership knew)
the societies were merely political associations. Their subversive
purpose was more frankly revealed as one penetrated into the
inner circles. Patriotic Union leagues organized to challenge the
societies and the secret services, both national and state, infiltrated
them so successfully that most of their more dangerous schemes
were uncovered before they came to fruition. The societies were
perhaps most successful in organizing resistance to the draft and
encouraging desertion.*

*The Knights of the Golden Circle, earliest of the brood, was
organized by the eccentric Dr. Bixley before the war. During the
first years of the conflict, its "castles" or local cells sprang up
throughout the midwest. Their prestige had already been considerably lowered, however, by a series of trials less than a year
before, following an exposure of their activities. George Fort
Milton describes an Indiana peace meeting in May, 1863, in
which the Knights took an unfortunate part.* [16]

Late in April, the heads of Indiana's Democratic State
organization called a mass meeting for Indianapolis, on May 20.
They expected such Indiana leaders as Daniel W. Voorhees and
Thomas A. Hendricks to make the welkin ring. . . . The purpose
was to stage a great party and public protest against the Lincoln
Administration policies, particularly the draft, suspension of
habeas corpus, the indemnity act, and emancipation. Nor would
they spare Governor Morton, whose course they regarded as
naked despotism.

The K.G.C. hierarchy determined to make use of the gathering
for another purpose. They would assemble their "troops" from

the castles all over the State, stage a military demonstration, and perhaps attack Camp Morton, release the Confederate prisoners, and seize the arsenal. The Grand Commander sent out orders for men to come armed and prepared for any eventuality. Many castles responded to these instructions, and their delegations arrived with arms and ammunition concealed on their persons, or under hay in the wagons that bore them. . . .

General Carrington, the commander of the Military District of Indiana, knew from his spies and informers the plans of the Copperheads. Governor Morton had his own secret-service tips. The two took measures to cope with any outbreaks. The Union troops in the city, together with the paroled Federal soldiers, were organized, and stationed over Indianapolis to guard the arsenal, military prisons, quartermaster depots, and so on. A heavy detachment at the Circle, just two blocks from the capitol, was ready with fixed bayonets, while a field gun was loaded and sighted at the State House.

Voorhees opened the meeting with a tribute to Vallandigham, who "has fallen a little sooner than the rest of us, perhaps, a victim to the base usurpation which has taken the place of public rights and of the Constitution." This gave the keynote for the day. The other speakers rang the changes on the loss of civil liberties, the outrages of the draft, and so forth. But none of them urged or intimated armed resistance to the constituted authorities.

While Hendricks was speaking, Federal troops took station around the capitol. Their orders were to check any "demonstration," but they took these as license to bait the crowd. Soon they began to cry "Copperhead," drew a cordon about the throng, and demanded three cheers for Abraham Lincoln.

About four o'clock, a squad with cocked rifles and fixed bayonets advanced through the crowd to the speaker's stand. No one knew what impended. Hendricks terminated his speech. Voorhees called for the report of the resolutions committee, put it to a vote, and adjourned the meeting.

The thousands of Democrats raged at this insolent troop interference with a public gathering. As they made their way from the scene, they expressed themselves loudly. The overbearing soldiers seized many as "traitors," and rushed them to the guardhouse.

Visitors from out of town went to the railroad stations. As one train left the Indiana Central station, a shot was fired from a car. This touched off the temper of the troops. The resulting scene has been described by W. D. Foulke, Governor Morton's friend and adulatory biographer, in these words:

"The intention to create an armed disturbance now seemed clear, and the soldiers determined to give the remaining Butternuts a lesson. When the Indiana Central train left the station, a cannon was placed in front of it. The train stopped. A small body of soldiers was collected; and a policeman, accompanied by the soldiers, demanded the surrender of all firearms in possession of the passengers. Nearly two hundred weapons were given up.

"The train to Cincinnati was also stopped, revolvers were taken, and many others were thrown by their owners into Pogue's Run, at the side of the track. Weapons had been given to the women, in the belief that they would not be searched. Seven were found upon one woman. A knife nearly two feet long was discovered in the stove of one of the cars. In all, about five hundred revolvers were taken from those who had attended the meeting."

This humiliating epilogue to the State-wide Democratic protest meeting angered the members of the party, irrespective of whether they sympathized with the Knights' plans or not. The jubilant way the *Journal*, Morton's organ, hailed the incident, led the Democratic *Sentinel* to term Indiana as thoroughly ruled by troops as was France, Austria, or Russia.

Whether cause or mere coincidence, this incident, still known in Indiana folklore as the Battle of Pogue's Run, marked the end of the menace of the Knights of the Golden Circle in that State. The Knights had initiated more members in their Indiana castles than in any other Loyal State. Their lodges had sprung up in practically every county in central and southern Indiana, and especially in those close to the Ohio River. But the organization was loose, unsupervised, and ineffective. It brought odium on its members, and an unjust condemnation of the Democrats as a party of traitors. It had no record of accomplishments to offset these failures.

By late 1863 the Knights of the Golden Circle had largely been absorbed into a new, more tightly organized order founded in Missouri by the visionary Phineas C. Wright. The Order of American Knights, with its secret military department sworn to the setting up of a Northwest Confederacy allied with that of the South, had a distinctly subversive character. But the atmosphere at this time was less favorable for such activities. After Gettysburg and Vicksburg the administration had regained much of its popularity.

In August Lincoln had hailed the turning of the tide in the confident, organlike prose of his famous letter to James C. Conkling: "The signs look better. The Father of Waters again goes unvexed to the sea. Thanks to the great Northwest for it. Nor yet wholly to them. . . ."[17] Later, the Republican disgrace of the year before was wiped out in the elections of 1863.

All of the war stresses, however, were to come into the open during the confused presidential election of 1864. The secret societies were to find in the bitter partisanship of a war-weary North their greatest opportunity. By 1864 both parties were deeply divided. Despite the recent success which had buoyed up Lincoln's administration, his enemies had been quieted but not converted. Although the people were with him, many politicians wished to replace him. The radicals especially were dead set against his announced reconstruction policies. Chase offered himself as a substitute but was rebuffed. In May Frémont had himself nominated on a dissident ticket at Cleveland by a rump convention of "strange odds and ends of parties, and factions, and disappointed and aspiring individuals" (as Welles noted in his diary) which conspicuously did not include any important Republicans.[18] But there seemed to be no strong contender for Lincoln's place. In early June he was renominated on a National Union party ticket (the Republican party renamed to make it sound more like a popular front) with Andrew Johnson, the War Democrat, as his running mate. Even the radicals, unable to find a substitute, sullenly went along with the renomination, although they managed to inject much of their philosophy into the platform. Lincoln took the news calmly. He assumed that the convention had concluded "that it is not best to swap horses while crossing the river. . . ."[19]

Then came the dark summer of '64. Hopes raised high by Grant's appointment sank to the lowest depths when the armies stalled before Petersburg and Atlanta, and Early marched almost unopposed toward the heart of the North. After the unbearable slaughter of Grant's spring campaign Lincoln was forced to schedule a new draft for September, a dangerous move in an election year. Lincoln was never more unpopular; he despaired of re-election. On August fifth Greeley's Tribune carried a manifesto, signed by Congressmen Wade and Davis, whose reconstruction bill Lincoln had vetoed. This savage attack by members of his own party led to a call by a group of Republican leaders for a convention in September to find a substitute for Lincoln, their own nominee. "There are no Lincoln men . . . ," a party worker wrote despairingly. "We know not which way to turn."[20]

The Democrats, hoping to capitalize on the troubles of the Republicans, had postponed their convention until August twen-

ty-ninth. They too faced a behind-the-scenes struggle between the eastern Democrats led by Governor Seymour and Samuel J. Tilden, and the Peace Democrats of the midwest. The moderate Seymour faction favored an end to emancipation, and prosecution of the war coupled with an attempt to secure reunion through negotiation. Their choice for the presidency was McClellan, still a general but inactive. The midwest, however, wanted more extreme measures. Vallandigham, who had turned up in Chicago without being molested by the authorities, was prepared to lead the convention fight and soon won for himself a crucial position on the drafting subcommittee of the Committee on Resolutions. George Fort Milton describes the climax of the Democratic convention.[21]

As soon as the members of the Committee on Resolutions assembled, the peace men tried to elect Vallandigham as their chairman. Only Tilden's quick work prevented this from being done. . . .

The critical struggle, both within the drafting group and in the full committee, was the paragraph about peace. Vallandigham dominated the group; his fanatic zeal, his extraordinary force, and his almost hypnotic personality made him a hard man to counter in an argument before a small group. The leader of the Union men was Tilden, but he was a man for an office and not for a fight. There was a curious subtlety, indirection, circumlocution, in him which did not permit him to join in a free-for-all.

The platform which came before the convention at four o'clock that Tuesday afternoon had the merit of brevity. It contained only six planks, each expressed in a single paragraph. The second of these read:

"*Resolved*, That this Convention does explicitly declare, as the sense of the American people, that after four years of failure to restore the Union by the experiment of war, during which, under the pretense of a military necessity, or war power higher than the Constitution, the Constitution itself has been disregarded in every part, and public liberty and private right alike trodden down, and the material prosperity of the country essentially impaired . . . justice, humanity, liberty, and the public welfare demand that immediate efforts be made for a cessation of hostilities, with a view to an ultimate convention of the States, or other peaceable means, to the end that, at the earliest practicable moment, peace may be restored on the basis of the Federal Union of the States."

This brought the issue of peace at any price right before the Democrats. It had been fought bitterly in the Resolutions Committee. Everyone expected that there would be an even more determined battle on the floor. The fatal section had been adopted in committee by a very slender margin. But there was no fight.

For some strange reason, Samuel J. Tilden did not challenge the Ohio incendiary. Confronted with such a situation, some men seated in the presiding officer's chair would have installed a substitute and taken the floor themselves to lead the fight. But Seymour did not do so.

The delegates were wild with excitement. They shrieked approval of the platform, and when no one stood up to oppose them, they proceeded to adopt it, almost in a shorter time than the telling, by a viva-voce vote.

The rest was anticlimax. When the excitement died down, the convention proceeded to choose its candidates. The call of States soon brought McClellan into the picture, together with a sharp attack upon him. An irate Maryland delegate protested the General's arrest of the legislature of that State in 1861, and sneered that "as a military man, he has been defeated everywhere." An Ohio man joined with the plea to the convention, "I beg of you to give us another candidate." This brought many cries of "Seymour of New York!"

But when Seymour's State was reached on the roll, the head of the delegation reported that "regretfully passing by her favorite son, who disclaims the candidacy," the Empire State casts its entire 33 votes for General McClellan. . . .

The Ohio delegation withdrew to caucus upon the action it should take. While it was out, Seymour made a little talk in which he said: "I cannot refrain from saying in behalf of General Mc-Clellan what in my heart I feel to be true, that when he is elected to the Presidential office, he will reflect with fidelity, boldness and zeal, the sentiments of patriotism and love of liberty and law, which animate the hearts of those who are here now assembled."

In a few minutes the Ohio delegation returned. Vallandigham cast its ballot for McClellan and moved that the choice be made unanimous. For running mate, the assemblage named Vallandigham's friend George H. Pendleton of Ohio. Thus the Democratic National Convention nominated a General who put Union first of all and instructed him to run on a Copperhead platform.

"If the dumb cattle are not worthy of another term of Lincoln then let the will of God be done & the murrain of McClellan fall on them" wrote young John Hay.[22] *Hay himself had been sent out to Missouri by Lincoln in June to investigate a report from General Rosecrans of "a conspiracy to overthrow the government" uncovered in that area. In St. Louis General Rosecrans, closeted with Hay, cast a glance over his shoulder and moved his chair nearer. "There is a secret conspiracy on foot against the Government, carried forward by a society called the Order of American Knights or, to use their initials, O.A.K.," he told Hay. "The head of the order, styled the high priest, is in the North, Vallandigham, and in the South, Sterling Price. . . ." The whole order, according to Rosecrans, was "in a state of intense activity." In the North it was doing everything it could to oppose the war while in the border states its mission was to protect, encourage and organize rebels coming north, as Hay put it, "out of the bush . . . with grass in their hair & the oath in their pocket—to*

plunder, steal, persecute and kill, and stand ready for insurrection or revolt."[23]

Rosecrans' spies had uncovered what is usually referred to as the "Northwest Conspiracy," hatched in most states not by the O.A.K. but by its even more dangerous successor, the Sons of Liberty. Central to the plot was the reappearance of Vallandigham in the United States. If not arrested, he was to go to the Chicago convention as a delegate from Ohio. By the time Hay reported back to Lincoln in Washington, Vallandigham had already reappeared in Ohio. Lincoln was not much alarmed by Hay's story and decided to leave the Copperhead leader alone. As he told Hay, "It cannot but result in a benefit to the Union cause to have so violent and indiscreet a man to go to Chicago as a firebrand to his own party."

Wood Gray sketches in the background of the Northwest Conspiracy in his The Hidden Civil War.[24]

On February 22, 1864, an important change took place in the affairs of the O.A.K. On that day a so-called national meeting of its moving spirits took place in New York in which the name was changed to the Sons of Liberty, thus claiming spiritual kinship with the patriotic society of the Revolutionary period. The ritual was reformed to delete any oaths of a treasonable nature, although a promise of strict obedience to the officers still left the way open for committing the membership to dangerous projects. On the way to the gathering two of the delegates went through Canada and secretly inducted Vallandigham into membership, at the same time securing his consent for his name to be proposed for the office of Supreme Commander. The proposal was submitted and adopted, and a leader of national importance for the first time was in direction of affairs . . .

The revolutionary schemes of the Sons of Liberty were now

to be given assistance and direction from a new source. With Grant and Sherman beginning to encircle the Confederacy in a crushing embrace while the blockade served to sap its energies for the critical encounter, the South was finally impelled to give direct attention to her last resource—the promotion of disaffection in the Midwest. On March 16, 1864, the Confederate Secretary of War placed the chief responsibility for such an undertaking in the hands of Captain Thomas H. Hines, formerly of Morgan's cavalry, a man who would in later years achieve the staid eminence of the chief justiceship of Kentucky but whose wartime exploits would merit the pen of an E. Phillips Oppenheim. . . .

About a month later President Davis appointed a commission consisting of Jacob Thompson, Secretary of the Interior under Buchanan, Clement C. Clay, member of the United States Senate and then the Confederate Senate from Alabama, and J. P. Holcomb, with directions to proceed through the blockade to Canada on a similar undertaking. After futile efforts to subsidize Northern newspapers for propaganda purposes and unproductive conferences at Niagara Falls with Horace Greeley and former Attorney General Jeremiah Black, the commission broke up. Holcomb proceeded to Europe. Clay elected to remain in eastern Canada to promote schemes of his own, and Thompson, from the safety of the Canadian side of the international boundary, turned his attention to the Midwest. On May 27 Captain Hines was directed to place himself under Thompson's direction, although he remained the real driving force in the schemes that followed. The possibility of utilizing the Sons of Liberty in measures favorable to the Confederacy was readily apparent. A meeting between Thompson and Vallandigham on June 11 was followed by other conferences. The Supreme Commander did Thompson the honor of initiating him into the Sons of Liberty and, although insisting upon his warm desire for the restoration of the Union on its original basis, was willing to discuss the practicability of creating a "Western Confederacy" through a revolutionary uprising. Other leaders of the order were even less circumspect in their discussions with the Confederate representatives. Gradually there evolved a scheme for the seizing of the governments of Illinois, Indiana, Ohio, Kentucky, and Missouri and the institution of provisional control by the officers of the Sons of Liberty. The armed forces that were to effect the overturn would consist of three contingents—Confederate refugees in Canada (chiefly soldiers escaped from Northern prison camps), the military section of the Sons of Liberty, and the prisoners still held in large numbers in camps of the Northwest. For the arming of the Sons of Liberty and their transportation to crucial points at the proper time money was lavishly provided by the Confederate commissioners, nearly $500,000 all told. Vallandigham, with that meticulous, legalistic desire to keep the record straight that was so characteristic of him, refused personally to accept the funds. But since he not only gave tacit approval of their purpose but recommended the adjutant-general of the order, James A. Barrett, as a proper person to distribute them, his later claims of perfect innocence in the matter became subject to something more than doubt.

Time and again dates were fixed for the rising, then postponed. The conspirators expected Vallandigham to be arrested on his reappearance in the United States. This was to be the first signal for revolt. Thanks to Lincoln's sagacity, the government refused to touch him. Next a series of mass meetings were supposed to trigger the explosion, but proved ineffectual. As it became increasingly apparent that the Copperhead fifth column was badly organized and poorly led the movement began to suffer from demoralization. The opposition of many of the northwestern Democrats, who realized that open sedition could ruin their party, further weakened the movement. Successful penetration of the Sons of Liberty by Union spies (especially the "master spy," Stidger) led to widespread arrests of the society's leaders in July. Under pressure from the Confederates, however, an uprising was finally scheduled to coincide with the Democratic convention at Chicago on August twenty-ninth. With the aid of some seventy ex-Confederate soldiers, attempts were to be made to release the Rebel prisoners in the camps in the Chicago area.

George Fort Milton takes the story through to its denouement:[25]

The approach of the opening date of the postponed Democratic National Convention brought huge throngs to Chicago. A day or so in advance, Hines and the other Confederate officers reached the city, and sought to appear and conduct themselves as though they were merely interested citizens coming to observe the political show. Other Southern soldiers came, in civilian clothes, through Indiana and Illinois. Many of the delegates to the convention were members of the secret order. . . .

The night before the convention opened its sessions, the Confederate leaders assembled the various Grand Commanders and other officers of the Sons of Liberty, to find out exactly how things stood. Hines and his subordinates reported that they had done everything they had agreed to do. The prisoners inside Camp Douglas were organized to attack their guards from within the instant they should hear the sound of the attack by the Sons of Liberty troops without the gates. The Confederate leaders then asked the Copperheads for specific information in regard to the strength of the armed forces they had ready for the morrow's battle.

The answers filled them with disgust. Vallandigham, Bowles, Dodd, Walsh, Piper, and the other O.S.L. committeemen and conferees in the meetings in Canada had failed to do almost everything that they had promised. The county and township lodges had not been notified, the members who had happened to come to Chicago had done so, with few exceptions, individually and without any organization or gathering-place. Nor was any among them ready to take the initiative in bringing order out of chaos.

While the meeting was in session, two further pieces of disturbing news were brought in. One was that Vallandigham had no chance to take over the Democratic National Convention and nominate a peace candidate. He might be able through some fluke of convention emotion, to get a peace plank in the platform, but this was problematical. General McClellan was likely to be the nominee. Were Seymour, the New York Governor, selected instead, the candidate would be for Union before he was for peace. Neither man would give any countenance at all to the idea of a new Northwest secession.

The second communication was equally ominous. The guard at Camp Douglas had been suddenly strengthened with several regiments of seasoned fighting men. No longer would it fall an easy prize to a surprise attack.

A near-panic swept the Sons of Liberty. A wave of disgust went over the Confederates. These last now had to admit to themselves the bitter fact that the Copperheads were no potential soldiers. They had neither the courage nor the organization to make a fight. Instead of wearing on the lapels of their coats the accustomed copper Liberty heads, they should wear white feathers.

Captain Hines was desperate. Was there anything that could be salvaged from this wreck of all their hopes? At dawn the next morning he gathered the Grand Commanders, to propose that they furnish the Confederates with five hundred dependable men. Hines and Castleman would take them, seize a passenger train due to leave for Rock Island at 9:00 that morning, cut the telegraph wires, capture the Rock Island arsenal, and release the Confederate prisoners there. Even this smacked too much of real danger for the champions of revolution. They preferred oratory in the secret sessions of the lodges. The Confederate money had been useful. But Confederate courage had no currency among the Copperheads.

That very day, Hines and his associates shook the dust of Chicago from their feet. The Northwest Conspiracy had failed, owing to no fault of the Confederates but because of the cowardice of the parlor, hotel-lobby, and barroom fifth-columnists. Camp Douglas was not attacked, Camp Morton remained undisturbed, and this chapter of attempted treason had been closed.

A series of military trials broke up the Sons of Liberty.[26] *Various Confederate attempts to subvert the North both before and after the abortive Northwest Conspiracy proved futile. Confederate General Morgan's daring cavalry raid into the northwest in July, 1863, had been supposed to coincide with fifth columnist uprisings. In October, 1864, Confederate agents from Canada raided St. Albans, Vermont, looted several banks and killed one man, and in November made their celebrated but ineffectual attempt to set fire to New York City. Repeated efforts to liberate Rebel prisoners from northern camps also failed. On the whole, subversive activity in the North had served chiefly to discredit the Democratic party. After the war it lacked the strength to act as an effective opposition, and left the Republicans unchallenged in their power.*

In more immediate terms, the debacle of the Northwest Conspiracy helped to re-elect Lincoln in November. The dark summer of '64 passed away. On September second Atlanta fell and the North went wild with joy. Six days later McClellan publicly repudiated Vallandigham's "peace-at-any-price" plank in the Democratic platform, and toward the end of the month Frémont, under pressure, sullenly withdrew his candidacy (as a result, it is said, of a bargain engineered by Senator Chandler: Montgomery Blair for Frémont). United again, the Republicans, led by Lincoln, launched an energetic campaign.

Returns from the earliest state elections in October were en-couraging. Hearing of the re-election of Governor Morton, Hay wrote, "I am deeply thankful. . . . I believe it rescues Indiana from sedition & civil war. . . ."[27] *Then it was November. Ben-jamin Thomas follows Lincoln through his hours of triumph.*[28]

Election day, November 8, found Washington quiet. Many persons had gone home to vote. A cold rain with wintry gusts kept people off the streets. Noah Brooks stopped at the White House and found Lincoln alone. The President felt gravely uncertain as the people registered their will.

"It is singular," Lincoln observed to John Hay later in the day, "that I, who am not a vindictive man, should always, except once, have been before the people in canvasses marked by great bitterness. When I came to Congress it was a quiet time, but al-ways, except that, the contests in which I have been prominent have been marked with great rancor."

About seven o'clock in the evening Lincoln and Hay splashed across the White House grounds to the side door of the War De-partment. A soaked and steaming sentry huddled against the wall. Few persons except the telegraph clerks remained in the building. Stanton was sick with chills and fever.

A dispatch from Indiana showed Lincoln well ahead. Philadel-phia Republicans reported 10,000 plurality. Party leaders in Bal-timore claimed the city by 15,000, and the state by 5,000. The Union ticket led in Massachusetts. The heavy storm delayed dispatches from distant states, but the trend continued to be favorable. McClellan led in New York City by 35,000, Lincoln in the state by 40,000. The President sent these first returns to Mrs. Lincoln. "She is more anxious than I," he said.

Gustavus Fox exulted over news that Henry Winter Davis had been defeated in Maryland. "You have more of that feeling of personal resentment than I," Lincoln replied. "Perhaps I have too little of it, but I never thought it paid. A man has no time to spend half his life in quarrels. If any man ceases to attack me I never remember the past against him."

Toward midnight Major Thomas T. Eckert provided supper. Lincoln awkwardly dished out the oysters. About half past two in the morning a band played under the window. In the course of the evening Lincoln, who was in a reminiscent mood, had told how, after the election of 1860, he went home utterly tired and threw himself down on a sofa. Opposite where he lay, a large mirror hung over a bureau. Looking in the glass, he saw himself nearly at full length, but his face had two distinct images, one nearly superimposed on the other. Perplexed and somewhat startled, he got up to study his reflection but the illusion vanished. When he lay down again, however, it reappeared, plainer than before, and he noticed that one face looked paler than the other. Again, when he rose, the vision disappeared. The phenomenon troubled him, and he had told his wife about it. Mrs. Lincoln had taken it for a sign—her husband would be elected for two terms, but the pale face signified that he would not live through the second one.

The complete election tally a few days later gave Lincoln 2,203,831 ballots to McClellan's 1,797,019—more than 400,000 plurality. With Lincoln carrying every state except Kentucky, Delaware, and New Jersey, the electoral vote would be 212 to 21. The soldier vote was an important factor in his triumph.

A few days later John Hay scribbled in his diary:[29]

November 11, 1864. This morning Nicolay sent a superb despatch from Illinois giving us 25,000 majority and 10 Congressmen, which we take to mean Wentworth, Farnsworth, Washburne, Cooke, Ingersoll, Harding, Cullom, Brownwell, Kuykendall, and Moulton at large, leaving the Copperheads Thornton, Morrison, Ross and Marshall.

At the meeting of the Cabinet today, the President took out a paper from his desk and said, "Gentlemen, do you remember last summer I asked you all to sign your names to the back of a paper of which I did not show you the inside? This is it. Now, Mr. Hay, see if you can get this open without tearing it?" He had pasted it up in so singular a style that it required some cutting to get it open. He then read as follows:

EXECUTIVE MANSION

WASHINGTON, *Aug. 23, 1864*

This morning, as for some days past, it seems exceedingly probable that this Administration will not be re-elected. Then it will be my duty to so cooperate with the President-elect, as to save the Union between the election and the inauguration; as he will have secured his election on such ground that he cannot possibly save it afterwards.

A LINCOLN

This was indorsed:

William H. Seward
W. P. Fessenden
Edwin M. Stanton
Gideon Welles
Edwd Bates
M. Blair
J. P. Usher

August 23, 1864

The President said, "You will remember that this was written at a time (6 days before the Chicago nominating Convention) when as yet we had no adversary, and seemed to have no friends. I then solemnly resolved on the course of action indicated above. I resolved, in case of the election of General McClellan, being certain that he would be the candidate, that I would see him and talk matters over with him. I would say, 'General, the election has demonstrated that you are stronger, have more influence with the American people than I. Now let us together, you with your influence and I with all the executive power of the Government, try to save the country. You raise as many troops as you possibly can for this final trial, and I will devote all my energies to assisting and finishing the war.'"

Seward said, "And the General would answer you 'Yes, Yes,' and the next day when you saw him again and pressed these views upon him, he would say, 'Yes, Yes'; & so on forever, and would have done nothing at all."

"At least," added Lincoln, "I should have done my duty and have stood clear before my own conscience."

6.

Lincoln in the White House

George Fort Milton has described wartime Washington as it might have appeared to a visitor making his first trip to the capital. This was the Washington that Lincoln knew.[1]

On his first visit to the city, the traveler could not but be impressed by the great Capitol which loomed before him as he left the station. When finished in Monroe's Administration, it had seemed "a grand affair," but the country's growth, together with the Congress's growing sense of self-importance, led to a great extension, which was started in 1850. Twelve years later workmen were still putting on the finishing touches, and had not yet capped the dome with its headpiece, the great statue of Freedom. The Capitol had been modernized considerably; its "members' baths," finished in black walnut, with marble-tiled floors, had showers as well as tubs. The Capitol restaurant offered every delicacy of the season on its bill of fare.

The structure housed the Library of Congress, which had bought Jefferson's private library. Visitors here were under strict rules. Under no circumstances would anyone less than sixteen years of age be admitted, while visitors must remove their hats and talk in whispers.

From the base of Capitol Hill, a visitor's hack would swing into Pennsylvania Avenue, which at the time of the fall of Sumter was paved with cobblestones all the way to Georgetown. By 1862, it had been so hammered by army wagons and other unexpected traffic that its surface suggested that of corrugated-iron roofing; in many places deep mud covered the pavement, and teams of army mules often mired down. The brick sidewalks along the Avenue and elsewhere were in sorry shape.

The Avenue was full of life and motion. On its corners were street vendors of an amazing variety. One sold "patent soaps warranted to remove grease spots most tenacious, in an amazingly short space of time." Near at hand, another sought to sell artificial insects attached to elastic strings. Candy men by the dozens stood by little stands chipping the hard sweets with little hammers. Then there were Italians roasting chestnuts, organ-grinders with dancing monkeys, telescope men proffering spyglasses at 10 cents a look. Bootblacks were everywhere, chiefly little inky fellows who would make a dive at your foot as you passed, and newsboys (exclusively white) were about as numerous. There were mounted guards at each street corner, swords drawn and waiting to seize the speeders of the day. Every two or three minutes horsecars clanked over the double track from Georgetown to the Navy Yard.

From early morn to latest night, wheeled traffic filled the avenue—hacks driven by Negroes being the most numerous, but with many private carriages with liveried coachmen, and government wagons and ambulances.

The Avenue was a museum without a Barnum. In one shop milady could buy a satin slipper, next door there was a load of hay for sale, and at the next, coffins up on end with a transparency suggesting that you be embalmed. The buildings on the north side were higher and more pretentious than the insignificant looking shacks on the south side.

For all this surface tinsel, to world travelers Washington was a rather shabby and disappointing capital. In 1862 it had only one theater, no modern school buildings, and an indifferent spattering of monuments and statues. North of K and west of Fourteenth, there were few private houses until one came to Georgetown. East of the Capitol, dwellings were similarly well scattered. The only imposing official structures were the Capitol, the White House, the Treasury, and the Interior Building. The State Department was housed in a tumble-down brick building at one end of the Treasury.

The War Department Building, to which Lincoln went so often and so anxiously, had originally been of two stories built of brick painted a drab color, having a wooden porch and heavy wooden columns. Already it looked battered and shattered. Not until the end of 1863 did the Post Office and the Patent Office near completion. The Center Market was a low row of sheds, open on both sides. The Washington Monument had climbed to only a third of its projected height, and ugly sheds and huge piles of rock and lumber clustered about its base.

The odorous B Street Canal and Tiber Creek ran through the center of the city—the last-named a little muddy stream which in summer was hardly liquid enough for geese; the two together made the city one vast stench. Other open pools, swamps, ditches, and sewers abounded, while horses, cows, goats, and pigs roamed at will.

Washington's noted hotels, the National, the Metropolitan, and Willard's, were all on Pennsylvania Avenue. The first-named, the city's largest, was at Pennsylvania Avenue and Sixth Street. Before the war it had been habited chiefly by Southerners, and during Buchanan's Administration a disease had been named for it— "the National Hotel disease"—the cause of which had been an oversimple kitchen sanitation. Across the street from it was Jesse Brown's establishment, first known as the Indian Queen, in the late 40's as Brown's Hotel, and in the Civil War bursting into the full effulgence of the title of the Metropolitan. On the Avenue at Twelfth was the Kirkwood House, unpretentious but bountiful.

Two blocks west, on the present site of the New Willard Hotel, was the inn of Caleb Willard, the most enterprising hotel-keeper the early capital had ever known. This was a rambling mass of rooms, six stories high. Obscure or unpretentious guests were assigned to the top-floor rooms farthest removed and had to climb five flights of steps; but the elite drew better quarters. Throughout the war Willard's was crammed to the eaves, and was said to house "more scheming, plotting, planning heads, more aching and joyful hearts, than any building of the same size ever held in the world."

Ladies visiting Willard's found a lavish drawing-room with pianos, sofas, and easy chairs. For the men there was a barber-shop, where shaving was conducted "to a high degree of pub-licity." The menus were varied and bountiful. An English visitor noted carefully what one American ordered for his breakfast: Black tea and toast, scrambled eggs, fresh spring shad, wild pigeons, pigs' feet, two robins on toast, oysters, Thomas bread, and an ample supply of waffles! From Willard's the visitor could walk west past the Treasury at the next corner and come to the President's House.

George Alfred Townsend, already at twenty-one a cynically brilliant reporter, was the youngest of the war correspondents. Later he became nationally known under his pen name, "Gath." Young Townsend had never liked Washington. In peacetime he had found it "A very dismal, a very dirty, and a very Democratic settlement" of "mammoth hotels, paltry dwellings, empty lots, prodigiously wide avenues, a fossil population, and a series of gigantic public buildings which seemed dropped by accident into a fifth-rate backwoods settlement." Townsend's wartime pieces have recently been republished under the title, Rustics in Rebellion: A Yankee Reporter on the Road to Richmond. *Here is his uncharitable view of Washington in 1862:*[2]

Even the war lost half its interest in Washington. A regiment marching down Broadway was something to see, but the same regiment on Pennsylvania Avenue looked mean and matter-of-fact. A general in the field, or riding uncovered through Boston or Baltimore, or even lounging at the bar of the Continental or the Astor House or the Tremont, was invested with an atmosphere half heroic, half poetic; but generals in Washington may be counted by pairs, and I used to sit at dinner with eight or a dozen of them in my eye. . . . The town, in fact, was overrun with troops. Slovenly guards were planted on horseback at crossings, and now and then they dashed, as out of a profound sleep, to chase some galloping cavalier. Gin and Jews swarmed along the Avenue, and I have seen gangs of soldiers of rival regiments, but oftener of rival nationalities, pummelling each other in the highways, until they were marched off by the Provosts. The number of houses of ill-fame was very great, and I have been told that generals and lieutenants of the same organization often encountered and recognized each other in them. Contractors and "jobbers" used to besiege the offices of the Secretaries of War and Navy, and the venerable Welles (who reminded me of Abraham in the lithographs), and the barnacled Stanton, seldom appeared in public. Simple-minded, straightforward A. Lincoln, and his ambitious, clever lady, were often seen of afternoons in their barouche; the little old-fashioned Vice-President walked unconcernedly up and down; and when some of the Richmond captives came home to the Capital, immense meetings were held, where patriotism bawled itself hoarse. A dining hour at Willard's was often wondrously adapted for a historic picture, when accoutred officers, and their beautiful wives —or otherwise—sat at the *table d'hôte,* and sumptuous dishes flitted here and there, while corks popped like so many Chinese crackers, and champagne bubbled up like blood. At night, the Provost Guard enacted the farce of coming by deputations to each public bar, which was at once closed, but reopened five minutes afterward. Congress water was in great demand for weak heads of mornings, and many a young lad, girt up for war, wasted his strength in dissipation here, so that he was worthless afield, and perhaps died in the hospital. The curse of civil war was apparent everywhere. One had but to turn his eye from the bare Heights of Arlington, where the soldiers of the Republic lay demoralized, to the fattening vultures who smoked and swore at the National, to see the true cause of the North's shortcomings— its inherent and almost universal corruption. Human nature was here so depraved, that man lost faith in his kind. Death lurked behind ambuscades and fortifications over the river, but Sin, its mother, coquetted here, and as an American, I often went to bed loathing the Capital, as but little better than Sodom, though its danger had called forth thousands of great hearts to throb out, in its defence. For every stone in the Capitol building, a man has laid down his life. For every ripple on the Potomac, some equivalent of blood has been shed.

As William O. Stoddard, one of Lincoln's secretaries, so aptly put it, Washington stood "a fortified post upon the Confederate frontier."³ The population was southern in manners and sentiment; high society reflected the long dominance of southern politicians in the government. Everywhere there were Confederate spies and sympathizers. "It is impossible in these days . . . to give readers of this later generation any adequate idea of the uneasiness that pervaded Washington. . . ." wrote Noah Brooks in later years.⁴ Secretary Welles added, "The atmosphere was thick with treason."⁵

Lincoln himself was manifestly uneasy in his new office. "He has not yet got out of Springfield," said Senator Douglas. "He *does not see that the shadow he casts is any bigger now than it was last year—but he will soon find out when he is once inside the White House."*[6] *Robert S. Harper samples the contemporary reaction to the lonely pair so newly installed in the White House.*[7*]

When the tall lawyer from Illinois took up his duties in the White House, he was both the man of the hour and the question mark. He was put under a microscope by an inquisitive press. He lived in a glass mansion, his every movement news. His personal appearance was intriguing; he did not even look like any of his predecessors in the lofty office.

A writer for an English magazine gave Great Britain this description of the new American President:

To say he is ugly is nothing; to add that his figure is grotesque is to convey no adequate impression. Fancy a man almost six feet high, and thin in proportion, with long bony arms and legs which somehow always seem to be in the way; with great rugged furrowed hands, which grasp you like a vise when shaking yours; with a long, scraggly neck, and a chest too narrow for the great arms at his side. Add to this figure a head, cocoanut shaped, and somewhat too small for such a stature, covered with rough, uncombed hair, that stands out in every direction at once; a face furrowed, wrinkled, and indented as though it had been scarred by vitriol; a high, narrow forehead, sunk beneath bushy eyebrows; two bright, somewhat dreamy eyes that seem to gaze through you without looking at you; . . . a close-set, thin-lipped stern mouth, with two rows of large white teeth, and a nose and ears which have been taken by mistake from a head twice the size. Clothe this figure then in a long, tight, badly-fitting suit of black. . . . Add to all this an air of strength, physical as well as moral, and a strange look of dignity . . . and you have the impression left on me by Abraham Lincoln.

In the eyes of the smart New York crowd, Lincoln was a dismal failure socially, always wearing the wrong clothes and saying the wrong thing. A reporter for the New York *Commercial Advertiser,* writing under the name of "Arabella Smith," dashed this off after an evening at the Executive Mansion:

> I don't believe first class people in Washington go to President Lincoln's levees. Why, I've seen more intelligence in a small drawing room in New York than I could see in the reception and ante-rooms together that evening at the White House. Mr. Lincoln is a good man, I am sure; and a modest man. Between ourselves, if he were my husband and President, too, I shouldn't like him to be so good-natured and free-and-easy in his manners. I should want him to look and act the Chief Magistrate a little more. . . .
>
> I'll tell you what I think. The President is Abraham Lincoln, as honest and upright a man as the world ever saw. But Abraham Lincoln, in one respect, is not yet a President. His speech, his bearing, and the society he seems most at home with show him to be still Mr. Lincoln only. He has not yet appreciated, socially, the position he has been called to occupy. . . .
>
> I saw Mrs. Lincoln and I don't think if I had been the President's wife I should dress exactly as she did. . . . And I wouldn't have talked quite so freely in a promiscuous crowd about my husband's affairs. Madam is a smart woman, however, with an indomitable spirit lurking behind her bright

eyes, and will not live four years in the White House without making her influence felt. . . .

Mary Clemmer Ames, a Washington correspondent for the *Springfield* (Mass.) *Republican*, wrote an equally unflattering picture of the new pair in the White House, saying, "Abraham Lincoln looks very awkward in white kid gloves and feels uncomfortable in new boots. Mrs. Lincoln is very dumpy and very good-natured and very gorgeous; she stuns me with her low-necked dresses and the flower beds which she carries on the top of her head."

Later in the war, William Stoddard noted the "sense of not breathing so easily here as elsewhere." "Inmates of the White House get accustomed, after a while, to this strange, unnatural, wartime atmosphere," he wrote, "but they cannot escape from some of its effects."[8] *Lincoln stood up with iron discipline to the ordeal of living in this "glass mansion." But the four years of the war (which he always called "this great trouble") told increasingly upon him. "Sometimes in Washington," Mary Lincoln later said, "being worn down, he spoke crabbedly to men, harshly so, and yet it seemed the people understood the conditions around him and forgave."*[9] *The burden of the war was, ultimately, his alone; and no part of it was harder for him to bear than the hurt of so many deaths. Stoddard recalled "the slow, heavy, regular tread of the President's feet" through the long night after Chancellorsville, "pacing up and down in his room" as he wrestled with himself, summoning his courage to go on.*[10]

The deep sadness noted by so many grew on Lincoln. "It is plain that this man has suffered deeply" de Chambrun wrote in 1865.[11] *Yet Lincoln could still laugh, and laugh heartily. He told Stoddard that "he must laugh sometimes, or he would surely die."*[12] *In the weeks before his death he was a broken man, worn out, ageing fast, as his last photographs attest. Opportunities to get away were rare—occasional visits to the theater and the army, summers in the rural cottage at the Soldiers' Home outside Washington. The Blairs' house at Silver Spring in nearby Maryland (they were the parents of Montgomery and Frank) was another refuge. Burton J. Hendrick has a few words to say on this:*[13]

The couple that presided over this suburban home, the elder Francis Preston Blair and his wife, Violet Gist, could offer all that personal charm, that sympathy, that understanding, that ever-ready advice and admonition so welcome to a man called every day to meet a hundred problems and beset on every hand by selfish intriguers. The very presence of these two experienced political and social leaders was a balm. Both had now passed their seventieth year and were basking in a life filled with beauty, culture, troops of friends, and all the other essentials of a contented old age. The sight of old man Blair, gray-headed, wrinkled, and stoop-shouldered, moving among his shrubberies, sipping his Madeira in the Acorn summerhouse, bending over his flower beds, lounging in his library with a favorite volume, or surrounded by a few companions at tea, formed perhaps the most soothing diversion in Lincoln's anxious days. Unforgettable was the rememberance of the old man, clad in silk dressing gown, in his beloved rose garden; he had the habit of picking his blooms by running his fingers up the stalks, a procedure that left nothing in his hands except the stemless flowers; he would thrust these into his large pocket, arranging them, after returning to the house, in a specially contrived silver dish.

And finally, life in the White House. What was it like for this harassed pair during the four years of the "great trouble"? Benjamin Thomas has rounded up a compact picture from scattered sources.[14]

A President's life is wearying and worrisome at best, but in Lincoln's case all the vast problems of the war were added to the normal tasks of office. Nicolay and Hay comprised his secretarial staff until William O. Stoddard was brought in to assist them midway of the war. Edward D. Neill succeeded Stoddard when the latter became ill, and was in turn succeeded by Charles Philbrick. These young men scrutinized and questioned visitors, prepared a daily digest of news and military information, read and sorted the mail, and took care of whatever other details happened to call for attention. They had rooms at the White House, but walked to Willard's for their meals.

Lincoln started his workday early, for he was a light and fitful sleeper, and sometimes walked alone across the White House lawn in the gray dawn to summon a newsboy. By eight o'clock, when breakfast was announced, he had already been at work for an hour or more. His morning meal consisted of an egg and a cup of coffee; he was so little concerned about eating that Mrs. Lincoln sometimes invited guests to breakfast to make sure he would come. After breakfast he put in another hour of work before his door opened to visitors.

Except for the hot summer months, when they lived at the Soldiers' Home, the Lincoln family occupied the west wing of the second floor of the White House. The east wing was devoted to business. Lincoln's office was a large room on the south, next to Nicolay's office in the southeast corner. Its furnishings were simple—a large oak table covered with cloth, around which the cabinet met; another table between the two long windows, at which Lincoln usually wrote, seated in a large armchair; a tall desk with pigeonholes for papers against the south wall; a few straight-backed chairs, and two plain, hair-covered sofas. A marble mantel surmounted the fireplace with its high brass fender and brass andirons. Glass-globed jets hung from the ceiling. The only wall adornments were an old discolored engraving of President Jackson above the mantel, a photograph of John Bright, the English liberal leader, and numerous military maps in wooden frames. One door opened into Nicolay's office and another into the hall, where a messenger sat to bring in the cards of visitors. A bell cord hung near the President's desk.

At first Lincoln refused to limit the visiting-hours. "They do not want much," he said of the throng waiting to see him, "and they get very little. . . . I know how I would feel in their place." So people began coming before breakfast, and some still remained late at night. Lincoln realized at last that something must be done to conserve his time, and agreed to restrict the visiting-period from ten o'clock in the morning till three in the afternoon. But his other work continued to pile up, and the hours were again shortened, from ten till one.

Priority was granted to cabinet members, senators, and representatives in that order; finally, if any time remained, ordinary citizens were admitted. Army officers, many of whom had made nuisances of themselves with requests for promotion or demands for redress from supposed injustices, were forbidden to come to Washington without special permission.

Notwithstanding Lincoln's wish to keep himself accessible, it was not easy to see him. His friend Dr. Anson G. Henry, who was a house guest at the White House in February 1863, noted that "nine times out of ten not half the Senators get in unless several go in to-gether & this is very often done, and they can take in with them as many of their friends and constituents as they please. It is no uncommon thing for Senators to try for ten days before they get a private interview." . . .

With only Edward Moran, a short, thin, humorous Irishman, who had served since President Taylor's time, stationed at the front door, and Louis Bardorf, another White House veteran, posted in the upstairs corridor, the throng enjoyed access to all the public rooms and trooped about unhindered. Lamon warned

Lincoln that eavesdroppers and traitors lurked among the crowd, and suggested that Allan Pinkerton or some other shrewd detective be employed to ferret them out. At least everyone should be kept downstairs until his name was called, he thought. But not until November 1864 were four District of Columbia policemen in plain clothes detailed to the White House. A secretary gave each visitor a final scrutiny, but even so, unworthy persons often managed to intrude upon the President.

Once a visitor had passed the outer barriers and entered Lincoln's office, he encountered no further formality. The President never effused: "I am delighted to see you," unless he meant it; he simply said: "How do you do?" or "What can I do for you?" with a pleasant nod and smile. Lincoln wore no outward signs of greatness. . . .

Samuel R. Suddarth, Quartermaster General of Kentucky, observed after an interview: "His conversational powers are fine—and his custom of interspersing conversation with incidents, anecdotes and witticisms are well calculated to impress his hearers with the kindheartedness of the man. And they are so adroitly and delicately mingled in the thread of his discourse that one hardly notices the digression. His language is good though not select. . . . He is dignified in his manners without austerity." Suddarth was one of very few persons who heard Lincoln use profanity; "He is a damned rascal," the President said of a certain politician, and then added hastily, as though surprised: "God knows I do not know when I have sworn before."

Nicolay always rejoiced when Congress adjourned. The members presented countless trivial demands that kept the President vexed and anxious and troubled him no end. Many private citizens were scarcely less considerate of Lincoln's time. "Going into his room this morning to announce the Secretary of War," Nicolay confided to his fiancée, "I found a little party of Quakers holding a prayer-meeting around him, and he was compelled to bear the affliction until the 'spirit' moved them to stop. Isn't it strange that so many and such intelligent people often have so little common sense?"

Nicolay and Hay noted that through all the stirring days of war Lincoln almost invariably remained assured and steady on the surface no matter how afflicted he might be within. One caller observed the same fund of anecdote in Lincoln, but not the old free, lingering laugh. Another remarked about "the two-fold working of the two-fold nature of the man: Lincoln the Westerner, slightly humorous but thoroughly practical and sagacious. . . . Lincoln the President and statesman . . . seen in those abstract and serious eyes, which seemed withdrawn to an inner sanctuary of thought, sitting in judgment on the scene and feeling its far reach into the future."

It always gave Lincoln pleasure to be able to grant a request. But the glibbest talkers could not back him down. He seldom gave an outright "No." He was more likely to make the necessity of saying it so obvious that refusal became unnecessary. Or he would turn the conversation with a story or a jest; when petitioners found themselves back in the hall, they wondered how he had got rid of them. Men of the strongest personalities felt Lincoln's quiet dominance. Thurlow Weed went home after a talk with him and wrote: "I do not, when with you, say half I intend, partly because I do not like to 'crank,' and partly because you talk me out of my convictions and apprehensions. So bear with me, please, now, till I free my mind."

Lincoln gave way to annoyance at times. "Now go away!" he told one visitor. "Go away! I cannot attend to all these details. I could as easily bail out the Potomac with a teaspoon!" He replied sharply to a lady who sent him a long, demanding letter that "the bare reading of a letter of that length requires more than any person's share of my time."

Usually, however, he kept his temper under tight control. "If I do get up a little temper," he wrote, "I have no sufficient time to keep it up." He refused to quarrel himself, and tried to keep others from quarreling. He wrote to Senator Pomeroy about a senatorial dispute over an appointment: "I wish you and Lane would make an effort to get out of the mood you are in—It does neither of you good—it gives you the means of tormenting my life out of me, and nothing else."

One time it became the President's duty to administer a rebuke to a young captain, James Madison Cutts, a brother-in-law of Stephen A. Douglas, who became involved in quarrels with brother officers. Evidently Lincoln drew up a memorandum of what he wished to say, for among his papers is a document which reads: "Although what I am now to say is to be, in form, a reprimand, it is not intended to add a pang to what you have already suffered upon the subject to which it relates. You have too much of life yet before you, and have shown too much of promise as an officer, for your future to be lightly surrendered. . . . The advice of a father to his son, 'Beware of entrance to a quarrel, but being in, bear it that the opposed may beware of thee,' is good, and yet not the best. Quarrel not at all. No man resolved to make the most of himself, can spare time for personal contention. Still less can he afford to take all the consequences, including vitiating of his temper, and the loss of self-control." . . .

With government officials and men of influence so often turned away from Lincoln's office, it is remarkable that so many humble people managed to get in. But if he learned that some anxious old lady or worried wife, or a young soldier in a private's uniform had been waiting patiently from day to day to see him, he would arrange an appointment and if necessary overstay his time to hear his story. His secretaries estimated that he spent at least three quarters of his time in meeting people, despite their efforts to shield him from annoyance. It was as though he tried to make himself the nation's burden-bearer; and when his door swung shut at last, he was often near exhaustion.

While these daily sessions wore on him physically, they refreshed his mind and spirit. Through them he measured the pulse-beat of the people and learned to key his actions to its changing throb, using caution when it slowed, moving boldly when he felt it quicken. He called them his "public opinion baths," but they were more than that, for they also enabled him to curb the undue harshness of subordinates, and to override bureaucratic arrogance and indifference.

Time and again, after listening to someone's woes, the President would send him to Stanton, Welles, Seward, or some other person in authority with a brief but precious missive: "Mr. Secretary, please see and hear this man"; "Please give this matter your immediate attention"; "Can this man be accommodated?" "Has the Sec. of the Navy any knowledge of this case? and if any, what?" "There is a mistake somewhere in this case. . . . Will the Secretary of War please have the matter corrected? or explain to me wherein the hitch is?" "Mr. Defrees—please see this girl who works in your office, and find out about her brother, and come and tell me." To Surgeon General William A. Hammond, Lincoln wrote: "A Baltimore committee called on me this morning, saying that city is full of straggling soldiers, half-sick, half-well, who profess to have been turned from the hospital with no definite directions where to go. Is this true? Are men turned from the hospitals without knowing where to go?"

An "influence peddler," who gave his name as Captain Parker, claimed to know Judge Advocate General Joseph Holt, and promised a Mrs. Anna S. King that for three hundred dollars he would obtain a pardon for her husband. It was all the money the poor woman had; and John Hay, when he heard the story, took her to the President. After listening to her, Lincoln telegraphed to General Meade: "An intelligent woman in deep distress called this morning, saying her husband, a Lieutenant in the A. P. was to be shot next morning for desertion." She had left without giving her name or that of her husband, but the President made sure that Meade would delay all executions, ran down the man's identity, and commuted his sentence to imprisonment. The doors of military prisons opened for untold numbers of repentant Confederates at the behest of Lincoln's terse endorsement: "Let this man take the oath and be discharged."

Times almost innumerable the President sent petitioners joyfully on their way to a department head with a brief but authoritative note: "Let this woman have her son out of Old Capital Prison"; "Attorney-General, please make out and send me a pardon in this case"; "Injustice has probably been done in this case, Sec. of War please examine it"; or a brief statement of a request followed by: "Let it be done." It would be difficult to estimate how many tired, scared, or homesick boys in the Union army who fell asleep on picket duty, ran away in battle, or slipped off without leave to visit wives or parents were spared from the death sentence by a terse telegram from Lincoln: "Suspend sentence of execution and forward record of trial for examination," or "Let him fight instead of being shot."

Lincoln's orders to Stanton often display sly humor. The crabbed Secretary must have snorted with disgust when he read Lincoln's order: "Please have the adjutant general ascertain whether second Lieutenant of Company D, 2nd infantry, Alexander E. Drake, is entitled to promotion. His wife thinks he is. Please have this looked into." Stanton had learned that he could oppose the President up to a point; but to go beyond that point might bring him a rebuff such as: "I personally wish Jacob R. Freese, of New Jersey, to be appointed a Colonel of a colored regiment—and this regardless of whether he can tell the exact shade of Julius Caesar's hair." On August 23, 1862 Lincoln wrote, either to Stanton or as a memorandum for himself: "Today,

Mrs. Major Paul of the Regular Army calls and urges the appointment of her husband as Brig-Genl. She is a saucy woman and I am afraid she will keep tormenting me till I have to do it." Less than two weeks later, Major Gabriel R. Paul was commissioned a brigadier general.

Many of Lincoln's instructions were subtly philosophical. "This man wants to work," he wrote, "so uncommon a want that I think it ought to be gratified." His most commonplace writings bear the stamp of individuality. "You request my autograph. Well here it is"—or "here 'tis. A. Lincoln," he scribbled many times.

This sort of work filled Lincoln's mornings. At one o'clock, or some time afterward, he made his way to the living-quarters through the still-crowded corridor. His passage gave the more intrusive callers an opportunity to intercept him, for his informal habits made him prone to stop and talk. In 1864 a door cut from his office gave direct access to the family apartment.

The visiting time ended early on Tuesdays and Fridays, when the cabinet met regularly at noon. On Mondays, when the President held a reception from one to two, he usually missed his lunch. This was of small concern to him, however, for he normally ate only a biscuit, with perhaps some fruit in season, and drank a glass of milk.

After lunch Lincoln might sprawl in a big armchair by the window in the family sitting-room to read for a few minutes, one leg crossed over the other and bouncing up and down as though to music. Corns bothered him—he wrote a testimonial for a Jewish chiropodist who also performed confidential missions for him: "Dr. Zacharie has operated on my feet with good success, and considerable addition to my comfort"—so he often slipped off his shoes and sat in his stocking feet, until Mrs. Lincoln noticed it and sent a servant for his slippers. Some time during the day a servant shaved his upper lip and trimmed his beard, and had been seen to shake the towel out of the White House window.

Early afternoon found Lincoln again at work. With the expansion of the army, thousands of commissions must be signed; later these became less numerous, but in their place came batches of court-martial sentences, amounting to thirty thousand in a year, for him to modify or approve. Those involving the death penalty received his closest attention, but none escaped his notice. John Hay told of six hours spent in such work on a humid July day and noted how eagerly Lincoln seized on any possible excuse to save a soldier's life. Only cases of meanness or cruelty failed to evoke his sympathy. He was especially averse to approving the death penalty for cowardice—"leg cases" he called those in which a soldier ran away in battle—and as he remitted sentence he said wryly: "It would frighten the poor fellows too terribly to kill them."

But while his impulse was always toward forgiveness, he could be hard when military discipline called for sternness. In the case of five bounty-jumpers sentenced to death for desertion, he wrote to General Meade: "I understand these are very flagrant cases and that you deem their punishment as being indispensable to the service. If I am not mistaken in this, please let them know at once that their appeal is denied."

Some time during the morning the secretaries had sorted the mail. Correspondence arrived in torrents: resolutions and petitions written in copperplate scroll, letters carefully composed, and almost illegible scrawls. Threatening or abusive letters were usually tossed into the wastebasket. Those of a routine nature went to various departments. Only a relatively small number reached the President's desk, usually with a secretarial notation— "Personal," "Political," or a brief summary of their contents written on the back.

Even after careful sifting they made a formidable pile. Lincoln

snatched what time he could to read them, but many suffered
the same fate as that of Dr. Henry P. Tappan, chancellor of the
University of Michigan. The well-meaning educator sent Lincoln fifteen pages of advice, routing his letter by way of David
Davis to make sure Lincoln would read it. Davis endorsed it.
"This letter is an elaborate one, written in good temper & from
the Christian character of the author entitled to be read." But
even such a testimonial was not enough; Lincoln wrote on the
back of the letter: "Mr. Nicolay, please run over this & tell me
what is in it."

John Hay answered some of Lincoln's mail, usually with the
introduction: "In reply to your letter, the President directs me
to say—" But in most cases where an answer was required, Lincoln penned it in longhand, and frequently took the trouble of
making a copy for his files. He employed the same rudimentary
filing system that he had used as a country lawyer; the pigeonholes of his tall desk were marked alphabetically, with a few of
the apertures assigned to individuals. Each cabinet member and
a number of generals had pigeonholes of their own. So did Horace
Greeley. One compartment marked "W. & W." aroused the
interest of Frank B. Carpenter, the artist, and Lincoln explained:
"That's Weed and Wood—Thurlow and Fernandy." "That's a
pair of 'em," he chuckled. . . .

The war time afflictions of friends and acquaintances never
failed to touch Lincoln deeply. When Lieutenant Colonel William
McCullough, of Bloomington, met death in the Vicksburg campaign, Lincoln learned that one of McCullough's daughters had
become inconsolable. And just before Christmas in 1862 a letter
came to young Fanny McCullough from a busy President: "It is
with deep grief that I learn of the death of your kind and brave
Father; and especially, that it is affecting your young heart beyond what is common in such cases. In this sad world of ours,
sorrow comes to all; and, to the young, it comes with bitterest

agony, because it takes them unawares. The older have learned to ever expect it. I am anxious to afford some alleviation of your present distress. Perfect relief is not possible, except with time. You can not now realize that you will ever feel better. Is not this so? And yet it is a mistake. You are sure to be happy again. . . . The memory of your dear Father, instead of an agony, will yet be a sad sweet feeling in your heart, a purer, and holier sort than you have known before." . . .

Lincoln's deep human sympathy reached beyond his acquaintances and made him kin to all. "I have been shown in the files of the War Department," he wrote to Lydia Bixby, a Boston widow, "a statement of the Adjutant General of Massachusetts that you are the mother of five sons who have died gloriously on the field of battle. I feel how weak and fruitless must be any word of mine which should attempt to beguile you from the grief of a loss so overwhelming. But I cannot refrain from tendering to you the consolation that may be found in the thanks of the republic they died to save. I pray that our heavenly Father may assuage the anguish of your bereavement, and leave you only the cherished memory of the loved and lost, and the solemn pride that must be yours to have laid so costly a sacrifice upon the altar of freedom."

Lincoln had been misinformed: Mrs. Bixby had only two sons killed; of the other three, two deserted and one was honorably discharged. But that he wrote under a misconception detracts in no wise from the nobility of his motives, nor from the beauty of his tribute to democratic motherhood.

Numerous inventors were to be found among the White House throng, each sure that his idea would win the war. Lincoln grasped mechanical principles quickly, and had a faculty for finding flaws in their devices. But if a new explosive or gun model offered promise, the President made sure that it reached the attention of the proper authorities. The new breech-loading rifles interested him keenly, and early morning might find him on the marsh south of the White House watching while they were tried, or perhaps taking a rifle to fire a few rounds himself. A rustic observer at one such experiment afforded him much merriment with the comment that "a good piece of audience hadn't ought to rekyle," and if it did, it should "rekyle a lettle forrid." Lincoln also visited the navy yard to watch tests of naval ordnance. He saw to it that a young chemist was detached from the Department of Agriculture to help Isaac Diller, a Springfield druggist who had sold the Lincolns their cough syrup and calomel, in experiments with a new gunpowder that Diller was trying to perfect.

Lincoln wrote his own speeches and prepared his own state papers in the midst of trivial duties that crowded his working day. Seward arranged for ceremonial introductions and formal interviews with foreign ministers and wrote the brief remarks Lincoln made on such occasions. The President had to receive various delegations and respond to them; parades must be reviewed, and serenaders greeted in the night.

Lincoln had been threatened with tuberculosis during his circuit days, and Mrs. Lincoln insisted that he have fresh air. So almost every day at four o'clock, unless bad weather interfered, the coachman brought a carriage to the White House portico, and the President and his wife went for a drive. They often stopped at some hospital, where Lincoln walked from cot to cot, taking the wan hands in friendly grip, joking with the convalescents, and offering cheer and comfort to those with more serious hurts. He was especially solicitous to the friendless Southern boys.

During the early years of his Presidency, Lincoln sometimes rode horseback in the late afternoon. . . .

The Lincolns dined at six o'clock, unless a state function had been planned, and again the President ate sparingly of one or two courses. Military uniforms sometimes lent splendor to the White

House dining-room. The artist Carpenter remembered a dinner attended by twelve officers; another time two generals and two colonels, captured at Bull Run and Seven Pines and recently exchanged, were honored guests. There was a splendid dinner for Prince Napoleon Jerome Bonaparte when he visited the United States during the summer of 1861, and another for officers of the Russian navy in 1863. Grant, Meade, and other officers were dinner guests soon after Grant's appointment as commander in chief.

A memorandum furnished by the State Department for the President's social guidance decreed that state dinners should begin at seven thirty o'clock. Correct dress for gentlemen was a black dress coat or one of blue with bright buttons—one should never wear a frock coat. Protocol determined those officials who must be invited to various functions, and the proper seating arrangement. The Lincolns followed the custom of serving wine at official dinners.

Once a week, except in summer, the President held an evening reception or levee. People came by thousands to shake his hand and perhaps steal an opportunity to ask a favor of him. Mrs. Lincoln offered a striking contrast to her husband as she stood beside him elegantly gowned, with a sprig or wreath of flowers in her carefully dressed hair, and jewels at her wrists and throat; for while she saw to it that he wore good clothes and kept them brushed and pressed, they never seemed to hang right on his tall, stooped frame. The white gloves that were the fashion at receptions made his big hands look enormous; once when his glove burst with a loud pop under an especially strong handclasp, he held it up ruefully and laughed. . . .

Most evenings when no formal function had been planned, found Lincoln back at his desk. Nicolay wrote that it was "impossible to portray by any adequate words, the labor, the thought, the responsibility, the strain of intellect and the anguish of soul" that he endured. Carpenter came into Lincoln's office at eleven o'clock one night and found him seated alone at his long table with a pile of military commissions before him. They were made of heavy, oily parchment, very hard to handle or sign, but he went about his labor with patient industry. "I do not, as you see, pretend to read over these documents," he said to Carpenter as the artist sat down beside him. "I see that Stanton has signed them so I conclude they are alright." He paused to read one. "John Williams is hereby appointed adjutant-general with the rank of captain, etc. E. M. Stanton, Secretary of War." "There," he said, adding his own signature, "that fixes him out." He went on chatting and writing till he reached the bottom of the stack. Then rising and stretching his long arms above his head, he remarked: "Well, I have that job *husked out;* now I guess I'll go over to the War Department before I go to bed and see if there is any news."

A visit to the War Department telegraph office was usually his last chore. The operators left copies of all military telegrams in a pile in a desk drawer for him, with the last dispatch on top. They noticed that as he read them he sat forward on the edge of his chair with one knee almost touching the floor. When he had worked through the pile to the messages he had read before, he put all of them back and said: "Well, I have got down to raisins."

The curiosity of the young operators got the better of them at last, and one of them asked the President what he meant by that remark. He told them he had known a little girl back home who once gorged herself with a stupendous meal of soup, chicken, ham, salad, potatoes and sundry other vegetables, ice cream and cake, and at last a handful of raisins. Things began coming up; and after she had been busily occupied for some time, she looked at her mother and said reassuringly: "I am all right now. I have got down to raisins."

Lincoln usually read a little before he went to bed. The telegraph operators noticed that he often carried a worn copy of *Macbeth* or *The Merry Wives of Windsor* under his arm when he made his last visit to their office. And John Hay told how at midnight, when he sat writing his diary, the President came into the office laughing to read him and Nicolay a funny story by Thomas Hood, "seemingly utterly unconscious that he with his short shirt hanging about his long legs, and setting out behind like the tail feathers of an enormous ostrich, was infinitely funnier than anything in the book he was laughing at." . . .

Occasionally in the evening Lincoln listened to music in the White House drawing-room. The massive Lamon had a deep, rich voice, and Lincoln loved to hear him sing. One of his special favorites was *The Blue-Tailed Fly*, and Lamon recalled how "he often called for that buzzing ballad when we were alone and he wanted to throw off the weight of public or private cares. . . . But while he had a great fondness for witty or mirth-provoking ballads, our grand old patriotic airs and songs of the tender and sentimental kind afforded him the deepest pleasure." The simple melodies of Stephen Foster never failed to move him deeply.

Lincoln enjoyed the Marine Band; it played twice weekly during the summer months on the south lawn of the White House. But the President was more of an attraction than the musicians, and Carpenter recalled how, when he appeared on the portico, the crowd loudly applauded and called for a speech. Lincoln bowed his thanks, stepped back into the parlor, and slumped down on a sofa. "I wish they would let me sit out there quietly, and enjoy the music," he said wistfully.

Henry C. Whitney, who had traveled the circuit with Lincoln, remembered how he often went alone to any sort of little show or concert and even slipped away one time to attend a magic-lantern show intended for children. Residence in Washington gave him his first chance to hear opera. He became very fond of it, as well as concert music, and as the war took a turn for the better, he attended the theatre, opera, or concerts whenever he could, usually with Mrs. Lincoln or a party of friends.

Among the operas that he heard were Gounod's *Faust,* Verdi's *Ballo in machera* and Boïeldieu's *La Dame blanche.* John W. Forney, of the *Philadelphia Press,* recalled an evening at the opera during which the President sat in a corner of his box the entire time, wrapped in a shawl, "either enjoying the music or communing with himself." A vicious battle was raging and Lincoln remarked afterward that he supposed some people would think it indiscreet of him to seek amusement at such a time. "But the truth is," he declared, "I must have a change of some sort or die."

Marshal Lamon never ceased worrying when Lincoln went to public functions without guards. On December 15, 1864 he wrote to Nicolay from New York that he had good reason to fear for the President's safety—"See that he don't go out alone either in the day or night time." Soon afterward, when Lamon made his customary inspection of the White House and found that the President had gone out, he left a note of warning on his desk: "Tonight, as you have done on several previous occasions, you went unattended to the theatre. When I say unattended I mean you went alone with Charles Sumner and a foreign minister, neither of whom could defend himself against an assault from any able-bodied woman in this city." . . .

While Lincoln derived much pleasure from concerts and the theatre, he spent most of his leisure evenings in his office, swapping yarns with friends who happened in. Such sessions found him at his best, according to John Hay, who remembered that "his wit and rich humor had free play, he was once more the Lincoln of the Eighth Circuit, the cheeriest of talkers, the riskiest of story tellers," as a long leg dangled over his chair arm or his ample feet adorned a desk. Seward, Senators Browning, Ira Harris, and James Harlan, Marshal Lamon, Congressmen Washburne of Illinois and W. D. Kelley of Pennsylvania, and Indian Commissioner Dole were among his most frequent evening visitors. Old friends from Illinois were usually present whenever they came to

Washington, and witty Sam Galloway, of Ohio, was always a welcome guest.

Courtly, polished Charles Sumner came so often that Harlan said: "Ah, Sumner, we are sure of finding you here." The fastidious Sumner with his elegantly tailored brown coat, maroon vest, and lavender pantaloons made a strange companion for the easygoing President, whose garb on these informal evenings was likely to be a faded, long-skirted dressing gown, belted around the waist, and an old, worn pair of carpet slippers. Lincoln's and Sumner's sharp disagreement over reconstruction policies never dampened their personal friendship. Mrs. Lincoln was also fond of Sumner and often invited him to drive with her and the President to attend their theatre parties. But whenever Lincoln, at ease in his office, heard Sumner's gold-headed cane thumping down the White House corridor, he deferred to the Senator's pompous dignity by dropping his feet to the floor.

If only one or two persons were with Lincoln in the evening, he liked to read aloud from Shakespeare, Robert Burns, or the works of the contemporary humorists Artemus Ward, Orpheus C. Kerr, or Petroleum V. Nasby. Bryant and Whittier also ranked among his favorites, and he never tired of Oliver Wendell Holmes's "The Last Leaf." Novels had no appeal for him; he had never been able to finish *Ivanhoe*. . . .

In summer the evening session in Lincoln's office must have resounded with slaps, for the White House windows had no screens or netting. Nicolay complained to his fiancée: "My usual trouble in this room (my office) is from . . . 'big bugs'—(oftener humbugs)—but at this present writing (10 o'clock p.m. Sunday night) the thing is quite reversed and *little bugs* are the pest. The gas lights over my desk are burning brightly and the windows of the room are open, and all bugdom outside seems to have organized a storming party to take the gas lights, in numbers that seem to exceed the contending hosts at Richmond. The air is swarming with them, they are on the ceilings, the walls and the furniture in countless numbers, they are buzzing about the room, and butting their heads against the window panes, they are on my clothes, in my hair, and on the sheet I am writing on."

Lincoln had a questing mind. He sometimes went to the Observatory to study the moon and stars, and it gave him unusual satisfaction to talk with men of broad intellect. Louis Agassiz, the scientist, and Dr. Joseph Henry, curator of the Smithsonian Institution, both marveled at his intellectual grasp. It must have delighted a man of his meager educational opportunities when Princeton (then known as the College of New Jersey), Columbia, and Knox College, in Illinois, saw fit to honor him with degrees of Doctor of Laws, and when Lincoln College, in Illinois, was named for him, as the town where it was located had been. . . .

Mrs. Lincoln regularly attended Sunday morning service at the New York Avenue Presbyterian Church of Dr. Phineas D. Gurley, and Lincoln went with her when he could. Sometimes they took the boys, but they were more likely to be found at the Fourth Presbyterian Church, where they attended Sunday school with their playmates Bud and Holly Taft. Browning remembered seeing Lincoln read the Bible in the White House, but he did not say grace before meals.

When the Lincolns moved into the White House in 1861, Willie (William Wallace) was ten and Tad (Thomas for his grandfather) was eight. For many years the venerable mansion had seen no children. Innumerable stories tell how the Lincoln boys, usually in league with their playmates of the same age, Bud and Holly Taft, turned the place inside out during the early years of the war. Robert Lincoln, the oldest son, was eighteen at the beginning of the war and already away at Harvard. Robert later became a lawyer, Secretary of War, and Minister to England. Tad died in his teens, in 1871. Willie's tragic death in 1862 threw a deep shadow over the remaining years in the White House.

"Willie Lincoln was the most lovable boy I ever knew, bright,

sensible, sweet-tempered and gentle-mannered," remembered
*Julia Taft, who was a grown-up of sixteen when she first met the
Lincoln boys in 1861. As Julia Taft Bayne she wrote it all down
many years later in her lively* Tad Lincoln's Father. *"Tad had a
quick fiery temper, very affectionate when he chose, but implaca-
ble in his dislikes. . . . They were two healthy, rollicking Western boys, never accustomed to restraint . . ."* Julia had many
affectionate memories of life in the White House:[15]

I ascended to the attic and as I opened the door,
Tad rushed at me, shouting, "Come quick, Julie. We're having a
circus. I've got to be blacked up and Willie can't get his dress on
and Bud's bonnet won't fit." They had two sheets pinned together for a curtain, behind which was a crowd of soldiers, sailors,
gardeners and servants. Anybody, white or black, who had five
cents, could go up the back stairs and see the show.

I took away from Tad the bottle of shoe blacking he was
flourishing and made him up with some burnt cork. I told him
burnt cork would do just as well and be easier to get off than
shoe blacking. Willie was struggling with a lilac silk of his
mother's. The gown had a long train and was cut in the expan-
sive Victorian decollété. I pinned it up so he could manage it,
then straightened the bonnet, which Bud had stuck sideways
firmly upon his head. He was wearing a white morning dress of
Mrs. Lincoln's pinned around him in billowy folds.

"Boys," I said, highly scandalized at these proceedings, "does
the President know about this?"

"Yep," said Tad. "Pa knows and he don't care, neither. He's
coming up when those generals go away."

Willie handed me a bottle of "Bloom of Youth," saying, "Put
some of this on Bud and me." I swabbed them both liberally with
the beautifier. Tad was singing at the top of his voice, "Old Abe
Lincoln came out of the wilderness."

"Tad, Tad," I remonstrated, "don't sing that. Suppose the President hears you."

"I don't care if he does," answered Tad. "Anyway, Pa won't care. I'm going to sing that song in the show." I don't think, however, that he did. At any rate, it wasn't listed on the "official program" gotten up by Willie.

I had had quite enough and, thoroughly disgusted, made my escape from the attic.

In his one-volume life of Lincoln, Carl Sandberg tells how Willie died:[16]

Willie Lincoln went riding on his pony in a chilly rain and fell sick with a cold and fever in February '62, at a time when a White House ball was planned. The President spoke of the ball to Miss Dorothea Dix, wanted to stop it, had it announced officially there would be no dancing. "But the Marine band at the foot of the steps filled the house with music while the boy lay dying above," wrote one woman. "A sadder face than that of the President I have rarely seen. He was receiving at the large door of the East Room, speaking to the people as they came, but feeling so deeply that he spoke of what he felt and thought, instead of welcoming the guests. To General Frémont he at once said that his son was very ill and he feared for the result . . . The ball was becoming a ghastly failure."

During the next few days Willie called for Bud Taft, who came and held his hand. The President would come in, lean over and stroke Willie's hair. "Better go to bed, Bud," he said one night. Bud answered, "If I go he will call for me." Still another night Lincoln came in, found Bud asleep, picked him up and carried him off to another room.

A few days later Willie lay still and cold. Elizabeth Keckley, the mulatto seamstress and Mrs. Lincoln's trusted companion, wrote, "The light faded from his eyes, and the death-dew gathered on his brow." She had been on watch but did not see the end, telling of it: "I was worn out with watching, and was not in the room when Willie died, but was immediately sent for. I assisted in washing and dressing him, and then laid him on the bed, when Mr. Lincoln came in." He lifted the cover from the face of his child, gazed at it long, and murmured, "It is hard, hard, hard to have him die!" The mother wept long hours, moaned and shook with grief.

They closed down the lids over the blue eyes of the boy, parted his brown hair, put flowers from his mother in his pale, crossed hands, and soldiers, Senators, Cabinet officers, foreign Ministers, came to the funeral. The mother, too far spent, could not come. The body was later sent west to Illinois for burial. And the mother clutched at his memory and if his name was mentioned her voice shook and the tears came. "She could not bear to look upon his picture," said Mrs. Keckley. "And after his death she never crossed the threshold of the Guest's Room in which he died, or the Green Room in which he was embalmed."

Two years later Julia Taft, who had been away at school, returned briefly to the White House. When Tad saw her he threw himself down on the floor and kicked and screamed until he had to be carried out. "You must excuse him, Julia. You know what he remembers," said Mrs. Lincoln.[17] After Willie's death Tad and his father drew close to each other. Sandburg continues:[18]

The boy Tad meant more to Lincoln than anyone else. They were chums. "Often I sat by Tad's father reporting to him about some important matter that I had been ordered to inquire into," wrote Charles A. Dana, "and he would have this boy on his knee; and, while he would perfectly understand the report, the striking thing about him was his affection for the child."

Tad usually slept with him, wrote John Hay. Often late at night the boy came to the President's office: "He would lie around until he fell asleep, and Lincoln would shoulder him and take him off to bed."

"Tad" was short for Tadpole, a wriggler, nervous, active. With a defective palate, his occasional "papa dear" sounded more like "pappy day." He could burst into the President's office and call out what he wanted. Or again Tad would give three sharp raps and two slow thumps on the door, three dots and two dashes he had learned in the war telegraph office. "I've got to let him in," Lincoln would say, "because I promised never to go back on the code." . . .

The boy did things with a rush. "I was once sitting with the President in the library," wrote Brooks, "when Tad tore into the room in search of something, and having found it, he threw himself on his father like a small thunderbolt, gave him one wild, fierce hug, and without a word, fled from the room before his father could put out a hand to detain him." Tutors came and went, Brooks noted. "None stayed long enough to learn much about the boy; but he knew them before they had been one day in the house." Of this the father would say: "Let him run. There's time enough yet for him to learn his letters and get poky."

The strain of the war years was almost as hard on Mary Lincoln as it was on her husband; but where Lincoln could exercise control Mary, already burdened with a growing emotional instability, could not stand up to the ordeal. She was completely prostrated by Willie's death. He was the second child she had lost. For almost three years she lived in virtual seclusion, emerging only at New Years in 1865. She resorted to mediums and spiritualists, and insisted that Willie came to her in the night. Lincoln was always gentle with her, but feared for her sanity. She could be sweet ("I have a very sweet and tender memory of her," wrote

Julia[19]*) but her aberrations, which eventually forced her son Rob-*
ert to commit her to an insane asylum after the war, grew on her
markedly. She was particularly erratic in money matters. She
over-spent a congressional appropriation for redecorating the
White House (much to Lincoln's embarrassment); piled up lavish
debts, without her husband's knowledge, for clothes she did not
need; and all of this while practicing the most absurd penny-
pinching in the management of the White House.

"It was not easy at first," wrote Stoddard, who of all the secre-
taries was closest to her, "to understand why a lady who could be
one day so kindly, so considerate, so generous, so thoughtful and
so hopeful, could, upon another day, appear so unreasonable, so
irritable, so despondent, so even niggardly, and so prone to see
the dark side. . . ." A talk with a physician, Stoddard continued,
made it easier for him to comprehend the "causes of a sudden
horror of poverty to come, for example, which, during a few
hours of extreme depression, proposed to sell the very manure in
the Executive stables, and to cut off the necessary expenses of the
household."[20] *In his private diary John Hay called her the "Hell-*
Cat," and John Nicolay was eventually forced to leave the White
House because once in 1865 he had incurred her displeasure by
remonstrating with her for omitting the names of Chase and his
daughter and son-in-law from the list for a Cabinet dinner. The
beautiful Kate Chase, who was married to Governor Sprague of
Rhode Island in wartime Washington's most ostentatious wed-
ding, was a particularly sharp thorn in poor Mary's side. Burton
Hendrick tells why.[21]

Her appearance at her first White House reception
almost immediately lifted Kate to the social leadership of the new
administration. Certainly the stately father and the brilliant, ani-
mated daughter made a handsome pair on entering the East Room.
As Mrs. Seward, wife of the "Premier," was an invalid and seldom

appeared in Washington, this left Kate, as hostess of the cabinet officer second in rank, virtually first lady of the cabinet and chief assistant to Mrs. Lincoln at state functions. But the post of second-in-command by no means satisfied her ambitions. At this first reception the girl of twenty-one, dressed in white silk with sprays of jasmine, made rather a pale figure of Mary Todd, in white satin and black lace, forty-three, mother of four children, who, if by no means the dowd that malicious gossip pictured her, could hardly compete with the tall, exquisitely framed figure—the brown eyes melting into blue, searching, demanding; the rust-gold hair; the small but willful mouth; the little, perfectly formed chin; the lively laughter and spirited talk of her youthful rival. For rival to the President's wife Kate became from the day she entered Washington. Just as Chase regarded himself as the man morally entitled to rule the administration, so his daughter believed that the position fate had intended for her was to be eventually mistress of the White House. That she sought to make herself the center of White House functions, generally with success —drawing to her circle the most distinguished, such as the French princes, with whom, thanks to a daily association for nine years with Mademoiselle Janon at Miss Haines's School in New York, she could easily converse in their own language—was perhaps natural enough, and it was also to be expected that Mrs. Lincoln would resent her pretensions and regard her soon as a presumptuous enemy. The fact that Lincoln, like all men, liked to bend over the lovely creature and bask in her entertaining talk did not improve Mary's fondness for the girl.

When discussing Mary Lincoln, it is indeed hard to distinguish between truth and slander. Mary was always in trouble. She fell prey, for instance, to a series of unscrupulous adventurers, and matters were not improved by the constant criticism of her in the press. She was condemned for abandoning the social life in the

*White House after Willie's death as she had been blamed for over-
doing it in the first years. While suffering private anguish at the
death of close relatives in the Southern armies, she had to endure
reiterated public reflections on her loyalty. Her excessive grief
for a single child came in for particular disapproval in a land
mourning its unnumbered dead. Certain deepening neurotic traits,
however, could not be explained away by the difficulties of her
position. In the later years of the war, for instance, she gave way
more and more to wholly unreasonable fits of jealousy.*

*And yet this strangely matched couple loved each other. In
her* Mary Lincoln: Biography of a Marriage, *Ruth Painter Randall
tells of their last afternoon ride together through the streets of
Washington.*[22] *It was April 14, 1865.*

Lincoln was happy that day. "Dear husband, you
almost startle me, by your great cheerfulness," Mary said to him
that afternoon when they went for their drive. There were just
the Lincolns in the carriage because he had wished it so. When
she asked him whether she should invite someone to go with them
he had answered, "No, I prefer to ride by ourselves today." He
wanted to talk to her about the future, the happy unstrained
days ahead. They could settle back now into the old familiar companionship of their marriage. That companionship was like an old
coat, stretched and frayed by long use but all the more comfortable for that reason. It did not matter that the coat had never
been a perfect fit; it was the coat he had selected from all others
because it was the one he liked; habit had adjusted it to his needs
and he felt at home in it.

He was supremely happy on that last ride together; ". . . well
I may feel so, Mary," he said, "I consider *this day*, the war has
come to a close—We must *both*, be more cheerful in the future
—between the war & the loss of our darling Willie—we have
both, been very miserable."

Mrs. Lincoln later told some of the plans for that cheerful future. "My husband intended, when he was through with his presidential terms, to take me and the family to Europe." Before their revived spirits was the lure and joy of travel and seeing new things. When they returned from abroad they would "go to California over the Rocky mountains, and see the prospects (prospectors' claims) of the soldiers, etc., digging out gold to pay the national debt." In this connection she mentioned again how "cheery and funny" he was. According to her understanding, Lincoln's intention up to 1865 had been ultimately to return to Springfield to live, but in that year he "Changed his opinion" though he had not "settled on any place particularly." Ahead of them stretched four peaceful years in Washington before that decision had to be made.

As they returned from the drive two friends were just leaving the White House. Friendships too could be on a relaxed basis now; the President called to the dignified gentlemen. "Come back, boys, come back." He visited with them, laughing and jesting, until he was late for dinner. Dinner must not be delayed too long as they were going to Ford's Theatre that evening.

7.

One War at a Time

*The diplomatic history of the Civil War reveals dramatic mo-
ments, but few which carry the impact of a Gettysburg or an
Appomattox. Yet these moments were often decisive for peace
or war, victory or defeat. Time after time England or France or
both together balanced on the edge of war with the North, then
drew back in response to some diplomatic threat or to changes in
the political or military scene. Only the double victories at Gettysburg and Vicksburg put an end at last to Southern hopes of
foreign intervention.*

*Lincoln's problem was to keep England and France from rec-
ognizing the Confederacy. Recognition would probably have led
to intervention, and since France was not disposed to move without England, it was important to keep the two from acting in
concert. In time Lincoln and Seward became adept at mingling
threats with conciliation to achieve their purposes. It is not really
necessary to assign the leading role in this partnership in diplomacy either to Lincoln or to Seward. Once the two had come to
an understanding they worked very closely together.*

*The first test of the partnership came in May, 1861, only a
month after Lincoln had been forced to show Seward who was*

*master. Seward still clung to his panacea of a foreign war. When
he heard that the British government was about to receive the
Confederate commissioners in London and was considering recognition of the Confederacy jointly with France, he drafted a dispatch so belligerent that it might well have provoked war. But
"Dispatch Number Ten" was never sent as written, for Lincoln
toned it down and directed his new minister in London, Charles
Francis Adams, to use it only at his discretion. Adams was thus
able to win from Lord John Russell, the British foreign secretary,
a promise not to receive the Confederate commissioners in the
future.*

*"One war at a time," Lincoln later cautioned Seward.[1] The
happy outcome of this first crisis with England seemed to give
Seward a new confidence in the judgment of his chief. But relations with England were still strained. The governing classes
sympathized with the South. Queen Victoria had recognized
Southern belligerency, and her government looked upon Seward,
with cause, as a dangerous Anglophobe. Then without warning
came the* Trent *affair, and Seward's diplomacy was put to the
test. Burton J. Hendrick examines the incident and then goes on
to discuss Seward's handling of foreign affairs during the war.[2]*

It seems almost as though a sardonic fate had created
the *Trent* crisis for the express purpose, in poker language, of
calling Seward's bluff. In late November, 1861, the golden opportunity for a war with England arrived, without any artificial
stimulation from the White House or State Department. When
the bumptious Captain Wilkes, in command of the sloop of war
San Jacinto, stopped the British packet *Trent* in the Bahama
Straits, forcibly removed from her deck four insurgent Americans
and lodged them as prisoners of war in Fortress Monroe, Virginia,
he presented Seward with that European war which several
months before had been the chief item in his statesmanship. The

mercurial gentleman, abruptly confronted with the fact, hesitated to seize this gift from heaven. It is the most picturesque contradiction in Seward's career that, in the *Trent* disturbance, he was almost the only member of the cabinet who kept his head. All of the seven, excepting Montgomery Blair and Seward, seemed ready to go to war with England rather than back down and surrender the prisoners. Even Lincoln, the most deliberate influence in the administration, inclined to the prevailing view that Captain Wilkes must not be disavowed. . . .

In its essentials, the *Trent* affair involved no diplomatic problem. Captain Wilkes, a troublesome officer whose insubordination had already involved him in one court-martial and was to involve him in another, had acted on his own responsibility, without the slightest suggestion of instructions from his government. In doing so, he had violated certain principles of international law of which the United States had been the champion for sixty years, and had acted in accordance with certain British practices against which this country had always protested. It was for doing precisely what Captain Wilkes had done in the *Trent* that the American government had declared war on England in 1812. Had the administration promptly disavowed Wilkes's act and restored the captives to the British guardianship from which they had been ravished, it not only would have acted in a way befitting the nation's dignity, but would have scored a diplomatic triumph. Mr. Seward would have upheld American principles, and would have compelled Great Britain to recognize interpretations of maritime law which it had been disregarding for centuries.

Not improbably Seward perceived this great opportunity, but certain demonstrations, both in England and in America, made such a course almost impossible. At no time in history, even in 1776 and 1812, had England been so unpopular in the United States. That English statesmen were deliberately planning to use American domestic troubles as an excuse for disrupting the Union, destroying its trade and merchant marine, and ending the Republic as a threat to the supremacy of the British Empire, was the conviction of most Americans. . . .

It is not strange therefore that the news of the capture of Mason and Slidell, two envoys sent by the Confederacy to England and France, to secure, among other things, recognition of Southern independence, was received with a frenzy of approbation. Captain Wilkes found himself the hero of the hour. . . . In England the seizure of Mason and Slidell still further enraged the enemies of the United States and dismayed its friends. Though the *Times* and other anti-American papers had seemed to have exhausted already their resources in lampooning their transatlantic kindred, they now burst out with a new fury of execration. Naturally the name of Seward loomed large in all this excitement. That Captain Wilkes had acted under his instructions, and that Seward's purpose was to start the war with England which he had long planned, seemed as clear as daylight. Seward's steady course of hostility to England in thirty years of public life, and the many unpleasant comments he had made on the British Empire and British "rapacity," were now brought forth as part explanation of the Mason-Slidell "outrage." . . . All over England rose an almost unanimous demand for war. The sentiment was general that only the most abject apology could save Uncle Sam from a trouncing at the hand of the British fleet. War preparations began in every British shipyard on a scale not known since the days of Napoleon. An army of twelve thousand men was assembled for immediate transport to Canada, and fortifications were thrown up in strategic places on the long undefended Canadian frontier. Under these circumstances—the roars of approval from the American population, the threat of annihilation from what was then regarded as America's most determined enemy—the likelihood that the question of the *Trent* could be settled on the basis of justice and the principles of law seemed slight.

The attitude of the seven cabinet members on the *Trent* issue thus figured large in the public mind. In some cases individual opinions were expressed with an emphasis that subsequently proved embarrassing. That roving pictorial historian Benson J. Lossing happened to be in the War Department on the morning when the news of the *Trent* "broke" in Washington. He has left a lively picture of Simon Cameron, Secretary of War, leading a large crowd of associates in three cheers for Captain Wilkes, one of the most enthusiastic of the group being Governor Andrew of Massachusetts. The usually placid and judicial Gideon Welles, Secretary of the Navy, indulged in extravagant praise that cost him in future years a vast amount of casuistry to explain away. . . . Chase, though, as always somewhat nebulous in his use of words, believed "that the circumstances under which the act of Captain Wilkes was done, not only repelled the imputation of aggressive or unfriendly intent, but entitled him to commendation for the motives by which his conduct was governed, and reduced the seizure and removal from the 'Trent' of the rebel commissioners to a mere technical violation of the neutral rights of England. . . . The capture was, of course, warranted, and Captain Wilkes, in making it, performed only his plain duty to his government." . . .

Only one member of the cabinet evidently believed, and so expressed himself, that the whole business was a mistake. Immediately on hearing the news Montgomery Blair declared that Wilkes had acted in violation of international law and that Mason and Slidell would have to be handed over to British custody. The proper course, he said, would be for Wilkes to take Mason and Slidell on the *Iroquois*, sail to England, and deliver them to the British government. Otherwise, resulting complications would fatally interfere with the attempt to put down rebellion. The elder Blair, at Silver Spring, fulminated against Seward, whom he mistakenly regarded as responsible for the crisis. Not only should

Mason and Slidell be restored to England, said old man Blair, but he suggested that "Billy Bowlegs"—he was now accustomed to refer to the Secretary of State in this unseemly fashion—should be added as a sacrificial offering on the altar of British revenge.

What was the real attitude of Seward and, an even more important matter, of his chief in the White House? According to Gideon Welles—the statement was made several years after the event—"no man was more elated or jubilant over the capture of the emissaries than Mr. Seward." This may have been true as a momentary impulse, but second sober thoughts soon gained control in Seward's mind, especially as he faced the practical issue involved—either to surrender the captives or to engage in war with England. Certainly his conduct in the six weeks of the *Trent* crisis—from November 8 to December 26—show the man at his best. . . .

It had been his lifetime habit to view problems in their practical, not their legalistic or idealistic, aspect, and the theories advanced by many respectable sources as to the rights and wrongs of Captain Wilkes's performance interested him far less than what was likely to be the definite outcome. His once cherished plan for a European war as a means of bringing North and South together no longer represented his ideal of statesmanship. "You will perhaps be surprised," wrote Lord Lyons to Lord John on December 23, while the negotiation was still pending, "to find Mr. Seward on the side of peace. He does not like the look of the spirit he has called up. Ten months in office have dispelled many of his illusions. I presume that he no longer believes in the existence of a Union party in the South; in the return of the South to the arms of the North in case of a foreign war; in his power to frighten the nations of Europe by great words; in the ease with which the U. S. could crush rebellion with one hand and chastise Europe with the other; with the notion that the relations with England in particular are safe playthings to be used for the amusement of the American people. He sees himself in a very painful dilemma. But he knows his countrymen well enough to believe that if he can convince them that there is a real danger of war, they may forgive him for the humiliation of yielding to England, while it would be fatal to him to be the author of a disastrous foreign war. How he will act eventually I cannot say. . . ."

Lincoln's position is more obscure. The conventional version shows the President as the dominant mind in the *Trent* excitement, as the cool statesman who at once perceived the realities of the situation and who compelled Seward to modify his attitude and find good reasons for giving up the captives. The known facts do not substantiate this view. Several witnesses, it is true, have recorded glimpses of Lincoln in the crisis that lend color to the legend. One of them, Benson J. Lossing, tells of meeting Lincoln on the day when the *Trent* news reached the Capital, and he portrays the President as the one man who seemed to be keeping his poise when the rest of the government had fallen victim to the prevailing madness. "I fear," he quotes Lincoln as saying, "the traitors will prove to be white elephants. We must stick to American principles concerning the rights of neutrals. We fought Great Britain for insisting, by theory and practice, on the right to do precisely what Wilkes has done. If Great Britain shall now protest against the act, and demand their release, we must give them up, apologize for the act as a violation of our doctrines and thus forever bind her over to keep the peace in relation to neutrals and so acknowledge that she has been wrong for sixty years." Gideon Welles quotes Lincoln as using this same phrase, "white elephants," in reference to the Southern gentlemen then languishing in Fort Warren, Boston Harbor (to which they had been removed), and Nicolay and Hay insist that he saw the issue correctly from the first. There are indications, however, that the idea of backing down before British threats rankled in Lincoln's breast, and that he was anxious to find some other solution. Charles Sumner proved to be a wholesome influence at this time. As chairman of the Senate Committee on Foreign Relations, Sumner had considerable claims to Lincoln's confidence, and spent a part of nearly every day with him discussing the *Trent* question. Sumner saw clearly the issues involved. From the first he was for a peaceful settlement, not only because England had justice on its side, but because he knew that a military conflict would sink his country in disaster. . . .

Though Lincoln gladly listened to Sumner, he was, as always, moving slowly, taking advice from all worth-while sources, but not committing himself. In his message, sent to Congress on December 1, the *Trent* affair was not even mentioned, greatly to the disgust of British statesmen. Sumner, like Lincoln, was seeking a way out that would not mean abject surrender, and the two men gave much consideration to arbitration. Sumner was willing to go to any extreme to avert war, but the President at first hesitated at complete acquiescence in the British viewpoint. That influences other than Seward and Blair and Sumner were working to smooth the way to American acceptance of British terms was not known then, but is known today. When Seward obtained his first view of Lord John's note, demanding the surrender of Mason and Slidell, the agreeable tone in which the message was framed gave him a pleasant surprise. Seward "told me that he was pleased to find that the despatch was courteous and friendly and not dictatorial or menacing," Lord Lyons wrote the Minister of Foreign Affairs. Had Russell's original paper been handed to the Secretary of State his satisfaction would not have been so pronounced. That the Queen and the Prince Consort had edited this curt ultimatum—for in its orginal form it was little less—cutting out the harsh phrases and writing in more polite ones, leaving the general implications the same yet transforming it into something that a proud nation could accept without humiliation, did not become known until long after the *Trent* had become part of history.

When the cabinet came together on Christmas Day, 1861, only Seward and Blair had taken a stand in favor of the British contention. It required the better part of two days' discussion to obtain that unanimity of decision desirable in the solution of such a momentous problem. Not improbably this session was the most fateful held in the course of the Civil War. The real issue hanging in the balance was the future of the United States. A stark alternative confronted the council: refusal to accept the British demand meant that, in addition to subduing the South, American army and naval forces would be compelled to add the British Empire to its foes. In all probability the French Empire would have joined England in hostilities, as well, for Napoleon III had from the beginning supported the British and it was no secret that the dismemberment and paralyzing of American power was regarded in the Tuileries as essential to the success of French imperial schemes in Mexico. . . .

Lord John Russell's letter to Seward, polite as was the phraseology, admitted of nothing but a "yes" or "no" answer. It demanded the return of Mason and Slidell to British custody and an apology for the insult to the British flag. In private instructions to Lord Lyons, Russell had said that Britain would probably be "easy" about the apology, in consideration of American sensitiveness. Seward's statement that Captain Wilkes had acted without instructions naturally made such an apology superfluous; no nation could be reasonably expected to apologize for an offense it had not committed. After reading Russell's note, Seward laid before his colleagues the reply which, shut up all alone in his office, he had spent two days in preparing. It was a clever political paper, and one of the most characteristic ones that ever came from Seward's pen; it was written not primarily for the attention of Her Majesty's law lords but for the ears of the American public. It was not intended to be a document that would stand the closest analysis from the standpoint of international law, but one that would show the man in the street that he was not kow-towing to the British lion when he gave up his unpopular guests. Seward's main contention was that envoys on a neutral ship, carrying dispatches, were contraband of war and subject to seizure. Captain Wilkes therefore had been within his rights in firing a shot across the bow of the *Trent,* boarding that vessel, demanding her papers, and searching for forbidden matériel and personnel of war. Seward granted, however, that Wilkes had ex-ceeded his right when he forcibly removed the suspected envoys to an American ship. He should have seized not only the "con-traband" but the ship itself, taken it into the nearest American port, and handed it over to a prize court. That had always been the American practice, and Wilkes, in disregarding it, and in adopting instead the British custom of violently removing passen-gers from merchant vessels, had followed a procedure which his government could not support. That is, in surrendering the South-ern envoys, the United States was observing principles for which it had been contending for the best part of a century. "These principles were laid down for us in 1804, by James Madison, when Secretary of State in the administration of Thomas Jefferson, in instructions given to James Monroe, our Minister to England." How could America remain true to its own doctrines and sustain Wilkes when he had violated them? "The four persons," con-cluded Seward, "in question are now held in military custody at Fort Warren in the State of Massachusetts. They will be cheer-fully liberated. Your lordship will please indicate a time and place for receiving them."

Adroit as Seward had shown himself to be in finding a way out of this deadlock, his colleagues were slow to be convinced. . . . Though the cabinet discussed the matter from ten o'clock in the morning till two in the afternoon, no conclusion had been reached. It was therefore decided to adjourn and meet the following morning. After all the others had left the cabinet room, Lincoln and Seward found themselves alone. "You will go on, of course," Lincoln said to Seward, "preparing your answer, which, as I understand it, will state the reasons why they ought to be given up. Now I have a mind to try my hand at stating the reasons why they ought *not* to be given up. We will compare the points on each side." Lincoln did formulate such an argument and it is now preserved among his papers. In it he approached the plan of arbitration—in this doubtless showing the influence of Charles Sumner, who had been at his elbow for several weeks pressing this solution. When the cabinet reconvened the next morning, however, Lincoln did not present his thesis. All seven men now accepted Seward's answer. After the cabinet broke up, Lincoln and Seward again held a private session. Seward referred to their talk of the day before. "You thought you might frame an argument for the other side?" Lincoln smiled and shook his head. "I found that I could not make an argument that would satisfy my own mind," he said. "That proved to me that your ground was the right one."

The *Trent* episode made clear that Seward had other resources of diplomacy than menacing threats against the most powerful nations of Europe. Perhaps his skillful behavior when confronted with the contingency he had apparently so long hoped for sheds a new light upon the motives which had inspired these explosive moments. Seward's great responsibility, as Secretary of State, was to prevent the recognition of the Confederacy by Great Britain and France. Such recognition, he believed—and most students of the period agree with him—would have resulted in a Confederate triumph. There is little question that Great Britain would have extended this friendly welcome to Jefferson Davis, except for one thing. That was fear of war with the United States. To fight such a war successfully, England would have had to dispatch practically her entire fleet to American waters, and in the tense situation prevailing at that time in Europe, this was too dangerous a hazard to risk. Seward perceived this last from the outset, and his genius as a diplomat consists in the ability with which he utilized it as the one possible way of forestalling British intervention. From this point of view his denunciation of England at private dinner parties in the secession winter of 1860-1861, and his declaration of war in case the Palmerston government meddled in American concerns, assume a new importance. . . .

The bad reputation which Seward enjoyed in Europe in itself proved to be an invaluable asset. In England no American, possibly excepting Charles Summer, was so well known. Any American who wins fame as an enemy of the British Empire is more likely to acquire notoriety in England than one who achieves high place in literature, science, art, or even statesmanship. And Seward meant to British statesmen the pre-eminent American jingo. American destiny, in the conviction to which he frequently gave expression, was to become mistress of the entire North American Continent, from the Arctic to Panama. . . .

The correspondence of Lord Lyons, British Minister at Washington, indicates the apprehension which Seward's advent as Secretary of State caused in England. He could not help fearing, Lyons wrote Russell that "Mr. Seward will be a dangerous Foreign Minister," and his anxiety was confirmed when, at a formal dinner party at the British Legation on March 25, the new Secretary began to lay down the law to all the foreign representatives present—not only the British Minister, but the French, Russian, and other distinguished emissaries. "Mr. Seward," Lord Lyons wrote his chief, "went off into a defiance of foreign nations, in a style of braggadocio which was formerly not uncommon with him, but which I had not heard from him since he had been in office." At times the Secretary of State used more subtle methods of threat. Thus on April 8, 1861, he sent for William H. Russell, correspondent of the London *Times,* and amid huge clouds of tobacco smoke entertained his guest by confidentially reading a dispatch which he was about to send to Charles Francis Adams, recently arrived American Minister in London. Russell expressed his misgivings at the menacing attitude towards Great Britain which Mr. Adams was instructed to adopt. Naturally, Russell dutifully reported the details to the British Minister, as Seward knew he would; that was the reason he had taken him into his confidence. He could not directly lay his dispatch to Mr. Adams before the British envoy, but this roundabout method served the purpose just as effectively.

Mad as all this seems, there was method in it; the one idea which Seward was determined to implant in the minds of British and French statesmen was that the recognition of the Confederacy would spell war with the United States. . . . In August 1862, there were signs in plenty that Earl Russell, goaded by Gladstone, was contemplating this fatal step. McClellan's reverses in the Peninsula had persuaded that statesman of the utter hopelessness of the Union cause. Minister Adams was instructed, on August 16, that if Britain took any step that indicated an intention "to dictate, or to mediate, or even to solicit or persuade, you will answer that you are forbidden to debate, to hear, or in any way receive, entertain, or transmit, any communication of the kind." If the South were "acknowledged" Adams was "immediately to suspend his function." . . .

Whatever may have been the shortcomings of Seward as a diplomat, he had one virtue, whose value in that evasive profession has been recognized only in modern times. He spoke in the plainest of terms; his correspondence was, indeed, "shirt sleeves" diplomacy at its best. Mr. Judah P. Benjamin, [Secretary of State in the Confederate cabinet] . . . gives Seward praise for "penetrating into the secret feelings of the British cabinet" and foreseeing that this "policy of intimidation" would be successful. . . .

Palmerston himself succinctly, if colloquially, summed up British policy when a delegation of British clergymen, noblemen, Members of Parliament, and other distinguished gentlemen called upon him, in July 1864, to urge mediation. "They who in quarrels interpose, Will often wipe a bloody nose," he reminded his visitors—"a quotation which," commented the *Index*, the pro-Confederate weekly published in London, "in the mouth of the Prime Minister of the British Empire, and on such an occasion, must be admitted as not unworthy of Abraham Lincoln himself."

Of all Seward's threats, his masterpiece was delivered in 1863, when the so-called "rams," under construction by the Lairds of Liverpool as Confederate raiders, were nearing completion. The *Alabama*, secretly built by the same firm a year before, was wreaking vast destruction at that time on American merchant shipping. These new ships were much more powerful, and should they be permitted to "escape" from the Liverpool docks, in the manner of the *Alabama*, the American flag would have vanished from the seas. Charles Francis Adams, under instructions from Seward, had been bringing pressure for months on Lord John Russell, presenting unmistakable evidence that the ships were Confederate property and demanding their detention by the British government. Mr. Adams, in September 1862, presented his protest, concluding an eloquent state paper with the famous words that if the rams became part of the Confederate navy, "it would be superfluous in me to point out to your Lordship that this is war." This declaration, and the apparent British backdown in face of it, have become one of the legends of the Civil War. The fact is that Russell, five days before this menacing note was received, had ordered the seizure of the ships, had stationed British war vessels in Liverpool Harbor to prevent their escape— with orders to sink them, if the attempt were made—and, soon after, purchased them and made them part of the British Navy. It was not Adams's threat, but the more subtle maneuvering of Seward that had persuaded the British government to change its policy.

In July 1862, a bill was introduced in Congress authorizing the President to issue letters of marque and reprisal—that is, to commission "privateers"—as a kind of "militia of the sea" to prey upon enemy commerce, just as Confederate "corsairs" were attacking Federal ships. There was only one defect in this otherwise desirable measure: the South had no merchant marine, and therefore there were no Southern ships to attack. Because of this absurdity, the bill was pigeonholed by both House and Senate, and lay unnoticed and unacted upon in committee until February 1863. Then Congress, prompted by Seward, took up the measure and quickly passed it, with little debate. When Charles Sumner, in the Senate, objected to the bill as senseless, since the South had no mercantile marine, Senator Grimes, who had the measure in charge, replied that that was true, but added that the administration desired the legislation to use "if need arose" and hinted that privateers might be useful against British ships that had "turned Confederate." While there was much puzzlement in the United States, and while Seward, in his statements to Lord Lyons and his instructions to Adams, was rather vague, in one quarter no doubt prevailed as to the value of the measure at this critical moment. British shipping interests quickly grasped its meaning. So did Palmerston and Russell. . . . A vast array of British merchant ships, during the Civil War, plied between home ports and the Confederacy, bringing munitions and other necessaries to the struggling South and transporting back most marketable cargoes of cotton, tobacco, and other Southern products. They had to take the chance of seizure, of course, but blockade running, despite many captures, proved to be a most profitable risk. A cordon of privateers placed out at sea, so numerous that few vessels could escape, would be a different matter. According to American law—for the United States was not a party to the Declaration of London, outlawing such procedures—enemy property in neutral ships was legally subject to attack and confiscation. That such a "flood of privateers" operating against British ships would incite war was evident. In a word, the privateering bill was Seward's reply to the construction of Confederate commerce destroyers in British shipyards.

The American war was fought in Europe with speeches and resolutions, at hurried cabinet meetings, private interviews and mass meetings, secret intrigues, sermons and lectures, with books and pamphlets and plays, and by means of the devious financial transactions and the profitable schemes of businessmen. The financial war was waged with a mounting tempo. British shipbuilding interests, championed by the politician William Schaw Lindsay, were responsible for several attempts in Parliament to force through recognition of the Confederacy. Lindsay, too, negotiated privately with Napoleon III of France for joint action. In the meantime, Slidell, the Confederate representative in Paris and the German banker, Erlanger, launched a huge bond issue backed by promises of Southern cotton to be delivered after the war. The proceeds were to be used for warships which France would build for the South. To counter such transactions, Lincoln sent over the financier, Robert J. Walker, and a merchant prince, William H. Aspinwall. Walker scattered leaflets over England from a balloon and dazzled London with his carriage drawn by six white horses.

Europe, in fact, swarmed with agents of both sides, official and unofficial. Those suave Northern diplomats, John Bigelow in Paris and Charles Francis Adams in London, kept close watch on the Confederate commissioners, Mason and Slidell, while doing their best to nullify the clever journalistic outpourings of the

*Southern propagandists, Hotze and DeLeon. To charm important
people Thurlow Weed was sent to Europe; old General Scott,
no diplomat, came too, blundered, and had to be extricated by
Weed. Lecturers and writers toured the provinces; the famous
preacher, Henry Ward Beecher, drew thousands to his meetings.*

*And both sides tried to exploit the deep class divisions in Eng-
land. The aristocrats, the governing classes, the shipping interests
growing wealthy by blockade-running, sympathized with the
Southern oligarchy. They were mortally afraid that the infection
of Northern democracy might upset their cherished institutions.
The working classes and much of the middle class, although suffering from the economic hardships caused by the war, nevertheless continued to look to the American Union as an example of
democratic progress and freedom. And always the fortunes of
diplomats, financiers, propagandists, and lecturers swayed un-
certainly in response to victories or reverses in America.*

*A passage from Jay Monaghan's study of Lincoln's foreign
policy,* Diplomat in Carpet Slippers, *gives the flavor of the American war as it was fought out in England.*[3] *It was the pivotal year
1863, when the South's hopes for foreign intervention were finally
dashed.*

Propaganda for recognition of the South in Parliament assumed carnival proportions in June 1863. Day after day
barrel organs played Southern tunes in London streets. Ragged
children ran after the music, hoping to see the monkey. Scullions,
on their knees scrubbing brownstone steps, stopped their work,
brushed grimy locks of hair back from dirty faces and listened. . . .

Carefully written leaders appeared in the *Herald* and *Standard.*
First one paper, then the other, on alternate days, urged Parliament to adopt the proposed motion for recognition of the Confederacy. A large open-air meeting at Sheffield passed resolutions
requesting the government to act. Confederate sympathizers

chuckled over the rams and other ships being built in British yards. Pro-Southern meetings were held at Manchester, at Preston and elsewhere.

The great day came. On June 30, 1863, [Charles Francis] Adams sent his son and secretary, Henry, to the House of Commons to report the result. These crises had become almost seasonal, like London fogs. Henry sat down under the gallery at the left. Out beyond the gangway he could see the profiles of the government, sharp and stolid as the profiles on his father's coins —faces ruled by expediency. Popular will in Britain seemed to have shifted completely away from the North. . . .

Before long, John Arthur Roebuck, an anti-Whig reactionary, introduced the dread resolution. John Bright glowered at him across the gangway. Henry Adams wondered why the Southern bloc selected so weak a man. Gregory in 1861 and Lindsay in 1862 had both been more able men. Had the Emancipation Proclamation made the Confederacy so odious that no other champion could be found? Roebuck was old and fatuous. . . .

The debate, before it was finished, became extremely personal, revealing all the secret negotiations of Lindsay and company with Napoleon. The British government was accused by one side of disclosing the contents of a confidential dispatch from the Emperor to America. The other side denied that any such dispatch existed. Soon the rafters of the great hall were ringing with a pertinent discussion as to whether Napoleon or Roebuck was a liar. The Emperor, when he heard of it, was not pleased. The gap between England and France widened—this time for good. Joint recognition became impossible. Henry Hotze admitted that the Southern cause was done in England. Recognition in Parliament, he said, would "never again receive serious attention, even if a man could be found bold enough to broach it." Jeff Davis notified Mason to withdraw from London, his mission at an end. . . .

Parliament's refusal to pass Roebuck's resolution was followed by startling news from America. The invasion of the North had been checked at Gettysburg and General Grant had captured Vicksburg—two of the greatest victories of the Civil War. The Jovelike Lee had been stopped at last, and the Confederacy was split down the Mississippi. Payday had come for democracy.

The strain at the American legation in London eased immediately. Monckton Milnes, Lord Houghton, scorned a possible overthrow of the British government. At a party he rushed through the throng "with a whoop of triumph," threw his arms around Henry Adams and kissed him on both cheeks. Minister Adams felt that the victory made him equal to any situation— Russell or Palmerston or anyone. Confederate shipbuilding in general and the ironclad rams in particular would stop now or he would know the reason why.

The diplomatic war centered in England, for England had the closest ties with America. Yet England, of all the European nations, was most hostile to the North. Generally the others disliked slavery and feared the example of rebellion, although Germany, with landowners and army officers arrayed against strong middle class commercial interests and the urban proletariat was divided along lines very similar to those in the United States. Russia, in a liberal mood and intensely jealous of British supremacy, favored the North and sent a fleet to visit the Union.

Outside of England, France posed the most dangerous threat to the North. Wily Napoleon III intrigued with both sides and was trusted by neither. Proposing mediation early in 1863 (which, translated out of the French, would have meant recognition of the South's independence) he was sharply rebuffed by the North. He allowed Confederate warships to be built in French yards, but when Union fortunes improved he had them seized. Taking advantage of America's preoccupation with its war, Louis Napoleon occupied Mexico in June, 1863, just before Gettysburg. Again Seward showed himself a great foreign secretary—"many believe

*the greatest who ever headed the Department of State," as Hen-
drick has written.*⁴ *Seward held off against intense pressure to attack the French in Mexico, merely warning Napoleon that he
would be dealt with in good time. Finally in 1866, pressure from
the United States, backed up by an army along the border, easily
brought the Mexican adventure to an end. France withdrew,
leaving its puppet emperor, Maximilian, to his tragic fate at the
hands of a Mexican firing squad.*

*The naval blockade of the Confederacy, designed to keep des-
perately needed European supplies from reaching the South, was
ultimately a decisive factor. The Union had to be tender with the
blockade-running ships of British merchants who developed almost a monopoly of this highly profitable business. On the other
hand, Northern diplomats sought persistently to prevent the
cruisers built in British yards for Confederate use from going
into action. Thanks largely to the brilliant work of Confederate
Captain James D. Bulloch in England, the South was able to acquire eighteen commerce destroyers in all. Supplemented by perhaps a dozen privateers, these ships harassed Union shipping in all
the seas. The imagination of the public has been captured by
the exploits of the big raiders, especially by the world-wide dep-
redations of the* Alabama, *followed by its dramatic sinking by
the U. S.* Kearsarge *outside Cherbourg harbor while thousands of
sightseers watched as at a football match.*

*The Northern blockade, however, was far more significant in
the developing pattern of the war. The following summary comes
from an article by Horatio Wait, a Union Navy paymaster, originally published in* The Century Magazine *in 1898.*⁵

At the beginning of the war in 1861, a perplexing
question arose as to whether it would be best for the government
to declare all the Southern ports of entry to be closed, or to
proclaim a blockade. . . . The urgency of the case caused President
Lincoln to act promptly. On April 19, 1861, six days after the

surrender of Fort Sumter, he issued a proclamation declaring a blockade of the entire coast of the Confederacy, from South Carolina to Texas; and on April 27 extended it to cover Virginia and North Carolina, making a coast-line of over three thousand miles to be blockaded, greater in extent than the Atlantic coast of Europe—an undertaking without precedent in history. . . .

When Mr. Lincoln issued this proclamation we had only forty-two ships in commission in our navy. Most of them were absent on foreign stations, and only one efficient war-ship, the *Brooklyn*, was available for immediate service.

How was it possible to undertake such a blockade as this, along such a vast extent of coast, when so few ships of any kind were available, without its being open to the charge of being a mere paper blockade? In the early part of the century European powers had attempted to enforce paper blockades, but the same nations were now the first to make merry over the subject of our paper blockade. Some of the most prominent European statesmen publicly declared it a "material impossibility to enforce it." . . .

When the Secretary of the Navy asked the principal shipping merchants and shipowners of New York to aid him in procuring vessels for the blockade, it is related that their committees decided that thirty sailing-ships would be needed. As it took over six hundred ships, mostly steamers, to do the work, it is manifest that they had a very faint conception of what was to be done. There were twenty-eight old ships of war lying dismantled at the various navy-yards. Those that were worth repairing were fitted for sea as rapidly as possible. All the available merchant vessels that could be made to carry a battery, including tugs and old New York ferry-boats, were purchased and converted into fighting ships as hastily as the limited facilities of the Northern ports would permit. The scanty resources of the navy-yards were inadequate. All the private ship-yards were crowded with work. There were

not enough skilled workmen to meet this sudden demand, and
the naval officers found it necessary personally to direct the un-
skilled artisans, or to assist with their own hands in fitting these
nondescript vessels for the mounting and working of heavy guns.
As fast as the vessels could be purchased, altered, and equipped,
they were stationed along the coast or sent to sea. Many such
vessels, by the tact and skill of the officers in charge of them,
were made to do good service. One of the most important prizes
captured, the steamer *Circassian*, was taken near the harbor of
Havana by one of the old Fulton Ferry boats.

The lack of men was as great an embarrassment as the want of
vessels. Three hundred and twenty-two officers of the old navy
joined the insurgent forces, many of them having already distinguished themselves in service. One of these, Commander John M.
Brooke, rendered very important services to the Southerners by
converting the ten-inch columbiads captured by them into rifled
guns. They proved to be very effective pieces, and were said to
be the best converted guns ever made. He also aided in devising
the simplest and best of the many kinds of torpedoes and fuses
used by the Confederates, as well as in designing the ram *Merrimac*.

The total number of seamen at all the Northern naval stations
available for immediate detail amounted to only two hundred and
seven; and it must be remembered that it was as important that
they should be trained to handle heavy guns at sea as that they
should be good seamen. The true sailor will soon make himself
efficient on board any ship, as far as the handling of the vessel is
concerned; but in the effective use of the battery only the trained
man-o'-war's-man can safely be relied upon; and there are many
other minor matters, such as the division of duties, the exercise
at quarters and in boats, forming essential features of the system
on a man-o'-war, that are unknown outside the naval service.
Officers and men from the merchant service freely offered them-

selves. Gunnery schools were established at the naval stations for their instruction. As fast as the volunteers could be given an elementary training in the handling of heavy guns, they were sent to sea. This was continued for three years, by which time we had six hundred and fifty vessels and over fifty thousand men afloat.

The service to be performed by this hastily improvised force was as unique as the fleet itself. The entire outer coast-line of the Confederacy was 3549 miles in extent, with several large seaports. To guard the ordinary entrances to these ports was comparatively a simple task. There was, however, a greater difficulty to be met; for the outer coast-line is only the exterior edge of a series of islands between which and the mainland there is an elaborate network of navigable sounds and passages, having numerous inlets communicating with the sea. These inlets were frequently changing under the influence of the great storms; new channels would be opened and old ones filled up. As soon as we closed a port, by stationing vessels at the main entrance thereto, the blockade-runners would slip in at some of the numerous remote inlets, reaching their destination by the inside passages; so that blockade-running flourished until we were able to procure as many blockaders as there were channels and inlets to be guarded. The extreme diversity of the services required of these blockading vessels made it difficult to obtain ships that could meet the varying necessities. They must be heavy enough to contend with the enemy's rams, or they would be driven away from the principal ports. They must be light enough to chase and capture the swift blockade-runners. They must be deep enough in the water to ride out in safety the violent winter gales, and they must be of such light draft as to be able to go near enough to the shallow inlets to blockade them efficiently.

The blockading fleets of all the important harbors were composed of several very heavy ships, with a few vessels of the lighter class; the rest of the fleet represented some of the other classes needed. But it was impossible to do this along the entire coast, and it sometimes happened that the Confederate ironclads perversely attacked the lighter vessels, as in the case of the rams at Charleston selecting for their victims the *Mercedita* and the *Keystone State*, instead of the heavier ships; while, on the other hand, the swift blockade-runners disclosed themselves most frequently to the ponderous and slow-moving ships that were least able to catch them. . . .

Supplies were brought to the South from various sources, but principally from European ports. At the beginning of the war the blockade-running was carried on from Chesapeake Bay to the mouth of the Rio Grande, by vessels of all sorts, sizes, and nationalities. The steamers formerly engaged in the coasting-trade, that had been interrupted in their regular business by the war, were at first the most successful. The small sailing-vessels did well for some time before the blockade became vigorous; but as the number of our warships increased, the earlier groups of blockade-runners were either captured, destroyed, or drawn off. This diminished the volume of supplies to the Confederates just at the time when the demand was greatly increased by the emergencies of warfare, causing general distress and embarrassment in the Confederacy. Prices reached an unprecedented height. Cotton was as low as eight cents a pound in the Confederacy, as high as sixty cents a pound in England, and over one dollar a pound in New York. The moment this state of affairs became known, the science, ingenuity, and mechanical skill of the British seemed to be directed to the business of violating our blockade. Stock companies were formed, by whom the swiftest steamers in the European merchant service were quickly freighted with the supplies that would bring the highest prices in the Confederacy. Officers of rank in the royal navy, under assumed names; officers of the Confederate navy, who had but just resigned from the United

States navy; and adventurous spirits from all quarters, flocked
to this new and profitable, though hazardous, occupation. The
Confederate government also embarked in the business, procuring swift steamers from English builders, officered with Confederate naval officers, and sailing under the British ensign. They
also shipped merchandise in other vessels on government account. . . .

When the blockade-running was at its height, in 1863, a Confederate officer stated that the arrivals and departures were
equal to one steamer a day, taking all of the Confederate ports
together. Prior to this no such attempts had ever been made to
violate a blockade. The industrial necessities of the principal maritime nations stimulated them to unusual efforts, in return for
which they looked forward to a rich harvest. The British especially had abundant capital, the finest and swiftest ships ever
built, manned by the most energetic seamen. They felt confident
that they could monopolize the Southern cotton and the markets
of the Confederacy; but when it was found that neither swift
steamers, skilled officers, nor desperate efforts could give security
to their best investments of capital, and that the perils to their
beautiful vessels and precious cargoes increased as fast as their
efforts to surmount them, ultimately becoming even greater in
proportion than the enormous gains of the traffic when successful,
they were at last driven off from our coast entirely, and kept at
bay, though armed and supported by the greatest of foreign
powers. They finally gave up the business, admitting that the
blockade was a success. A Confederate officer stated that when
Fort Fisher fell their last port was gone, and blockade-running
was at an end.

*The blockade made European interference costly and danger-
ous. The Emancipation Proclamation of January, 1863, on the
other hand, furnished a decisive moral argument to those groups*

in Europe which supported the Northern side. Abhorrence of slavery was general throughout Europe; for a time, however, the British upper classes, sympathetic with the Southern oligarchy and profitably engaged in blockade-running and cruiser-building, seemed quite ready to ignore the underlying problem of slavery. Indeed, until Lincoln himself came to see Emancipation as a weapon against the South, even the middle and lower classes of England, always sympathetic with the North, had been confused by the Southern argument that the war was simply a struggle for power. The Emancipation Proclamation made it clearly a crusade against slavery and for freedom everywhere.

The new note was sounded in the famous letter from the workingmen of Manchester, England, which follows, with Lincoln's reply. It was a cry of hope from the very people who had been hardest hit by the war-induced cotton famine.[6]

December 31, 1862

To Abraham Lincoln, President of the United States:

As citizens of Manchester, assembled at the Free-Trade Hall, we beg to express our fraternal sentiments toward you and your country. We rejoice in your greatness as an outgrowth of England, whose blood and language you share, whose orderly and legal freedom you have applied to new circumstances, over a region immeasurably greater than our own. We honor your Free States, as a singularly happy abode for the working millions where industry is honored. One thing alone has, in the past, lessened our sympathy with your country and our confidence in it—we mean the ascendency of politicians who not merely maintained Negro slavery, but desired to extend and root it more firmly.

Since we have discerned, however, that the victory of the free North, in the war which has so sorely distressed us as well as afflicted you, will strike off the fetters of the slave, you have attracted our warm and earnest sympathy. We joyfully honor you, as the President, and the Congress with you, for many decisive steps toward practically exemplifying your belief in the words of your great founders: "All men are created free and equal." You have procured the liberation of the slaves in the district around Washington, and thereby made the centre of your Federation visibly free. You have enforced the laws against the slave-trade, and kept up your fleet against it, even while every ship was wanted for service in your terrible war. You have nobly decided to receive ambassadors from the Negro republics of Hayti and Liberia, thus forever renouncing that unworthy prejudice which refuses the rights of humanity to men and women on account of their color. In order more effectually to stop the slave-trade, you have made with our Queen a treaty, which your Senate has ratified, for the right of mutual search. Your Congress has decreed freedom as the law forever in the vast unoccupied or half unsettled Territories which are directly subject to its legislative power. It has offered pecuniary aid to all States which will enact emancipation locally, and has forbidden your Generals to restore fugitive slaves who seek their protection. You have entreated the slave-masters to accept these moderate offers; and after long and patient waiting, you, as Commander-in-Chief of the Army, have appointed to-morrow, the first of January, 1863, as the day of unconditional freedom for the slaves of the rebel states.

Heartily do we congratulate you and your country on this humane and righteous course. We assume that you cannot now stop short of a complete uprooting of slavery. It would not become us to dictate any details, but there are broad principles of humanity which must guide you. If complete emancipation in some States be deferred, though only to a predetermined day, still in the interval, human beings should not be counted chattels. Women must have the rights of chastity and maternity, men the rights of husbands, masters the liberty of manumission. Justice demands for the black, no less than for the white, the protection of law—that his voice be heard in your courts. Nor must any such abomination be tolerated as slave-breeding States, and a slave market—if you are to earn the high reward of all your sacrifices, in the approval of the universal brotherhood and of the Divine Father. It is for your free country to decide whether any thing but immediate and total emancipation can secure the most indispensable rights of humanity against the inveterate wickedness of local laws and local executives.

We implore you, for your own honor and welfare, not to faint in your providential mission. While your enthusiasm is aflame, and the tide of events runs high, let the work be finished effectually. Leave no root of bitterness to spring up and work fresh misery to your children. It is a mighty task, indeed, to reorganize the industry not only of four millions of the colored race, but of five millions of whites. Nevertheless, the vast progress you have made in the short space of twenty months fills us with hope that every stain on your freedom will shortly be removed, and that the erasure of that foul blot upon civilization and Christianity—chattel slavery—during your Presidency will cause the name of Abraham Lincoln to be honored and revered by posterity. We are certain that such a glorious consummation will cement Great Britain to the United States in close and enduring regards. Our interests, moreover, are identified with yours. We are truly one people, though locally separate. And if you have any ill-wishers here, be assured they are chiefly those who oppose liberty at home, and that they will be powerless to stir up quarrels between us, from the very day in which your country becomes, undeniably and without exception, the home of the free.

Accept our high admiration of your firmness in upholding the proclamation of freedom.

January 19, 1863.

To the Working-Men of Manchester:

I have the honor to acknowledge the receipt of the address and resolutions which you sent me on the eve of the new year. When I came, on the 4th of March, 1861, through a free and constitutional election to preside in the Government of the United States, the country was found at the verge of civil war. Whatever might have been the cause, or whosoever the fault, one duty, paramount to all others, was before me, namely, to maintain and preserve at once the Constitution and the integrity of the Federal Republic. A conscientious purpose to perform this duty is the key to all the measures of administration which have been and to all which will hereafter be pursued. Under our frame of government and my official oath, I could not depart from this purpose if I would. It is not always in the power of governments to enlarge or restrict the scope of moral results which follow the policies that they may deem it necessary for the public safety from time to time to adopt.

I have understood well that the duty of self-preservation rests solely with the American people; but I have at the same time been aware that favor or disfavor of foreign nations might have a material influence in enlarging or prolonging the struggle with disloyal men in which the country is engaged. A fair examination of history has served to authorize a belief that the past actions and influences of the United States were generally regarded as having been beneficial toward mankind. I have, therefore, reckoned upon the forbearance of nations. Circumstances—to some of which you kindly allude—induce me especially to expect that if justice and good faith should be practised by the United States, they would encounter no hostile influence on the part of Great Britain. It is now a pleasant duty to acknowledge the demonstration you have given of your desire that a spirit of amity and peace toward this country may prevail in the councils of your

Queen, who is respected and esteemed in your own country only more than she is by the kindred nation which has its home on this side of the Atlantic.

I know and deeply deplore the sufferings which the working-men at Manchester, and in all Europe, are called to endure in this crisis. It has been often and studiously represented that the attempt to overthrow this government, which was built upon the foundation of human rights, and to substitute for it one which should rest exclusively on the basis of human slavery, was likely to obtain the favor of Europe. Through the action of our disloyal citizens, the working-men of Europe have been subjected to severe trials, for the purpose of forcing their sanction to that attempt. Under the circumstances, I cannot but regard your decisive utterances upon the question as an instance of sublime Christian heroism which has not been surpassed in any age or in any country. It is indeed an energetic and reinspiring assurance of the inherent power of truth and of the ultimate and universal triumph of justice, humanity, and freedom. I do not doubt that the sentiments you have expressed will be sustained by your great nation; and on the other hand, I have no hesitation in assuring you that they will excite admiration, esteem, and the most reciprocal feelings of friendship among the American people. I hail this interchange of sentiment, therefore, as an augury that whatever else may happen, whatever misfortune may befall your country or my own, the peace and friendship which now exist between the two nations will be, as it shall be my desire to make them, perpetual.

ABRAHAM LINCOLN

8.

A New Birth of Freedom

Secretary Chase's diary contains the following entry:[1]

Monday, Sept. 22, 1862.

To Department about nine. State Department messenger came, with notice to Heads of Departments to meet at 12. Received sundry callers. Went to White House.

All members of the Cabinet were in attendance. There was some general talk; and the President mentioned that Artemus Ward had sent him his book. Proposed to read a chapter which he thought very funny. Read it, and seemed to enjoy it very much—the Heads also (except Stanton) of course. The Chapter was "Highhanded Outrage at Utica."

The President then took a graver tone and said:—

"Gentlemen: I have, as you are aware, thought a great deal about the relation of this war to Slavery; and you all remember that, several weeks ago, I read to you an Order I had prepared on this subject, which, on account of objections made by some of you, was not issued. Ever since then, my mind has been much occupied with this subject, and I have thought all along that the

time for acting on it might very probably come. I think the time
has come now. I wish it were a better time. I wish that we were
in a better condition. The action of the army against the rebels
has not been quite what I should have best liked. But they have
been driven out of Maryland, and Pennsylvania is no longer in
danger of invasion. When the rebel army was at Frederick, I
determined, as soon as it should be driven out of Maryland, to
issue a Proclamation of Emancipation such as I thought most
likely to be useful. I said nothing to any one; but I made the
promise to myself, and (hesitating a little)—to my Maker. The
rebel army is now driven out, and I am going to fulfil that
promise. I have got you together to hear what I have written
down. I do not wish your advice about the main matter—for
that I have determined for myself. This I say without intending
anything but respect for any one of you. But I already know the
views of each on this question. They have been heretofore expressed, and I have considered them as thoroughly and carefully
as I can. What I have written is that which my reflections have
determined me to say. If there is anything in the expressions I
use, or in any other minor matter, which any one of you thinks
had best be changed, I shall be glad to receive the suggestions.
One other observation I will make. I know very well that many
others might, in this matter, as in others, do better than I can;
and if I were satisfied that the public confidence was more fully
possessed by any one of them than by me, and knew of any
Constitutional way in which he could be put in my place, he
should have it. I would gladly yield it to him. But though I believe that I have not so much of the confidence of the people as
I had some time since, I do not know that, all things considered,
any other person has more; and, however this may be, there is
no way in which I can have any other man put where I am. I
am here. I must do the best I can, and bear the responsibility of
taking the course which I feel I ought to take."

The President then proceeded to read his Emancipation Proclamation, making remarks on the several parts as he went on, and showing that he had fully considered the whole subject, in all the lights under which it had been presented to him. . . .

The next morning the newspapers carried Lincoln's warning that on January 1, 1863, all slaves in any state still in rebellion would be declared free. The news was received with rejoicing and that evening Lincoln was greeted with a serenade. In his diary, John Hay describes the jubilation of Secretary Chase and his friends.[2]

At Governor Chase's there was some talking after the serenade. Chase and Clay made speeches and the crowd was in a glorious humor. After the crowd went away to force Mr. Bates to say something, a few old fogies staid at the Governor's and drank wine. Chase spoke earnestly of the Proclamation. He said, "This was a most wonderful history of an insanity of a class that the world had ever seen. If the slaveholders had staid in the Union they might have kept the life in their institution for many years to come. That what no party and no public feeling in the North could ever have hoped to touch they had madly placed in the very path of destruction." They all seemed to feel a sort of new and exhilarated life; they breathed freer; the Prest[s] Proc[n] had freed them as well as the slaves. They gleefully and merrily called each other and themselves abolitionists, and seemed to enjoy the novel sensation of appropriating that horrible name.

Although Chase might rejoice, since he had been for many years a leader of the antislavery forces, the Preliminary Emancipation Proclamation was coldly received in the North. It was, of course, far too mild for the radical Republicans and the abolitionists; whereas the Democrats felt betrayed. In their eyes the war for the Union had been turned overnight into a crusade to liberate the black man. Resentment helped to turn the fall elections of 1862 disastrously against the Republicans.

All the signs seemed to indicate that Lincoln had made a mistake in announcing his change of policy when he did, and the President himself seemed unhappy with his work. Just before the Preliminary Proclamation appeared, he gave this curiously uneasy interview to a pro-emancipation delegation from Chicago.[3]

What good would a proclamation of emancipation from me do, especially as we are now situated? I do not want to issue a document that the whole world will see must necessarily be inoperative, like the Pope's bull against the comet. Would my word free the slaves, when I cannot even enforce the Constitution in the rebel States? Is there a single court, or magistrate, or individual that would be influenced by it there? And what reason is there to think it would have any greater effect upon the slaves than the late law of Congress, which I approved, and which offers protection and freedom to the slaves of rebel masters who come within our lines? Yet I cannot learn that that law has caused a single slave to come over to us. . . .

Now, then, tell me, if you please, what possible result of good would follow the issuing of such a proclamation as you desire? Understand, I raise no objections against it on legal or constitutional grounds; for, as commander-in-chief of the army and navy, in time of war I suppose I have a right to take any measure which may best subdue the enemy; nor do I urge objections of a moral nature, in view of possible consequences of insurrection and massacre at the South. I view this matter as a practical war measure, to be decided on according to the advantages or disadvantages it may offer to the suppression of the rebellion. . . .

I will also concede that emancipation would help us in Europe, and convince them that we are incited by something more than ambition. I grant, further, that it would help somewhat at the North, though not so much, I fear, as you and those you represent imagine. Still, some additional strength would be added in that way to the war, and then, unquestionably, it would weaken the rebels by drawing off their laborers, which is of great importance; but I am not so sure we could do much with the blacks. . . . I will mention another thing, though it meet only your scorn and contempt. There are fifty thousand bayonets in the Union armies from the border slave States. It would be a serious matter if, in consequence of a proclamation such as you desire, they should go over to the rebels. I do not think they all would—not so many to-day as yesterday. Every day increases their Union feeling. They are also getting their pride enlisted, and want to beat the rebels. Let me say one thing more: I think you should admit that we already have an important principle to rally and unite the people, in the fact that constitutional government is at stake. This is a fundamental idea going down about as deep as anything.

The final Emancipation Proclamation had almost no immediate effect upon the institution of slavery. It looked indeed as if Lincoln had issued a document which "must necessarily be inoperative, like the Pope's bull against the comet." Richard Hofstadter sums it up.[4]

The Emancipation Proclamation of January 1, 1863 had all the moral grandeur of a bill of lading. It contained no indictment of slavery, but simply based emancipation on "military necessity." It expressly omitted the loyal slave states from its terms. Finally, it did not in fact free any slaves. For it excluded by detailed enumeration from the sphere covered in the

Proclamation all the counties in Virginia and parishes in Louisiana that were occupied by Union troops and into which the government actually had the power to bring freedom. It simply declared free all slaves in "the States and parts of States" where the people were in rebellion—that is to say, precisely where its effect could not reach. Beyond its propaganda value the Proclamation added nothing to what Congress had already done in the Confiscation Act.

Seward remarked of the Proclamation: "We show our sympathy with slavery by emancipating the slaves where we cannot reach them and holding them in bondage where we can set them free." The London *Spectator* gibed: "The principle is not that a human being cannot justly own another, but that he cannot own him unless he is loyal to the United States."

Yet everybody knows that Lincoln, the "Great Emancipator," won undying glory throughout the world by "freeing the slaves." The paradox lies in confusing the cumulative, final impact of the Proclamation with the limited, immediate purpose for which it was designed. Although Lincoln's judgment as well as his timing were in the long run fully vindicated, it is perhaps easier to understand the Proclamation in the terms in which Lincoln himself presented it—as a war measure, issued on the narrow grounds of military necessity, and designed to hurt the enemy both at home and abroad. Today we would call such a maneuver "psychological warfare," just as we would refer to Lincoln's reconstruction policies for the South as "postwar planning."

The unifying theme in all of Lincoln's planning was his insistence that the war must be fought primarily to save the Union. As his remarks to the Chicago delegation indicate, he never really abandoned this conviction, and it formed the basis for his policies both in emancipation and in reconstruction. In 1861, near the beginning of hostilities, he told Hay: "I consider the central idea pervading this struggle is the necessity that is upon us, of proving that popular government is not an absurdity. We must settle this question now, whether the minority have the right to break up the government whenever they choose."⁵ But when he felt it had become expedient (a word he often used) to add the dynamic element of emancipation to this basic purpose, he did not hesitate to do so. "If I could save the Union without freeing any slave I would do it, and if I could save it by freeing all the slaves, I would do it; and if I could save it by freeing some and leaving others alone I would also do that."⁶ When he wrote these words to Horace Greeley in the summer of 1862 he had already made up his mind to issue the Proclamation at the first favorable opportunity.

Lincoln was certainly not insensitive, on the other hand, to the humanitarian and idealistic overtones of his Emancipation Proclamation, and he deserves the fame it brought him. The fact is that Lincoln's stubbornly moderate attitude toward slavery had changed little between the time of his first forays into politics in 1836 and the publishing of the Proclamation in 1863. He had always preached the containment of slavery rather than its abolition. After the renewal of the slavery controversy in 1854, he added to his views a strong note of moral condemnation which brought him into public prominence. In 1855 he wrote to his old friend, Joshua F. Speed.⁷

In 1841 you and I had together a tedious low-water trip, on a Steam Boat from Louisville to St. Louis. You may remember, as I well do, that from Louisville to the mouth of the Ohio, there were, on board, ten or a dozen slaves, shackled together with irons. That sight was a continued torment to me; and I see something like it every time I touch the Ohio, or any other slave-border. It is hardly fair for you to assume that I have no interest in a thing which has, and continually exercises, the power of making me miserable. You ought rather to appreciate how much the great body of the Northern people do crucify their feelings, in order to maintain their loyalty to the Constitution and the Union.

I do oppose the extension of slavery, because my judgment and feelings so prompt me; and I am under no obligation to the contrary. If for this you and I must differ, differ we must. . . .

I am not a Know-Nothing. That is certain. How could I be? How can any one who abhors the oppression of Negroes, be in favor of degrading classes of white people? Our progress in degeneracy appears to me to be pretty rapid. As a nation, we began by declaring that "*all men are created equal.*" We now practically read it "all men are created equal, *except Negroes.*" When the Know-Nothings get control, it will read "all men are created equal, except Negroes, *and foreigners, and Catholics.*" When it comes to this I should prefer emigrating to some country where they make no pretence of loving liberty—to Russia, for instance, where despotism can be taken pure, and without the base alloy of hypocrisy.

In the passage below on Lincoln's prewar attitude toward slavery, Richard Hofstadter, possibly by way of reaction against more conventional views, somewhat minimizes Lincoln's genuine moral repugnance toward the institution.[8]

      His later career as an opponent of slavery extension must be interpreted in the light of his earlier public indifference to the question. Always moderately hostile to the South's "peculiar institution," he quieted himself with the comfortable thought that it was destined very gradually to disappear. Only after the

Kansas-Nebraska Act breathed political life into the slavery issue did he attack it openly. His attitude was based on justice tempered by expediency—or perhaps more accurately, expediency tempered by justice.

Lincoln was by birth a Southerner, a Kentuckian; both his parents were Virginians. His father had served on the slave patrol of Hardin County. The Lincoln family was one of thousands that in the early decades of the nineteenth century had moved from the Southern states, particularly Virginia, Kentucky, and Tennessee, into the Valley of Democracy, and peopled the southern parts of Ohio, Indiana, and Illinois.

During his boyhood days in Indiana and Illinois Lincoln lived in communities where slaves were rare or unknown, and the problem was not thrust upon him. The prevailing attitude toward Negroes in Illinois was intensely hostile. Severe laws against free Negroes and runaway slaves were in force when Lincoln went to the Springfield legislature, and there is no evidence of any popular movement to liberalize them. Lincoln's experiences with slavery on his journeys to New Orleans in 1828 and 1831 do not seem to have made an impression vivid enough to change his conduct. Always privately compassionate, in his public career and his legal practice he never made himself the advocate of unpopular reform movements. . . .

When Lincoln returned to active politics the slavery issue had come to occupy the central position on the American scene. Stephen Douglas and some of his colleagues in Congress had secured the passage of the Kansas-Nebraska Act, which, by opening some new territory, formally at least, to slavery, repealed the part of the thirty-four-year-old Missouri Compromise that barred slavery from territory north of 36° 30'. The measure provoked a howl of opposition in the North and split Douglas's party. The Republican Party, built on opposition to the extension of slavery, began to emerge in small communities in the Northwest. Lincoln's ambitions and interests were aroused, and he proceeded to rehabilitate his political fortunes.

His strategy was simple and forceful. He carefully avoided issues like the tariff, internal improvements, the Know-Nothing mania, or prohibitionism, each of which would alienate important groups of voters. He took pains in all his speeches to stress that he was not an abolitionist and at the same time to stand on the sole program of opposing the extension of slavery. On October 4, 1854, at the age of forty-five, Lincoln *for the first time in his life* denounced slavery in public. In his speech delivered in the Hall of Representatives at Springfield (and later repeated at Peoria) he declared that he hated the current zeal for the spread of slavery: "I hate it because of the monstrous injustice of slavery itself." He went on to say that he had no prejudice against the people of the South. He appreciated their argument that it would be difficult to get rid of the institution "in any satisfactory way." "I surely will not blame them for not doing what I should not know how to do myself. If all earthly power were given me, I should not know what to do as to the existing institution. My first impulse would be to free all the slaves and send them to Liberia, to their own native land." . . .

And yet nothing could justify an attempt to carry slavery into territories now free, Lincoln emphasized. For slavery is unquestionably wrong. "The great mass of mankind," he said at Peoria, "consider slavery a great moral wrong. [This feeling] lies at the very foundation of their sense of justice, and it cannot be trifled with. . . . No statesman can safely disregard it." The last sentence was the key to Lincoln's growing radicalism. As a practical politician he was naturally very much concerned about those public sentiments which no statesman can safely disregard. . . .

He had now struck the core of the Republican problem in the Northwest: how to find a formula to reconcile the two opposing points of view held by great numbers of white people in the North. Lincoln's success in 1860 was due in no small part to his ability to bridge the gap, a performance that entitles him to a place among the world's great political propagandists.

To comprehend Lincoln's strategy we must keep one salient fact in mind: the abolitionists and their humanitarian sympathizers in the nation at large and particularly in the Northwest, the seat of Lincoln's strength, although numerous enough to hold the balance of power, were far too few to make a successful political party. Most of the white people of the Northwest, moreover, were in fact not only not abolitionists, but actually— and here is the core of the matter—Negrophobes. They feared and detested the very thought of living side by side with large numbers of Negroes in their own states, to say nothing of competing with their labor. Hence the severe laws against free Negroes, for example, in Lincoln's Illinois. . . .

If the Republicans were to succeed in the strategic Northwest, how were they to win the support of both Negrophobes and antislavery men? Merely to insist that slavery was an evil would sound like abolitionism and offend the Negrophobes. Yet pitching their opposition to slavery extension on too low a moral level might lose the valued support of the humanitarians. Lincoln, perhaps borrowing from the old free-soil ideology, had the right formula and exploited it. He first hinted at it in the Peoria speech:

The whole nation is interested that the best use shall be made of these Territories. *We want them for homes of free white people. This they cannot be, to any considerable extent, if slavery shall be planted within them.* Slave States are places for poor white people to remove from, not to remove to. New free States are the places for poor people to go to, and better their condition. For this use the nation needs these Territories.

Here was the answer to the Republican problem. Negrophobes and abolitionists alike could understand this threat; if freedom should be broken down they might themselves have to compete with the labor of slaves in the then free states—or might even be reduced to bondage along with the blacks! Here was an argument that could strike a responsive chord in the nervous system of every Northern man, farmer or worker, abolitionist or racist: *if a stop was not put somewhere upon the spread of slavery, the institution would become nation-wide.* Here, too, is the practical significance of the repeated statements Lincoln made in favor of labor at this time. Lincoln took the slavery question out of the realm of moral and legal dispute and, by dramatizing it in terms of free labor's self-interest, gave it a universal appeal. . . .

The importance of this argument becomes increasingly clear when it is realized that Lincoln used it in every one of his recorded speeches from 1854 until he became the President-elect. He once declared in Kansas that preventing slavery from becoming a nation-wide institution "is *the purpose* of this organization [the Republican Party]." The argument had a great allure too for the immigrants who were moving in such great numbers into the Northwest. . . .

During the debates with Douglas, Lincoln dwelt on the theme again and again, and added the charge that Douglas himself was involved in a Democratic "conspiracy . . . for the sole purpose of nationalizing slavery." Douglas and the Supreme Court (which a year before had handed down the Dred Scott decision) would soon have the American people "working in the traces that tend to make this one universal slave nation." . . . So also the theme of the "House Divided" speech:

I do not expect the Union to be dissolved—I do not expect the House to fall—but I do expect it to cease to be divided. It will become all one thing or all the other. Either the opponents of slavery will arrest the further spread of it, and place it where the public mind shall rest in the belief that it is in the course of ultimate extinction; or its advocates will push it forward, till it shall become alike lawful in all the States, old as well as new, North as well as South.

Have we no tendency to the latter condition?

The last sentence is invariably omitted when this passage is quoted; perhaps from a literary standpoint it is anticlimactic. But in Lincoln's mind—and, one may guess, in the minds of those who heard him—it was not anticlimactic, but essential. Lincoln was *not* emphasizing the necessity for abolition of slavery in the near future; he was emphasizing the immediate "danger" that slavery would become a nation-wide American institution if its geographical spread were not severely restricted at once.

Once this "House Divided" speech had been made, Lincoln had to spend a great deal of time explaining it, proving that he was not an abolitionist. These efforts, together with his strategy of appealing to abolitionists and Negrophobes at once, involved him in embarrassing contradictions. In northern Illinois he spoke in one vein before abolition-minded audiences, but farther south, where settlers of Southern extraction were dominant, he spoke in another. It is instructive to compare what he said about the Negro in Chicago with what he said in Charleston.

Chicago, July 10, 1858:

Let us discard all this quibbling about this man and the other man, this race and that race and the other race being inferior, and therefore they must be placed in an inferior position. Let us discard all these things, and unite as one people throughout this land, until we shall once more stand up declaring that all men are created equal.

Charleston, September 18, 1858:

I will say, then, that I am not, nor ever have been in favor of bringing about in any way the social and political equality of the white and black races [applause]: that I am not, nor ever have been, in favor of making voters or jurors of negroes, nor of qualifying them to hold office, nor to inter-marry with white people. . . .

And inasmuch as they cannot so live, while they do re-main together there must be the position of superior and inferior, and I as much as any other man am in favor of having the superior position assigned to the white race.

It is not easy to decide whether the true Lincoln is the one who spoke in Chicago or the one who spoke in Charleston. Pos-sibly the man devoutly believed each of the utterances at the time he delivered it; possibly his mind too was a house divided against itself. In any case it is easy to see in all this the behavior of a professional politician looking for votes.

As Hofstadter notes, Lincoln's Southern background cannot be ignored in evaluating his attitude toward slavery. A minority of informed men and women in the South realized that slavery was doomed. As Allan Nevins says, they fought for the right to deal with it, and the related problem of race adjustment, "on their own time and on their own terms."⁹ One thinks of that valiant southern woman, Mrs. Chesnut, who wrote in her diary, "I say we are no better than our judges in the North, and no worse. We are human beings of the nineteenth century and slav-ery has to go, of course. . . . The slave owners, when they are good men and women, are the martyrs. I hate slavery."¹⁰ This is almost a paraphrase of Lincoln's attitude toward slavery. It was the attitude of those to whom slavery had been a living presence rather than an abstract question of morality, an entrenched institution which could not simply be wished out of existence. James G. Randall, in Lincoln and the South, *elaborates on the theme of Lincoln's Southern antecedents.*[11]

But Lincoln left Kentucky at the age of seven and never after that was his home in a Southern state. What of those later years, which were nearly his whole life? The answer is that as a boy and growing youth in the woods of southern Indiana, as a young man in New Salem, Illinois, and as a mature man in the fuller years, Lincoln was still immersed in Southern influences. The dispersion of Southern human types, mores, and thought patterns, throughout the West and Northwest was a notable thing; Lincoln was precisely a part of that transit of culture by which Southern characteristics took hold in Northern states. . . .

It was so also in Illinois, which kept many of the characteristics of a slave state at least as late as 1840, and which, from Springfield south to picturesque Shawneetown and Cairo, presented in marked degree those human aspects, cultural types, and mannerisms that characterized Dixie. . . .

All three of Lincoln's Springfield law partners—John Todd Stuart, Stephen T. Logan, and William H. Herndon—were born in Kentucky. In the case of Stuart and Logan, their backgrounds, eminently typical of pioneer Kentucky, were on the more favored social level. . . .

Though Abraham Lincoln is often thought of as a backwoods character, partly because of overemphasis on his sobriquet of "railsplitter," yet when he was only thirty-four years old and not yet widely prominent, he was actually regarded as "the candidate of pride, wealth, and aristocratic family distinction." . . .

This more favored family connection brings us to the subject of Lincoln's marriage to a Southerner and what it meant in his life and achievement. . . .

Mary Todd's early background included the richness and beauty of life found in a prominent family of the Old South: stately home in Lexington, Kentucky (now fallen into decay and degradation), fine family carriage with liveried coachman, beloved house servants, beautiful clothes, extensive hospitality, picturesque and spacious living. The Todds were a proud Kentucky family and there was reason for their pride even if there is point to the tradition of Lincoln's once saying that, while one *d* was enough to spell God, it took two *d's* for Todd! . . .

Lexington exhibited varying phases of slavery. In one corner of the public square stood the slave auction block, in another corner the whipping post. Frequent gangs of slaves were taken through the town on their way to slave markets in the deep South. From the home of Mrs. Lincoln's grandmother, Mrs. Parker, one could see the slave jail of a Negro dealer, with dismal slavepens in its yard. Records show that a hundred and fifty slaves went on the auction block within the probable dates of Lincoln's visit in 1849.

Mary Todd knew all the aspects of slavery from what she had witnessed and from the political discussion she had heard in the Todd home. Emilie Todd Helm, her sister, is authority for the statement that Lincoln discussed all important topics with his wife. Mary Lincoln's approach was that of the governing class of the South. From his wife through the years in Springfield and from his visits to her old home in Kentucky, Lincoln had unique opportunity, not only as to slavery but in other matters, to know and understand the mind of "the people on the other side of the line."

One could even speak of Lincoln's political views as Southern. Coming from Kentucky and southern Indiana he could be correctly described in his Illinois period, at least down to the late forties, as a Clay Whig, which meant that he was at one with the large and influential brotherhood of Southern Whigs. . . .

In becoming a Republican Lincoln forfeited that political harmony between North and South which was natural and obvious so long as there was a Whig party to which he could belong. Yet in the troubled fifties when parties were changing and signs of conflict growing, Lincoln still looked South in wistfulness for the old Whig days. If ever a man's reorientation was painful it was so in Lincoln's case. . . .

Lincoln was, of course, conservative in his dislike of the "radicals" of his day; but these radicals were themselves reactionaries, so that Lincoln's opposition to them must be counted for liberalism. He understood the meaning of democracy only in the liberal sense. We may truly call it the Southern liberal sense: it would have been acceptable to a Willie Jones, a John Taylor of Caroline, a George Mason, or a Thomas Jefferson. . . .

In earliest life, in years of growth, in love and friendship, in the family circle, in the tough substance of democratic thought, Lincoln's mind and character were molded by Southern influences. In wistfulness for other days when sectionalism was raging, in the midst of tragic strife as at Gettysburg where he uttered not a syllable of hatred, Lincoln gave evidence of Southern understanding. In his closeness to border-state opinion, in his design for freedom, in incidents of presidential helpfulness to friends on the other side, and at the last in his pattern for peace without vindictiveness, Lincoln kept his sympathy for the people of the South.

When some Unionists from East Tennessee visited Lincoln in 1863, John Hay noted: "They talked in a very friendly way with the President; I never saw him more at ease than he is with those first rate patriots of the border. He is of them really."[12] *Since most of the border was slave territory, it presented an additional reason for Lincoln's reluctance to embark on a policy of emancipation before he had bound the border states firmly to the Union. James G. Randall turns next to the problem of the border states.*[13]

As to Lincoln's attitude toward this huge border region, one finds a paradox: Lincoln understood the border people, but they did not understand Lincoln. In his office of President, Lincoln had to reckon with the border. He had to take it into his every calculation. Yet it was a region in which he had but the weakest support. Lincoln could not expect the border people to favor his party or be attached to his administration. There was no chance of that. He had therefore to assume that people in this region would make a distinction between the Republican party and the Union cause. . . .

He could not win his war for the Union without remaining wedded to the border, no matter how difficult the domestic adjustments of this marriage. . . .

Lincoln showed himself a diplomat in his handling of the Kentucky situation. He did not rush proceedings or force the issue. . . . His Kentucky policy was such a balancing of delicacy with firmness, of delay with watchfulness, of Unionism with self-determination, that he, as much as any man, must be given the credit for keeping Kentucky. Since he considered holding or losing Kentucky the equivalent of gaining or forfeiting the cause itself, the keeping of this state, viewed from the Union standpoint, was no small achievement. From the Confederate standpoint the Kentucky development was regrettable; it constituted the loss of an important trick. . . .

The union cause held good also in other parts of the border. In Delaware and Maryland secession was avoided and the Federal government substantially supported. In eastern Tennessee Union sentiment was strong, though a separate-state movement in that area was frustrated. . . .

Missouri resembled other border areas, but with some differences. Missouri had many Germans; it had Republicans; it had a border on Iowa and another on Kansas; it had St. Louis, which was a military center in the West; it had Frémont; and it had Mrs. Frémont. The state was a battleground between opposing forces so intermingled and so complexly interlocked that the struggle could not be considered merely as a regular war or a conflict of armies in the usual sense. Perhaps none of the states manifested so strikingly the governmental disruption, private feuds, irregular tactics, ambitious jealousies, sniping, guerrilla warfare, popular excitement, pervasive turbulence, and contending governmental structures that accompany civil war within a state. . . .

The United States had a President, and Missouri had a governor—or rather two of them, one Union and the other Confederate—but Frémont reached out for civil as well as military power; and on August 31, 1861, he issued a stirring proclamation in which he "assumed the military powers of the State," whatever that meant. He proclaimed martial law throughout Missouri, ordering that persons taken with arms in their hands be shot if convicted by court-martial. The property of persons hostile to the United States he declared confiscated; their slaves he declared "free men." Here was military emancipation proclaimed by a general without presidential authority. Here was a ringing battle cry for abolitionists. Here was swift punishment for rebels; here to many was a Joshua ready to lead the hosts of the Lord.

Lincoln was most deeply worried by the possible reaction of the other border states to Frémont's highhanded act, despite the storm of approval it aroused throughout the North. Taking all possible precautions against a revolt of Frémont's followers, Lincoln relieved him of his command in October, 1861. Lincoln's agitation in his difficult and lonely position is dramatically conveyed through an excerpt from a letter to his close friend, O. H. Browning, who had queried his stand on Frémont's proclamation.[14]

Private & Confidential
EXECUTIVE MANSION
WASHINGTON, Sept. 22d 1861

Hon. O. Browning
My dear Sir.

. . . Genl. Fremont's proclamation, as to confiscation of property, and the liberation of slaves, is *purely political*, and not within the range of *military* law, or necessity. If a commanding General find a necessity to seize the farm of a private owner, for a pasture, and encampment, or a fortification, he has the right to do so, and to so hold it, as long as the necessity lasts; and this is within military law, because within military necessity. But to say the farm shall no longer belong to the owner, or his heirs forever; and this as well when the farm is not needed for military purposes as when it is, is purely political, without the savor of military law about it. And the same is true of slaves. If the General needs them, he can seize them, and use them; but when the need is past, it is not for him to fix their permanent future condition. That must be settled according to laws made by lawmakers, and not by military proclamations. The proclamation in the point in question, is simply "dictatorship." It assumes that the general may do *anything* he pleases—confiscate the lands and free the slaves of *loyal* people, as well as of disloyal ones. And going the whole figure I have no doubt would be more popular with some thoughtless people, than that which has been done! But I cannot assume this reckless position, nor allow others to assume it on my responsibility. You speak of it as being the only means of *saving* the government. On the contrary it is itself the surrender of the government. Can it be pretended that it is any longer the Government of the U. S.—any government of Constitution and laws,—wherein a General, or a President, may make permanent rules of property by proclamation?

I do not say Congress might not with propriety pass a law, on the point, just such as General Fremont proclaimed. I do not say I might not, as a member of Congress, vote for it. What I object to is, that I as President, shall expressly or impliedly seize and exercise the permanent legislative functions of the government.

So much as to principle. Now as to policy. No doubt the thing was popular in some quarters, and would have been more so if it had been a general declaration of emancipation. The Kentucky Legislature would not budge till that proclamation was modified; and Gen. Anderson telegraphed me that on the news of Gen. Fremont having actually issued deeds of manumission, a whole company of our Volunteers threw down their arms and disbanded. I was so assured, as to think it probable, that the very arms we had furnished Kentucky would be turned against us. I think to lose Kentucky is nearly the same as to lose the whole game. Kentucky gone, we can not hold Missouri, nor, as I think, Maryland. These all against us, and the job on our hands is too large for us. We would as well consent to separation at once, including the surrender of this capital. On the contrary, if you will give up your restlessness for new positions, and back me manfully on the grounds upon which you and other kind friends gave me the election, and have approved in my public documents, we shall go through triumphantly. . . .

James G. Randall concludes:[15]

It is sometimes said that Lincoln went over to the radicals, but this is far from true. Radical opposition to him became an increasing crescendo of bitterness in the later years of the war. In the Frémont matter he put his foot down in the anti-radical sense. He kept the border states in the Union, which he could hardly have accomplished on the basis of any surrender to the radicals. He did not get all the border-state support he wanted, but perhaps he got all that the cards allowed. He endured abuse for the sake of holding the border. He took pride in reporting to Congress the number of Union soldiers furnished by Delaware, Maryland, Kentucky, and Missouri. He kept a strategic eye upon operations in the West. When uneasiness for Kentucky subsided, Tennessee became a kind of specialty with him in this respect. When he reached the point of proclaiming emancipation he did not apply his edict to border states. . . .

All told, Kentucky and her neighbors had great significance for Lincoln. That significance was a matter of birth and boyhood, native hills, underlying origins, marriage, cultural ties, close friendships, and challenging problems in the field of statesmanship. To subtract Kentucky with its influences and with the huge border area is to leave out much of Lincoln's personal life and public history.

The storm over Frémont's emancipation proclamation showed how far Northern sentiment had swung toward approval of a war on slavery during the first six months of the conflict. Yet Lincoln held stubbornly to the original conception of the war embodied in the Crittenden resolution of July, 1861, which had implied that the South might be brought back with slavery intact. Although in December the House refused to re-enact the Crittenden resolution, Lincoln continued to maintain the status quo, scrupulously enforcing the Fugitive Slave Law. When General David Hunter took it upon himself to free the slaves in Georgia, Florida and South Carolina in May, 1862, the President peremptorily countermanded the order.

He explored every possible means for settling the slavery problem short of emancipation. He proposed gradual emancipa-

tion with federal-assisted compensation for the owners, to be followed by voluntary deportation of the freedmen to colonies abroad. He urged this program upon the border states, but they would have none of it. Still he listened hopefully to ideas for colonies in Central America and the Caribbean, but eventually he had to recognize the futility of such plans.

George Fort Milton, in his Conflict: The American Civil War, *has reviewed the incidents of this transitional period.*[16]

From the outbreak of the war until July, 1862, Lincoln's public attitude on emancipation was to reprehend it. Welles testifies that, in all Cabinet discussions prior to that time, whenever emancipation or the mitigation of slavery was brought up, the President had been "prompt and emphatic in denouncing any interference by the General Government." Likewise this sentiment pervaded the whole Cabinet.

At the beginning it pervaded Congress as well. As has been seen, the tone of the special session of the Summer of 1861 had been pacific on the abolition question. Not only had John J. Crittenden's resolution of the Union as it was and the Constitution as it is passed both Houses by large majorities; but also the legislation regarding emancipation had been almost negligible. Indeed, the only item of any consequence had been the Act of August 6, 1861, confiscating any slaves who had been used for a military purpose against the United States.

This Act, incidentally, had as one of its purposes the legalizing and regularizing of the position Ben Butler had taken in his famous "contraband" order. When in command at Fortress Monroe, he had the chance to see, at first hand, how valuable the Negro slaves were to the Confederacy, not only on the plantations but also in the camps and on the fortifications and other works of defense. Therefore he issued an order that such property within his lines was "contraband of war" and would be confiscated whenever needed. The idea and the phrase caught on, and were adopted throughout the Army. The Act of Congress merely cloaked with law Butler's flashing phrase.

When the Congress assembled again in December, 1861, its tone was much more vigorous. The Radical Republicans, under the lead of Thad Stevens in the House, and Chandler and Wade in the Senate, were itching to take over the control of policy for the war. Not only did they institute the Joint Committee on the Conduct of the War, an increasing source of annoyance to the Executive, but also they moved step by step toward emancipation.

On December 16, Senator Wilson, of Massachusetts, introduced a measure to abolish slavery in the District of Columbia. Still there was an effort at temperateness in terms, and the debate was not fever-heated.

The President, in his annual message on the state of the Nation, had set forth the three main points of his then view of any emancipation program. To begin with, it should be voluntary, not forced, on the part of any loyal slave State. Next compensation should be paid slave-owners in such States. Then, finally, the freedmen in such States should be colonized. Henry Wilson, who brought in the District bill, followed the Presidential ideas. The debate was temperate, for the circumstances, and on April 16, 1862, it passed and was signed by the Chief Executive.

Lincoln kept urging compensated emancipation. On March 6, he sent a message requesting a Congressional Joint Resolution "that the United States ought to cooperate with any State which may adopt gradual abolishment of slavery, giving to each State which may adopt gradual abolishment, pecuniary aid" and other assistances. This, he felt, was both just and economical. Were the nation to be able to put its daily cost of war for 87 days into paying for slave manumissions, it could buy all in Missouri, Kentucky, Maryland, Delaware and the District of Columbia. In essence, this offer, if embraced by the South, would have meant $400 for each slave.

This message gathered laurels practically nowhere. The Border State Conservatives, "set in their ways," would have none of it— they feared any sort of social change. Economics seemed relatively unimportant to them in comparison with an upturning of the social pyramid. Equally the message upset the Radical Republicans, such as Thad Stevens, who termed it "the most diluted milk and water-gruel proposition ever made to the American nation." It did not go. Doubters and extremists on both sides would not accept a sensible accommodation course.

Thenceforward, the continuous battle was, on the President's part, not to have Congress take any attitude that would alienate the Border States; and on the part of the Radical Republicans in Congress, no matter how thin their majority in and control of the two Houses, to be truculent and belligerent.

At the immediate juncture, however, Lincoln was given the resolution he had asked for, and on March 10 he gathered the delegates from the Border States and asked them to accept a plan of compensated emancipation. He did not ask that the freedom be given immediately; rather, the "decision at once to emancipate gradually." Thirty members of Congress listened to him, but only a minority acquiesced in his view. This was one of the President's greatest defeats in persuading policy.

The Congress continued its program of whittling away at the legal establishment of slavery. On March 13, 1862, it prohibited officers returning to their masters fugitive slaves who had taken refuge with the Army, irrespective of whether the masters were loyal or disloyal. In June it passed an act prohibiting slavery "in the present Territories of the United States, and in any that shall hereafter be acquired."

The next month it voted a measure Senator Trumbull had introduced, extending greatly the scope of confiscation of slaves held by disloyal masters. The old act had applied only to slaves who had been used for a military purpose. The new one declared that all slaves "escaping from such persons and taking refuge within the lines of the Army; and all slaves captured from such persons or deserted by them and coming under the control of the Government . . . and all slaves found on or being within any place occupied by rebel forces and afterward occupied by forces of the United States, shall be deemed captives of war, and shall be forever free of their servitude."

Trumbull's bill went a step further, in that it authorized the President "to employ as many persons of African descent as may seem necessary and proper for the suppression of this rebellion." In effect, this committed the Federal Government to the use of Negro troops.

By these successive steps, the Congress had gone to the uttermost limits it could go on emancipation. Indeed, it had gone much further than the contemporary views of its Constitutional powers envisaged it as being able legitimately to proceed. Suffice it to say that Lincoln hesitated, on Constitutional grounds as well as those of Border State policy, before signing the Trumbull measure. For he knew that real emancipation could come only by act of the President, out of his power as Commander-in-Chief, and residual powers he might use in order to win the war. . . .

It was the course of the war rather than the views of the Radicals which caused the President to turn more and more to the idea of emancipation as a military aid. As 1862 proceeded, he became more and more concerned over the failure of the military effort, more and more convinced of the need for extraordinary measures to preserve the National existence. His disappointments as to McClellan's failure to take Richmond aided the growth, and the latter's political demands brought to fruit his determination for action. Indeed, Lincoln is said to have written the first draft of the eventual Emancipation Proclamation, on the steamer that brought him back from Harrison's Landing to Washington, early in July, 1862.

At any event, on July 13, shortly after his return from McClellan's Headquarters, the President, in the course of a carriage ride with Seward and Welles, advised them, as the latter noted in his diary, that he had been earnestly considering "emancipating the slaves by proclamation, in case the Rebels did not cease to persist in their war on the Government and the Union, of which he saw no evidence." He had come to the conclusion "that it was a military necessity absolutely essential for the salvation of the Union, that we must free the slaves or be ourselves subdued."

"We have about played our last card," he went on, "and must change our tactics or lose the game." This was the first time he had mentioned the matter to anyone. Would these gentlemen tell him frankly what they thought?

Seward's spot reaction was that probably the measure was justifiable, and perhaps expedient and necessary. Father Gideon concurred in this. As they parted, Lincoln asked them to think the matter over and advise him of their matured views.

Once Lincoln had concluded that there was no acceptable alternative to emancipation, he went about drafting his proclamation in the greatest secrecy, consulting no one. Major Eckert, Superintendent of the Military Telegraph, has left us an intimate picture of Lincoln at work on a draft of the proclamation in the War Department Telegraph Office near the White House, as told in David H. Bates' Lincoln in the Telegraph Office.[17]

He would look out of the window a while and then put his pen to paper, but he did not write much at once. He would study between times and when he had made up his mind he would put down a line or two, and then sit quiet for a few minutes. After a time, he would resume his writing, only to stop again at intervals to make some remark to me or to one of the cipher operators as a fresh dispatch from the front was handed to him.

Once his eyes were arrested by the sight of a large spiderweb stretched from the lintel of the portico to the side of the outer window sill. This spiderweb was an institution of the cipher room and harbored a large colony of exceptionally big ones. We frequently watched their antics, and Assistant Secretary Watson dubbed them "Major Eckert's lieutenants." Lincoln commented on the web, and I told him my lieutenants would soon report and pay their respects to the President. Not long after a big spider appeared at the crossroads and tapped several times on the strands, whereupon five or six others came out from different directions. Then what seemed to be a great confab took place, after which they separated, each on a different strand of the web. Lincoln was much interested in the performance and thereafter, while working at the desk, would often watch for the appearance of his visitors.

On the first day, Lincoln did not cover one sheet of his special writing paper (nor indeed on any subsequent day). When ready to leave, he asked me to take charge of what he had written and not allow any one to see it. I told him I would do this with pleasure and would not read it myself. "Well," he said, "I should be glad to know that no one will see it, although there is no objection to your looking at it; but please keep it locked up until I call for it tomorrow." I said his wishes would be strictly complied with.

When he came to the office on the following day he asked for the papers, and I unlocked my desk and handed them to him and he again sat down to write. This he did nearly every day for several weeks, always handing me what he had written when ready to leave the office each day. Sometimes he would not write more than a line or two, and once I observed that he put question marks on the margin of what he had written. He would read over each day all the matter he had previously written and revise it, studying carefully each sentence.

On one occasion, he took the papers with him, but he brought them back a day or two later. I became much interested in the matter and was impressed with the idea that he was engaged upon something of great importance, but did not know what it was until he had finished the document and then for the first time he told me that he had been writing an order giving freedom to the slaves in the South, for the purpose of hastening the end of the war.

On July twenty-second Lincoln read his final draft to the Cabinet. All except Seward and Welles, to whom he had earlier confided his plans, were taken by surprise. It was Seward's shrewd advice (which Lincoln followed) to wait for a military victory lest publication in a time of reverses might be looked upon "as the last measure of an exhausted government." But during the summer of 1862 the pressure on Lincoln to declare for emancipation became frenzied. Finally the partial victory at Antietam provided the occasion. Lincoln had now publicly promised to implement emancipation if the rebellious states had not returned to the fold by the new year. But many wondered if he would fulfil his pledge, for in December he once again proposed a scheme for compensated emancipation, this time in a plan so gradual that it would not have been completed until 1900! This plan unleashed a furious campaign by the outraged radicals. In consequence, on New Year's Day, 1863, with scant ceremony, Lincoln signed the final Proclamation.

Again the paradox must be faced. How was it possible for this ineffectual pronouncement to make its way not only into the select company of great state documents but even into the folk heritage of the country? One is reminded of that verse of the rousing Civil War song "When Johnny Comes Marching Home":

> In eighteen hundred and sixty three,
> Hurrah! Hurrah!
> Abe Lincoln set the darkies free,
> Hurrah! Hurrah!

James G. Randall gives part of the answer.[18]

Negative points, however, do not form the whole story. What Lincoln did not do, what Congress and the states failed to do on Lincoln's urging, what the proclamation did not provide, and what it encountered in the way of opposition, have received attention because of the necessity of remembering authentic history. To leave the subject there, however, would be to omit a great deal. Somehow, despite all its limitations, the proclamation did become a force. Perhaps it became more of a slogan than an enforced edict, but as such it had vitality. Freedom was something in the air. Inspirational aspects of the proclamation at the North—or in certain Northern circles—were tremendous. For the stirring of men's souls the war took on new meaning. Good people, Christians, humanitarians, hailed it with delight; their speeches, hosannas, and prayers had an effect upon home morale. It was the Victorian age. . . .

One should look twice before thinking too cynically of all this. People thought of Lincoln as a divine instrument. They thought of something greater than any President, of Providence intervening in the affairs of men, using the rough hand of war to accomplish a holy purpose. That the edict came at New Year's gave it a kind of Messianic quality, a note of ringing out the old and ringing in the new. It was another "Battle Hymn of the Republic." A deed had been done for freedom. God was keeping watch above his own. Something was happening that had to do with Lincoln's fame. World concepts of the man as well as traditional national memories of him were taking shape.

The Proclamation did its work because it gave the North the initiative in the war of ideas. It provided a rallying point for public opinion and immeasurably strengthened the pro-Union sentiment in Europe. Above all, the Proclamation did free the slaves. As the Northern armies fought their way through the Confederacy, they brought the Proclamation with them. Freedom for the slaves no less than force of arms destroyed the rebellious aristocracy. Lincoln's words in his 1862 Message to Congress had been justified:

> We know how to save the Union. . . . In giving freedom to the slave, we assure freedom to the free—honorable alike in what we give, and what we preserve. We shall nobly save, or meanly lose, the last, best, hope of earth. Other means may succeed; this could not fail. The way is plain, peaceful, generous, just—a way which, if followed, the world will forever applaud, and God must forever bless.[19]

Lincoln now turned with enthusiasm to the problems of reconstruction. John Hay noted in July, 1863: "It deeply interests him now. He considers it the greatest question ever presented to practical statesmanship. While the rest are grinding their little private organs for their own glorification the old man is working with the strength of a giant and the purity of an angel to do this great work."[20]

What the radicals and their followers were after was inadvertently blurted out by a Yankee colonel in the South as early as 1862:[21]

The thing we seek is *permanent* dominion & what instance is there of permanent dominion without changing, revolutionizing, absorbing, the institutions, life, and manners of the conquered peoples? . . . They think we mean to take their *Slaves.* Bah! We must take their *ports,* their *mines,* their *water power,* the *very soil* they plough, and develop them by the hands of our *artisan* armies. . . . *This army must not come back.* Settlement, migration must put the seal on battle, or we gain nothing.

Although the radicals moved cautiously, their drift was revealed as the antagonists clashed repeatedly over certain basic issues: was the President, or Congress, to control reconstruction? Were the rebellious states of the South to be considered "conquered provinces" to be carved up and readmitted on some entirely new basis, or had they, as Lincoln maintained, never left the Union? And what was to be done with the freed slaves? The evolution of Lincoln's plans has been described by Benjamin Thomas.[22]

Lincoln wanted to achieve a peace worth keeping, not the sort that breeds another war. He realized the necessity of careful planning—the terms of peace must be thought out, and perhaps applied, in time of war. From the beginning of the conflict he had seized every opportunity, however small, to bring disaffected areas and individuals within the Union fold again. His terms were not exacting: it was enough for him that persons in rebellion should repent. During the first six months of 1862 he had established military governments in Louisiana, Arkansas, and Tennessee, not as a means of suppression, but to bring order so that loyal state governments could be organized.

The chief obstacle to such a program was not the vanquished. Lincoln's problem, as has been the case with other wartime Presidents, was to win acceptance of his terms at home. The radical leaders of his party, wishing to impose stiff penalties on the conquered South, had so far balked his plans. Pontifical Charles Sumner raised the question of Lincoln's authority to deal with the conquered states at all. . . .

With the assembling of Congress in December 1863, however, Lincoln believed the time had come to offer a general plan of reconciliation to the South. He supplemented his annual message with the proclamation guaranteeing a full pardon to persons implicated in the rebellion—except a few major offenders—who would take an oath of loyalty to the Constitution, and swear to support the Emancipation Proclamation, together with all acts of Congress dealing with slaves. The proclamation further promised that when, in any rebellious state, a number of citizens equal to one tenth of the voters in the election of 1860 should reestablish a democratic government, in conformity with the oath of allegiance, it should be recognized as the true government of the state and receive Federal protection.

Lincoln offered no threats if the Southern states rejected his plan. He contemplated no reprisals, no wholesale hangings of "traitors," no transformation of the South into a "desert," no imposition of vengeful military rule. He sought for a genuine reconciliation without retribution or revenge.

In a letter to General Banks in Louisiana four months before, Lincoln had expressed the hope that the people, in establishing a new state government, would adopt some practical system whereby whites and blacks "could gradually live themselves out of their old relation to each other, and both come out better prepared for the new. Education for young blacks should be included in the plan." . . . If a new state government would recognize the permanent freedom of the Negroes and take measures to prepare them for their new status, Lincoln would not object to temporary restrictions made necessary by "their present condition as a laboring, landless, and homeless class." Provided certain overriding principles were respected, he would allow the Southern people to solve their own race problem.

Generally, Lincoln's plan of 1863 had been favorably received in the North, but when new governments actually were formed, radical opposition flared. Friction first developed in Louisiana in late 1862 when Lincoln replaced the flamboyant General Butler, a radical, with the milder Banks. General Banks put the freedmen into a forced labor system (instead of recruiting them into the army, as the radicals desired) and then proceeded to organize a state government under Lincoln's plan.

Unfortunately, a state government meant nothing from the national standpoint unless state representatives were allowed to sit in Congress. Hence the radical answer to Lincoln was the Wade-Davis Bill of 1864 defining congressional terms for readmission of states to the federal legislature. Although mild compared to later radical plans, the Wade-Davis Bill required a majority of white voters for the re-establishment of a state government instead of only ten per cent, and set up other stringent limitations. The battle was really joined when Lincoln killed the bill with a pocket veto in July, 1864. That summer, the dark summer of 1864, Wade and Davis published their vitriolic attack upon Loncoln. T. Harry Williams describes the course of the reconstruction debate.[23]

The problem of reconstruction and who should control its process, Congress or the president, had lain dormant since before the election. Now in the early months of 1865 it was clear to all observers that the Confederacy would soon collapse. With the approach of victory and peace, reconstruction became a dominant issue to the exclusion of all other questions. Upon what terms were the Southern states to be received back into

the Union? Who would determine the conditions of readmission
—Wade and Chandler or Lincoln? . . . The Jacobins had moved
far beyond their position as announced in the Wade-Davis bill.
No longer were they content to accept emancipation as the great
result of the war. Now they demanded as the price of readmission a program which would insure Republican political control
of the South. They had no mind to see unrepentant Southern
Democrats returning to Congress and in alliance with their
Northern fellows, destroying the economic measures passed by
the Republicans during the war: the protective tariff, the national banking system, and the homestead bill. They demanded
the suffrage for the freed slaves and the disfranchisement of a
substantial portion of the Southern white population. Some of
them, like Stevens, advocated the distribution of confiscated
rebel property among former slaves. They demanded that until
their policies became a reality the seceded states be governed by
the military as "conquered provinces." Over the issue of reconstruction Lincoln and the Jacobins fought their last titanic battle.
Again the Jacobins were to defeat their great antagonist. . . .

Early in February the radicals prepared to jam through Congress a resolution declaring that the eleven seceded states were
not entitled to representation in the electoral college. This struck
directly at Lincoln's four reconstructed states. Wade, who led
the debate for the Jacobins, bitterly denounced Lincoln's reconstruction plan as "the most absurd and impracticable that ever
haunted the imagination of a statesman." The proclamation which
Lincoln had issued when he pocketed the Wade-Davis bill was,
cried Wade, "the most contentious, the most anarchical, the
most dangerous proposition that was ever put forth for the government of a free people." The resolution passed both houses, and
Lincoln signed it under protest. He may have hoped to conciliate
the Jacobins by yielding. It was a useless concession. The radicals
had the bit in their teeth and they were running hard.

Late in February the senators and representatives elected by reconstructed Louisiana knocked at the doors of Congress asking for recognition and admission. This the Jacobin chieftains were determined to prevent. Wade, Chandler, and Sumner led the fight to deny seats to the petitioners. Fearful that they could not command a majority to defeat the resolution recognizing the Louisiana government, the three resorted to obstruction and delay. They spoke interminably, they demanded the yeas and nays on every question. And finally they triumphed. The Senate, its patience worn thin, "dispensed" with the resolution.

No Southern state was actually restored to the Union under Lincoln's plan, although he had considered his terms fulfilled in North Carolina, Tennessee, Arkansas and Louisiana. The radicals had won their fight—for the time being. But Lincoln was a patient and a resourceful man and the events of the last weeks of his life show that he had by no means given up the struggle. Indeed, the radicals secretly considered his death "a godsend" to their cause.[24]

In March he delivered his famous Second Inaugural: "With malice toward none; with charity for all . . . let us strive on . . . to do all which may achieve and cherish a just and lasting peace. . . ." On the evening of April eleventh, three days before the assassination, a crowd hysterical with joy at the end of the war gathered on the White House lawn to serenade the President. Lincoln spoke a few words to them. Instead of the expected salute to victory, he pleaded with the crowd to help him carry through his plans for a lasting peace, a peace tempered with mercy.

Reconstruction, he warned, "is fraught with great difficulty. . . . We simply must begin with, and mould from, disorganized and discordant elements. Nor is it a small additional embarrassment that we, the loyal people, differ among ourselves as to the mode, manner, and means of reconstruction." *What matter, he continued, if the new government of Louisiana had been elected under his plan by only twelve thousand people? By supporting it we "encourage the hearts, and nerve the arms of the twelve thousand to adhere to their work, and argue for it, and proselyte for it, and fight for it, and feed it, and grow it, and ripen it to a complete success. . . . Concede that the new government of Louisiana is only to what it should be as the egg is to the fowl, we shall sooner have the fowl by hatching the egg than by smashing it.*"[25]

A few days earlier, in newly surrendered Richmond, he had promised Judge Campbell (that same Southern judge who had negotiated with Seward over Fort Sumter) that he would consent to recognize the wartime legislature of Virginia if it would agree to vote to restore the state to the Union. Back in Washington the radicals raised such a row over this concession that Lincoln was forced to rescind his promise. But in Lincoln's mind the struggle over reconstruction was just beginning, and his views, which were the antithesis of those of the radicals, were already firmly fixed. The Marquis de Chambrun, in a passage from his Impressions of Lincoln and the Civil War, *underlined the profundity of Lincoln's longing for a magnanimous peace.*[26] *The Marquis, who had visited captured Petersburg with Lincoln at the close of the war, accompanied him on his return to Washington.*

On Sunday, April 9th, we were proceeding up the Potomac. That whole day the conversation turned on literary subjects. Mr. Lincoln read aloud to us for several hours. Most of the passages he selected were from Shakespeare, especially *Macbeth.* The lines after the murder of Duncan, when the new king falls a prey to moral torment, were dramatically dwelt on. Now and then he paused to expatiate on how exact a picture Shakespeare here gives of a murderer's mind when, the dark **deed** achieved, its perpetrator already envies his victim's calm sleep. He read the scene over twice. . . .

Our party dispersed on arriving at the Potomac wharf. Mr. and Mrs. Lincoln, Senator Sumner and I drove home in the same carriage. As we drew near Washington, Mrs. Lincoln, who had hitherto remained silently looking at the town, said: "That city is full of enemies." The President, on hearing this, retorted with an impatient gesture: "Enemies, never again must we repeat that word."

When success at last had crowned so many bloody efforts it was impossible to discover in Lincoln any thought of revenge or feeling of bitterness toward the vanquished. His only preoccupation was to recall the Southern States into the Union as soon as possible. When he encountered opposition on this point, when many of those surrounding him insisted on the necessity of strong reprisals, he would exhibit signs of impatience, for though uninfluenced by such opinions, on hearing them, he gave evident signs of a nervous fatigue which he partially controlled but was unable to dissimulate entirely.

9.

War's End

During the fall of 1864 the Union forces closed in on the Confederacy by sea and by land. While Grant pinned down Lee at Petersburg, Sheridan cleaned out the Valley of Virginia, destroying Early's army, and held himself in readiness to join Grant. Further south Sherman took Atlanta in September, marched boldly to the sea, and presented Lincoln with Savannah as a Christmas present. Along the coasts meanwhile the blockade tightened. Admiral ("Damn the torpedoes!") Farragut had closed the port of Mobile in August. As Sherman prepared to march northward through the Carolinas to join Grant, Admiral David Dixon Porter stormed Fort Fisher on the coast of North Carolina, denying the port of Wilmington to the blockade runners. Charleston fell on February eighteenth, leaving only distant Galveston in Texas open to the sea.

.The Confederacy had been cut in two, its eastern heartland had been encircled and invaded, and Lee's depleted army in Virginia was nearing exhaustion. It had long been Lincoln's plan to isolate the rebellious states, then starve and batter them into submission. His plan was at last taking visible shape.

Of all the closing exploits of the war, Sherman's march through Georgia and the Carolinas is best remembered, and can still raise hot sparks of controversy. Ordered to move east into the heart of the Confederacy, Sherman left Chattanooga in May, 1864, but did not reach Atlanta until July, so brilliant were General Johnston's delaying actions amidst the rugged mountains. Nevertheless, Johnston's Fabian tactics displeased President Davis, who replaced him with General John B. Hood. Hood promptly took the offensive against Sherman, lost heavily, and was forced out of Atlanta in September.

Hoping to lure Sherman out of Atlanta again, Hood marched inland and sent his cavalry to harass the over-extended Union supply lines stretching back into Tennessee. Then came the bold decision. Sherman, dispatching nearly half his army under General Thomas with orders to hold off Hood, asked Grant to let him march with the remainder of his troops in the opposite direction, forward to the sea, abandoning his communications with Chattanooga and living off the land. Grant and Lincoln hesitated, but finally agreed. When the decision had been made, Stanton wired Sherman, for the President: "Whatever the result, you have the confidence and support of the Government."[1]

Sherman ordered the evacuation of Atlanta, then burned its public buildings and military installations to render the city useless to the enemy. When the City Council remonstrated, he dashed off the famous letter giving his philosophy of "total war."

You cannot qualify war in harsher terms than I will. War is cruelty, and you cannot refine it; and those who brought war into our country deserve all the curses and maledictions a people can pour out. I know I had no hand in making this war, and I know I will make more sacrifices to-day than any of you to secure peace. But you cannot have peace and a division of our country. . . . The United States does and must assert its authority, wherever it once had power. . . . Once more admit the Union, once more acknowledge the authority of the national Government, and, instead of devoting your houses and streets and roads to the dread uses of war, I and this army become at once your protectors and supporters. . . .

You might as well appeal against the thunder-storm as against these terrible hardships of war. . . .

But, my dear sirs, when peace does come, you may call on me for any thing. Then will I share with you the last cracker, and watch with you to shield your homes and families against danger from any quarter.[2]

Sherman marched through Georgia virtually unopposed, cutting a swath of destruction three hundred miles long and sixty miles wide. He arrived before Savannah on December tenth. Back in Tennessee the methodical General Thomas, who had been biding his time, smashed Hood's army at Nashville on the fifteenth and sixteenth, and lifted the threat from that quarter. Sherman himself, in an excerpt from his Memoirs, *recalled the first few days of his epic march through Georgia.*[3]

About 7 A.M. of November 16th we rode out of Atlanta by the Decatur road, filled by the marching troops and wagons of the Fourteenth Corps; and reaching the hill, just outside of the old rebel works, we naturally paused to look back upon the scenes of our past battles. We stood upon the very ground whereon was fought the bloody battle of July 22d, and could see the copse of wood where McPherson fell. Behind us lay Atlanta, smouldering and in ruins, the black smoke rising high in air, and hanging like a pall over the ruined city. Away off in the distance, on the McDonough road, was the rear of

Howard's column, the gun-barrels glistening in the sun, the white-topped wagons stretching away to the south; and right before us the Fourteenth Corps, marching steadily and rapidly, with a cheery look and swinging pace, that made light of the thousand miles that lay between us and Richmond. Some band, by accident, struck up the anthem of "John Brown's soul goes marching on;" the men caught up the strain, and never before or since have I heard the chorus of "Glory, glory, hallelujah!" done with more spirit, or in better harmony of time and place. . . .

The day was extremely beautiful, clear sunlight, with bracing air, and an unusual feeling of exhilaration seemed to pervade all minds—a feeling of something to come, vague and undefined, still full of venture and intense interest. Even the common soldiers caught the inspiration, and many a group called out to me as I worked my way past them, "Uncle Billy, I guess Grant is waiting for us at Richmond!" Indeed, the general sentiment was that we were marching for Richmond, and that there we should end the war, but how and when they seemed to care not. . . .

The first night out we camped by the road-side near Lithonia. Stone Mountain, a mass of granite, was in plain view, cut out in clear outline against the blue sky; the whole horizon was lurid with the bonfires of rail-ties, and groups of men all night were carrying the heated rails to the nearest trees, and bending them around the trunks. Colonel Poe had provided tools for ripping up the rails and twisting them when hot; but the best and easiest way is the one I have described, of heating the middle of the iron-rails on bonfires made of the cross-ties, and then winding them around a telegraph-pole or the trunk of some convenient sapling. I attached much importance to this destruction of the railroad, gave it my own personal attention, and made reiterated orders to others on the subject.

The next day we passed through the handsome town of Covington, the soldiers closing up their ranks, the color-bearers unfurling their flags, and the bands striking up patriotic airs. The white people came out of their houses to behold the sight, spite of their deep hatred of the invaders, and the negroes were simply frantic with joy. Whenever they heard my name, they clustered about my horse, shouted and prayed in their peculiar style, which had a natural eloquence that would have moved a stone. I have witnessed hundreds, if not thousands, of such scenes; and can now see a poor girl, in the very ecstasy of the Methodist "shout," hugging the banner of one of the regiments, and jumping up to the "feet of Jesus." . . .

The skill and success of the men in collecting forage was one of the features of this march. Each brigade commander had authority to detail a company of foragers, usually about fifty men, with one or two commissioned officers selected for their boldness and enterprise. This party would be dispatched before daylight with a knowledge of the intended day's march and camp; would proceed on foot five or six miles from the route traveled by their brigade, and then visit every plantation and farm within range. They would usually procure a wagon or family carriage, load it with bacon, corn-meal, turkeys, chickens, ducks, and every thing that could be used as food or forage, and would then regain the main road, usually in advance of their train. When this came up, they would deliver to the brigade commissary the supplies thus gathered by the way. . . . No doubt, many acts of pillage, robbery, and violence, were committed by these parties of foragers, usually called "bummers"; for I have since heard of jewelry taken from women, and the plunder of articles that never reached the commissary; but these acts were exceptional and incidental. I never heard of any cases of murder or rape; and no army could have carried along sufficient food and forage for a march of three hundred miles; so that foraging in some shape was necessary. The country was sparsely settled, with no magistrates or civil authorities who could respond to requisitions, as is done in all the wars of Europe; so that this system of foraging was simply indispensable to our success. By it our men were well supplied with all the essentials of life and health, while the wagons retained enough in case of unexpected delay, and our animals were well fed. Indeed, when we reached Savannah, the trains were pronounced by experts to be the finest in flesh and appearance ever seen with any army. . . .

Lincoln's terms for peace were simple but inexorable: "Once more admit the Union," as Sherman had put it, "once more acknowledge the authority of the national Government. . . ." But the proud Confederacy preferred destruction to submission on these terms. The cry for peace came rather from the North, warweary and discouraged; and no one, during the dark days of the summer of 1864, cried more loudly for a negotiated peace than Horace Greeley. Informed that Confederate commissioners waited on the Canadian side of Niagara Falls, the excitable editor of the Tribune *badgered the skeptical Lincoln into action. The wily President insisted that Greeley go to Canada himself. When the negotiations came to nothing, Greeley was the laughingstock of the country. Dana called the incident, "One of the cleverest minor political moves which Mr. Lincoln ever made. . . ."*[4]

By 1865, however, the possibility of peace began to be taken more seriously. Although Lincoln still felt that negotiations would be fruitless, he allowed Frances P. Blair, the elder statesman, to go to Richmond at the end of the year. After lengthy talks with President Davis, Blair returned with a promise from Davis to send emissaries immediately "with a view to secure peace to the two countries." Well aware of Davis's implication, Lincoln countered with an offer to receive agents at any time "with the view of securing peace to the people of our one common country." Nevertheless, Davis appointed three peace commissioners, Vice-President Alexander H. Stephens, Judge John A. Campbell of

Alabama, and R. M. T. Hunter of Virginia. They met with Lincoln and Seward at Hampton Roads on February third. Benjamin Thomas describes the scene.[5]

On February 3 Lincoln and Seward sat down with the three Confederates in the cabin of the *River Queen* under the guns of Fortress Monroe. Frail Alexander H. Stephens, for whom Lincoln had entertained a genuine fondness and admiration since their days in Congress, arrived bundled in a tremendous overcoat with numerous scarves and vestments. The President watched him good-humoredly as he unwrapped his puny body, and remarked later to Grant that it was the smallest nubbin for so much shucking that he had ever seen.

For four hours there was a swift interplay of acute minds across the council table. Lincoln would make no bargain with an enemy in arms. When Hunter retorted that Charles I had negotiated with persons in arms against his government, the President replied that he was not posted on history; all that he distinctly remembered about the matter was that Charles had lost his head. Hunter said he understood that Lincoln looked upon the leaders of the Confederacy as traitors. Lincoln granted that was "about the size of it." There was a moment's silence. Then Hunter smiled. "Well, Mr. Lincoln," he observed, "we have about concluded that we shall not be hanged as long as you are President —if we behave ourselves."

Lincoln let it be known that he still favored compensation to owners of emancipated slaves. It had never been his intention to interfere with slavery in the states; he had been driven to it by necessity, he explained. He believed that the people of the North and South were equally responsible for slavery, and if hostilities should cease and the states would voluntarily abolish slavery, he thought the government should indemnify the owners—to the extent, possibly, of $400,000,000.

The conference came to nothing. Two days later, however, Lincoln read his cabinet a proposal to appropriate $400,000,000 for reimbursement to slave-owners, provided hostilities stopped by April 1. With victory imminent, it was the ultimate in magnanimity. But the cabinet unanimously disapproved this generous gesture, and Lincoln regretfully abandoned the idea.

The North was distracted briefly from the closing drama of the war by Lincoln's second inauguration, on March 4, 1865. Noah Brooks wrote the classic account of the occasion, which saw the delivery of one of Lincoln's greatest orations.[6]

All eyes were turned to the main entrance, where, precisely on the stroke of twelve, appeared Andrew Johnson, Vice-President elect, arm in arm with Hannibal Hamlin, whose term of office was now expiring. They took seats together on the dais of the presiding officer, and Hamlin made a brief and sensible speech, and Andrew Johnson, whose face was extraordinarily red, was presented to take the oath. It is needless to say here that the unfortunate gentleman, who had been very ill, was not altogether sober at this most important moment of his life. In order to strengthen himself for the physical and mental ordeal through which he was about to pass, he had taken a stiff drink of whisky in the room of the Vice-President, and the warmth of the Senate chamber, with possibly other physical conditions, had sent the fiery liquor to his brain. He was evidently intoxicated. As he went on with his speech, he turned upon the cabinet officers and addressed them as "Mr. Stanton," "Mr. Seward," etc., without the official handles to their names. Forgetting Mr. Welles's name, he said, "and you, too, Mr.—," then, leaning over to Colonel Forney, he said, "What is the name of the Secretary of the Navy?" and then continued as though nothing had happened. Once in a while, from the reporters' gallery, I could observe Hamlin nudging Johnson from behind, reminding him that the hour for the inauguration ceremony had passed. The speaker kept on, although President Lincoln sat before him, patiently waiting for his extraordinary harangue to be over. . . .

When Johnson had repeated inaudibly the oath of office, his hand upon the Book, he turned and took the Bible in his hand, and, facing the audience, said, with a loud, theatrical voice and gesture, "I kiss this Book in the face of my nation of the United States."

This painful incident being over, Colonel Forney, the secretary of the Senate, read the proclamation of the President convoking an extra session, and called the names of the members elect. Thereupon the newly chosen senators were sworn in, and the procession for the inauguration platform, which had been built on the east front of the Capitol, was formed. There was a sea of heads in the great plaza in front of the Capitol, as far as the eye could reach, and breaking in waves along its outer edges among the budding foliage of the grounds beyond. When the President and the procession of notables appeared, a tremendous shout, prolonged and loud, arose from the surging ocean of humanity around the Capitol building. Then the sergeant-at-arms of the Senate, the historic Brown, arose and bowed, with his shining black hat in hand, in dumb-show before the crowd, which thereupon became still, and Abraham Lincoln, rising tall and gaunt among the groups about him, stepped forward and read his inaugural address, which was printed in two broad columns upon a single page of large paper. As he advanced from his seat, a roar of applause shook the air, and, again and again repeated, finally died far away on the outer fringe of the throng, like a sweeping wave upon the shore. Just at that moment the sun, which had been obscured all day, burst forth in its unclouded meridian splendor, and flooded the spectacle with glory and with light. Every heart beat quicker at the unexpected omen, and doubtless not a few mentally prayed that so might the darkness which had obscured the past four years be now dissipated by the sun of prosperity.

> Till danger's troubled night depart,
> And the star of peace return.

The inaugural address was received in most profound silence. Every word was clear and audible as the ringing and somewhat shrill tones of Lincoln's voice sounded over the vast concourse. There was applause, however, at the words, "both parties deprecated war, but one of them would *make* war rather than let the nation survive, and the other would *accept* war rather than let it perish"; and the cheer that followed these words lasted long enough to make a considerable pause before he added sententiously, "and the war came." There were occasional spurts of applause, too, at other points along this wonderful address. Looking down into the faces of the people, illuminated by the bright rays of the sun, one could see moist eyes and even tearful cheeks as the good President pronounced these noble words: "With malice toward none, with charity for all, with firmness in the right as God gives us to see the right, let us strive on to finish the work we are in; to bind up the nation's wounds; to care for him who shall have borne the battle, and for his widow and his orphan; to do all which may achieve and cherish a just and a lasting peace among ourselves and with all nations."

Early in March Lee tried to negotiate a "military convention" with Grant, but Lincoln insisted upon keeping the peace negotiations in his own hands. Later in the month, anticipating an early surrender, Lincoln appeared at Grant's headquarters at City Point. As Welles put it in his diary, "The President has gone to the front, partly to get rid of the throng that is pressing upon

*him. . . . There is no doubt that he is much worn down; besides
he wishes the War terminated, and, to this end, that severe terms
shall not be exacted of the Rebels."*[7] *Lincoln discussed with Grant
and Sherman the broad lines of policy from which stemmed the
generous terms imposed upon Lee by Grant and upon Johnston
by Sherman. He left nothing to chance. He was determined upon
an easy peace in order to hasten the reunion of North and South.*

*In the meantime Sheridan moved toward Richmond from
the Valley. To escape the closing net, Lee abandoned Petersburg
and Richmond on April second and fled west along the Appomattox. Lincoln had time to visit both fallen cities, but was forced
to hurry back to Washington before Lee's surrender when news
reached him that Seward had been seriously injured in an accident.*

*Admiral David Porter, who saw much of Lincoln during his
trip to the front, described these last, climactic days of Lincoln's
life in his* Incidents and Anecdotes of the Civil War. *Sometimes
an excitable and inaccurate reporter, the Admiral may well have
exaggerated what Lincoln actually said to Grant and Sherman
about reconstruction.*[8]

The President was evidently nervous; the enormous
expense of the war seemed to weigh upon him like an incubus;
he could not keep away from General Grant's tent, and was constantly inquiring when he was going to move; though, if he had
looked at the wagons, stuck fast in the thick red mud of the
surrounding country, he would have known why no army could
operate.

I attached myself to the President at his own request, and did
all I could to interest him by taking him up and down the river
in my barge, or driving about the country in General Ingals's
buggy with two fine horses. I saw that, without being aware of
it, he was pushing General Grant to move more than circum-

stances justified, and I did all I could to withdraw his attention from the subject.

Mr. Lincoln had a wonderful faculty for understanding the topography of a country, and he was quite familiar with the one in which the army was about to operate; he carried a small chart in his pocket, on which were marked all the rivers and hills about Richmond, with the city itself, and the different points where General Lee had his forces posted, the lines of defense, and, in fact, all the information that a general of an army wanted. . . .

Leaving General Schofield in command of the army, Sherman took the small steamer Russia from Morehead City and proceeded in her to City Point, arriving on March 27th. He was received on board the River Queen by the President with that warmth of feeling which always distinguished him when meeting any of the brave men who had devoted their lives to crushing out the great Rebellion.

General Sherman spent a long time with the President, explaining to him the situation in his department, which was very encouraging.

At this moment Sherman's army was holding General Joe Johnston's forces in North Carolina in a position from which he could not move without precipitating a battle with some eighty thousand of the best troops in our army. . . .

The morning after Sherman's arrival the President held a council on board the River Queen, composed of General Grant, General Sherman, and myself, and, as considerable controversy was caused by the terms of surrender granted to General Joe Johnston, I will mention here the conversation which took place during this meeting in the River Queen's cabin.

I made it a rule during the war to write down at night before retiring to rest what had occurred during each day, and I was particularly careful in doing so in this instance.

At this meeting Mr. Lincoln and General Sherman were the

speakers, and the former declared his opinions at length before Sherman answered him. The President feared that Lee—seeing our lines closing about him, the coast completely blockaded, his troops almost destitute of clothing and short of provisions— might make an attempt to break away from the fortified works at Richmond, make a junction with General Joe Johnston, and escape South or fight a last bloody battle. . . .

The President's mind was made easy on this score, yet it was remarkable how many shrewd questions he asked on the subject, and how difficult some of them were to answer. He stated his views in regard to what he desired; he felt sure, as did every one at that council, that the end of the war was near at hand; and, though some thought a bloody battle was impending, all thought that Richmond would fall in less than a week.

He wanted the surrender of the Confederate armies, and desired that the most liberal terms should be granted them. "Let them once surrender," he said, "and reach their homes, they won't take up arms again. Let them all go, officers and all. I want submission, and no more bloodshed. Let them have their horses to plow with, and, if you like, their guns to shoot crows with. I want no one punished; treat them liberally all round. We want those people to return to their allegiance to the Union and submit to the laws. Again I say, give them the most liberal and honorable terms." . . .

As the army advanced, a telegraph-wire was laid out and a telegraph-office established under the direction of Colonel Bowers, who collected all the dispatches. The President used to sit there nearly all day receiving telegrams, and I sat there with him. "Here," he said once, taking out his little chart, "they are at this point, and Sheridan is just starting off up this road. That will bring about a crisis."

"Now let us go to dinner; I'd like to peck a little."

Then we came back and received the news of the evacuation of Petersburg. "We will go there to-morrow," he said. . . .

We spent a most agreeable day at Petersburg. The streets were alive with negroes, who were crazy to see their savior, as they called the President; and it was found necessary at last to eject them from the doorways *vi et armis.*

The tobacco-stores were all open, and every one seemed to be helping himself to the delicious weed. It was mostly put up in small bales of three pounds each. Some one presented me with four packages, and I tied them upon the saddle of my horse, which I had determined to ride back again by way of enjoying a better horse in case I should ever come across one.

The President took a fancy to have four little bales also; they were a genuine curiosity to him, and Tad wanted four bales because his father had them.

The next day Admiral Porter escorted Lincoln up the James River to visit newly conquered Richmond.

When the channel was reported clear of torpedoes (a large number of which were taken up), I proceeded up to Richmond in the Malvern, with President Lincoln on board the River Queen, and a heavy feeling of responsibility on my mind, notwithstanding the great care that had been taken to clear the river.

Every vessel that got through the obstructions wished to be the first one up, and pushed ahead with all steam; but they grounded, one after another, the Malvern passing them all, until she also took the ground. Not to be delayed, I took the President in my barge, and, with a tug ahead with a file of marines on board, we continued on up to the city. . . .

The street along the river-front was as deserted as if this had been a city of the dead. The troops had been in possession some hours, but not a soldier was to be seen. . . .

There was a small house on this landing, and behind it were some twelve negroes digging with spades. The leader of them was an old man sixty years of age. He raised himself to an upright position as we landed, and put his hands up to his eyes. Then he dropped his spade and sprang forward. "Bress de Lord," he said, "dere is de great Messiah! I knowed him as soon as I seed him. He's bin in my heart fo' long yeahs, an' he's cum at las' to free his chillun from deir bondage! Glory, Hallelujah!" And he fell upon his knees before the President and kissed his feet. The others followed his example, and in a minute Mr. Lincoln was surrounded by these people, who had treasured up the recollection of him caught from a photograph, and had looked up to him for four years as the one who was to lead them out of captivity. . . .

It was a minute or two before I could get the negroes to rise and leave the President. The scene was so touching I hated to disturb it, yet we could not stay there all day; we had to move on; so I requested the patriarch to withdraw from about the President with his companions and let us pass on. . . .

Our progress was very slow; we did not move a mile an hour, and the crowd was still increasing.

Many poor whites joined the throng, and sent up their shouts with the rest. We were nearly half an hour getting from abreast of Libby Prison to the edge of the city. The President stopped a moment to look on the horrid bastile where so many Union soldiers had dragged out a dreadful existence, and were subjected to all the cruelty the minds of brutal jailers could devise.

"We will pull it down," cried the crowd, seeing where his look fell.

"No," he said, "leave it as a monument." . . .

It was a warm day, and the streets were dusty, owing to the immense gathering which covered every part of them, kicking up the dirt. The atmosphere was suffocating, but Mr. Lincoln could be seen plainly by every man, woman, and child, towering head and shoulders above that crowd; he overtopped every man there. He carried his hat in his hand, fanning his face, from which the perspiration was pouring. He looked as if he would have given his Presidency for a glass of water—I would have given my commission for half that. . . .

We were brought to a halt by the dense jam before we had gone a square into the city, which was still on fire near the Tredegar Works and in the structures thereabout, and the smoke, setting our way, almost choked us. . . .

While we were stopped for a moment by the crowd, a white man in his shirt-sleeves rushed from the sidewalk toward the President. His looks were so eager that I questioned his friendship, and prepared to receive him on the point of my sword; but when he got within ten feet of us he suddenly stopped short, took off his hat, and cried out, "Abraham Lincoln, God bless you! You are the poor man's friend!" Then he tried to force his way to the President to shake hands with him. He would not take "No" for an answer until I had to treat him rather roughly, when he stood off, with his arms folded, and looked intently after us. The last I saw of him he was throwing his hat into the air.

Just after this a beautiful girl came from the sidewalk, with a large bouquet of roses in her hand, and advanced, struggling through the crowd toward the President. The mass of people endeavored to open to let her pass, but she had a hard time in reaching him. Her clothes were very much disarranged in making the journey across the street.

I reached out and helped her within the circle of the sailors' bayonets, where, although nearly stifled with the dust, she gracefully presented her bouquet to the President and made a neat little speech, while he held her hand. The beauty and youth of the girl—for she was only about seventeen—made the presentation very touching.

There was a card on the bouquet with these simple words: "From Eva to the Liberator of the slaves." She remained no longer than to deliver her present; then two of the sailors were sent to escort her back to the sidewalk. There was no cheering at this, nor yet was any disapprobation shown; but it was evidently a matter of great interest, for the girl was surrounded and plied with questions. . . .

In a short time we reached the mansion of Mr. Davis, President of the Confederacy, occupied after the evacuation as the headquarters of Generals Weitzel and Shepley. It was quite a small affair campared with the White House, and modest in all its appointments, showing that while President Davis was engaged heart and soul in endeavoring to effect the division of the States, he was not, at least, surrounding himself with regal style, but was living in a modest, comfortable way, like any other citizen. . . .

After this inspection I urged the President to go on board the Malvern. I began to feel more heavily the responsibility resting upon me through the care of his person. The evening was approaching, and we were in a carriage open on all sides. He was glad to go; he was tired out, and wanted the quiet of the flag-ship.

Carl Sandburg describes the surrender of Lee at Appomattox. It was Palm Sunday, April 9, 1865.[9]

Across the path of Lee's army and blocking its way this morning stood the cavalry of Phil Sheridan. At five o'clock this morning General Lee on high ground studied the landscape and what it held. Through a fog he looked. What had arrived yonder? Was it Sheridan only, or did the horse have supporting foot troops? He would wait. He had seen his troops breakfast that morning on parched corn, men and horses having the same food. He had seen his officers breakfast on a gruel of meal and water. He had not been seen to eat any breakfast himself. He had put on his handsomest sword, coat, hat, boots and spurs looking new and fresh, the array topped with a sash of deep-red silk, saying when General Pendleton asked about this gay garb, "I have probably to be General Grant's prisoner and thought I must make my best appearance."

Eight o'clock came. Also came word that Sheridan's cavalry had fallen slowly back and widened out. Behind the cavalry and screened by woodland waited heavy bodies of infantry in blue; these were the troops of Ord and Griffin, who had made an almost incredible march of thirty miles the night and day before, coming up at daybreak to support Sheridan and invite battle. To the left, to the rear, were other Union lines. Their circle of campfires reflected on clouds the night before told of their surrounding the Army of Northern Virginia.

Robert E. Lee now had three choices. He could go into frontal battle, fight the last, bloody, forlorn conflict of the war. He could escape with a thin remnant to mountains lying westward and carry on guerrilla warfare. Or he could surrender.

He asked Longstreet and other generals whether the sacrifice of his army in battle would help the Confederate cause elsewhere. They said in effect that a battle lost now against overwhelming numbers and resources would be of no use. To General Alexander, Lee spoke of the lawless futility of bushwhacking and guerrilla fighting, which "would bring on a state of affairs it would take the country years to recover from."

Lee's staff officers heard him say, "There is nothing left for me to do but to go and see General Grant, and I would rather die a thousand deaths."

"Oh, General," protested one, "what will history say of the surrender of the army in the field?"

"Yes, I know they will say hard things of us! They will not understand how we were overwhelmed by numbers. But that is not the question, Colonel: The question is, is it right to surrender this army. If it is right, then I will take all the responsibility."

He looked over the field at a lifting fog and spoke as though tempted to go out where, the war being still on, he would be one easy target. "How easily could I be rid of this, and be at rest! I have only to ride along the line and all will be over!" For a moment he seemed almost hopeless, then recovered. "But it is our duty to live."

Lee wrote a note asking Grant for an interview "with reference to the surrender of this army." Grant on receiving it at once wrote Lee to name the place for their meeting. Grant riding toward the front said to Colonel Horace Porter, "The pain in my head seemed to leave me the moment I got Lee's letter."

And it became a folk tale and a school-reader story how at the McLean house on the edge of Appomattox village, ninety-five miles west of Richmond, the two great captains of men faced each other in a little room and Lee gave over his army to Grant, and the two men looked so different from each other. Lee tall and erect, Grant short and stoop-shouldered. Lee in a clean and dazzling military outfit, Grant in a rough-worn and dusty blouse telling his high rank only by the three stars on the shoulders, Grant apologizing to Lee that he had come direct from the field and hadn't time to change his uniform. Lee fifty-eight years old with silver hair, near the evening of life, Grant forty-two with black hair and unspent strength of youth yet in him. . . .

"I met you once before, General Lee," began Grant in even voice, "while we were serving in Mexico. . . . I have always remembered your appearance, and I think I should have recognized you anywhere."

"Yes, I know I met you on that occasion, and I have often thought of it and tried to recollect how you looked, but I have never been able to recall a single feature."

Talk about Mexico ran into memories of that war when they both wore blue. Grant just about forgot why they were there, it seemed, or else the old and early bashfulness of Grant was working. Lee brought him to the point. "I suppose, General Grant, that the object of our present meeting is fully understood. I asked to see you to ascertain upon what terms you would receive the surrender of my army."

Not a shading of change crossed Grant's face. He went on as between two good neighbors. "The terms I propose are those stated substantially in my letter of yesterday—that is, the officers and men surrendered to be paroled and disqualified from taking up arms again until properly exchanged, and all arms, ammunition and supplies to be delivered up as captured property."

Lee nodded assent. This was what he had hoped for, though one of his generals had predicted that the army would be marched off to prison in shame and disgrace. "Those," said Lee to Grant, "are about the conditions I expected would be proposed."

Grant, seated at a table, put it in writing, his staff aides and corps commanders standing by, Lee seated with his aide Colonel Charles Marshall standing behind his chair. Grant rose, stepped over to Lee, and handed him the paper scrawled in pencil. Lee took out spectacles from a pocket, pulled out a handkerchief and wiped the glasses, crossed his legs, and read slowly and carefully the strangest and most consequential paper for him that had ever met his eyes.

At the words "until properly" he suggested that General Grant must have meant to add the word "exchanged."

"Why, yes," said Grant, "I thought I had put in the word 'exchanged.' "

Lee said that with Grant's permission he would mark where the word "exchanged" should be inserted. "Certainly," said Grant. Lee felt his pockets for a pencil and seemed that day to have no pencil. Colonel Horace Porter stepped forward with a pencil. Lee thanked him, put a caret where the word "exchanged" was to go in, read to the finish, and then with his first touch of warmth said to Grant, "This will have a very happy effect on my army."

Grant asked for any further suggestions. Lee had one. In his army the cavalrymen and artillerists owned their horses. He wanted these men who owned their mounts to have them on their farms for spring plowing. Grant said this subject was quite new to him. He hadn't known that private soldiers owned their horses. In his own army the rank and file had only government horses and mules. However, "I take it that most of the men in the ranks are small farmers, and as the country has been so raided by the two armies, it is doubtful whether they will be able to put in a crop to carry themselves and their families through the next winter without the aid of the horses they are now riding." So without changing the written terms he would instruct officers receiving paroles "to let all the men who claim to own a horse or mule take the animals home with them to work their little farms."

Lee showed relief. "This will have the best possible effect upon the men. It will be very gratifying and will do much toward conciliating our people."

Lee shook hands with some of Grant's generals who offered theirs, bowed, said little, was too heavy of heart to join in a pleasantry from one old West Point acquaintance, then turned to Grant saying that a thousand Union prisoners, including some officers, had been living the last few days on parched corn only; they required attention, and of provisions "I have, indeed, nothing for my own men." This was discussed briefly and Grant directed that 25,000 rations be sent to Lee's men.

Lee wrote an acceptance of Grant's terms, signed it, and at 3:45 in the afternoon of this Palm Sunday, April 9, 1865, the documents of surrendering an army were completed. There remained only such formalities as roll call and stacking of arms. Union gunners made ready to fire a salute of grand national triumph, but Grant forbade any signs of rejoicing over a broken enemy that he hoped hereafter would no longer be an enemy. Grant directed his men that no cheers, no howls of triumph, were wanted—and few were heard. The rank and file of these two armies, "bluebelly" and "butternut," had traded tobacco and coffee and newspapers on the picket lines enough to have a degree of fellowship and affection for each other. Too often this fraternizing on the front lines had troubled commanders who felt it was interfering with the war.

Lee rode among his men—who crowded around him crying, "We'll fight 'em yet"—and explained, with tears and in a choked voice, that they had fought the war together, he had done his best, and it was over. Many were dazed. Some wept. Others cursed and babbled. The army could die but never surrender, they had hoped. Yet they still worshiped Lee. They touched his hands, his uniform; they petted Traveller and smoothed his flanks with their hands. One man, throwing down his musket, cried to the blue heaven: "Blow, Gabriel, blow! My God, let him blow, I am ready to die!"

For a wild week or more the North celebrated, first the fall of Richmond and finally the surrender at Appomattox. The scene in Washington, for four years the heart of the Union's mighty effort, is described by Margaret Leech.[10]

From Fourteenth and M Streets sounded a deafening salute of eight hundred guns—three hundred for Petersburg and five hundred for Richmond—and one hundred more boomed from the Navy Yard wharf. Every Government building spilled out shouting clerks. The circuit and criminal courts adjourned. Workers tumbled out of banks and offices and shops. Gleeful colored folk came running, convalescents panted out of the hospitals, and children skipped from the public schools to swell the holiday crowds. By noon, in streets dizzy with clanging church bells and waving flags, the entire population of Washington seemed to be abroad, shaking hands and embracing, throwing up their hats, shrieking and singing, like a carnival of lunatics.

Oratory burst spontaneously from the steps of public buildings, and hotels. Most impressive of all was the scene at the War
Department, where Secretary Stanton faltered out a solemn
speech to the multitude that packed the park. In a phrase that
might have been Lincoln's, he asked his hearers to beseech Providence "to teach us how to be humble in the midst of triumph."
The crowd yelled applause for his pious sentiments, though some
called "Let her burn!" at the news that Richmond was on fire.
There were tears in Stanton's eyes, as people rushed forward to
grip his hand, even to try to throw their arms about him. He had
suddenly become the most popular man in Washington. "I forgive ye all yer sins, ye old blizzard!" a soldier shouted. . . .

As though by prearrangement, bands turned out, blaring the
national airs, and the crowds marched in time to "Yankee Doodle"
and "Rally 'Round the Flag." Two squadrons of cavalry and
a brigade of Veteran Reserves formed a parade, and found themselves being reviewed by General Augur in the grounds south of
the White House. Carriages, draped with flags, went rolling along
the Avenue. The fire departments galloped through town, blowing off blasts of steam.

Black and white, the people of Washington whooped it up
through the whole delirious afternoon. Fraternizing patriots went
arm in arm to drink together, and nightfall failed to quiet their
exuberance. That evening, the celebrated comedienne, Miss Laura
Keene, opened a two weeks' engagement at Ford's in a composition of her own, *The Workmen of Washington*, a moral drama
directed at exposing the evils of intemperance. It was a timely, if
uninfluential, production. Champagne corks were popping all
over Washington, and the drinking saloons were jammed. To
assist the night force, the day police remained on duty until
eleven. The patrolmen looked with tolerance on boisterous parties
of songsters, escorting helpless drunks home, and arrested only
flagrant offenders. . . .

The State Department had recommended a grand illumination for Tuesday evening in honor of the victory. All day the public buildings swarmed with workmen. The White House and its neighboring departments grew gay with decorations. Patriotic mottoes embellished the State Department. The War Department was smothered in flags and ensigns. The Navy hung out a large model of a full-rigged ship. Over the main entrance of the Treasury was a transparency of a ten-dollar, interest-bearing United States note.

The big Treasury, with its many windows, was bound to outshine the rest in concentrated splendor, and Mr. Stanton bestirred himself to make a striking effect at the War Department. Though it was a diminutive structure, it had overflowed into eleven buildings, some of which, like Winder's and the Corcoran Art Gallery, were of imposing size. As the dark-blue evening fell, a man was stationed, matches in hand, in every window. Other men stood ready at a row of fireballs in the department park. There was a trumpet blast, a band crashed into "The Star-Spangled Banner," and instantaneously, "like lighting gas-jets by electricity," the branch offices gleamed in a comet's tail along Seventeenth Street, while the little War Department swam in colored flame.

From basement to dome, the Capitol burned like a beacon on its hill. Over the western pediment, Major French had contrived a great, gaslighted transparency, printed in enormous letters. The words could be read far up Pennsylvania Avenue: "This is the Lord's doing; it is marvellous in our eyes." There were illuminations at the Patent Office and the Post-Office, at all the army headquarters, the Marine Barracks, the Navy Yard, the National Conservatory and the hospitals. Superintendent Wood had been at pains to make the First Street prison brilliant. The Insane Asylum glittered like a star. . . .

All Washington turned out to see the show. Throngs gathered

in the Capitol grounds, and around the furnace glow of the Treasury. There were music and fireworks in F Street, where thousands stood wedged before the Patent Office at a Republican mass meeting. Under the gas jets which spelled "Union," Judge Cartter of the District supreme court stepped forward on the Patent Office portico to speak of Jefferson Davis, "the flying rascal out of Richmond." He made dark allusions to the national military institution which educated traitors to cut the nation's throat, and hesitated not to say "that those who have been fed, clothed and taught at the public expense ought to stretch the first rope." F Street rang with cheers for Judge Cartter, and for Vice-President Johnson, who dwelt on the same theme. Jefferson Davis, Andy ranted, had plunged the sword given him by his country in his mother's bosom. Calls of "Hang him!" rose from the crowd; and Johnson shouted yes, hang him twenty times, for treason was the greatest of crimes.

The President was at Richmond, watching the last struggles of Lee's hard-pressed and starving troops, and Washington could hear no word from him on that night of celebration.

Mrs. Lincoln had returned to Washington on Sunday, but on Wednesday she again left for City Point with a party of notables. That same day, an accident occurred in Washington which was influential in hastening the President's return. While Mr. Seward was taking his afternoon drive, his horses became frightened, and bolted. The Secretary jumped from the carriage, and was violently thrown to the ground. He was picked up unconscious, suffering from concussion, a broken right arm and a shattered jaw. . . .

The *River Queen* docked early on the evening of Palm Sunday, April 9. Lincoln went immediately to Seward's residence, and was admitted to the sick chamber. Seward lay on the side of the bed away from the door, precariously stretched along the edge, so that his painful broken arm projected, free from any pressure. His face, swathed in bandages, was so swollen and discolored as to be nearly unrecognizable. He managed to whisper, "You are back from Richmond?" "Yes," the President told him, "and I think we are near the end, at last." Lincoln sprawled across the bed, resting on his elbow with his face close to Seward's, and related the story of the last two weeks. At last, the Secretary of State fell into a feverish sleep, and Lincoln slipped softly from the room.

Before he went to rest, the President learned from Stanton that Lee's army had surrended that morning at Appomattox. Few were abroad in the dark and damp to join the jollification of the newspaper reporters. Most people in the capital were informed of the surrender when, at daybreak next morning, their beds were shaken by the repercussions of the guns. The battery was stationed on Massachusetts Avenue, behind Lafayette Square, and cracking windowpanes in that aristocratic neighborhood provoked some of the residents to wish an end to the Union's rejoicing. A large crowd of patriots was soon hurrahing in the bleak dawn. Many loyal persons, however, remained abed, satisfied to know that the tongues of the guns proclaimed victory for General Grant. . . .

There was not the wild hysteria that had greeted the fall of Richmond. Popular emotion had been too freely spent to repeat that outburst in a single week. Yet there was one new factor which made the strongest excitement on April 10. The President was back in Washington, and to the White House, from breakfast time on, people went running like joyful children eager to see their father. Several times, Lincoln, hard at work in his office, sent out word to disperse the crowds, but twice he appeared briefly at the window. In the forenoon, a procession followed in the wake of the Navy Yard workmen, who had been rampaging through the streets with bands and noisy boat howitzers. While the little showoff, Tad, waved a captured rebel flag, there were shouts for a speech. The President's appearance was the signal for pandemonium. Throwing their hats in the air again and again, men gave vent to throat-splitting yells of exultation. Lincoln briefly excused himself. He supposed that there would be some general demonstration, and he would say something then. He called on the musicians to play the good old tune of "Dixie," which he declared had now become the lawful property of the Union. Late in the afternoon, he again responded to rousing calls by saying that he would defer his remarks; preferably until the following evening, as he would be better prepared.

The President's features had lost their look of illness and fatigue. His thin face was shining. The burden of "this great trouble" was about to be lifted from his shoulders; but there was no elation in his happiness. Absorbed in thoughts of rebuilding the Union, his joy was sobered by the heavy responsibilities of victory.

10.

The Moral Force

To say that Lincoln's literary style and his private religious views had a lot to do with winning the war is a paradox which yet contains much truth. Lincoln was a master of communication. To understand the importance of his gift requires a re-examination of his training and his personality.

Horace White, later editor of the New York Evening Post, *who knew Lincoln well during the prewar period, launches the discussion with an analysis of the elements which made up Lincoln's oratorical skill. "The ambitious young men of the day,"* he wrote, *"must make their mark by oratory or not at all. . . . If a man was to gain any popularity he must gain it by talking into the faces of the people. He must have a ready tongue, and must be prepared to meet all comers and to accept all challenges. Stump-speaking, wrestling, story-telling, and horse-racing were the only amusements of the people. In the first three of these Mr. Lincoln excelled." It was a hard school for the rising politician, who could expect no help from public address systems, radio or television. Yet in White's opinion it was "the best possible school" for Lincoln, who also had the advantage of being pitted against able opponents like Douglas. "It was in restless competition and rough-and-tumble with Douglas and others,"*

White concluded, "that Mr. Lincoln acquired that rare power of expression, by mouth and pen, which drew to himself the attention of the State and afterward of the nation and the world."[1]

Story-telling was a cherished art on the frontier. "In early times," wrote Joseph Gillespie, a youthful crony of Lincoln's, "Illinois was conspicuous for the number of its story tellers. The prevailing taste at that time took that direction."[2] *Lincoln's fame as a raconteur spread throughout Illinois; yet few of his anecdotes were his own. "I do generally remember a good story when I hear it," Lincoln told Noah Brooks many years later, "but I never did invent anything original; I am only a retail dealer."*[3]

Although these "backwoods allegories" all but disappeared from Lincoln's public speech in later life, he continued to use his rich gift in private for a variety of social purposes: to drive home a point in conversation, to set people at their ease, to get rid of unwelcome visitors, to conceal his real opinions, even to achieve the ingratiating ambiguity so necessary at times to the politician and statesman. Nevertheless his enemies constantly ridiculed him for his "vulgar, backwoods jokes" and in time Lincoln grew sensitive about his reputation as a teller of stories.

The point is illustrated by a touching anecdote. Colonel Silas W. Burt, on the wartime staff of Governor Seymour of New York, found it necessary late one night to rouse Lincoln out of bed at the Soldiers' Home with an urgent message from his Governor. Two companions came with Burt, one of them a coarse army major who had already drunk too much. It was 1863 and the eve of Gettysburg.[4]

After the servant returned and announced that the President would receive us, we sat for some time in painful silence. At length we heard slow, shuffling steps come down the carpeted stairs, and the President entered the room as we respectfully rose from our seats. That pathetic figure has ever remained indelible in my memory. His tall form was bowed, his hair disheveled; he wore no necktie or collar, and his large feet were partly incased in very loose, heel-less slippers. It was very evident that he had got up from his bed or had been very nearly ready to get into it when we were announced, and had hastily put on some clothing and those slippers that made the flip-flap sounds on the stairs.

It was the face that, in every line, told the story of anxiety and weariness. The drooping eyelids, looking almost swollen; the dark bags beneath the eyes; the deep marks about the large and expressive mouth; the flaccid muscles of the jaws, were all so majestically pitiful that I could almost have fallen on my knees and begged pardon for my part in the cruel presumption and impudence that had thus invaded his repose. As we were severally introduced, the President shook hands with us, and then took his seat on a haircloth-covered sofa beside the Major, while we others sat on chairs in front of him. Colonel Van Buren, in fitting words, conveyed the message from Governor Seymour. . . .

The merely formal talk being over, something was said about the critical condition of military matters, and the President observed that he had no fears about the safety of Washington, and was certain that the attempted invasion of the Northern States would be arrested. He said the latest intelligence from the Army of the Potomac was favorable, but gave no details, and it was not until the next day that we learned that General Meade had succeeded General Hooker.

A little pause in the conversation ensued. The gaunt figure of the President had gradually slid lower on the slippery sofa, and his long legs were stretched out in front, the loose slippers half-fallen from his feet, while the drowsy eyelids had almost closed over his eyes, and his jaded features had taken on the suggestion of relaxation in sleep. . . .

Deeply moved by the President's evident fatigue, and by his cordial treatment of us in spite of our presumptuous call, Colonel Van Buren and I were about rising to make our adieux when, to our dismay, the Major slapped the President on his knee and said: "Mr. President, tell us one of your good stories."

If the floor had opened and dropped me out of sight, I should have been happy.

The President drew himself up, and turning his back as far as possible upon the Major, with great dignity addressed the rest of us, saying: "I believe I have the popular reputation of being a story-teller, but I do not deserve the name in its general sense; for it is not the story itself, but its purpose, or effect, that interests me. I often avoid a long and useless discussion by others or a laborious explanation on my own part by a short story that illustrates my point of view. So, too, the sharpness of a refusal or the edge of a rebuke may be blunted by an appropriate story, so as to save wounded feeling, and yet serve the purpose. No, I am not simply a story-teller, but story-telling as an emollient saves me much friction and distress." These are almost his exact words, of which I made a record that very night.

Lincoln found the telling of stories a useful device in the building of his career, but in later life the writing and the delivery of speeches became vastly more important as a means of bringing his ideas and his personality before the people. As Horace White has pointed out, the study and practice of oratory was a major concern for all public men. Walt Whitman, for instance, trained himself in oratory, practicing in the solitude of the woods and along the shores until the cadences of the public speaker came to permeate his poetry. Lincoln's own intense interest in "declamation" was remembered by a boy who chanced to visit him in his Springfield law office shortly before the war:[5]

Evidently Mr. Lincoln was in a talkative mood, for, in the absence of an older person, he seemed pleased to see me. He put me through a course of questions, probably to get at the thoughts and interests of the boy of the day. One discovery was that the thing in which I was most interested at school—probably because I had a knack of doing it fairly well for a boy—was declamation. Nothing would do but I must repeat an oration. To this day I wonder at and admire the tact with which he overcame my great embarrassment. The place and conditions were such as to make a boy resolve to perish before raising his voice in a school declamatory exercise. Yet before I quite knew it, or knew how he did it, he had me standing at the table and shouting a tribute to Washington. He was really interested, for he went over the piece himself, to give his notion of the emphasis and inflection; and he undertook to make me explain why "he needs no marble monument, no consecrated pile." To illustrate some point he recalled one of the many speeches which he said he had "learned by heart" when he began the study of law, hesitating now and then, but always getting the word at last. He mentioned many famous addresses all of which he knew at one time, when he was forming what he called "an unnatural style of speech" for professional use.

"Try to think they're your own words, and talk them as you would talk them to me," was his advice after I had ranted in school-boy manner. He insisted, too, on the importance of learning, in early life, sentiments expressed by verse. In effect he said that as a man grows older lines which he learned because of their pleasant sound come to have a meaning; just as old saws show their truth in later life; "It is a pleasure," he said, "to be able to quote lines to fit any occasion," and he noted that the Bible is the richest source of pertinent quotations. I think Mr. Lincoln had much to do with creating whatever ambition I had for the reading of history, on which he placed great stress.

Lincoln's masterful literary style, distinguished by its clean use of words, its power, its rhythmical balance, and its subtle responsiveness to the occasion, was only in part a development of his study of "declamation." He was a born literary artist, and his style

*grew and changed as he grew. As a fledgling politician, for in-
stance, Lincoln was given to flights of purple rhetoric in the
manner of the time: "I know that the great volcano at Washington, aroused and directed by the evil spirit that reigns there,"
he declaimed in the peroration of a speech on the Sub-Treasury
in 1839, "is belching forth the lava of political corruption, in a
current broad and deep, which is sweeping with frightening
velocity over the whole length and breadth of the land, bidding
fair to leave unscathed no green spot or living thing, while on its
bosom are riding like demons on the waves of Hell, the imps of
that evil spirit, and fiendishly taunting all those who dare resist
its destroying course, with the hopelessness of their effort; and
knowing this, I cannot deny that all may be swept away."[6]*

*The turning point in Lincoln's personality, and consequently in
his style, seems to have come during those reflective years of
political retirement between 1849 and 1854. It was perhaps the
practice of the law during these years as much as Horace White's
"school of the stump" that sharpened and refined the style. In
the legal turmoil Lincoln learned how to reach and sway men
through the power of words. He became an acknowledged master
at addressing juries. ". . . there is no false glitter, no sickly senti-
mentalism to be discovered" the Danville Illinois Citizen wrote
in 1850 about Lincoln's way with a jury. "In vain we look for
a rhetorical display. . . . Bold, forcible and energetic, he forces
conviction upon the mind, and, by his clearness and conciseness,
stamps it there, not to be erased. . . ."[7]*

In an article on Lincoln, written for The Cambridge History
of American Literature, *Nathaniel W. Stephenson finds the clue
to Lincoln's style in the unfolding of his personality.[8]*

Here is an original literary artist who never did any
deliberate literary work, who enriched English style in spite
of himself under pressure of circumstances. His style is but the

flexibility with which his expression follows the movements of a peculiar mind. And as the mind slowly unfolds, becomes overcast, recedes, advances, so, in the main, does the style. The usual symptoms of the literary impulse are all to seek. He is wholly preoccupied with the thing behind the style. Again the idea of a nature shrouded, withdrawn, that dwells within, that emerges mysteriously. His youth, indeed, has a scattered, unemphatic intimation of something else. What might be called the juvenilia of this inscrutable mind include some attempts at verse. They have no literary value. More significant than his own attempts is the fact that verse early laid a strong hold upon him. Years later, when the period of his juvenilia may be counted in the past, as late as 1846, in denying the authorship of a newspaper poem he added: "I would give all I am worth and go in debt to be able to write so fine a piece." Even in the first period of his maturity he could still lapse into verse. A visit to his former home in 1844 called forth two poems that have survived. One was a reverie in the vein of

> O Memory! thou midway world
>   Twixt earth and Paradise,
> Where things decayed and loved ones lost
>   In dreamy shadows rise.

The other was a description of an idiot, long a familiar village figure. Commenting on this poem, Lincoln refers to his "poetizing mood." His official biographers tell us that his favourite poets were Shakespeare, Burns, Byron, and Tom Hood, and add that his taste was "rather morbid." Byron's *Dream* was one of his favourites. It is a commonplace that he never tired of the trivial stanzas beginning

> Oh why should the spirit of mortal be proud.

. . . Lincoln's sense of rhythm was far deeper, far more subtle, than mere cadence. In time it became a marvellous power for arranging ideas in patterns so firmly, so clearly, with such unfaltering disposition of emphasis that it is impossible to read them into confusion—as is so easy to do with the idea-patterns of ordinary writers. And with this sense of the idea-pattern grew up at last a sense of cadence most delicately and beautifully accompanying, and reinforcing, the movement of the ideas. In 1832 there were but gleams of all this—but genuine gleams.

The ten years following, sterile from the point of view of production, are none the less to the student of Lincoln's mind most important. . . . Is it fanciful to find a connection between the way in which his mysticism develops—its atmospheric, non-dogmatic pervasiveness—and the way in which his style develops? Certainly the literary part of him works into all the portions of his utterance with the gradualness of the daylight through a shadowy wood. [The] seven years following 1842 show a gradual change; but it is extremely gradual. And it is to be noted that the literary quality, so far as there is any during these years—for it comes and goes—is never incisive. It is of the whole, not of the detail. It does not appear as a gift of phrases. Rather it is the slow unfolding of those two original characteristics, taste and rhythm. What is growing is the degree of both things. The man is becoming deeper, and as he does so he imposes himself, in this atmospheric way, more steadily on his language.

Curiously enough it is to this period that his only comic writings belong. Too much has been said about Lincoln's humour. Almost none of it has survived. Apparently it was neither better nor worse than the typical American humour of the period. . . .

A speech which he made in Congress, a landmark in his development, shows the quality of his humour, and shows also that he was altogether a man of his period, not superior in many small ways to the standards of his period. The Congress of the United

States has never been distinguished for a scrupulous use of its time; today, however, even the worst of Congresses would hardly pervert its function, neglect business, and transform itself into an electioneering forum, with the brazenness of the Congresses of the middle of the last century. In the summer of 1848, with Zachary Taylor before the country as the Whig nominee for president, Lincoln went the way of all flesh political, squandering the time of the House in a jocose electioneering speech, nominally on a point before the House, really having no connection with it—in fact, a romping burlesque of the Democratic candidate, Cass. As such things went at that day, it was capital. It was better than most such speeches because, granting the commonplace thing he had set out to do, Lincoln's better sense of language gave even to his romp a quality the others did not have. . . .

Another period in Lincoln's literary life extends from his return to politics to the First Inaugural. Of all parts of his personal experience it is the most problematic. At its opening there rises the question why he returned to politics. Was there a crisis of some sort about 1855 as, surely, there was about 1849? His official biographers are unsatisfying. Their Lincoln is exasperatingly conventional—always the saint and the hero, as saint-heroes were conceived by the average American in the days when it was a supreme virtue to be "self-made." That there was some sort of failure of courage in the Lincoln who gave up politics in 1849 is of course too much for official biography to be expected to consider. But it might perceive something besides pure devotion to the public weal in Lincoln's return. That this successful provincial lawyer who had made a name for conscientiousness should be deeply stirred when politics took a turn that seemed to him wicked, was of course quite what one would expect. And yet, was the Lincoln who returned to the political arena the same who had withdrawn from it? Was there not power in him in 1855 that was not in him in 1849? May it not be that he had fled from his

ambition in an excess of self-distrust, just as in his love affair
doubt of himself had led him for a time to forsake what he most
desired? And may not the new strength that had come to him
have revived the old ambition, blended it with his zeal for service,
and thus in a less explicit way than his biographers would have
us think, faced him back toward politics. Be that as it may, his
literary power, which took a bound forward in the excitement
following the Nebraska Bill, holds itself at a high level for several
years, and then suddenly enters into eclipse. Beginning with the
speech at Springfield on the Dred Scott case, including the
"house divided" speech, the Douglas speeches, and closing with
the Cooper Union speech in February, 1860, there are a dozen
pieces of prose in this second manner of Lincoln's that are all
masterly. . . .

Then, in the later winter, between his determination of the new
policy and his inauguration, came the eclipse. All the questions
roused in the past by his seasons of shadow, recur. Was it super-
stition? Was it mystical premonition? Was there something here
akin to those periods of intense gloom that overtook the Puritans
of the seventeenth century? . . . No recollection of Lincoln is
more singular than one preserved by his law partner with regard
to this period of eclipse. He tells of Lincoln's insistence that their
sign should continue to hang over the office door; of his sad
eagerness to have everyone understand that his departure was not
final; of his reiteration that some day he would come back, that
his business would be resumed in the plain old office just as if
nothing had happened. . . .

The notions of the time required the President-elect to talk all
the way from his home to the White House. This group of
speeches forms an interlude in Lincoln's development so strange
that the most psychological biographer might well hesitate to
attack its problem. As statecraft the speeches were ruinously
inopportune. Their matter was a fatuous assurance to the country
that the crisis was not really acute. As literature, his utterances

have little character. The force, the courage, the confident note of the second manner had left him. His partisans were appalled. One of the most sincere among them wrote angrily "Lincoln is a Simple Susan."

And then, lightning-like, both as statecraft and as literature, came the First Inaugural. Richard was himself again. He was much more, he was a new Richard. The final manner appeared in the First Inaugural. All the confident qualities of the second manner are there, and with them something else. Now, at last, reading him, we are conscious of beauty. Now we see what the second manner lacked. Keen, powerful, full of character, melodious, impressive, nevertheless it had not that sublimation of all these, and with that the power to awaken the imagination which, in argumentative prose, is beauty.

Lincoln had apparently passed through one of those indescribable inward experiences—always, it seems, accompanied by deep gloom—which in mystical natures so often precede a rebirth of the mind. Psychology has not yet analyzed and classified them. But history is familiar with a sufficient number to be sure of their reality. From Saul agonizing in his tent to Luther throwing his inkpot at the devil; from Cromwell wrestling with the Lord to Lincoln striving to be vocal when his mind was dumb—in a hundred instances there is the same range of phenomena, the same spiritual night, the same amazing dawn.

To Stephenson, Lincoln was above all an artist in temperament. It was Stephenson's theme, as developed in his biography of Lincoln, that the artist in Lincoln lay deeply buried during the brash years of his youth and the self-distrust of his middle years. Only with the release of this sensitive inner personality did the transformed Lincoln of the war years emerge. "The dreamer had learned to translate his intuitive knowledge into action; he had become the artist as executive. . . ." Stephenson summed it up: "The fusion of the outer and inner person was the result of a profound interior change. Those elements of mysticism which were in him from the first, which had gleamed darkly through such deep overshadowing, were at last established in their permanent form. The political tension had been matched by a spiritual tension with personal sorrow as the connecting link. In a word, he had found his religion."[9]

It was religion in the mystical sense which infused Lincoln's great speeches with deep emotion. And it was this emotional drive which enabled him to impose his view of the war with such force upon a nation which believed as a matter of course that a guiding Providence directed the affairs of men. Under the stress of war Lincoln's religious expression took on an almost biblical tone, close to that of New England Puritanism. In his eyes the war had become a mighty struggle between the powers of good and evil. In The Lincoln Legend Roy P. Basler marshals evidence to show that Lincoln identified himself and his wartime mission with the purposes of God.[10] Nevertheless, Lincoln could never have been called religious in the conventional sense. T. V. Smith put it succinctly: "He did not join a church, nor could he have joined one, churches being what they were and his sense of fitness being what it was."[11] He had rebelled against organized religion in his youth, and as late as 1858, in a talk with Henry Villard about "infidels" in Villard's native Germany, admitted that "my own inclination is that way."[12]

Yet the substance of religion, if not the outward forms, illuminated his entire life. The frontier environment of his youth offered little in the way of formal religious training, but the hard and lonely conditions of life in the wilderness instilled a mystical sense of powerful natural forces. A fragment from 1862, usually called "A Meditation on the Divine Will," brings out both the questing skepticism of Lincoln's mind and his deep if undefined feeling for the immanence of God.

The will of God prevails. In great contests, each party claims to act in accordance with the will of God. Both may be, and one must be wrong. God cannot be both for and against the same thing at the same time. In the present Civil War it is quite possible that God's purpose is something quite different from the purpose of either party; and yet the human instrumentalities working just as they do, are the best adaptation to effect His purpose. I am almost ready to say that this is probably true; that God wills this contest and wills that it shall not end yet. By His mere great power on the minds of the now contestants, He could either have saved or destroyed the Union without a human contest. Yet the contest began. And, having begun, He could give the final victory to either side any day. Yet the contest proceeds.

Watching Lincoln at the second inauguration, De Chambrun felt the underlying reverence: "I had not fully comprehended up to this moment his attitude of selfless modesty, nor conceived that such an exalted position could be sustained with so much religious feeling."[13] *And who should know better than Mary Lincoln, fundamentally an understanding woman despite her eccentricities? She told Herndon after Lincoln's death: "Mr. Lincoln had no faith and no hope in the usual acceptation of those words. He never joined a church; yet still, as I believe, he was a religious man by nature. He first seemed to think about the subject when our boy Willie died, and then more than ever about the time he went to Gettysburg; but it was a kind of poetry in his nature, and he was never a technical Christian."*[14]

In his introduction to Lincoln's Speeches and Writings, *Roy P. Basler has searched out the religious element in the Gettysburg Address.*[15]

The emergence of this new feeling was significantly coincident with his assumption of what he seemed to consider his supreme task—the preservation of the Union, and with it democracy. His utterances regarding slavery, in fact, his words on all other subjects, fine as many of them are, fall into place near or far from the high words in which he defended and pleaded for democracy as symbolized in the Union. Alexander Stephens once said that the Union with Lincoln rose in sentiment to the "sublimity of a religious mysticism." The "Gettysburg Address" is excellent literary evidence in support of Stephen's opinion, for it reveals Lincoln's worship of the Union as the symbol of an ideal yet to be realized.

Lincoln's problem at Gettysburg was to do two things: to commemorate the past and to prophesy for the future. To do these things he took the theme dearest to his audience, honor for the heroic dead sons and fathers, and combined it with the theme nearest to his own heart, the preservation of democracy. Out of this double theme grew his poetic metaphor of birth, death, and spiritual rebirth, of the life of man and the life of the nation. To it he brought the fervor of devoutly religious belief. Democracy was to Lincoln a religion, and he wanted it to be in a real sense the religion of his audience. Thus he combined an elegiac theme with a patriotic theme, skillfully blending the hope of eternal life with the hope of eternal democracy.

"Short, short, short" was Lincoln's description of the speech he intended to deliver at the dedication of the Union cemetery at Gettysburg, when Noah Brooks asked him about it the day before.[16] *John Hay described the ceremonies of November 19, 1863: "In the morning I got a beast and rode out with the President's suite to the Cemetery in the procession. The procession formed itself in an orphanly sort of way & moved out with very little help from anybody & after a little delay Mr. Everett took his place on the stand—and Mr. Stockton made a prayer which thought it was an oration; and Mr. Everett spoke as he always*

does, perfectly—and the President, in a fine, free way, with more grace than is his wont, said his half dozen words of consecration, and the music wailed and we went home through crowded and cheering streets." [17]

Into these "half dozen words of consecration" Lincoln had distilled his entire vision of the war. It was a testament of faith, composed with the terseness of true poetry and embodying his most deeply felt ideas. But unfortunately, we have heard these words too often; they have turned dull in the mind like a record played over and over again until the meaning of the notes is lost. Yet the speech may once again come alive in all its greatness if you will read it as Lincoln felt it—as a testament of his leadership, as a poem built around the central theme for which he lived and died—the struggle to preserve a people's government in this land.

Fourscore and seven years ago our fathers brought forth on this continent a new nation, conceived in liberty, and dedicated to the proposition that all men are created equal.

Now we are engaged in a great civil war, testing whether that nation, or any nation so conceived and so dedicated, can long endure. We are met on a great battlefield of that war. We have come to dedicate a portion of that field, as a final resting place for those who here gave their lives that that nation might live. It is altogether fitting and proper that we should do this.

But, in a larger sense, we cannot dedicate—we cannot consecrate—we cannot hallow—this ground. The brave men, living and dead, who struggled here, have consecrated it, far above our poor power to add or detract. The world will little note, nor long remember, what we say here, but it can never forget what they did here. It is for us the living, rather, to be dedicated here to the unfinished work which they who fought here have thus far so nobly advanced. It is rather for us to be here dedicated to the great task remaining before us—that from these honored dead we take increased devotion to that cause for which they gave the last full measure of devotion—that we here highly resolve that these dead shall not have died in vain—that this nation, under God, shall have a new birth of freedom—and that government of the people, by the people, for the people, shall not perish from the earth.

In the heat of Lincoln's moral conviction, the artist and the statesman had fused into a new and compelling personality, one which was created, in a sense, by the literary artistry of the words themselves. Many of Lincoln's most memorable passages haunt the memory as much for their sound as for their meaning. Listen, as an example, to the magnificent rhetoric at the close of the Second Inaugural. "This was like a sacred poem," said Carl Schurz. "No American President had ever spoken words like these to the American people."[18]

Fondly do we hope—fervently do we pray—that this mighty scourge of war may speedily pass away. Yet, if God wills that it continue, until all the wealth piled by the bond-man's two hundred and fifty years of unrequited toil shall be sunk, and until every drop of blood drawn with the lash, shall be paid by another drawn with the sword, as was said three thousand years ago, so still it must be said "the judgments of the Lord, are true and righteous altogether."

With malice toward none; with charity for all; with firmness in the right, as God gives us to see the right, let us strive on to finish the work we are in; to bind up the nation's wounds; to care for him who shall have borne the battle, and for his widow, and his orphan—to do all which may achieve and cherish a just and lasting peace, among ourselves, and with all nations.

*Lincoln acted out a supreme part on the stage of history. It was
a role consciously assumed, and poetically expressed in the words
of his great speeches; a role which enabled him to lift the minds
and hearts of his people toward victory. And he acted it out to
the bitter end. Recurrent dreams and premonitions seemed to
foreshadow his inevitable assassination. A few days before his
death he heard in a dream the sounds of weeping and sobbing
throughout the White House and wandering into the East Room
found his own body laid out in death. "In the poem that Lincoln
lived," Edmund Wilson has written, "the tragic conclusion was
necessary to justify all the rest. It was dramatically and morally
inevitable that this prophet who had overruled opposition and
sent thousands of men to their deaths should finally attest his
good faith by laying down his own life with theirs."[19]*

*But in the poignancy of this almost religious drama Abraham
Lincoln, the man, has too often been forgotten. Hofstadter com-
passionately sketches in what the war and the presidency did to
the body and soul of Lincoln.[20]*

Lincoln was shaken by the presidency. Back in Spring-
field, politics had been a sort of exhilarating game; but in the
White House, politics was power, and power was responsibility.
Never before had Lincoln held executive office. . . .

Lincoln's rage for personal success, his external and worldly
ambition, was quieted when he entered the White House, and he
was at last left alone to reckon with himself. To be confronted
with the fruits of his victory only to find that it meant choosing
between life and death for others was immensely sobering. That
Lincoln should have shouldered the moral burden of the war was
characteristic of the high seriousness into which he had grown
since 1854; and it may be true, as Professor Charles W. Ramsdell
suggested, that he was stricken by an awareness of his own part

in whipping up the crisis. This would go far to explain the desperation with which he issued pardons and the charity that he wanted to extend to the conquered South at the war's close. In one of his rare moments of self-revelation he is reported to have said: "Now I don't know what the soul is, but whatever it is, I know that it can humble itself." The great prose of the presidential years came from a soul that had been humbled. Lincoln's utter lack of personal malice during these years, his humane detachment, his tragic sense of life, have no parallel in political history. . . .

Is it possible to recall anyone else in modern history who could exercise so much power and yet feel so slightly the private corruption that goes with it? Here, perhaps, is the best measure of Lincoln's personal eminence in the human calendar—that he was chastened and not intoxicated by power. It was almost apologetically that he remarked in response to a White House serenade after his re-election that "So long as I have been here, I have not willingly planted a thorn in any man's bosom." . . .

The presidency was not something that could be enjoyed. Remembering its barrenness for him, one can believe that the life of Lincoln's soul was almost entirely without consummation. Sandburg remarks that there were thirty-one rooms in the White House and that Lincoln was not at home in any of them. This was the house for which he had sacrificed so much!

As the months passed, a deathly weariness settled over him. Once when Noah Brooks suggested that he rest, he replied: "I suppose it is good for the body. But the tired part of me is *inside* and out of reach." There had always been a part of him, inside and out of reach, that had looked upon his ambition with detachment and wondered if the game was worth the candle. Now he could see the truth of what he had long dimly known and perhaps hopefully suppressed—that for a man of sensitivity and compassion to exercise great powers in a time of crisis is a grim and agonizing thing. Instead of glory, he once said, he had found only "ashes and blood." This was, for him, the end product of that success myth by which he had lived and for which he had been so persuasive a spokesman. He had had his ambitions and fulfilled them, and met heartache in his triumph.

11.

Death

The "poem that Lincoln lived" now culminates in that "tragic conclusion that was necessary to justify all the rest." Booth murdered a man, shooting from behind like a coward. But Booth's bullet did more than kill the weary body of a leader. That sudden, shocking deed quickened into vigorous life one of the great legends of the world. In discussing the Lincoln legend, Richard Hofstadter elaborates still futher the role that Lincoln played, in death as well as in life.[1]

The Lincoln legend has come to have a hold on the American imagination that defies comparison with anything else in political mythology. Here is a drama in which a great man shoulders the torment and moral burdens of a blundering and sinful people, suffers for them, and redeems them with hallowed Christian virtues—"malice toward none and charity for all"—and is destroyed at the pitch of his success. The worldly-wise John Hay, who knew him about as well as he permitted himself to be known, called him "the greatest character since Christ," a comparison one cannot imagine being made of any other political figure of modern times.

If the Lincoln legend gathers strength from its similarity to the Christian theme of vicarious atonement and redemption, there is still another strain in American experience that it represents equally well. Although his métier was politics and not business, Lincoln was a preeminent example of that self-help which Americans have always so admired. He was not, of course, the first eminent American politician who could claim humble origins, nor the first to exploit them. But few have been able to point to such a sudden ascent from relative obscurity to high eminence; none has maintained so completely while scaling the heights the aspect of extreme simplicity; and none has combined with the attainment of success and power such an intense awareness of humanity and moral responsibility. It was precisely in his attainments as a common man that Lincoln felt himself to be remarkable, and in this light that he interpreted to the world the significance of his career. Keenly aware of his role as the exemplar of the self-made man, he played the part with an intense and poignant consistency that gives his performance the quality of a high art. The first author of the Lincoln legend and the greatest of the Lincoln dramatists was Lincoln himself.

In the beginning of his The Lincoln Legend, *Roy P. Basler has gone more deeply into the elements of the legend.*[2]

It is difficult now to comprehend the wave of hero-worship which swept over the country after Lincoln's assassination. In reality the tide had already set in before, and his death was but an opening of the flood-gates of emotion. The state of the public mind was then, as it has always been, exceedingly delirious after a period of war and national stress. The populace must, it seems, have its periods of emotional unbalance even during quiet times. So at a period when the nation's emotions were all but out of control, when half a million soldiers were dead in their uniforms and thirty millions of people were so spent with grief that no man could be quite sane any more, it is not surprising that the entire populace reverted in its mental processes to something common to the childhood of a race—the creation of a hero-myth. Drunk with success, the North was ready to apotheosize the leader who had preserved the Union and abolished slavery.

Lloyd Lewis has given, in *Myths After Lincoln* (1929), a vivid account of the hysteria that reigned during the days of "Black Easter" and the reaction of the popular imagination to the assassination. Lincoln was suddenly lifted into the sky as the folk-hero, the deliverer, and the martyr who had come to save his people and to die for them. There is a striking similarity between this popular conception of Lincoln as the dying god and the similar myths of many lands and peoples. In the chronicle of folk-beliefs the list of dying gods is long and their stories are longer. Sir James George Frazier has traced, in *The Golden Bough*, the myth of the dying god through many ancient and modern religions. Osiris died each year to bring life to the dormant grain. Adonis was a parallel divinity in Greek mythology. In addition to these there were, to mention only a few, Apollo, Attis, Balder the Beautiful, and we might add King Arthur. As had the dying gods of older times, Lincoln came up from the people. He was mocked and unrecognized for what he was until he had died. As Osiris carried his evil brother Set into myth as his slayer, and King Arthur took with him the dark Sir Modred, so Lincoln snatched John Wilkes Booth from oblivion.

In the years that followed the assassination, the folk-mind was enraptured with the stories of how Lincoln had suffered, prayed, dreamed, and loved mankind and conquered his enemies. How he had doubted, despaired, cunningly schemed, and contrived to effect his ends, no one wanted to hear. His kind face and sad smile were infinitely more appealing than the cool, slow brain that thwarted the enemies of the Union and brought order out of chaos. To have done what he had, he must have been superhuman, a mysterious symbol of the god of the common humanity in whose flesh he had lived. Man has always felt, somehow, that a divine guide is required to help him through the thorny thicket of life. He has felt, likewise, that a chosen one must die in retribution for the sins of the race or of the world. It is a doubly significant myth that combines the deliverer and the dying god. So the myth of Lincoln grew in its various phases. In one phase it was primarily mystical and religious; in another it was intensely national.

The news of the fall of Richmond had reached Washington on April third. On April tenth the capital heard from Appomattox. Lincoln's work was done; the war which he had made his own had blazed out in victory. For twelve wild days the capital cele-brated with joyful abandon. Then on Good Friday, April 14, 1865, came the assassination. Washington was plunged suddenly into the depths of fear, grief, and rage. Here indeed was the macabre setting for the birth of a legend.

In meticulous detail Carl Sandburg describes the killing in Ford's Theater.[3]

      Out in a main-floor seat is one Julia Adelaide Shepard, writing a letter to her father about this Good Friday evening at the theater. "Cousin Julia has just told me," she reports, "that the President is in yonder upper right hand private box so handsomely decked with silken flags festooned over a picture of George Washington. The young and lovely daughter of Senator Harris is the only one of his party we see as the flags hide the rest. But we know Father Abraham is there like a Father watching what interests his children. The American cousin has just been making love to a young lady who says she'll never marry but for love but when her mother and herself find out that he has lost his prop-erty they retreat in disgust at the left hand of the stage while the American cousin goes out at the right. We are waiting for the next scene."

And the next scene? The next scene is to crash and blare and flare as one of the wildest, one of the most inconceivable, fateful and chaotic that ever stunned and shocked a world that heard the story.

The moment of high fate is not seen by the theater audience. Only one man sees that moment. He is the Outsider, the one who waited and lurked and made his preparations. He comes through the outer door into the little hallway, fastens the strong though slender bar into the two-inch niche in the brick wall, and braces it against the door panel. He moves softly to the box door and through the little hole studies the box occupants and his Human Target seated in an upholstered rocking armchair. Softly he opens the door and steps toward his prey, in his right hand a one-shot brass derringer pistol, a little eight-ounce vest-pocket weapon winged for death, in his left hand a steel dagger. He is cool and precise and times his every move. He raises the derringer, lengthens his right arm, runs his eye along the barrel in a line with the head of his victim less than five feet away—and pulls the trigger.

A lead ball somewhat less than a half-inch in diameter crashes into the left side of the head of the Human Target, into the back of the head, in a line with and three inches from the left ear. "The course of the ball was obliquely forward toward the right eye, crossing the brain in an oblique manner and lodging a few inches behind that eye. In the track of the wound were found fragments of bone, which had been driven forward by the ball, which was embedded in the anterior lobe of the left hemisphere of the brain." . . .

Near the prompt-desk off stage stands W. J. Ferguson, an actor. He looks in the direction of the shot he hears, and sees "Mr. Lincoln lean back in his rocking chair, his head coming to rest again the wall which stood between him and the audience . . . well inside the curtains"—no struggle or move "save in the slight backward sway." Of this the audience knows nothing.

Major Rathbone leaps from his chair. Rushing at him with a knife is a strange human creature, terribly alive, a lithe wild animal, a tiger for speed, a wildcat of a man bareheaded, raven-haired—a smooth sinister face with glaring eyeballs. He wears a dark sack suit. He stabs straight at the heart of Rathbone, a fast and ugly lunge. Rathbone parries it with his upper right arm, which gets a deep slash of the dagger. Rathbone is staggered, reels back. The tigerish stranger mounts the box railing. Rathbone recovers, leaps again for the stranger, who feels the hand of Rathbone holding him back, slashes again at Rathbone, then leaps for the stage.

This is the moment the audience wonders whether something unusual is happening—or is it part of the play? From the box railing the Strange Man's leap for the stage is slightly interrupted. The draped Union flag of silk reaches out and tangles itself in the spur of one riding boot, throwing him out of control. He falls perhaps ten feet to the stage, landing on his left leg, breaking the shinbone a little above the instep.

Of what he has done the audience as yet knows nothing. They wonder what this swift, raven-haired, wild-eyed Strange Man portends. They see him rush across the stage, three feet to a stride, and vanish. Some have heard Rathbone's cry "Stop that man!" Many have seen a man leap from a front seat up on the stage and chase after the weird Stranger, crying "Stop that man!" It is less than half a minute since the Strange Man mounted the box railing, made the stage and strode off.

Off stage between Laura Keene and W. J. Ferguson he dashes at breakneck speed, out of an entrance, 40 feet to a little door opening on an alley. There stands a fast bay horse, a slow-witted chore boy nicknamed John Peanuts holding the reins. He kicks the boy, mounts the mare; hoofs on the cobblestones are heard but a few moments. In all it is maybe 60 or 70 seconds since he loosed the one shot of his eight-ounce brass derringer.

Did the Strange Man now riding away on a fast bay horse pause a moment on the stage and shout a dramatic line of speech? Some said he ran off as though every second of time counted and his one purpose was escape. Others said he faced the audience a moment, brandished a dagger still bloody from slashing Rathbone, and shouted the state motto of Virginia, the slogan of Brutus as he drove the assassin's knife into imperial Caesar: *"Sic semper tyrannis"*—"Thus be it ever to tyrants."

The audience is up and out of its 1,000 seats, standing, moving. Panic is in the air, fear over what may happen next. Many merely stand up from their seats, fixed and motionless, waiting to hear what has happened. The question is spoken quietly or is murmured anxiously—"What is it? What has happened?" The question is yelled with anguish—"For God's sake, what is it—what has happened?"

A woman's scream pierces the air. Some say afterward it was Mrs. Lincoln. The scream carries a shock and a creeping shiver to many hearing it. "He has shot the President!" Men swarm up to the edge of the stage, over the gas-jet footlights onto the stage. The aisles fill with people not sure where to go.

Some 200 soldiers arrive to clear the theater. The wailing and the crazy chaos let down in the emptying playhouse—and flare up again in the street outside, where some man is accused of saying he is glad it happened, a sudden little mob dragging him to a lamppost with a ready rope to hang him when six policemen with clubs and drawn revolvers manage to get him away, and jail him for safekeeping.

Mrs. Lincoln in the box sees her husband seated in the rocking chair, his head slumped forward. With little moaning cries she springs toward him and with her hands keeps him from tumbling to the floor. Major Rathbone has shouted for a surgeon, has run out of the box into the narrow hallway, and with one arm bleeding and burning with pain he fumbles to unfasten the bar between wall and door panel. An usher from the outside tries to help him. They get the bar loose. Back of the usher is a jam of people. He holds them back, allowing only one man to enter, a young-looking man with mustache and sideburns, 23-year-old Charles A. Leale, assistant surgeon, U. S. Volunteers.

Dr. Leale holds Mrs. Lincoln's outstretched hand while she cries, "Oh, Doctor! Is he dead? Can he recover? Will you take charge of him? Do what you can for him. Oh, my dear husband! my dear husband!" He soothes her a little; he will do all that can possibly be done.

The man in the chair at first scrutiny seems to be dead, eyes closed, no certainty he is breathing. Dr. Leale with help from others lifts the man from the chair and moves him to a lying position on the floor. Dr. Leale lifts the eyelids and sees evidence of a brain injury. He rapidly passes the separated fingers of both hands through the blood matted hair of the head, finding a wound and removing a clot of blood, which relieves pressure on the brain and brings shallow breathing and a weak pulse.

Dr. Leale bends over, puts a knee at each side of the body, and tries to start the breathing apparatus, attempts to stimulate respiration by putting his two fingers into the throat and pressing down and out on the base of the tongue to free the larynx of secretion. Dr. Charles Sabin Taft, an army surgeon lifted from the stage into the box, now arrives. Another physician, Dr. Albert F. A. King, arrives. Leale asks them each to manipulate an arm while he presses upward on the diaphragm and elsewhere to stimulate heart action. The body responds with an improvement in the pulse and the irregular breathing.

Dr. Leale is sure, however, that with the shock and prostration the body has undergone, more must now be done to keep life going. And as he told it later: "I leaned forcibly forward directly over his body, thorax to thorax, face to face, and several times drew in a long breath, then forcibly breathed directly into his mouth and nostrils, which expanded his lungs and improved his respirations. After waiting a moment I placed my ear over his thorax and found the action of the heart improving. I arose to the erect kneeling posture, then watched for a short time and saw that the President could continue independent breathing and that instant death would not occur. I then pronounced my diagnosis and prognosis: 'His wound is mortal; it is impossible for him to recover.' "

Brandy and water arrive. Dr. Leale slowly pours a small quantity into the President's mouth. It is swallowed and retained. While they are waiting for the President to gain strength, wrote Leale later, Laura Keene "appealed to me to allow her to hold the President's head. I granted this request, and she sat on the floor of the box and held his head in her lap. We decided that the President could now be moved to a house where we might place him on a bed in safety."

Four soldiers from Thompson's Independent Battery C, Pennsylvania Light Artillery, lift the President by the trunk and legs, Dr. Taft carrying the right shoulder, Dr. King the left shoulder, Dr. Leale the head. They come to the door of the box. Dr. Leale sees the passageway packed with people. He calls out twice, "Guards, clear the passage!" A captain goes into action with troopers. They show muskets, bayonets, sabers. "Clear out!" rings the repeated order. "Clear out!" they cry to the curiosity seekers, and to some who hesitate and still insist on blocking passage, "Clear out, you sons of bitches!"

Then the solemn little group with their precious freight carried headfirst moves slowly through a space lined by protecting soldiers. At the stair head they shift so the feet are carried first. Two more soldiers join the original four in holding the President and moving him. As they go out of the door of the theater Dr. Leale is again asked if the President can be taken to the White House and answers, "No, the President would die on the way." . . .

Packing Tenth Street straight across from the front door of
Ford's Theater is a crowd so massed that there is no hope of a
path for those carrying the President unless something is done.
The same captain who had managed clearance inside the theater
comes to Leale: "Surgeon, give me your commands and I will
see that they are obeyed." Leale asks the captain to clear a passage
to the nearest house opposite. The captain draws a sword, commands the people to make an opening; they move back, and the
procession begins its slow crossing. Several times they stop while
Dr. Leale removes the newly gathered blood clots on the head
wound. A barrier of men forms to keep back the crowds on each
side of an open space leading to the house. Now comes the report
that this house is closed. At the next house, Mr. Peterson's, No.
453 Tenth Street, Dr. Leale sees a man standing at the door with
a lighted candle, beckoning them to come in. "This we did," ran
Leale's account, "not having been interrupted in the slightest by
the throngs in the street; but a number of the excited populace followed us into the house."

There they lay their stricken Friend of Man in the rented room
of William Clark, a boarder in the house of William Peterson—on
a plain wooden bed—at about 10:45 o'clock, somewhat less
perhaps than a half-hour after the moment the trigger of the
little eight-ounce derringer was pulled.

The President lies on his back in the center of the humble
walnut bed. Now Dr. Leale holds the face upward to keep the
head from rolling to either side. The long knee elevation troubles
Leale. He orders the foot of the bed removed. Dr. Taft and Dr.
King report it is a fixture. Leale requests it be broken. This it
seems cannot be done with any satisfaction. Leale then has Lincoln moved so he lies diagonally across the bed and, propped
with extra pillows, is gently slanted with a rest for head and
shoulders, finally in a position of repose. . . .

The breath comes hard; pulse 44, feeble; the left pupil much
contracted, the right widely dilated; both eyes totally insensible

to light. The President is completely unconscious, an occasional sigh escaping with the labored breath.

In a nearby room Mrs. Lincoln has the company of Miss Harris, of several women who have arrived, and of the Reverend Dr. Gurley. Major Rathbone has fainted from loss of blood and is taken home. At intervals Mrs. Lincoln is notified she may visit her husband. Once she cries to him, "Live! you must live!" and again, "Bring Tad—he will speak to Tad—he loves him so."

Dr. Robert K. Stone, the Lincoln family physician, arrives, followed soon by Surgeon General Joseph K. Barnes and his assistant Dr. Charles H. Crane, who take charge. Dr. Leale reports to his chief what he has done. At 2 A.M. Dr. Barnes tries to locate the bullet and after a time further exploration for the bullet is considered of no avail. . . .

Two friends of Chase drop in to tell the Chief Justice the President has been shot. "My first impulse," Chase writes in his diary for April 14, "was to rise immediately and go to the President, but reflecting that I could not possibly be of any service, I resolved to wait for morning and further intelligence."

Secretary Welles is just falling asleep about 10:30 when his wife calls him. His messenger James Smith has arrived, excited, saying the President has been shot. In the Peterson house at the bedside of "the giant sufferer" Welles' outstanding impressions were: "He had been stripped of his clothes. His large arms, which were occasionally exposed, were of a size which one would scarce have expected from his fair appearance. His slow, full respiration lifted the clothes with each breath that he took. His features were calm and striking. I had never seen them appear to better advantage than for the first hour, perhaps, that I was there. After that, his right eye began to swell and that part of his face became discolored."

One by one the other Cabinet members arrive till all are in the Peterson house except Seward and McCulloch. Vice-President Andrew Johnson comes early for a brief visit.

At one in the morning, wrote the New York *Herald* man, "Senator Sumner was seated on the right of the President's couch, near the head, holding the right hand of the President in his own. He was sobbing like a woman, with his head bowed down almost on the pillow of the bed on which the President was lying."

Nerves are wearing away, faces haggard. Dr. Leale continues the one expedient of keeping the wound opening free from blood clot. The surgeons direct or perform every necessary act that comes to mind. They are supposed to be coldly practical, with no emotion to interfere with clear thinking, yet Surgeon Taft noted moments when "there was scarcely a dry eye in the room." To Dr. Leale it is vastly more than one more surgical case. From a distance he had loved the President. He had gone to Ford's Theatre chiefly to have a look at a public man he admired as a heroic character. So he is softly moved to a procedure he later described: "Knowledge that frequently just before departure recognition and reason return to those who have been unconscious caused me for several hours to hold his right hand firmly within my grasp to let him in his blindness know, if possible, that he was in touch with humanity and had a friend."

The one man dominant in the house is Edwin McMasters Stanton. He seems to have lived for this night, for the exercise of the faculties on which he prided himself. Over Washington wild rumors were running that a new uprising of the Confederacy was breaking, a city guerrilla warfare—that secretly armed secessionists were to swarm from their hiding places, take strategic points, and make a last desperate stand for the Confederate cause. "Stanton," wrote one of his friends, "instantly assumed charge of everything near and remote, civil and military." He ordered troops to keep clear the spaces around the house, to let no one enter the house except high Government officers and persons on special business. He sent for the District of Columbia Chief Justice David K. Cartter, who arrived soon and in an adjoining room began taking testimony, with a shorthand reporter present, of persons who might have evidence bearing on the high crime. To Charles A. Dana, Assistant Secretary of War, who could write shorthand, Stanton dictated telegrams to all parts of the country. . . .

As daylight began to slant through the windows, with its white clarity making the yellow gas jets and lamplights look garish and outdone, it became evident the President was sinking. Surgeon General Barnes, seated near the head of the bed, occasionally held his finger over the carotid artery to note its pulsation. Dr. Stone sat on the edge of the foot of the bed. Dr. Leale held the President's right hand, with an extended forefinger on the pulse.

At 5 A.M. the oozing from the wound ceased entirely and the breathing became stertorous and labored. On the haggard faces of the silent ones circled about, it was written more than once they thought the end had come.

From 11 at night until six in the morning Welles had "remained in the room . . . without sitting or leaving it." At six o'clock he went out of the house, tasted a deep breath of fresh air, looked up at a gloomy sky, and took a 15-minute walk. Every few rods were huddles and bunches of people, all anxious, all wanting to know what of the night, some of them having stood waiting all night and into the morning. One or more would step out from each of these groups and ask Welles, bearded and fatherly-looking, about the President. "Is there no hope?" He was impressed, reading "intense grief" on every face at his answer that the President could survive but a short time. "The colored people especially—and there were at this time more of them, perhaps, than of whites—were overwhelmed with grief."

A cold rain began falling. Out of a monotonous sky inexorably gray a cold rain began falling. . . .

The last breath was drawn at 21 minutes and 55 seconds past 7 A.M. and the last heart beat flickered at 22 minutes and 10 seconds past the hour on Saturday, April 15, 1865. Dr. Barnes' finger was over the carotid artery, Dr. Leale's finger was on the right wrist pulse, and Dr. Taft's hand was over the cardium when the great heart made its final contraction.

The Pale Horse had come. To a deep river, to a far country, to a by-and-by whence no man returns, had gone the child of Nancy Hanks and Tom Lincoln, the wilderness boy who found far lights and tall rainbows to live by, whose name even before he died had become a legend inwoven with men's struggle for freedom the world over.

The voice of Phineas D. Gurley: "Let us pray." Kneeling at the bedside, his sonorous tones shook with submission to the Everlasting, to the Heavenly Father, with pleading that the dead man's country and family be comforted.

The widow was told. She came in and threw herself with uncontrollable moaning on the body. When later she went away the cry broke from her, "O my God, and I have given my husband to die!"

Over the drawn face muscles Dr. Leale moved a smoothing hand, took two coins from his pocket, placed them over the eyelids, and drew a white sheet over the face. Over the worn features had come, wrote John Hay, "a look of unspeakable peace." Stanton, it was said afterward, pronounced the words: "Now he belongs to the ages." By his wish this became legend.

The attempted assassination of Seward, the hunting down of Booth, the uncovering of the plot and the wild surmises as to its purpose and scope, the trial of the conspirators and the hanging of four of them seem irrelevant after the irrevocable fact of Lincoln's death. But the nation's grief and shock are a part of the story.

"This is the hour of our greatest peril," wrote Orville H. Browning, a close friend of the President's, shortly after the

shooting. ". . . anarchy and the wildest scenes of confusion and bloodshed, ending in military Despotism" seemed all too possible.[4] *Julia Shephard, hardly recovered from the confusion and horror in Ford's Theater, lay awake most of that dreadful night listening to the sounds of the cavalry "rushing through the echoing street."*

The day before the assassination Julia had driven into the city and had found it still delirious with joy at the ending of the war. She wrote: ". . . all along our route the city was one blaze of glorious light. From the humble cabin of the contraband to the brilliant White House light answered light down the broad avenue. The sky was ablaze with bursting rockets. Calcium lights shone from afar on the public buildings. Bonfires blazed in the streets and every device that human Yankee ingenuity could suggest in the way of mottoes and decoration made noon of midnight." Overwhelmed by the spectacle, she added, "it seemed as though heaven smiled upon the rejoicings." After the crime at Ford's Theater, she and her family took trembling refuge in their rooms. Next day, continuing the letter she had been writing in Ford's Theater, she confided to her father, "I feel like a frightened child. I wish I could go home and have a good cry. I can't bear to be alone. . . . Sleeping or waking, that terrible scene is before me."[5]

About eleven on the night of the murder Elizabeth Keckley, the mulatto seamstress who had become Mrs. Lincoln's confidante, ventured outside in an attempt to reach her mistress in the White House. "The streets were alive with wondering, awestricken people," she wrote afterward. "Rumors flew thick and fast, and the wildest reports came with every new arrival." She passed Seward's residence, closely guarded by soldiers with bayonets, then came to the White House only to find it guarded too, and no one allowed to pass. She wandered down the street. "A gray-haired old man was passing. I caught a glimpse of his face, and it seemed so full of kindness and sorrow that I gently touched his arm, and imploringly asked: 'Will you please, sir, to tell me whether Mr. Lincoln is dead or not?' 'Not dead,' he replied, 'but dying. God help us!'" And Elizabeth Keckley added, "Not dead, but dying! then indeed God help us!"[6]

Noah Brooks did not hear of the assassination until the next morning.[7]

I was awakened in the early dawn by a loud and hurried knocking on my chamber door, and the voice of Mr. Gardner, the landlord, crying, "Wake, wake, Mr. Brooks! I have dreadful news." I slipped out, turned the key of the door, and Mr. Gardner came in, pale, trembling, and woebegone, like him who "drew Priam's curtain at the dead of night," and told his awful story. At that time it was believed that the President, Mr. Seward, Vice-President Johnson, and other members of the Government, had been killed; and this was the burden of the tale that was told to us. I sank back into my bed, cold and shivering with horror, and for a time it seemed as though the end of all things had come. I was aroused by the loud weeping of my comrade, who had not left his bed in another part of the room.

When we had sufficiently collected ourselves to dress and go out of doors in the bleak and cheerless April morning, we found in the streets an extraordinary spectacle. They were suddenly crowded with people—men, women, and children thronging the pavements and darkening the thoroughfares. It seemed as if everybody was in tears. Pale faces, streaming eyes, with now and again an angry, frowning countenance, were on every side. Men and women who were strangers accosted one another with distressed looks and tearful inquiries for the welfare of the President and Mr. Seward's family. The President still lived, but at half-past seven o'clock in the morning the tolling of the bells announced to the lamenting people that he had ceased to breathe. . . .

Instantly flags were raised at half-mast all over the city, the bells tolled solemnly, and with incredible swiftness Washington went into deep, universal mourning. All shops, government departments, and private offices were closed, and everywhere, on the most pretentious residences and on the humblest hovels, were the black badges of grief. Nature seemed to sympathize in the general lamentation, and tears of rain fell from the moist and somber sky. The wind sighed mournfully through the streets crowded with sad-faced people, and broad folds of funeral drapery flapped heavily in the wind over the decorations of the day before. Wandering aimlessly up F street toward Ford's Theatre, we met a tragical procession. It was headed by a group of army officers walking bareheaded, and behind them, carried tenderly by a company of soldiers, was the bier of the dead President, covered with the flag of the Union, and accompanied by an escort of soldiers who had been on duty at the house where Lincoln died. As the little cortège passed down the street to the White House, every head was uncovered, and the profound silence which prevailed was broken only by sobs and by the sound of the measured tread of those who bore the martyred President back to the home which he had so lately quitted full of life, hope, and cheer.

On the night of the 17th the remains of Lincoln were laid in the casket prepared for their reception, and were taken from the large guest-chamber of the house to the famous East Room, where so many brilliant receptions and so many important public events had been witnessed; and there they lay in state until the day of the funeral (April 19). The great room was draped with crape and black cloth, relieved only here and there by white flowers and green leaves. The catafalque upon which the casket lay was about fifteen feet high, and consisted of an elevated platform resting on a dais and covered with a domed canopy of black cloth which was supported by four pillars, and was lined beneath with fluted white silk. In those days the custom of sending "floral tributes" on funeral occasions was not common, but the funeral of Lincoln was remarkable for the unusual abundance and beauty of the devices in flowers that were sent by individuals and public bodies. From the time the body had been made ready for burial until the last services in the house, it was watched night and day by a guard of honor, the members of which were one major-general, one brigadier-general, two field officers, and four line officers of the army and four of the navy. Before the public were admitted to view the face of the dead, the scene in the darkened room—a sort of *chapelle ardente*—was most impressive. At the head and foot and on each side of the casket of their dead chief stood the motionless figures of his armed warriors.

When the funeral exercises took place, the floor of the East Room had been transformed into something like an amphitheatre by the erection of an inclined platform, broken into steps, and filling all but the entrance side of the apartment and the area about the catafalque. This platform was covered with black cloth, and upon it stood the various persons designated as participants in the ceremonies, no seats being provided. . . .

The sight of the funeral pageant will probably never be forgotten by those who saw it. Long before the services in the White House were over, the streets were blocked by crowds of people thronging to see the procession, which moved from the house precisely at two o'clock, amid the tolling of bells and the booming of minute-guns from three batteries that had been brought into the city, and from each of the many forts about Washington. The day was cloudless, and the sun shone brilliantly upon cavalry, infantry, artillery, marines, associations, and societies, with draped banners, and accompanied in their slow march by mournful dirges from numerous military bands. . . . The casket rested on a high platform eight or ten feet above the level of the street. As it passed many shed tears, and all heads were uncovered. The car was inclosed in a hollow square formed by a guard of honor consisting of mounted and non-commissioned officers of various light artillery companies from Camp Berry. . . .

One noticeable feature of the procession was the appearance of the colored societies which brought up the rear, humbly, as was their wont; but just before the procession began to move, the Twenty-Second United States Colored Infantry (organized in Pennsylvania), landed from Petersburg and marched up to a position on the avenue, and when the head of the column came up, played a dirge, and headed the procession to the Capitol. The coffin was taken from the funeral car and placed on a catafalque within the rotunda of the Capitol, which had been darkened and draped in mourning.

The coffin rested in the rotunda of the Capitol from the 19th of April until the evening of the 20th. During that time many thousands of people from every part of the United States paid to the dead form of the beloved President their last tearful tribute of affection, honor, and respect. . . .

While this solemn pageant was passing, I was allowed to go alone up the winding stairs that lead to the top of the great dome of the Capitol. Looking down from that lofty point, the sight was weird and memorable. Directly beneath me lay the casket in which the dead President lay at full length, far, far below; and, like black atoms moving over a sheet of gray paper, the slow-moving mourners, seen from a perpendicular above them, crept silently in two dark lines across the pavement of the rotunda, forming an ellipse around the coffin and joining as they advanced toward the eastern portal and disappeared. When the lying in state at the Capitol was over, the funeral procession from Washington to Springfield, Illinois, began, the cortège passing over the same route which was taken by Abraham Lincoln when he left his home for the national capital to assume the great office which he laid down only with his life. . . .

History has recorded how thousands of the plain people whom Lincoln loved came out from their homes to stand bareheaded and reverent as the funeral train swept by, while bells were tolled and the westward progress through the night was marked by campfires built along the course by which the great emancipator was borne at last to his dreamless rest.

Charles Sabin Taft, the young surgeon who had ministered to Lincoln through the long agonizing night after the assassination, was the brother of that Julia Taft who had frequented the White House in happier days. Like Dr. Leale, he had wandered out, exhausted, into the drizzling rain. "The yard of the house where Lincoln died," wrote Julia Taft many years later, "was full of blossoming lilacs, and as long as Charlie Taft lived the scent of lilacs would turn him sick and faint, as it brought back the black horror of that dreadful night."[8]

The poet, Walt Whitman, noted too the lilacs with their "mastering odor," blooming in those weeks. But for Whitman the death was not the immediate, sickening experience it had been for Leale and Taft. Fashioning a stately anthem, he captured for all time, not the immediate horror of Lincoln's murder, but the mood of a people's grief amidst the onward-moving stream of life in America. "Death does its work," he wrote in Specimen Days, *"obliterates a hundred, a thousand—President, general, captain, private—but the nation is immortal."*

I

When lilacs last in the dooryard bloom'd,
And the great star early droop'd in the western sky in the night,
I mourn'd, and yet shall mourn with ever-returning spring.

Ever-returning spring, trinity sure to me you bring,
Lilac blooming perennial and drooping star in the west,
And thought of him I love.

2

O powerful western fallen star!
O shades of night—O moody, tearful night!
O great star disappear'd—O the black murk that hides the star!
O cruel hands that hold me powerless—O helpless soul of me!
O harsh surrounding cloud that will not free my soul.

3

In the dooryard fronting an old farm-house near the white-wash'd
          palings,
Stands the lilac-bush tall-growing with heart-shaped leaves of rich
          green,
With many a pointed blossom rising delicate, with the perfume
          strong I love,
With every leaf a miracle—and from this bush in the dooryard,
With delicate-color'd blossoms and heart-shaped leaves of rich
          green,
A sprig with its flower I break.

4

In the swamp in secluded recesses,
A shy and hidden bird is warbling a song.

Solitary the thrush,
The hermit withdrawn to himself, avoiding the settlements,
Sings by himself a song.

Song of the bleeding throat,
Death's outlet song of life, (for well dear brother I know,
If thou wast not granted to sing thou would'st surely die.)

5

Over the breast of the spring, the land, amid cities,
Amid lanes and through old woods, where lately the violets
      peep'd from the ground, spotting the gray debris,
Amid the grass in the fields each side of the lanes, passing the end-
      less grass,
Passing the yellow-spear'd wheat, every grain from its shroud in
      the dark-brown fields uprisen,
Passing the apple-tree blows of white and pink in the orchards,
Carrying a corpse to where it shall rest in the grave,
Night and day journeys a coffin.

6

Coffin that passes through lanes and streets,
Through day and night with the great cloud darkening the land,
With the pomp of the inloop'd flags, with the cities draped in
      black,
With the show of the States themselves as of crape-veil'd women
      standing,
With processions long and winding and the flambeaus of the
      night,
With the countless torches lit, with the silent sea of faces and the
      unbared heads,
With the waiting depot, the arriving coffin, and the sombre faces,
With dirges through the night, with the thousand voices rising
      strong and solemn,

With all the mournful voices of the dirges pour'd around the
    coffin,
The dim-lit churches and the shuddering organs—where amid
    these you journey,
With the tolling tolling bells' perpetual clang,
Here, coffin that slowly passes,
I give you my sprig of lilac.

7

(Not for you, for one alone,
Blossoms and branches green to coffins all I bring,
For fresh as the morning, thus would I chant a song for you O
    sane and sacred death.

All over bouquets of roses,
O death, I cover you over with roses and early lilies,
But mostly and now the lilac that blooms the first,
Copious I break, I break the sprigs from the bushes,
With loaded arms I come, pouring for you,
For you and the coffins all of you O death.)

8

O western orb sailing the heaven,
Now I know what you must have meant as a month since I walk'd,
As I walk'd in silence the transparent shadowy night,
As I saw you had something to tell as you bent to me night after
    night,
As you droop'd from the sky low down as if to my side, (while
    the other stars all look'd on,)
As we wander'd together the solemn night, (for something I know
    not what kept me from sleep,)

As the night advanced, and I saw on the rim of the west how full
      you were of woe,
As I stood on the rising ground in the breeze in the cool transpar-
      ent night,
As I watch'd where you pass'd and was lost in the netherward
      black of the night,
As my soul in its trouble dissatisfied sank, as where you sad orb,
Concluded, dropt in the night, and was gone.

9

Sing on there in the swamp,
O singer bashful and tender, I hear your notes, I hear your call,
I hear, I come presently, I understand you,
But a moment I linger, for the lustrous star has detain'd me,
The star my departing comrade holds and detains me.

10

O how shall I warble myself for the dead one there I loved?
And how shall I deck my song for the large sweet soul that has
      gone?
And what shall my perfume be for the grave of him I love?

Sea-winds blown from east and west,
Blown from the Eastern sea and blown from the Western sea, till
      there on the prairies meeting,
These and with these and the breath of my chant,
I'll perfume the grave of him I love.

11

O what shall I hang on the chamber walls?
And what shall the pictures be that I hang on the walls,
To adorn the burial-house of him I love?
Pictures of growing spring and farms and homes,
With the Fourth-month eve at sundown, and the gray smoke lucid
    and bright,
With floods of the yellow gold of the gorgeous, indolent, sinking
    sun, burning, expanding the air,
With the fresh sweet herbage under foot, and the pale green
    leaves of the trees prolific,
In the distance the flowing glaze, the breast of the river, with a
    wind-dapple here and there,
With ranging hills on the banks, with many a line against the sky,
    and shadows,
And the city at hand with dwellings so dense, and stacks of
    chimneys,
And all the scenes of life and the workshops, and the workmen
    homeward returning.

12

Lo, body and soul—this land,
My own Manhattan with spires, and the sparkling and hurrying
    tides, and the ships,
The varied and ample land, the South and the North in the light,
    Ohio's shores and flashing Missouri,
And ever the far-spreading prairies cover'd with grass and corn.

Lo, the most excellent sun so calm and haughty,
The violet and purple morn with just-felt breezes,

The gentle soft-born measureless light,
The miracle spreading, bathing all, the fulfill'd noon,
The coming eve delicious, the welcome night and the stars,
Over my cities shining all, enveloping man and land.

13

Sing on, sing on you gray-brown bird,
Sing from the swamps, the recesses, pour your chant from the
        bushes,
Limitless out of the dusk, out of the cedars and pines.

Sing on dearest brother, warble your reedy song,
Loud human song, with voice of uttermost woe.

O liquid and free and tender!
O wild and loose to my soul—O wondrous singer!
You only I hear—yet the star holds me, (but will soon depart,)
Yet the lilac with mastering odor holds me.

14

Now while I sat in the day and look'd forth,
In the close of the day with its light and the fields of spring, and
        the farmers preparing their crops,
In the large unconscious scenery of my land with its lakes and
        forests,
In the heavenly aerial beauty, (after the perturb'd winds and the
        storms,)
Under the arching heavens of the afternoon swift passing, and
        the voices of children and women,
The many-moving sea-tides, and I saw the ships how they sail'd,

And the summer approaching with richness, and the fields all busy
    with labor.
And the infinite separate houses, how they all went on, each with
    its meals and minutia of daily usages,
And the streets how their throbbing throbb'd, and the cities pent
    —lo, then and there,
Falling upon them all and among them all, enveloping me with
    the rest,
Appear'd the cloud, appear'd the long black trail,
And I knew death, its thought, and the sacred knowledge of
    death.

Then with the knowledge of death as walking one side of me,
And the thought of death close-walking the other side of me,
And I in the middle as with companions, and as holding the hands
    of companions,
I fled forth to the hiding receiving night that talks not,
Down to the shores of the water, the path by the swamp in the
    dimness,
To the solemn shadowy cedars and ghostly pines so still.

And the singer so shy to the rest receiv'd me,
The gray-brown bird I know receiv'd us comrades three,
And he sang the carol of death, and a verse for him I love.

From deep secluded recesses,
From the fragrant cedars and the ghostly pines so still,
Came the carol of the bird.

And the charm of the carol rapt me,
As I held as if by their hands my comrades in the night,
And the voice of my spirit tallied the song of the bird.

Come lovely and soothing death,
Undulate round the world, serenely arriving, arriving,
In the day, in the night, to all, to each,
Sooner or later delicate death.

Prais'd be the fathomless universe,
For life and joy, and for objects and knowledge curious,
And for love, sweet love—but praise! praise! praise!
For the sure-enwinding arms of cool-enfolding death.

Dark mother always gliding near with soft feet,
Have none chanted for thee a chant of fullest welcome?
Then I chant it for thee, I glorify thee above all,
I bring thee a song that when thou must indeed come, come un-
        falteringly.

Approach strong deliveress,
When it is so, when thou hast taken them I joyously sing the
        dead,
Lost in the loving floating ocean of thee,
Laved in the flood of thy bliss O death.

From me to thee glad serenades,
Dances for thee I propose saluting thee, adornments and feast-
        ings for thee,
And the sights of the open landscape and the highspread sky are
        fitting,
And life and the fields, and the huge and thoughtful night.

The night in silence under many a star,
The ocean shore and the husky whispering wave whose voice I
        know,

And the soul turning to thee O vast and well-veil'd death,
And the body gratefully nestling close to thee.

Over the tree-tops I float thee a song,
Over the rising and sinking waves, over the myriad fields and the
     prairies wide,
Over the dense-pack'd cities all and the teeming wharves and
     ways,
I float this carol with joy, with joy to thee O death.

15

To the tally of my soul,
Loud and strong kept up the gray-brown bird,
With pure deliberate notes spreading filling the night.

Loud in the pines and cedars dim,
Clear in the freshness moist and the swamp-perfume,
And I with my comrades there in the night.

While my sight that was bound in my eyes unclosed,
As to long panoramas of visions.

And I saw askant the armies,
I saw as in noiseless dreams hundreds of battle-flags,
Borne through the smoke of the battles and pierc'd with missiles
     I saw them,
And carried hither and yon through the smoke, and torn and
     bloody,
And at last but a few shreds left on the staffs, (and all in silence,)
And the staffs all splinter'd and broken.

I saw battle-corpses, myriads of them,
And the white skeletons of young men, I saw them,

I saw the debris and debris of all the slain soldiers of the war,
But I saw they were not as was thought,
They themselves were fully at rest, they suffer'd not,
The living remain'd and suffer'd, the mother suffer'd,
And the wife, and the child and the musing comrade suffer'd,
And the armies that remain'd suffer'd.

16

Passing the visions, passing the night,
Passing, unloosing the hold of my comrades' hands,
Passing the song of the hermit bird and the tallying song of my
    soul,
Victorious song, death's outlet song, yet varying ever-altering
    song,
As low and wailing, yet clear the notes, rising and falling, flood-
    ing the night,
Sadly sinking and fainting, as warning and warning, and yet again
    bursting with joy,
Covering the earth and filling the spread of the heaven,
As that powerful psalm in the night I heard from recesses,
Passing, I leave thee lilac with heart-shaped leaves,
I leave thee there in the dooryard, blooming, returning with
    spring.

I cease from my song for thee,
From my gaze on thee in the west, fronting the west, commun-
    ing with thee,
O comrade lustrous with silver face in the night.

Yet each to keep and all, retrievements out of the night,
The song, the wondrous chant of the gray-brown bird,
And the tallying chant, the echo arous'd in my soul,

With the lustrous and drooping star with the countenance full
of woe,
With the holders holding my hand nearing the call of the bird,
Comrades mine and I in the midst, and their memory ever to
keep, for the dead I loved so well,
For the sweetest, wisest soul of all my days and lands—and this
for his dear sake,
Lilac and star and bird twined with the chant of my soul,
There in the fragrant pines and the cedars dusk and dim.

Reference Notes and Bibliography

INTRODUCTION: THE MAKING OF A LEADER

1. William H. Herndon and Jesse W. Weik, *Herndon's Life of Lincoln* (World, 1942) pp. 468-469. Hereafter: *Herndon's Lincoln*.

2. William H. Herndon, *Abraham Lincoln. The True Story of a Great Life*, 2 vols. (Appleton, 1892), I, xxvi.

3. Rufus Rockwell Wilson, *Intimate Memories of Lincoln* (Primavera Press, 1945), p. 409.

4. The quotations in following character sketch have been taken from: *Herndon's Lincoln*, esp. pp. 468-490; Francis B. Carpenter, *The Inner Life of Abraham Lincoln* (Hurd and Houghton, 1868), pp. 80 and 150; Charles A. Dana, *Recollections of the Civil War* (Appleton, 1898), pp. 172-173; Marquis Adolphe de Chambrun, *Impressions of Lincoln and the Civil War* (Random House, 1952), p. 100; Rufus Rockwell Wilson, *Lincoln Among His Friends* (Caxton, 1942), pp. 418-435; Allen Thorndike Rice, *Reminiscences of Abraham Lincoln by Distinguished Men of His Time* (North American Publ. Co., 1886), pp. 477-500. The quotations from Swett and Hay appear in *Herndon's Lincoln*, pp. 269-270, 425-433 and 415 ff.

5. Richard Hofstadter, *The American Political Tradition and the Men Who Made It* (Knopf, 1948), p. 128. Hereafter: Hofstadter, *American Political Tradition*.

6. David Donald, *Lincoln Reconsidered* (Knopf, 1956), p. 131.

7. Jay Monaghan, *Diplomat in Carpet Slippers* (Bobbs-Merrill, 1945), p. 324.

8. Hofstadter, *American Political Tradition*, pp. 93-94.

9. Hofstadter, *American Political Tradition*, pp. 98 ff.

10. James G. Randall, *Lincoln the President: Springfield to Gettysburg*, 2 vols. (Dodd, Mead, 1945), I, p. 121. Hereafter: Randall, *Lincoln the President*.

11. Benjamin P. Thomas, *Abraham Lincoln* (Knopf, 1952), pp. 208 ff. Hereafter: Thomas, *Lincoln*.

12. H. G. and Oswald G. Villard, editors, *Lincoln on the Eve of '61: A Journalist's Story* (Knopf, 1941), pp. 13 ff.

13. Allan Nevins, *The Emergence of Lincoln*, 2 vols. (Scribners, 1950), II, pp. 316-317.

LINCOLN AND THE CIVIL WAR

Chapter 1. The Union Breaks Apart

1. Roy P. Basler, *The Collected Works of Abraham Lincoln*, 8 vols. (Rutgers, 1953), IV, pp. 149-150. Hereafter: Basler, *Collected Works*.

2. Carl Sandburg, *Abraham Lincoln: The War Years*, 4 vols. (Harcourt, Brace, 1939), I, pp. 8-12. Hereafter: Sandburg, *War Years*.

3. Basler, *Collected Works*, IV, p. 204.

4. F. Lauriston Bullard, editor, *Diary of a Public Man* (Rutgers, 1946), p. 51.

5. Margaret Leech, *Reveille in Washington, 1860-1865* (Harper, 1941), pp. 35 ff. Hereafter: Leech, *Reveille in Washington*.

6. Henry S. Commager, editor, *The Blue and the Gray*, 2 vols. (Bobbs-Merrill, 1950), I, p. 14. Hereafter: Commager, *Blue and the Gray*.

7. Thomas, *Lincoln*, pp. 246 ff.

8. Hofstadter, *American Political Tradition*, pp. 19 ff. Italics in original.

9. Roy P. Basler, editor, *Abraham Lincoln: His Speeches and Writings* (World, 1946), pp. 594 ff. Hereafter: Basler, *Speeches*.

10. Commager, *Blue and the Gray*, I, pp. 43-45.

11. Colin R. Ballard, *The Military Genius of Abraham Lincoln* (World, 1952), pp. 42 ff. Hereafter: Ballard, *Military Genius*.

12. John G. Nicolay and John Hay, *Abraham Lincoln, A History*, 10 vols. (Century, 1890), IV, pp. 365-366.

CHAPTER 2. COMMANDER-IN-CHIEF

1. T. Harry Williams, *Lincoln and His Generals* (Knopf, 1952), pp. 3 ff. Hereafter: Williams, *Lincoln and His Generals*.

2. Sir Frederick Maurice, *Statesmen and Soldiers of the Civil War* (Little, Brown, 1926), pp. 65-68. Hereafter: Maurice, *Statesmen and Soldiers*.

3. William H. Russell, *My Diary North and South*, edited by Fletcher Pratt (Harper, 1954), p. 256.

4. Ballard, *Military Genius*, p. 106.

5. Ballard, *Military Genius*, pp. 105 ff.

6. Sandburg, *War Years*, I, p. 553.

7. Tyler Dennett, editor, *Lincoln and the Civil War in the Diary and Letters of John Hay* (Dodd, Mead, 1939), p. 176. Hereafter: Dennett, *Hay Diary*.

8. Sandburg, *War Years*, I, p. 552.

9. Basler, *Speeches*, p. 659.

10. Maurice, *Statesmen and Soldiers*, p. 89.

11. Williams, *Lincoln and His Generals*, pp. 199 ff.

12. Williams, *Lincoln and His Generals*, p. 212.

13. Basler, *Speeches*, pp. 693 ff.

14. Noah Brooks, *Washington in Lincoln's Time* (Century, 1895), pp. 47 ff. Hereafter: Brooks, *Washington*.

15. Brooks, *Washington*, p. 57.

16. Basler, *Speeches*, p. 698.

17. Williams, *Lincoln and His Generals*, p. 253.

18. Commager, *Blue and the Gray*, II, 642 ff.

19. Ballard, *Military Genius*, pp. 168 ff.

CHAPTER 3. GRANT AND VICTORY

1. To James C. Conkling, August 26, 1863. Basler, *Speeches*, p. 720.

2. Thomas, *Lincoln*, p. 372 ff.

3. John T. Morse, Jr., editor, *The Diary of Gideon Welles*, 3 vols. (Houghton Mifflin, 1911), I, pp. 364-365. Hereafter: Morse, *Welles Diary*.

4. David Homer Bates, *Lincoln in the Telegraph Office* (Century, 1907), p. 123.

5. Basler, *Collected Works*, V, pp. 91-92 and 95.

6. Sandburg, *War Years*, I, pp. 460 ff.

7. Alexander K. McClure, *Abraham Lincoln and Men of War-Times* (Times Publ. Co., 1892), pp. 193-196.

8. Williams, *Lincoln and His Generals*, p. 184.

9. Sandburg, *War Years*, II, pp. 420 ff.

10. Dennett, *Hay Diary*, p. 93.

11. Sandburg, *War Years*, II, p. 425.

12. Basler, *Collected Works*, VI, pp. 480-481.

13. William O. Stoddard, *Inside the White House in War Times* (Webster & Co., 1890), p. 220. Hereafter: Stoddard, *Inside the White House*.

14. Leech, *Reveille in Washington*, pp. 311 ff.

15. Williams, *Lincoln and His Generals*, pp. 311 ff.

16. Bruce Catton, *A Stillness at Appomattox* (Doubleday, 1954), pp. 109-110.

17. Maurice, *Statesmen and Soldiers*, pp. 100 ff.

18. Bruce Catton, *U.S. Grant and the American Military Tradition* (Little, Brown, 1954), p. 124 ff.

CHAPTER 4. LINCOLN'S CABINET

1. Dennett, *Hay Diary*, p. 76.

2. David Donald, *Inside Lincoln's Cabinet, The Civil War Diaries of Salmon P. Chase* (Longmans, 1954), p. 17.

3. Morse, *Welles Diary*, I, p. 136.

4. Burton J. Hendrick, *Lincoln's War Cabinet* (Little, Brown, 1946), pp. 3 ff. Hereafter: Hendrick, *Lincoln's War Cabinet*.

5. Randall, *Lincoln the President*, pp. 257-258.

6. Jay Monaghan, *Diplomat in Carpet Slippers* (Bobbs-Merrill, 1945), p. 14.

7. Thomas, *Lincoln*, pp. 232 ff.

8. Hendrick, *Lincoln's War Cabinet*, pp. 127 ff.

9. Leech, *Reveille in Washington*, p. 51.

10. Hendrick, *Lincoln's War Cabinet*, p. 168.

11. Same source, pp. 171-172.

12. Frederick W. Seward, editor, *William H. Seward: An Autobiography. A Memoir of His Life, with Selections from His Letters*, 3 vols. (Derby & Miller, 1891), II, p. 535. Hereafter: Seward, *Autobiography*.

13. Basler, *Speeches*, pp. 590-591.

14. Seward, *Autobiography*, II, p. 590.
15. Morse, *Welles Diary*, I, p. 136.
16. F. Lauriston Bullard, editor, *Diary of a Public Man* (Rutgers, 1946), pp. 55-56.
17. Hendrick, *Lincoln's War Cabinet*, p. 289.
18. Hendrick, *Lincoln's War Cabinet*, pp. 306 ff.
19. Morse, *Welles Diary*, I, pp. 101-102.
20. Hendrick, *Lincoln's War Cabinet*, pp. 315-316.
21. James G. Randall and Theodore Calvin Pease, editors, *The Diary of Orville Hickman Browning*, 2 vols. (Illinois State Historical Library, 1927, 1933), I, pp. 600-601.
22. Randall, *Lincoln the President*, II, pp. 244 ff.
23. Hendrick, *Lincoln's War Cabinet*, pp. 369-370.
24. A. G. Riddle, *Recollections of War Times*, 1860-1865 (Putnam, 1895) p. 273.
25. Thomas, *Lincoln*, p. 412.
26. Hendrick, *Lincoln's War Cabinet*, pp. 426-427.
27. George S. Merriam, *Life and Times of Samuel Bowles* (Century, 1885), I, p. 413.
28. Jim Bishop, *The Day Lincoln Was Shot* (Harper, 1955), pp. 121 ff.

CHAPTER 5. THE POLITICAL WAR

1. Emanuel Hertz, editor, *The Hidden Lincoln, From the Letters and Papers of William H. Herndon* (Viking, 1938), p. 295 ff. Hereafter: Hertz, *Hidden Lincoln*.
2. James G. Randall, *Lincoln The Liberal Statesman* (Dodd, Mead, 1947), pp. 65-66.
3. Brooks, *Washington*, p. 170.
4. T. Harry Williams, *Lincoln and the Radicals* (Univ. of Wisconsin Press, 1941). pp. 4 ff. Hereafter: Williams, *Lincoln and the Radicals*.
5. Dennett, *Hay Diary*, p. 31.
6. Williams, *Lincoln and the Radicals*, pp. 64 ff.
7. Nathaniel W. Stephenson, *Abraham Lincoln and the Union* (Yale Univ. Press, 1918), pp. 142 ff. Hereafter: Stephenson, *Abraham Lincoln*.
8. Stephenson, *Abraham Lincoln*, pp. 152 ff.

9. George Fort Milton, *Abraham Lincoln and the Fifth Column* (Vanguard, 1942), pp. 137 ff. Hereafter: Milton, *Fifth Column*.

10. Stephenson, *Abraham Lincoln*, pp. 168 ff.

11. Milton, *Fifth Column*, pp. 203 ff.

12. Wood Gray, *The Hidden Civil War* (Viking, 1942), pp. 119-120.

13. Robert S. Harper, *Lincoln and the Press* (McGraw-Hill, 1951), pp. 239 ff.

14. Stephenson, *Abraham Lincoln*, pp. 163 ff.

15. James G. Randall, *The Civil War and Reconstruction* (D. C. Heath, 1937), pp. 402 ff.

16. Milton, *Fifth Column*, pp. 89 ff.

17. August 26, 1863. Basler, *Speeches*, p. 720.

18. Morse, *Welles Diary*, II, p. 41.

19. Thomas, *Lincoln*, p. 429.

20. Thomas, *Lincoln*, p. 443.

21. Milton, *Fifth Column*, pp. 226 ff.

22. Dennett, *Hay Diary*, pp. 211-212.

23. Dennett, *Hay Diary*, pp. 189 ff.

24. Wood Gray, *The Hidden Civil War* (Viking, 1942), pp. 166 ff.

25. Milton, *Fifth Column*, pp. 302 ff.

26. The findings of these military commissions were to be declared invalid by the Supreme Court after the war in the famous decision, *Ex Parte Milligan*.

27. Dennett, *Hay Diary*, p. 229.

28. Thomas, *Lincoln*, p. 452 ff.

29. Dennett, *Hay Diary*, pp. 237-238.

CHAPTER 6. LINCOLN IN THE WHITE HOUSE

1. Milton, *Fifth Column*, pp. 59 ff.

2. George Alfred Townsend, *Rustics in Rebellion: A Yankee Reporter on the Road to Richmond, 1861-1865* (Univ. of North Carolina Press, 1950), pp. 189 ff.

3. Stoddard, *Inside the White House*, p. 177.

4. Brooks, *Washington*, p. 11.

5. Morse, *Welles Diary*, I, p. 10.

6. Helen Nicolay, *Personal Traits of Abraham Lincoln* (Century, 1912), p. 168.

7. Robert S. Harper, *Lincoln and the Press* (McGraw-Hill, 1951), pp. 92 ff.

8. Stoddard, *Inside the White House*, p. 37.

9. Ruth Painter Randall, *Mary Lincoln: Biography of a Marriage* (Little, Brown, 1953), p. 312. Hereafter: Ruth P. Randall, *Mary Lincoln*.

10. Stoddard, *Inside the White House*, pp. 201 ff.

11. Marquis Adolphe de Chambrun, *Impressions of Lincoln and the Civil War* (Random, 1952), pp. 21-22. Hereafter: de Chambrun, *Impressions*.

12. Stoddard, *Inside the White House*, p. 165.

13. Hendrick, *Lincoln's War Cabinet*, p. 385.

14. Thomas, *Lincoln*, pp. 456 ff.

15. Julia Taft Bayne, *Tad Lincoln's Father* (Little, Brown, 1931), p. 8, pp. 102 ff. Hereafter: Bayne, *Tad Lincoln's Father*.

16. Carl Sandburg, *Abraham Lincoln: The Prairie Years and the War Years* (Harcourt, Brace, 1954), pp. 290 ff. Hereafter: Sandburg, *Prairie Years*.

17. Sandburg, *War Years*, I, p. 458.

18. Sandburg, *Prairie Years*, pp. 393-396.

19. Bayne, *Tad Lincoln's Father*, p. 9.

20. Stoddard, *Inside the White House*, p. 62.

21. Hendrick, *Lincoln's War Cabinet*, pp. 376-377.

22. Ruth P. Randall, *Mary Lincoln*, pp. 380-381.

CHAPTER 7. ONE WAR AT A TIME

1. Thomas, *Lincoln*, p. 282.

2. Hendrick, *Lincoln's War Cabinet*, pp. 199 ff.

3. Jay Monaghan, *Diplomat in Carpet Slippers* (Bobbs-Merrill, 1945), pp. 316 ff.

4. Hendrick, *Lincoln's War Cabinet*, p. 216.

5. Commager, *Blue and the Gray*, II, pp. 848 ff.

6. Commager, *Blue and the Gray*, I, pp. 549-552.

CHAPTER 8. A NEW BIRTH OF FREEDOM

1. David Donald, *Inside Lincoln's Cabinet, The Civil War Diaries of Salmon P. Chase* (Longman's, 1954), pp. 149 ff.

2. Dennett, *Hay Diary*, p. 50.

3. Paul M. Angle, *The Lincoln Reader* (Rutgers, 1947), pp. 409 ff.

4. Hofstadter, *American Political Tradition*, p. 131.

5. Dennett, *Hay Diary*, p. 19.

6. Basler, *Speeches*, p. 651.

7. Basler, *Speeches*, p. 332.

8. Hofstadter, *American Political Tradition*, pp. 106 ff. Italics in original.

9. Allan Nevins, *The Statesmanship of the Civil War* (Macmillan, 1953), pp. 51-52.

10. Ben Ames Williams, editor, *A Diary From Dixie* (Houghton Mifflin, 1949), p. 164.

11. James G. Randall, *Lincoln and the South* (Louisiana State University Press, 1946), pp. 11 ff. Hereafter: Randall, *Lincoln and the South*.

12. Dennett, *Hay Diary*, p. 104.

13. Randall, *Lincoln and the South*, pp. 62 ff.

14. Basler, *Speeches*, pp. 613-614.

15. Randall, *Lincoln and the South*, pp. 79 ff.

16. George Fort Milton, *Conflict: The American Civil War* (Coward-McCann, 1941), pp. 222 ff.

17. David Homer Bates, *Lincoln in the Telegraph Office* (D. Appleton, Century, 1939), pp. 139-141.

18. Randall, *Lincoln and the South*, pp. 107 ff.

19. Basler, *Speeches*, pp. 666 ff.

20. Dennett, *Hay Diary*, p. 73.

21. Thomas, *Lincoln*, p. 357.

22. Thomas, *Lincoln*, pp. 405 ff.

23. Williams, *Lincoln and the Radicals*, pp. 356 ff.

24. David Donald, *Lincoln Reconsidered* (Knopf, 1956), p. 4.

25. Basler, *Speeches*, p. 796.

26. de Chambrun, *Impressions*, pp. 83 ff.

CHAPTER 9. WAR'S END

1. Thomas, *Lincoln*, p. 488.

2. Commager, *Blue and the Gray*, II, pp. 947-948.

3. William T. Sherman, *Memoirs of General William T. Sherman* (Appleton, 1875), pp. 178 ff.

4. Charles A. Dana, *Recollections of the Civil War* (Appleton, 1898), p. 178.

5. Thomas, *Lincoln*, pp. 502-503.

6. Brooks, *Washington*, pp. 237 ff.

7. Morse, *Welles Diary*, II, p. 264.

8. David Dixon Porter, *Incidents and Anecdotes of the Civil War* (Appleton, 1885), pp. 282 ff.

9. Sandburg, *War Years*, IV, pp. 198 ff.

10. Leech, *Reveille in Washington*, pp. 378 ff.

CHAPTER 10. THE MORAL FORCE

1. William H. Herndon, *Abraham Lincoln. The True Story of a Great Life*, 2 vols. (Appleton, 1892), I, pp. xix-xxiii.

2. Hertz, *Hidden Lincoln*, p. 324.

3. Rufus Rockwell Wilson, *Lincoln Among His Friends* (Caxton, 1942), pp. 418-435.

4. Same source, pp. 331-333.

5. Same source, pp. 92-93.

6. Basler, *Speeches*, p. 90.

7. Willard King, "Riding the Circuit with Lincoln," *American Heritage* (February, 1955), p. 106.

8. W. P. Trent, John Erskine, Stuart P. Sherman and Carl Van Doren, editors, *The Cambridge History of American Literature* (Macmillan Co. and Cambridge Univ. Press, 1954), III, pp. 368 ff.

9. Nathaniel W. Stephenson, *Lincoln* (Bobbs-Merrill, 1922), p. 261.

10. Roy P. Basler, *The Lincoln Legend* (Houghton Mifflin, 1953), pp. 169 ff.

11. T. V. Smith, *Abraham Lincoln and the Spiritual Life* (Beacon, 1951), p. 10.

12. H. G. and Oswald G. Villard, editors, *Lincoln on the Eve of '61: A Journalist's Story* (Knopf, 1941), p. 7.

13. de Chambrun, *Impressions*, p. 37.

14. *Herndon's Lincoln*, p. 359.

15. Basler, *Speeches*, p. 42.

16. Brooks, *Washington*, p. 286.

17. Dennett, *Hay Diary*, p. 121.

18. D. K. Dodge, *Abraham Lincoln, Master of Words* (Appleton, 1924), p. 85.

19. Edmund Wilson, *Eight Essays* (Doubleday Anchor Books, 1954), p. 202.

20. Hofstadter, *American Political Tradition*, pp. 132 ff.

CHAPTER 11. DEATH

1. Hofstadter, *American Political Tradition*, pp. 92-93.

2. Roy P. Basler, *The Lincoln Legend* (Houghton Mifflin, 1953), pp. 3 ff.

3. Sandburg, *Prairie Years*, pp. 709 ff.

4. James G. Randall and Theodore Calvin Pease, editors, *The Diary of Orville Hickman Browning*, 2 vols. (Illinois State Historical Library, 1927, 1933), II, p. 19.

5. Rufus Rockwell Wilson, *Lincoln Among His Friends* (Caxton, 1942), pp. 391 ff.

6. Elizabeth Keckley, *Behind the Scenes* (Carleton & Co., 1868), pp. 184-185.

7. Brooks, *Washington*, pp. 259 ff.

8. Bayne, *Tad Lincoln's Father*, pp. 203-204.

Index